# Experiential Psychotherapy: Basic Practices

# Experiential Psychotherapy: Basic Practices

By

## Alvin R. Mahrer, Ph.D.

*Professor of Psychology,*
*School of Psychology,*
*University of Ottawa*
*Ottawa, Ontario, Canada*

BRUNNER/MAZEL *Publishers*  •  New York

Library of Congress Cataloging in Publication Data

Mahrer, Alvin R.
  Experiential psychotherapy.

  Bibliography: p.
  Includes index.
  1. Existential psychotherapy. I. Title. [DNLM:
1. Psychotherapy—Methods. WM 420 M217e]
RC489.E93M34    1983    616.89'14    82-17782
ISBN 0-87630-318-1

Published by
BRUNNER/MAZEL, INC.
19 Union Square West, New York, N.Y. 10003

Distributed in Canada by BOOK CENTER
1140 Beaulac St., Montreal, Quebec H4R-1R8

MANUFACTURED IN THE UNITED STATES OF AMERICA

# Contents

# Prologue

## SOME OF THE DIFFICULTIES IN WRITING THIS BOOK

One of the difficulties was that of bracketing sheer enthusiasm. There is a part of me which bounds around and yells: "Experiential therapy is great! It works! If you follow the method, real changes happen! There's no other therapy like it. It gets real changes going!" It was difficult to set this part aside when I sat down each day at my desk and my typewriter. Writing is hard for me. I work one or two hours every day on a project, and the last year or so has been spent editing, reorganizing, changing something here and there. It is work. And it is difficult to do this work when a part of me is just pleased as hell with experiential therapy and is shouting out to anyone how wonderful it is.

A second difficulty was that of being fair to both this experiential psychotherapy and also to others in what I regard as the family of experiential psychotherapies. I regard this therapy as fresh and new, qualitatively different from all other therapies, and qualitatively different from the rest of the experiential family. Yet I also regard this experiential psychotherapy as growing out of, as related to, as part of the family of experiential psychotherapies. It was difficult to acknowledge family kinship while developing a psychotherapy which is distinctive, fresh, and different.

A third difficulty was that of being fair to both my own version of existential and humanistic thought (Mahrer, 1978a) and also to that whole body of thought. This experiential psychotherapy comes out of my own version of an existential and humanistic conception of human beings. Some psychotherapies, including other experiential psychotherapies, come out of the larger body of that thought. It was difficult to maintain a fair perspective between this therapy, my own theory of human beings, other therapies, and the larger body of existential and humanistic theories of human beings.

## THE PARTS OF THE BOOK

Part I is titled An Overview of Experiential Psychotherapy. In order for the basic practices to be sensible, I believe that the reader's way of understanding human beings should be cordial either with my own humanistic theory (Mahrer, 1978a) or with the general body of existential and humanistic thought. Experiential psychotherapy also derives from practice. An overview means showing how this therapy grows both from theory and from practice, and how theory and practice can and should work with one another in the development and growth of psychotherapies. That is Chapter 1.

An overview also tells what experiential psychotherapy is in general, and how it works. Chapter 2 gives an overview of all the steps in this therapy, the entire process. It goes over the fundamental initial steps (basic practices) as well as the subsequent or advanced practices.

An overview also pertains to the various practical considerations in this therapy, ranging from the seating posture to post-therapy conversation, initial openings in the first session to a discussion of appropriate and inappropriate persons for this therapy. This is Chapter 3. Chapter 4 is a script of a complete session, based upon an actual session, and designed to illustrate all the steps and practices, basic and advanced.

Part II is titled Requiem for Therapist-Patient Relationships. The purpose of Chapters 5 and 6 is to present a set of conceptual and clinical arguments aimed at letting go of the therapist-patient relationships used in virtually all therapies, and inviting therapists to adopt the phenomenological paradigm of experiential psychotherapy. Now the therapist is ready to undertake the basic practices of this therapy.

Part III is titled The Basic Practices of the Experiential Psychotherapist. Each session opens with the therapist showing the patient how to focus attention so that a working level of experiencing is reached. This is

Chapter 7. Then the therapist must enter into and share the patient's phenomenological world. This is Chapter 8. Chapter 9 shows how the therapist then shares what occurs in the patient's phenomenological world; this is called "experiential listening." Basic practices culminate with the therapist's sharing of the patient's phenomenological world and engaging in experiential listening. However, the processes of therapeutic change have only begun with the basic practices.

Each session of experiential psychotherapy proceeds through five steps, as described in Part I. The purpose of this book is to describe the basic practices which culminate with the first of these five steps, and which are necessary for the subsequent four steps. Accordingly, Chapter 10 carries the reader through all of the subsequent steps in a kind of illustration of the methods and steps which complete each session. It is an adumbrative sampler of the advanced practices of experiential psychotherapy.

## A FEW EDITORIAL AND VOCABULARY MATTERS

I refer to an experiential psychotherapist and a patient. The word "patient" was selected on the understanding that "client" might easily have been used instead. Similarly, the word "counselor" or even "existential analyst" might have been used instead of "psychotherapist." However, with regard to this choice, I do prefer the word "psychotherapist." "Counselor" calls to my mind too broad a range of persons doing too broad a range of practices, and any phrase using the word "analyst" tends to invite professional pettiness, I believe. Nor does it fit the spirit or the meaning of experiential psychotherapy. Accordingly, one person is termed the psychotherapist, and the other is the patient.

On the other hand, the sexes of these two persons are all mixed up. Sometimes they are referred to in neutral ways, sometimes as "he," and sometimes as "she." If the topic is general, I tend to refer to them in neutral ways. But frequently I have in mind a particular female therapist or a particular male patient. Then I use the appropriate words. The words reflect what I had in mind rather than conforming to some effort at being sexist or nonsexist.

## WHAT THE BOOK INVITES READERS TO DO

This book is intended to invite some of the readers to undertake experiential psychotherapy, either as therapists or as patients.

This book is for persons who want to undergo significant and substantive change. Experiential psychotherapy is proposed as a method of enabling the most profound and pervasive therapeutic processes to occur. In this sense, I regard its competitor as psychoanalysis. Whereas psychoanalysis aims, in my opinion, at important personality change, I consider experiential psychotherapy as a method of carrying forward more profound and deeper personality processes. Whereas psychoanalysis seems to have equivocally limited success in achieving its aims, I am more sanguine about the capability of the experiential method. Accordingly, the invitation is extended both to patients and to psychotherapists who are ready for significant and substantive personality change.

This book is for patients and therapists for whom therapy is short-term, long-term, or forevermore. It is not a therapy which is universal, either for therapists or for patients (see Chapter 3). But it is for patients and for therapists who want to get something done in a short time, who have a long-term therapy in mind, or who regard therapy as a continuous part of their lives.

This book is for patients and therapists whose way of understanding persons is cordial to the existential-humanistic way. I am referring more to the ingrained, implicit ways of making sense of human beings than to explicit theories of personality. If the existential-humanistic way of conceptualizing human beings makes sense, then the invitation to both patients and therapists is to undertake experiential psychotherapy. If you are not yet undertaking some form of experiential psychotherapy, then try it out.

This book is for psychotherapists who are already in the experiential family. Lots of psychotherapists already carry out some of the methods and procedures which are part of the basic practices of experiential psychotherapy. For these persons, the invitation is to consider some of the other methods and procedures. In a way, it is like introducing an organized set of basic practices to a large group of people who already use little bits and pieces of them.

All of this has to do with plunging into the actual practice of experiential psychotherapy. That is the main invitation. There are two secondary invitations. One is to contribute to this therapy: Make it better. Take next steps in improving the practice. I regard most therapies as having a career. They come about, move ahead a little, and then their career comes to an end. In this book I have taken the family of experiential therapies and tried to move a chunk of that family ahead a little.

This book is an invitation to others to keep the career moving ahead. The other invitation is related, namely to undertake the kind of research study I describe in this book in order to make this therapy better. Improve its methods and procedures; improve its theory of practice. Study psychotherapy in the way I describe and make contributions to the forward movement of experiential psychotherapy.

## WHAT THE BOOK DOES NOT INVITE READERS TO DO

This book is not for psychotherapists (counselors, case workers, psychoanalysts) who already operate out of some implicit or explicit conception of human beings other than that of the existential-humanistic way of understanding human beings. Most practitioners already regard people, including themselves and their patients, in some way. It may be a biopsychological way, a psychoanalytic way, a sociopsychological or any other way which makes sense to the practitioner. This book is not an invitation to give up whatever conceptualization is there; indeed, deep-seated convictions will block these practitioners from a cordial grasp and understanding of experiential psychotherapy. With regard to these practitioners, my attitude is one of letting-be. I consider that the whole field of psychotherapy will profit from the moving forward of each approach. Accordingly, for those practitioners, the invitation is little more than to appreciate the gradual development of an experiential psychotherapy out of an existential-humanistic conceptualization of human beings.

## SOME EXPERIENCES AROUND THE BOOK

Francyne Dufault typed the manuscript. That was much of what she did for about five months, in her office at the Centre for Psychological Services at the University of Ottawa. One experience remains especially fresh. I brought the next chapter over to her office for typing, worried that she might have found the earlier chapters boring. Or maybe she would be eager to type the next one because the material was so captivating. With a cardboard smile and a tight chest, I inquired how she found the last chapter. She even used the right word: The last chapter was boring. I still see the twinkle in her eye as she did what the last chapter says to do when a defensive clod invites you to join in on his defensive world.

It is probably a small part of the job of an editor to insure that paragraphs make some sort of reasonable points, and that they chunk along the right path. It is probably a part of the job to insure that several pages of text can be said better in a paragraph or so, and even to turn this sloppy organization into that more creditable organization. On the other hand, there is something very special when she seems to know the material so knowledgeably and so realistically that she can point out the nature of a missing chapter, reinforced by solid reasons for adding the chapter, and even adding some general guidelines about its contents. That calls for acknowledgment, and, accordingly, I want to express my appreciation and thanks to Susan E. Barrows, Editorial Vice-President at Brunner/Mazel.

I remember sitting in our kitchen. The table was filled with coffee cups, papers, notes, pens, and the manuscript. Patricia Gervaize and I were proofreading. First she read a paragraph, then I read one. The exciting diversions consisted of our talking about experiential psychotherapy. I kept the pad of paper to take notes on what we talked about so that I could then add a few points here and there in the book. Later, at the kitchen table, we read what I had typed to see if I put it in the right way. For at least five years, Pat helped me with the book, gave me reactions to the parts over which I fretted, suggested some things I should read, and gave the book an existence as part of her life, my life, and our life together.

# Experiential Psychotherapy: Basic Practices

# I

# *An Overview of Experiential Psychotherapy*

# 1

# *A Theory of Psychotherapeutic Practice: Meaning and Development*

The purpose of this chapter is to answer two questions. The first may be phrased in several ways: What are the criteria of a good theory of psychotherapeutic practice? What are the ways in which a theory of psychotherapy may be considered useful, effective, adequate? I have in mind the experiential psychotherapy that I describe in this book, as well as all other approaches to psychotherapy. My first purpose is to propose some characteristics of a good theory of psychotherapy.

The second question also may be phrased in several ways: How may we make our theories of psychotherapy better? How may we go about developing them, advancing them? How may we study them so as to help them become more effective, more useful, more adequate? I am concerned that we are much too inefficient in trying to improve our theories of psychotherapeutic practice. We have much to learn about where and how to expend our energies if we want to contribute to the genuine development of these theories. My aim is to suggest some ways of improving and advancing experiential psychotherapy, and to invite others to consider adopting these ways in order to improve and advance their own psychotherapies.

## CHARACTERISTICS OF A GOOD THEORY
## OF PSYCHOTHERAPEUTIC PRACTICE

*It Is a Working Theory of Conditions-Operations-Consequences*

A good theory of psychotherapeutic practice helps the therapist to know what to do. It enables the therapist to practice, to do psychotherapy, to carry out operations. It is functional; it is operational. A good theory of psychotherapeutic practice tells the therapist that he should carry out this operation when the patient does this or does that. A good theory of practice lets the therapist know that when he carries out a particular operation, here are the likely consequences. In other words, a good theory of practice tells the therapist that when the patient is doing this or being this way (condition), here is what the therapist should do (operation), and the patient will then do that or be that way (consequence). The more a theory of practice can provide such explicit and workable guidelines, the better it is.

When the theory says the patient is doing this or that (condition), the actual referent may be the immediately preceding patient statement, or it may be something about the patient a little earlier. The size of the window may be larger or smaller, but there is some kind of antecedent patient condition, some kind of therapist operation, and some kind of patient consequence. A good theory will include principles or statements which relate condition, operation, and consequence.

It seems to me that in the field of psychotherapy, there are a few statements which come reasonably close to meeting this criterion. Here is an example: Under nearly all conditions (regardless of what the patient does or is being like), the therapist is to offer an appropriately empathic reflection, and the consequence is that the patient will tend to engage in self-exploration. Using our criterion, this qualifies as a fair theoretical statement of patient condition, therapist operation, and patient consequence. Unfortunately, most statements in the field of psychotherapy fail to meet this criterion. They are generally so vague and so loose that the working therapist does not know what to do, when to do it, and what the more or less immediate patient consequences might be.

In this book, my aim is to provide a set of statements (conditions-operations-consequences) for the experiential therapist in order to help move our theory of psychotherapy a little along the avenue from a loose art toward a working science (cf. Colby, 1962; Matarazzo, 1971).

*It is a working theory of therapeutic conditions.* A good working theory of psychotherapeutic practice will help the therapist to know what is going on in this patient, to grasp and to understand this specific person right here, to have some way of knowing what the patient is doing or expressing or being. A psychoanalytic therapist may grasp what the patient is doing in terms of the concept of transference. This patient is being demanding of her therapist in an unconscious effort to prove that her father really loves her. Accordingly, she is angrily accusing her therapist of not really caring, and she is demanding evidence of his concern and love. On the basis of this description of the immediate therapeutic conditions, certain therapist operations become appropriate. For example, the psychoanalytic therapist may remain silent in an effort further to build the transference relationship. Or the therapist may interpret her behavior in the light of childhood relationships with her father.

Other therapeutic approaches may offer different ways of making sense of what that patient is doing or expressing or being. For example, the patient may be described as beginning to express feelings of hurtful rejection. This kind of therapeutic condition may be coupled with therapeutic operations of empathic reflection aimed at enabling the patient to explore further these deeply felt feelings. There are many ways of describing this immediate therapeutic condition. For example, the same patient may be described as choosing to risk the anxiety of a direct encounter with the real and authentic therapist. This way of describing the therapeutic condition may be followed by therapist operations aimed at furthering the sheer experiencing of this person-to-person encounter:

> The concept of "transference" as such has often been used as a convenient protective screen behind which both therapist and patient hide in order to avoid the more anxiety-creating situation of direct confrontation. For me to tell myself, say, when especially fatigued, that the patient-is-so-demanding-because-she-wants-to-prove-she-can-make-her-father-love-her may be a relief and may also be in fact true. But the real point is that she is doing this to me in this given moment, and the reasons it occurs at this instant of the intersection of her existence and mine are not exhausted by what she did with her father. Beyond all considerations of unconscious determinism . . . she is at some point choosing to do this at this specific moment. Furthermore, the only thing that will grasp the patient, and in the long run make it possible for her to change, is to experience fully and deeply that she is doing precisely this to a real person, myself, in this real moment (May, 1958, p. 83).

A theory of practice is good to the extent that it provides the therapist with some way of grasping the patient condition, some way of understanding what the patient is doing or being like right now so that the therapist can carry out some operation. Many theories fall short of meeting this criterion.

*It is a working theory of therapeutic operations.* A good theory of psychotherapeutic practice tells the therapist that (a) under these conditions, here are the appropriate therapist operations, and (b) given these therapist operations, here are the likely patient consequences. When the patient is being this way, when these particular conditions occur, here is what you do. When you do that operation properly, here is what ought to happen.

As long as your eye is on the therapeutic operation, you may look either to the preceding conditions or the consequences. The conditions and the consequences are both related to a good therapist operation. Gendlin emphasizes the consequence or effect: "A helping person's responses, therefore, must at least sometimes have an effective experiential *effect*, if they are to have any problem resolution at all. The question: 'What is the best sort of therapist response?' leads us to the question: 'How can the therapist's response have a concrete experiential effect on the individual?' " (Gendlin, 1968, p. 208). A good theory of practice ties the therapist response or operation to both what precedes and what follows. Indeed, the closer you come to an actual description of concrete therapist operations, the more necessary it is to tie them to antecedent patient conditions and to patient consequences. The therapist interprets or reflects or is silent under these conditions and to achieve those patient consequences. A good theory of psychotherapy provides us with such information on our therapeutic operations.

*It is a working theory of patient consequences.* A good theory of psychotherapeutic practice will spell out the consequences of therapist operations. If you do this or that, here is what should occur. The consequence refers to the patient, and to what the patient then does or how the patient then is. The key is that the theory should spell out the therapeutic operation and the consequences which are expected to occur. What is important is that there be some connection between what the therapist does and a patient consequence. To the extent that a theory identifies such connections, it is a good working theory of therapeutic practice.

Too many of our theories of practice fail to meet this criterion. They point vaguely toward some characteristics about the patient, but they tell us very little about what the patient is doing or being like right now. We are given very little help in knowing what to do under what conditions. Nor do we know what consequences to expect following some operation by the therapist. We are left with vague and general notions of what to do, when to do it, and what will happen if we do it. My aim is to work toward a theory of experiential psychotherapy which meets this criterion.

### It Is a Growing, Practical, Heuristic, Not a Static Vocabulary

A good theory of psychotherapeutic practice is like an exciting storehouse of ideas. If you study the theory, you should be able to figure out more about how to do that psychotherapy. The test is whether that theory leads to new ideas about patient conditions, therapist operations, and patient consequences. The test is whether the theory leads to more effective interconnections among conditions, operations, and consequences. In this sense, a good theory grows; it leads to more practical therapeutics.

*Not a static vocabulary to describe other therapies.* It is not a criterion for one therapeutic approach to describe other therapeutic approaches within its vocabulary. We often act as if a therapeutic approach is somehow good to the extent that it can describe other therapies within its language system. It is all too common to engage in this game of mutual vocabulary-flexing. In fact, all this shows is that virtually any therapeutic vocabulary is able to incorporate any other vocabulary. The net result is a series of static vocabularies, each capable of describing the others.

It is all too easy for behavioral therapists to describe what happens in psychoanalytic therapy by using the vocabulary of learning theory. Client-centered therapists have an easy time using their vocabulary to redescribe what occurs in behavioral therapies. The psychoanalytic vocabulary easily incorporates what occurs in client-centered therapy. These are easy exercises in vocabulary, and tell us little or nothing about the worth or effectiveness of the theory of practice. If your vocabulary includes the construct of reinforcement, then you can easily describe the client-centered facilitating conditions in terms of reinforcement. But of course this is a two-way street, and every therapy can reduce everything done by other therapies to its own favorite vocabulary. Basically, every other therapy can be understood as operating on the basis of my constructs. If I favor the importance of client-centered facilitating conditions, then it is no feat to describe any change occurring in virtually any therapy in terms of the vocabulary of client-centered facilitating conditions (e.g., Patterson, 1968). Or, all therapeutic change can easily be described in terms of social influence (e.g., Poppen, Wandersman, & Wandersman, 1976), or experiencing (Gendlin, 1969), or insight and understanding, or the favorite constructs of any therapy. It is not a criterion of the worth of any theory of practice to flex its vocabulary muscles by describing any or all other approaches within its language system. We can all do that.

In the continuing effort to be king of the therapeutic mountain, one strategy is to rise to the level of a parent theory of personality and to show that the whole field of psychotherapy can be framed within the constructs of that theory of personality. In the first half of this century, the prevailing vocabulary was that of a psychoanalytic theory of personality. The field of psychotherapy lent itself to understanding and description in terms of that theory of human beings. Then, in the 1950s, the vocabulary of the learning theories rose to challenge the supremacy of the psychoanalytic vocabulary. In this fight, the big blows consist of demonstrations of how the whole field of psychotherapy can be reduced to, redescribed in terms of, or expressed as common denominators of one vocabulary or another. Occasionally, the generals of one side capitulate by declaring the supremacy of the other. Alexander (1963), for example, finally saw the light and publicly embraced the vocabulary of the learning theories. Meanwhile, the fight goes on, with every large theory of personality confidently proving that psychotherapy can easily be described in the vocabulary of learning theory, or social learning theory, or psychobiological theory, or social psychology, or cognitive psychology, or existential-humanistic psychology, or any other general theory of human beings.

All that such energetic enterprises show is that practically any therapeutic vocabulary is able to describe what occurs in other therapies. This enterprise is easy and cheap. Any therapeutic vocabulary can do it with some success. I do not regard this as a criterion of a theory of psychotherapeutic practice.

*Not a static vocabulary of extant therapeutic operations.* It is not a criterion of a good theory of psychotherapeutic practice to dress up old therapeutic operations in its own vocabulary. Many therapies use therapeutic operations which have been in the public marketplace for decades or even centuries. All the therapy does is redescribe the operation within its own language, with its own technical jargon, and hold it out as something new. All this shows is that we can easily borrow old therapeutic operations and describe them with our own vocabulary.

Consider a man who gets upset at work, especially at another fellow. Long before we had a profession of psychotherapy there were all sorts of prescriptions for such problems. If you are upset, get your mind off of it by doing something you like—eat some food that you like, sing a favorite song—that will help. Cautela (1965) used this therapeutic operation for a patient who became upset at work: ". . . treatment consisted in asking the patient, after the first session, to eat a candy bar whenever he felt fearful at work" (p. 451). Adopting this age-old method is one thing. But dressing up the method in technical vocabulary is quite another: "It was reasoned that anxiety acted on a response and drive producing capacity, thus starting a spiral of total drive (D) increasing reaction potentiality which caused a further increase in drive followed by an even further increase in reaction potential. Eating food would act to reduce the total drive state and to introduce a pleasant competing response to the fear stimulus. . . . The hope was that this would stop the spiral effect and establish competing responses to allow autosuggestion techniques to exert their influence" (p. 451).

If a person gets especially upset at another fellow, another age-old prescription is to try and imagine that the other fellow is really friendly and nice. This prescription is hundreds of years old. Cautela uses this method, and describes its use within Wolpe's therapeutic vocabulary: "The problem . . . was to directly reduce the reaction potential (readiness to respond with anxiety) to work (S) situation. According to Guthrie, one way to weaken or eliminate a particular S-R relation is to present the S and prevent the R from occurring so that another R may be connected to the original S. In the Hullian model, the reaction potential to a stimulus may be forced below the reaction threshold by either building up total inhibitory potential or by reinforcing a competing response tendency to a greater degree than the original. A combination of the interference method of Guthrie and the reinforcement method of Hull has been adapted by Wolpe in his reciprocal inhibition therapy" (Cautela, 1965, p. 450). Take away the impressive technical vocabulary, and we have two simple operations, each hundreds of years old. One is to take your mind off of it by doing something you like, something like eating a candy bar. The other is to try and imagine that the person who upsets you is really nice and friendly. It is not a criterion of the worth of a theory of psychotherapeutic practice to dress up (describe, explain) some old and simple operation within one's own technical vocabulary.

I have selected one case from one behavior therapy. Examples may be taken from all kinds of psychoanalytic therapies, humanistic therapies, cognitive therapies, and essentially every other therapy, including experiential therapies. All this shows is that each vocabulary is exceedingly capable of describing its operations (what the therapist does) within its own static, technical vocabulary. Demonstrations of this capability are not demonstrations of the worth of a theory of psychotherapeutic practice.

### It Tells What Falls Within and Without Its Domain

A good theory of psychotherapeutic practice enables the therapist to say that these psychotherapeutic issues (phenomena, events, concerns) fall inside or outside my particular domain. It is a theory of *psychotherapeutic practice*. That means some issues or phenomena fall inside and some fall outside my domain of psychotherapeutic practice. As indicated in Figure 1.1, we can divide the whole range of psychotherapy issues and phenomena into those which fall within the domain of psychotherapeutic practice, and those which may be considered as psychotherapeutic issues and phenomena but which are outside the domain of psychotherapeutic practice. If some issue falls within the domain of a theory of practice, studying the issue will tell us something about practice. Studying the issue will help us to know what to do, when to do it, and what the consequences are. These issues have relevance for a theory of psychotherapeutic practice. On the other hand, as indicated in Figure 1.1, there are loads of issues (and events and phenomena) which have something to do with psychotherapy, but fall outside the domain of psychotherapeutic practice. Talking about and studying these issues have little or any bearing on psychotherapeutic practice—even though they involve psychotherapy. A good theory of psychotherapeutic practice will help me say that these issues (phenomena, events) fall within its domain, and these others simply fall outside.

Consider such issues and phenomena as the following, all of which bear on the field of psychotherapy but fall outside a good theory of psychotherapeutic practice: advantages and disadvantages of a consultant, the religious meanings of patient's self-images, relationships between length of treatment and psychodiagnosis, sexual experience and orgasmic competency, changes in social desirability scores, comparisons of treatment approaches to essential hypertension, burnout in psychotherapists, midlife crises in male patients, physiological correlates of patients in paying their bills, psychotherapy as a problem of locus of control, changes in sex-role identification in psychotherapy, and on and on. There are hundreds of issues and phenomena which have something to do with psychotherapy, but which have little or no bearing on what the therapist does right now with this patient under these conditions, and therefore fall outside the domain of a theory of psychotherapeutic practice. A good theory of psychotherapeutic practice identifies these issues and phenomena as falling either inside or outside its domain.

## It Is Linked Both to Practice and to Its Parent Theory of Human Beings

A good theory of psychotherapeutic practice is linked to the actual data of practice; it tells what operations to carry out, the conditions under which they are carried out, and the consequences of carrying them out. In addition, a good theory of psychotherapeutic practice is linked to a parent theory of human beings.

A theory of human beings deals with issues and phenomena such as the structure of personality, the ways in which human beings develop, how change occurs in human beings, relationships with other human beings, happiness and sadness, feelings and emotions. A theory of human beings is much broader than a theory of psychotherapeutic practice. A good theory of human beings does not have to have something to say about psychotherapy, but a good theory of psychotherapy will, according to our criterion, have to have a parent theory of human beings.

A good theory of psychotherapeutic practice will be able to say, "Here is my answer to that question, and here is the answer from the perspective of my parent theory of human beings," or "On that question or issue, I have nothing to say; that is a matter for my parent theory of human beings."

Suppose that we are interested in the therapist's use of interpretation. We inquire why the therapist interprets. The therapist answers that it is intended to heighten the patient's insight on some matter. So far we are staying within a theory of psychotherapeutic practice. However, we go on. Why is insight important? What is the value or significance of insight on that matter? The therapist may answer from the perspective of a theory of psychotherapeutic practice. The answer relates to a therapeutic condition, to a subsequent therapist operation, to some subsequent therapeutic consequence. The answer stays within the domain of psychotherapeutic practice. On the other hand, the therapist may an-

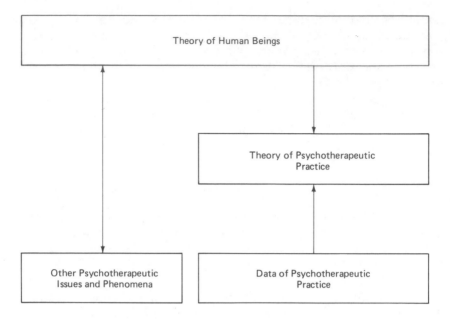

Figure 1.1. Relations Between Theory of Practice, Theory
of Human Beings, and Psychotherapy

swer from the perspective of a parent theory of human beings. Increased
insight is related to particular notions about the structure of personality;
insight is related to particular notions of personality change; insight is
related to particular ideas about human development. One answer may
be given from within the perspective of a theory of psychotherapeutic
practice, and another answer may be given from within the perspective
of a theory of human beings. The answers are different, and usually
they are consistent with each other.

   On psychotherapeutic issues and phenomena other than the data of
psychotherapeutic practice (see Figure 1.1), a good theory of psychotherapeutic practice will say, "I have no answer. That falls outside my
domain. But here is what my parent theory of human beings has to say
about that." Suppose that we are interested in how a patient happens
to become a person who sees things that no one else seems to see, or
how we can understand this patient who has had a series of miscarriages,
or how cancer seems to come and go, or what kind of a person this
patient may become ultimately. On these issues, questions, and phenomena, the theory of psychotherapeutic practice has little or nothing

to say. The parent theory of human beings, however, may have a great deal to say about such issues, questions, and phenomena.

A good theory of psychotherapeutic practice is linked to a parent theory of human beings. It can deal with psychotherapeutic events from its perspective, and also from the perspective of its parent theory of personality. And it knows where it stops and the parent theory of human beings takes over.

*The relationship with its parent theory of human beings.* The theory of psychotherapeutic practice derives from the parent theory of human beings. Advances and changes in the parent theory can have profound influence on the theory of practice; the reverse is much less true. Study the parent theory and you may well get ideas about practice; the reverse is much less true. The parent theory sets the boundaries and the contours of the theory of practice; the reverse is much less true. Much of what you have to know for practice is dependent upon and comes from the parent theory; most of what the parent theory deals with does not depend upon the theory of psychotherapy. In at least these ways, the relationship goes from the parent theory of human beings down to the theory of psychotherapeutic practice. This is indicated as the arrow from the former to the latter in Figure 1.1.

This means that a good theory of psychotherapeutic practice is a good tool of the parent theory of human beings. Its form and shape are logically derived from and generated by the parent theory.

It is my impression that psychoanalytic theories of practice fare somewhat questionably on this criterion. Indeed, Condrau and Boss (1971) forcibly argue that there are jarring inconsistencies and incompatibilities between psychoanalytic theories of practice and a psychoanalytic theory of human beings in general. Although this is a highly sensitive issue to psychoanalytic therapists, it also has an exciting aspect. Perhaps there is considerable room to develop whole new theories of psychoanalytic practice from a return to a careful study of a psychoanalytic theory of human beings. On the other hand, my impression is that the various behavioral theories score rather well on this criterion (e.g., Bergin, 1966). Given an overall conceptualization of human beings as learning organisms, there is a rather high goodness of fit between the behavioral theories of practice and their parent theory of human beings.

It is the parent theory of human beings which sets the ground rules for the conceptualization of human beings, their personality structure, the ways in which development and change occur, what human beings can become, the relationship between human beings and both the ex-

ternal and "internal" worlds, the basic foundations of personality structure, the relationships between psychological concepts and those of
other sciences, and everything else determining the conceptual context
of the theory of psychotherapeutic practice. Accordingly, the destiny of
each theory of psychotherapeutic practice is to grow and develop to its
own limits. Let each theory of practice flourish, nourished by its parent
theory of human beings. These theories of practice have careers and
destinies whose outer boundaries are already set by their parent theories
of human beings. In this sense, I favor the wholesale development of
each theory of psychotherapeutic practice. By the same line of thinking,
however, I am unimpressed by most of the arguments and fightings
between theories of practice. I am also of the opinion that a systematic
unfolding of a theory of practice will further its career more than attempts
to assemble packages of methods and techniques derived from different
parent theories of human beings. This kind of eclectic packaging may
have short-term appeal, but when the various practices are linked to
different parent theories of human beings, the long-term results seem
quite poor, at least to me. To the extent that theories of practice accept
a criterion of a goodness of fit with their parent theories of human
beings, these theories of practice will learn from their parent theories
and will develop and grow along the avenues laid out by these parent
theories.

*The relationship with other issues and phenomena of psychotherapy.* As indicated in Figure 1.1, there are data which comprise the guts of actual
psychotherapeutic practice. They consist of actual therapeutic conditions, actual therapeutic operations, and actual therapeutic consequences. These are the data of psychotherapeutic practice. Separate and
aside from this, there are issues and phenomena which have to do with
psychotherapy. As discussed above, these include such issues and phenomena as the role of values in psychotherapy, burnout in psychotherapists, physiological correlates of anxiety in patients, relationships
between treatment length and psychodiagnosis. While these issues and
phenomena are germane to the parent theory of human beings, they
fall outside the domain of a theory of psychotherapeutic practice. As
shown in Figure 1.1, there may well be a two-way interaction between
these issues and phenomena and the parent theory of human beings.
When the parent theory makes conceptual sense of these issues and
phenomena, the theory of practice can learn from its parent theory.
Therefore, once again, the theory of practice is at the dependent end,

profiting from such issues and phenomena of psychotherapy through its parent theory of human beings.

A good theory of psychotherapeutic practice will identify such issues and phenomena as falling outside its particular domain. However, these issues and phenomena are worthwhile areas of study for the parent theory of human beings, and the theory of practice profits thereby from what the parent theory of human beings learns from a study of these issues and phenomena. Not only is this a criterion for a good theory of practice, but it is also a guideline for one way in which a theory of psychotherapy grows and develops. That is, such issues and phenomena are most profitably studied from within the context of the parent theory of human beings.

*The relationship with the actual data of psychotherapeutic practice.* The theory of practice is most intimately related to the actual data of psychotherapy. Whereas the theory of practice learns from, is generated by, and fits in with the parent theory of human beings, the relationship with its actual data of psychotherapy is the reverse. The actual data of psychotherapy are what the theory of psychotherapeutic practices studies. It learns (and changes and develops) on the basis of the actual data of therapeutic practice. These data are the priceless stuff we study. These data teach us about our practice. By studying these data, we modify our theories of practice. We test out our theories by seeing the actual data of psychotherapeutic practice. This is why, in Figure 1.1, the arrow goes from the data of psychotherapeutic practice to the theory of psychotherapeutic practice. The balance of this chapter deals with how a theory of psychotherapy moves ahead by studying the actual data of psychotherapy.

## Some Concluding Propositions

These are some of the criteria of a good theory of psychotherapeutic practice. At least these are the criteria I am setting for an experiential theory of practice, and I invite other approaches to name their own criteria. If I were to measure our current theories of psychotherapy on these criteria, it would be almost easy to wonder if we have any theories of practice at all (cf. Matarazzo, 1971). One proposition is that these serve as the criteria of a good theory of psychotherapeutic practice. A second proposition is that our current crop of theories generally fails to meet these criteria. I am especially aware that experiential psychotherapies fail to meet these criteria. If we are going to make matters a little better, Figure 1.1 tells us that we can move the theory of experiential practice ahead by studying its parent theory of human beings and also by studying the data of psychotherapeutic practice. We now turn to the second of these two options.

## DEVELOPING A THEORY OF PSYCHOTHERAPY
## BY STUDYING PRACTICE

By "developing" a theory of psychotherapeutic practice, I mean helping it to grow, to advance, to become more useful. If an experiential psychotherapist wants to help develop the experiential theory of psychotherapeutic practice, I suggest the following ways of getting ready:

(a)  Be in experiential psychotherapy, preferably throughout your whole career.
(b)  Study those areas of the philosophy of science which deal with psychological theorizing and research.
(c)  Study theories of human beings. Pay special attention to existential-humanistic theories of human beings, but know the others. Learn the history of these theories.
(d)  Study the theories of psychotherapeutic practice. Pay special attention to experiential theories, but learn the others as well. Learn the history of these theories of psychotherapeutic practice.
(e)  Study actual psychotherapeutic practices. Learn from tapes, verbatim transcripts, live demonstrations, descriptions of actual practice. Concentrate on experiential therapy, but study all other approaches as well. Study the history of actual psychotherapeutic practice.
(f)  Do psychotherapy under helpful supervision. Concentrate on experiential psychotherapy, but gain some experience in other approaches as well.
(g)  Study the methods and the findings of psychotherapy research.

To the extent that you have progressed along the above lines, you are ready to contribute to the development of a theory of psychotherapeutic practice, and especially to an experiential theory. How, then, may we go about developing our theories of psychotherapeutic practice? One way, as indicated in Figure 1.1, is by moving down from a theory of human beings. The other way is by studying the actual data of practice.

My aim is to approach the actual data of psychotherapy in as careful and rigorous a manner as will enable me to learn something new. I want to develop hypotheses about what occurs in psychotherapy and about what seems to be related to the kinds of events that have special meaning for me. I am looking for a way of studying psychotherapy so that I can increase my knowledge and my effectiveness, so that I can know more and function better.

I am certain that precious little of the ordinary methods and procedures of psychological research will help me. Virtually the whole field of psychological research is useful in testing out formulated hypotheses and is essentially useless in the development and formulation of hypotheses. If my aim is to gain knowledge, to arrive at hypotheses which are new, I can expect little if any help from principles and methods of research, experimentation, and statistics. These come into play once someone has developed hypotheses to examine.

Indeed, the net result of psychological research is the gradual reduction in the body of knowledge we do have about psychotherapy, or any other area of psychology. Research principles and methods allow us to have more or less confidence in some hypotheses, and the result is a gradual shrinkage in the statements we can, with some confidence, make about psychotherapy. We test hypotheses, gradually finding that some are less tenable than we had thought. On the other hand, we are careful and rigorous in examining other hypotheses, the net result being that we are slowly confirmed in holding these hypotheses. With some knowledge made less tenable and with other pieces of knowledge somewhat confirmed, the best we can hope for is only a slight reduction in the body of knowledge. Psychologists like to refer to the accumulating body of knowledge, for example about psychotherapy. What that means, as I see it, is that such research tends to shrink the size of this body of knowledge to a smaller and smaller domain of statements which we can hold with some reasonable confidence. What cumulates is the degree of research-based confidence, not the size of the package.

What are the sources of new ideas, of hunches, of the kinds of research questions to ask, of hypotheses? The sources do not include research principles, tools, statistics, methods, or procedures. One source is the careful, rigorous process of working down from a theory. We can begin with a theory of human beings and we can be rigorously systematic in deducing ideas about a theory of psychotherapy, and from that making statements about the events of psychotherapy. That is one way. Another way is by studying the actual events of psychotherapy and working our way up to new ideas, hunches, research questions, and hypotheses.

This is the way of logical induction, of naive observation, of wallowing in the data itself, of the systematic methods of phenomenology. In this second way, precious little of ordinary research methods and procedures, experimental design and statistics is of any significant use. We turn now to this second way of learning something about psychotherapy by studying the actual events of psychotherapy.

## The Conditions-Operations-Consequences Paradigm

I suggest that the practice of psychotherapy can be studied by asking the following questions:

(a) How do you make sense of the patient, of what the patient is doing, expressing, being like? This is the patient condition.
(b) Given that condition, what operations are appropriate? What does the therapist do? This is the therapist operation.
(c) What are the consequences of those therapist operations? Given that therapist operation, how would you make sense of what the patient is now doing, expressing, being like? This is the patient consequence.

I suggest that most therapists do this most of the time. Implicitly or explicitly, most therapists have some answers to these questions as they work. Sometimes the answers refer to specific statements by patients and therapists; sometimes the "windows" are larger. Yet most therapists have ongoing notions about what the patient is doing, what therapist operations are appropriate, and what the likely patient consequences are. In other words, most therapists are already "doing research." The trouble is that most of the questions and answers are poorly formulated, loose, and unsystematic. We can move from casual researchers to more rigorous researchers by using this paradigm more carefully. Kiesler (1966) tells us how:

> . . . the basic skeleton of a paradigm for psychotherapy seems to be something like the following: The patient communicates something; the therapist communicates something in response; the patient communicates and/or experiences something different; and the therapist, patient, and others like the change. . . . The enormous task of psychotherapy theory and research is that of filling in the variables of this paradigm (pp. 129-130).

The window may be little or big. If the window is little, we look at what the patient says, what the therapist says, what the patient then says, and so on. Here is an example from the very beginning of an initial session:

Pt 1: Hi, Dr. Nelson.
T 1: I'm glad to meet you.
Pt 2: Thank you. (short pause) . . . uh . . .
T 2: I don't have any idea what sorts of things you want to bring up, but I would like to hear whatever concerns you.
Pt 3: I'm not quite sure where to begin.

How would you describe what the patient is doing in the first statement? Is the patient being sociable, taking the initiative, being dominant? However you describe the way the patient is being, what is the appropriate therapist operation? Is Dr. Nelson to be sociable, guarded, friendly but not revealing? How would you describe the therapist's first statement? How would you describe the second patient statement? Is the patient being sociable, leaving the next step up to the therapist, being somewhat uncomfortable? This second patient statement may be regarded as the consequence of the first therapist statement, and it also may be regarded as the "condition" for the next therapist statement (T2). Would you describe this second therapist statement as putting the patient at ease, taking control, providing structure, defining the therapist's role? How would you describe the consequence of the second therapist statement (that is, Pt 3)?

We have observed what the patient does, what the therapist then does, and what the patient then does. We are studying psychotherapy by looking at the process in terms of condition-operation-consequence. We may open the window a bit by studying the therapist operation as including more therapist statements than just one, by relating this operation to a patient condition which includes a larger number of antecedent patient statements, and by looking at patient consequence as referring to a larger number of patient statements. Regardless of the size of the window, we are using the same paradigm.

Beginning in the 1940s, Carl Rogers and his colleagues pioneered this simple way of looking at what actually happens in psychotherapy. I believe we owe these people a debt of gratitude for using this method, for writing about their results so candidly, and for further developing one of the first genuine theories of psychotherapeutic practice:

Sometime in 1940 a group of us at Ohio State successfully recorded a complete therapeutic interview. Our satisfaction was great
but it quickly faded. As we listened to this material, so formless,
so complex, we almost despaired of fulfilling our purpose of using
it as the data for research investigations. It seemed almost impossible to reduce it to elements which could be handled objectively.
Yet, progress was made. . . . The raw data of psychotherapy was
transformed by ingenious and creative thinking into crude categories of therapist techniques and equally crude categories of client
responses . . . and little by little the possibility of research in this
field became a reality (Rogers, 1970, p. 247).

If we acknowledge that there is meager research knowledge about the
actual practice of psychotherapy (cf. Frank, 1961) and if we accept the
challenge laid down by Truax and Carkhuff (1967) that virtually all forward movement in the theory of psychotherapeutic practice has emerged
from a study of actual clinical practice, then I suggest that an effective
way of studying the actual data of psychotherapeutic practice is by means
of the conditions-operations-consequences paradigm.

In order to do this, we need libraries of the work of psychotherapists
with actual patients (Mahrer, 1979). This library may include videotapes,
audiotapes, and verbatim transcripts. It should include the work of all
kinds of psychotherapists with all kinds of patients. It should include
single sessions from the beginning, middle, and ending phases of psychotherapy. It should include complete sessions, from the beginning to
the end of psychotherapy. It should include representative sessions and
sessions containing interesting and special psychotherapeutic happenings. The data contained in such libraries are the precious material from
which theories of psychotherapeutic practice may be further developed.

*The study of patient conditions.* This consists of studying what patients
do or how patients are antecedent to therapist operations. Suppose that
the patient says, "I know I have to be more assertive. I'm just a wimp.
Everyone walks all over me. I have to be more assertive." Or, "Well I
know I should be tough. I can be confident. I just need a little help and
everything'll be better." How do you go about making sense of that?
Would your theory tell you that the patient may be defining the problem
which therapy is to address? Do you regard the patient as self-critical
and self-derogatory? Is the patient being a parent to his child? Is the
patient defining the role to be ascribed to the therapist? Is the patient
being passive and dependent? Is the patient warding off an inner fear

that there will be no change? Is the patient expressing a current residual of an early situation in which parental figures are critical and rejecting of the child? Each theory of psychotherapeutic practice has some way of making sense of these data.

What are the key components the theory uses in making sense of what the patient does? Do we listen for the symbolic meanings? What symbolic meanings do we use? Do we listen by noticing the effects on the therapist? What effects? Do we listen for the degree of feeling or experiencing? How do we judge that? Do we pay attention to the facts included in what the patient says? Which facts are the more important ones?

When the patient is judged as doing this or that (or being like this or like that), what therapist operations are then in order? What are the relationships between the patient condition and the ensuing therapist operations? In this functional sense, how many categories does the theory use to make sense of what the patient does and how the patient is? Are there two or three major categories or are there 10 or 20? What are they? If the patient is regarded as being self-critical and self-derogatory, what are the likely therapist operations? Does the therapist demonstrate acceptance of the patient, describe the patient's feelings, explain why the patient is this way, discuss the likely underlying cognitive assumptions?

*The study of patient consequences.* We may further the development of theories of practice by studying particular patient consequences. First we flag certain patient consequences or events. Then we study the relationships between these patient consequences and antecedent events (cf. Eldred et al., 1954). Our center of study may be a single patient statement or a cluster of patient statements. In its simple form, we may study the therapist operations which more or less immediately precede that patient consequence, i.e., the immediate therapist statement or the three or four therapist statements preceding the patient consequence. Or we may examine the patterning of therapist and patient interchanges which precede our flagged patient consequence by a few minutes or more.

How do you go about selecting the kinds of patient consequences you want to study? One way is to look for whatever you regard as indications that something good is happening. These may include moments when therapy is working, when progress is occurring, either in general or specifically with regard to this patient in this session. Rogers regarded these as special "moments of movement":

. . . during this past year I have spent many hours listening to recorded interviews—trying to listen as naively as possible. I have endeavored to soak up all the cues I could capture as to the process, as to what elements are significant in change. Then I have tried to abstract from that sensing the simplest abstractions which would describe them. . . . I came . . . to appreciate what I think of as "moments of movement"—moments when it appears that change actually occurs (1970, pp. 128, 130).

Look for those moments in the session when you know that something important is going on right here. Therapy is working. A real change is occurring. Some of these events may be important mainly because the therapeutic method is moving along. Here is where the patient was undergoing intense experiencing. Here is where the patient moved from fighting the therapist to being wholly preoccupied with something that really bothered her. Here is where the patient seemed to have insight into the problem. Others of these events are important because they contain welcomed changes in the person who is the patient. Right here, and from here on, the continuous headache went away, or the stuttering was replaced by fluent speech. Here is where the patient became a different person: She was now sure of herself and on top of things; he is now being free and liberated; for the first time she is actually being a person in her own right, intact and independent.

Choose whatever moments are important to you, moments which compel you and excite you. Look for those moments which you would like to have happen again. Once you have located such important patient consequences, try to find what the therapist did, or what the therapist and patient together did, which may have helped bring about that consequence. Look back over the last few therapist statements and over the last few therapist-patient interchanges. Look back still further. Somewhere in those data may well be hints and cues about what helped to bring about the significant moments. By doing this, you are engaged in an enterprise (if you do this with some rigor, we call it research) which may well suggest further developments in the theory of psychotherapy.

There is a kind of disturbing and exciting risk in studying psychotherapy in this way. The risk is that you will actually learn something which does not fit too well with your theory of psychotherapeutic practice. Lambert and Bergin (1976) warn that therapists may be confronted with hard data which may not fit well with their theory of psychotherapeutic practice. As indicated in Figure 1.1, these data will have little or no impact upon the parent theory of human beings, but they open the door to possible changes (further developments) in the theory of practice—for those who are ready and willing to see the opening.

*The study of therapist operations.* The theory of psychotherapeutic practice can be further developed by looking carefully at therapeutic operations. With your attention on some therapist operation, ask such questions as the following:

(a)  What are the conditions under which the therapist does this? Does the therapist do this more when the patient is this way or that way?
(b)  What are the consequences of the therapist doing this? When the therapist does this, how many consequences seem to occur and what are they?
(c)  When the therapist does this under these conditions, what are the consequences, and when the therapist does this under those other conditions, what are the consequences?

Consider any therapist operation, phrased as carefully or as generally as you wish, and ask the above questions. For example, if you like to use reflections or if you like to interpret or if you like to invite a patient to carry out some prescribed task ("Tell your stomach that you are disappointed with it"), then study the antecedents and consequences of that operation. Under what patient conditions are reflections used? Under what conditions is this kind of interpretation used? What are the consequences of this kind of reflection or interpretation? When reflection or interpretation is used under these conditions, how do the consequences compare with its use under these other conditions?

Once again, the disturbingly exciting risk is that one may learn something which may or may not fit with the theory of practice. The theory of practice may say that reflections are to be used under these conditions; the consequences of a good interpretation are supposed to look like that. Maybe the actual data confirm the expectations, and maybe they do not. Through a systematic and honest study of therapist operations, it is possible further to develop the theory of psychotherapeutic practice.

## The Kinds of Category Systems We Need

In order to study conditions-operations-consequences in a way which can help us further develop theories of psychotherapeutic practice, we need systems of categorizing what patients and therapists do. We need one set of categories for patient conditions and consequences, and another set of categories for therapist operations.

Each category system must make sense in terms of its theory of psychotherapeutic practice, and it must make sense of the actual data of patients and therapists. This means that an experiential theory of practice will have its category system, each behavioral theory of practice will have its own category system, and so will every other theory of practice. With regard to categories of therapist operations, there likely may be a fair measure of commonality across many category systems, as well as a fair measure of differences. Some therapist operations are shared by several theories of practice. Other therapist operations are unique to particular theories of practice.

On the other hand, the categories of patient behavior (how the patient is being, what the patient is doing) come largely from the theory of practice, and therefore will generally have much less commonality across different category systems. By assembling a rather large set of therapist categories, it is possible to incorporate most of what most therapists do. In other words, it seems quite possible to assemble a single therapist category system to accommodate most therapists. However, it seems unlikely to assemble a patient category system which would cut across most or even many therapies. Each theory of practice has its own way of making sense of (categorizing) what patients do and how they are.

Each category system must make sense in terms of the theory of practice. That is, it must refer to and have direct implications for practice. It may make all sorts of sense in terms of the larger theory of human beings, but if it fails to make much sense in terms of practice, it just is not worth much. Gendlin (1972) shows how the usual psychodiagnostic system makes little sense in terms of practice:

> Few terms from psychopathology tell us what to do in psychotherapy. For example, if the patient is "schizophrenic—undifferentiated tendencies," what does that tell me about how to approach him? Little can be said about what to do which would be applicable to all who are given this label and are not applicable to many patients with other labels. Compare this diagnostic label with the category: "If the patient is quite verbal, but speaks only about externals and daily events. . . ." This category requires certain kinds of therapist procedures and allows us to discuss what we do. Notice that this is not a category of psychopathology! Some

schizophrenic individuals, some neurotics, and some normals will present a therapist with this problem. Nor is it a class of patients. The same individual who presents one type of in-therapy behavior now may present a different sort later (p. 345).

The experiential theory of practice has no use for a category system based upon standard diagnostic nomenclature. On the other hand, other theories of practice may well use categories from that nomenclature. Each theory of practice is free to develop its own category system for what therapists and patients do. My suggestion is that we acknowledge the importance of developing different category systems and that each system needs to make sense in terms of both the theory of human beings and the conditions-operations-consequences paradigm.

*Other Advantages of Using The Conditions-Operations-Consequences Paradigm*

*We can learn from other approaches to practice.* Any theory of practice can study the actual data of other approaches by using the conditions-operations-consequences paradigm. An experiential theory of practice can study the transcripts (or audiotapes or videotapes) of psychoanalytic therapists, cognitive behavioral therapists, any therapists whatsoever. We can do this by using our own category system and examining these other data in terms of patient conditions, therapeutic operations, and patient consequences. In the same way, any theory of practice may study the work of therapists from any other approach.

By studying the work of other therapists, we may learn that there are additional patient conditions under which our own methods can be used. We may learn that other therapist operations are followed by the kinds of patient consequences which we value. We may learn that our therapist operations, used under these new patient conditions, are linked with patient consequences which are of value to us. Looked at in terms of conditions-operations-consequences, each approach can learn a fair amount from other approaches.

*Students can learn the practice of psychotherapy.* The conditions-operations-consequences paradigm serves as an effective way of learning the practice of psychotherapy. The data consist of one's own tapes and transcripts as well as a library of tapes and transcripts of experienced therapists.

Students would be able to follow the whole sequence of conditions-operations-consequences from the beginning to the end of sessions by experienced therapists of identified persuasions. When the patient does this, what do I do? When I do that, what are the consequences? Students would be able to study ways in which experienced therapists deal with given patient conditions. What do I do at the very beginning of sessions? What do I do when the patient attacks me? What do I do when there is a long silence and I begin thinking about my own personal problems? Students would be able to study the kinds of patient consequences they want to learn to help bring about. How do I bring the patient to a point where she has such emotionally laden insight? How do I help bring about such a washing away of the nagging headache? Students would be able to learn when to use specific therapeutic operations and the consequences of using them that way. Self-disclosure used under these conditions seems to be followed by those consequences. When the patient is being this way, if I reflect, those seem to be the consequences. If I carry out this operation under that condition, here is the likely consequence.

Students can approach the conditions-operations-consequences way of studying from either an artistic, highly individualistic perspective or from a rigorously technical perspective. One views either the artist or the technician at work. The conditions-operations-consequences way of studying accommodates either preference.

In addition to studying other therapists, students can study their own work by attending to patient conditions or therapist operations or patient consequences. Each of these, and their interrelationships, can be looked at in terms of some sort of problem, some sort of accomplishment, or some sort of puzzlement. For example, the student may be compelled by a patient consequence, some patient happening or occurrence. It is meaningful because it is a problem for the student. Look what awful thing happened here. What could possibly account for that? I am ashamed and worried about this. Or it is meaningful because it is delightful. Look what wonderful thing happened. How did this precious event ever come about? Or the patient consequence may be compelling because of its unusualness. This is odd. What accounts for something like this? I am puzzled and bewildered by this occurrence. Students can follow whole sessions by allowing themselves to be compelled by these kinds of questions about the progressive flow of conditions-operations-consequences throughout the session.

*The Role of "Outcome" Research: Essentially Useless*

My proposition is that a theory of psychotherapy is further developed by studying the actual data of psychotherapeutic practice. More specifically, the proposition is that we can further develop an experiential theory of psychotherapeutic practice by studying the relationships between patient conditions, therapist operations, and patient consequences. I suggest that our ways of studying psychotherapy by means of "outcome research" are essentially useless if our aim is to further develop an experiential theory of psychotherapeutic practice or any other theory of practice.

I suggest that "outcome" research is essentially useless in answering such questions about patient conditions as the following: How do you go about making sense of what patients do and say? What are the useful data in the process of making sense of what patients do and say? When the patient is judged as doing this or that (or being like this or like that), what therapist operations are then in order? What are the relationships between the patient condition and the ensuing therapist operations? I suggest that "outcome" research is essentially useless in answering such questions about patient consequences as the following: What kinds of therapist operations (or therapist-patient conjoint operations) are antecedent to selected patient consequences? What seemed to help bring about those patient consequences? I suggest that "outcome" research is essentially useless in answering such questions about therapist operations as the following: What are the patient conditions under which the therapist carries out this operation? What are the patient consequences of this therapist operation? When the therapist carries out this operation, how many consequences are there, and what are they? When the therapist carries out this operation under these conditions, what are the patient consequences, and when the therapist carries out this operation under those other conditions, what are the patient consequences? If outcome research is essentially useless in answering such questions, it is unable to provide data which would help further develop a theory of experiential practice or any other theories of practice. For these purposes, such outcome research is useless.

On the other hand, outcome research is designed to answer its own set of questions. However, the answers to these questions shed little light on the further development of theories of psychotherapeutic practice. Here are some of the questions outcome research is designed to answer: Is psychotherapy effective, especially compared with other modes of treatment? Given this problem (difficulty, complaint, symptom, target behavior, psychiatric illness), to what extent does psychotherapy alleviate the problem? How does psychotherapy compare with other modes of alleviating the problem? How does this therapeutic approach compare with other therapeutic approaches in dealing with a given problem? To what extent does psychotherapy achieve the goals it says it wants to accomplish? Which mode of treatment is more cost-efficient? Are there any differences among psychologists and psychiatrists and psychoanalysts and social workers in regard to their therapeutic effectiveness? Are there differences in outcome between short-term and long-term therapies? Are there differences between therapists with more experience and those with less experience in regard to outcome? What are the outcomes of psychotherapy in general? What are the outcomes of this or that kind of psychotherapy? If the therapist uses client-centered facilitating conditions, or psychoanalytic interpretations (or anything else a therapy considers useful), is the therapy effective? Are there any differences in outcome between therapies that require patients to come once a week, twice a week, five times a week, once every two weeks, for 50-minute sessions, sessions of 20 minutes, 10-minute sessions? What kinds of therapies are comparatively more effective with what kinds of problems in what kinds of patients under what kinds of circumstances?

To the extent that these are legitimate questions touching legitimate concerns, outcome research may very well provide some useful answers. However, such research offers a low yield for questions relating to our patient conditions, therapist operations, and patient consequences. Such research sheds minimal light on actual therapist operations, the conditions under which they are used, and the consequences of their use. Such research fails to provide data which can be used effectively to contribute to the further development of a theory of psychotherapeutic practice.

If you look again at Figure 1.1, most of the issues and questions about the "outcome" of psychotherapy fall in the domain of "other psychotherapeutic issues and phenomena." They have little relationship to the actual data of psychotherapeutic practice. The job of defining the goals of psychotherapy, its outcomes, is the province of the parent theory of human beings. An existential-humanistic theory of human beings will outline its own brand of goals, the outcomes of psychotherapy, the avenues along which persons (including patients) can progress. So too will a biopsychological theory, a social learning theory, a psychoanalytic theory, and every other theory of human beings. The results of research will have little serious effect upon the parent theory's notions of the goals and outcomes of psychotherapy. If research suggests that clients are not necessarily internally freer following psychoanalytic therapy, that may have little impact on the parent psychoanalytic theory of what the outcomes of therapy ought to be, or how persons can become. While concerns about outcomes are of central importance to administrators and other groups in the psychotherapy marketplace, only a slim portion of the results will be of interest to the parent theory of human beings, and virtually none of the results relates in any systematic manner to the theory of psychotherapeutic practice. The net result is that such studies make little difference to the theories of human beings and perhaps even less difference to the further development of theories of psychotherapeutic practice.

### The Study of "In-therapy Outcomes"

There is a way of studying the outcomes (or results or consequences) of psychotherapy so as to contribute to the further development of the theory of psychotherapeutic practice. The key proposition is that some of the consequences in the conditions-operations-consequences paradigm are coterminal with welcomed and desirable "outcomes of psychotherapy." By studying the actual data of psychotherapeutic practice, by studying what occurs in psychotherapy, we can use the conditions-operations-consequences paradigm, and thereby we can answer the question: What therapeutic operations, carried out under what patient conditions, lead to those patient consequences which are regarded as welcomed, desirable therapeutic outcomes?

Kiesler (1966) is representative of those who call attention to these in-therapy outcomes and who suggest the importance of studying them. From the perspective of an experiential theory of practice, some patient consequences (in the conditions-operations-consequences paradigm) involve actual changes in the personality and behavior of the patient. These are the in-therapy payoffs of effective experiential psychotherapy. Much, if not all, of what would be considered the outcome of effective experiential psychotherapy shows itself in the therapeutic session itself. This consists of the patient consequences which are important, valuable, welcomed, desirable happenings or events in the psychotherapy session. These are the consequences we can study by following the conditions-operations-consequences paradigm. They are present in experiential psychotherapy, and I am sure that they are also present in most other psychotherapies.

There are other consequences in the conditions-operations-consequences paradigm which are not valuable in-therapy outcomes. Although they may be important because they are part of the process of psychotherapy, they are not regarded as valuable in-therapy outcomes. For example, in experiential therapy, it is an important consequence when the patient is able to achieve a high level of experiencing. It is important when the patient is able to pour most of her attention onto some meaningful focal center. But these are not personality/behavioral changes; they are not what is ordinarily meant by the outcomes of psychotherapy. They are, instead, instrumental consequences, process consequences, consequences which are intended to pave the way for subsequent in-therapy outcomes. Experiential therapy has a set of these process consequences, and it has a set of in-therapy outcome consequences. Undoubtedly, other theories of practice likewise have these two kinds of consequences, both of which can be studied through the conditions-operations-consequences paradigm.

If our aim is to contribute to the further development of the theory of experiential practice, to what extent are there significant extra-therapy outcomes over and above in-therapy outcomes? Extra-therapy outcomes are studied by going outside the therapy session and looking at the patient before therapy, after therapy, during the course of therapy, but outside the actual sessions themselves. From the perspective of experiential therapy, our answer is that few if any extra-therapy outcomes have significance for the further development of the experiential theory of practice. I suspect that this is true for most other theories of practice also. However, the answer must be given by proponents of each theory on this question.

To what extent do in-therapy outcomes include extra-therapy outcomes? That is, to what extent do the outcomes (personality/behavioral changes) which occur outside of the therapy session occur in the therapy session itself? From the perspective of experiential therapy, the answer to the first question is very much and the answer to the second question is very little. This therapy is expressly designed so that virtually all the classes or kinds of extra-therapy personality/behavioral changes occur in the therapy session itself. I suspect that this is much less true of most other therapies. Here is an issue which lends itself to interesting theoretical and research study. However, there is one glaring exception.

Many therapies may be described as more or less direct training in being the ways the therapy holds as welcomed and desirable extra-therapy outcomes. This point calls for some discussion.

*In many therapies, the method is the outcome.* Many psychotherapies consist of methods and procedures which are direct training and practice in being the way the therapy says the patient is to be at the conclusion of successful and effective therapy. To the extent that the patient can follow the therapeutic method, the patient is practicing being a successful outcome.

In some therapies, both the method and the outcome are for the patient to allow a stream of thoughts and feelings and ideas to flow along easily. The patient is not to fight the flow, not to interfere with it, not to be overcome by the flow of material. This is formalized as the method of free association. It is also one mark of the successful outcome of those therapies. "The ability to free associate may be considered a criterion for termination of analysis. . . . The psychoanalytic patient is required to do (as a means for his cure) what he cannot possibly do" (Naranjo, 1969, p. 60). The method and the outcome are one and the same. The method is direct training and practice in being the outcome.

Some therapies regard entrusting oneself to others as a mark of successful therapeutic achievement. The patient is to be trusting rather than pulled back, resistant, seeking to preserve oneself. Yet these therapies require that the patient be this way in order to follow the method. For example, the patient is to lie down and not see the therapist who sits up and observes him. The patient is to trust that the therapist knows the patient better than the patient does. The patient is to entrust himself to the better judgment of the therapist. This is a direct training in what is considered an outcome measure. The method is the outcome. By following the method, the patient is getting direct practice in the outcome.

In some therapies, the outcome of therapy includes being able to step out of one's personality and to identify with or be empathic with or "be" whatever parts of one's personality the patient avoids or "projects" onto the external world. It is quite an achievement to be free enough to step out of what one is and to "be" that which one avoids or defends against. Yet that is what the method requires when the Gestalt therapist tells the patient to "be" his hated father or his menacing cancer or the derailed locomotive. The method is direct training in outcome.

Some therapies value the outcome of patients' being able to discuss their feelings, to attend to their feelings, to explore and talk about their feelings. The method of accomplishing this goal is for patients to discuss, attend to, explore, and talk about their feelings. It is curious to note how few methods we really use and what a large proportion of our methods are direct training in outcome. It may even be more illuminating to add to this proportion the so-called "methods" which may easily be described as providing a model or exemplar for the patient (cf. Jourard, 1968, 1976). If you do as I do, you will be the outcome I want. In these ways, many in-therapy outcomes (happenings, events) are also extra-therapy outcomes. This is a large and special class of extra-therapy outcomes which occur in the therapy session itself.

*How to derive in-therapy outcomes.* The proposition is that if you are interested in carrying forward a theory of practice, it can be done by studying those patient consequences which are also in-therapy outcomes. All right, how are these in-therapy outcomes identified? Two ways have been mentioned. One is by examining the large group of patient consequences which the therapist regards as welcomed and desirable. Right here, in this part of the session, the patient stopped stuttering or was able to cry or the headache washed away or he was being confident and sure of himself; for this patient, these are new and welcomed ways of being because of this and that consideration. This is one way. The second way is by examining the method itself and by identifying certain therapist operations as direct training in welcomed and desirable patient consequences, i.e., in-therapy outcomes.

There is a third way. Every therapist operation, every statement or behavior by the therapist, can be studied from the perspective of these questions: What is the patient invited (asked, told, instructed, directed) to do or be like? As a consequence of this therapist statement, what is the patient supposed to do or be like? Some therapist statements contain few or no such invitations or directives. However, other therapist statements emerge with moderate or high loadings. They are quite explicit in inviting or directing the patient to do this, be that way, change in this direction, undergo that way of being. The patient is given explicit tasks or directions; the patient is told what to do and how to be.

A careful study of therapist statements and operations will yield a set of explicit changes the patient is to carry out, specific behaviors for the patient, concrete ways of being. When all of these are carefully sifted and organized, either in a single session or across many sessions, for this patient or for many patients, a singularly interesting picture emerges. Included in this picture is the way the patient (or patients) is to be. In short, what will emerge is an organized picture of in-therapy outcomes, what the therapist is inviting this patient (or many patients) to be, to become. By a careful study of therapist statements, we can derive that therapist's version of welcomed and desirable changes or in-therapy outcomes or ways the patient is to be.

With rare exception, virtually all therapist statements lend themselves to such study, across all therapeutic approaches and all sessions with all patients. In this way, by studying what is simply present in many therapist statements, we can derive in-therapy outcomes which are functionally present and real. The data are right there in front of us.

*In-therapy outcomes which are the consequences of therapist operations.* What are the in-therapy outcomes of experiential psychotherapy? What are the consequences of therapist operations, carried out under given conditions, which are considered welcomed and desirable from the perspective of our humanistic-existential theory of human beings? What follows is the answer as given by the theory of experiential psychotherapy. The invitation is for other theories of practice to identify their own in-therapy outcomes.

1) There is an increase in the depth and breadth of what this person has available to experience; this includes changes in behaviors which provide for these experiencings, changes in the constructed worlds which provide appropriate contexts for these experiencings, and a heightening of accompanying good bodily sensations and feelings.

If this person has a potential for experiencing warm and tender sexuality, one welcomed and desirable therapeutic consequence (in-therapy outcome) is that the person experience this more deeply, more fully. The patient may have experienced this mildly or seldom or practically not at all. One change is that the sheer experiencing of warm and tender sexuality occurs more fully and deeply. A related change is that the person is able to behave in ways which provide for this fuller amplitude of experiencing. The person also is able to behave in ways which construct the kinds of worlds which are appropriate for the fuller and deeper experiencing of this potential. Finally, the change is toward a heightening of good bodily sensations and feelings accompanying the carrying forward of this experiencing (e.g., excitement, aliveness, vitality). Whatever this person has available to experience is carried forward in these ways.

2) There is an increase in the experiencing of "integrative" relationships between and among this person's potentials. That is, there is a
change in the bodily feelinged relationships between and among this
person's potentials for experiencing. The change is from disintegrative
relationships (e.g., those which are bothersome, painful, disturbing) to
integrative (e.g., those which are peaceful, harmonious).

The relationship between the patient and a deeper potential may be
distinctly disintegrative. If, for example, the deeper potential consists
of the experiencing of aggressive defiance, stubborn resistance, then the
patient may virtually never experience this. Instead she may be sweet,
smiling, cooperative, helpful, and never aggressively defiant. Should
therapy bring her into a somewhat more imminent proximity with the
deeper potential, she becomes short of breath, with a rushing in her
ears; she gets a little dizzy and light-headed; she feels tight and full of
tension; she becomes withdrawn and pulled away. In short, the relationship between the patient and the deeper potential is a disintegrative
one. In the course of the session, the welcomed and desirable consequence is that now there is an integrative relationship with this deeper
potential. She can play with the aggressive defiance. Interacting with
the aggressive defiance is accompanied with pleasant bodily sensations,
feelings of peacefulness, inner harmony, wholeness. She can relate to
the stubborn resistance, touch and fondle it, look it straight in the face,
and all with good integrative bodily sensations and feelings.

Likewise, there is an analogous change in the patient's constructed
worlds, as well as in the behavioral means of instituting relationships
between the patient and these worlds. As her own relationships with
the aggressive defiance move from disintegrative toward integrative,
there is an analogous change away from disintegrative relationships and
toward integrative relationships with constructed parts of the patient's
worlds. For example, no longer are there sensations of anxiety and
tension in relationship with such internal bodily phenomena as ulcers
or lower back pains or that constant hurtful heaviness in the head region.
In effect, these internal bodily phenomena recede and wash away. Likewise, the patient may no longer experience the anxiety and tension in
relationships with the aggressively defiant spouse or child or parent. In
effect, these external phenomena also wash away, together with the
behaviors which served to construct them in the patient's world and to
insure the former disintegrative relationship between the patient and
the spouse or child or parent.

The point is that all of these changes occur within the therapy session, and thereby constitute a second class of in-therapy outcomes which occur as consequences of therapist operations under particular patient conditions.

3) There is a qualitative disengagement from the patient's whole identity, the ordinary, continuing personhood in which the patient had existed. Instead, the nuclear personality change is one of being the good form of the deeper personality process; the patient now experiences as the good form of the deeper potential. This is a substantive, nuclear personality change.

If the deeper potential includes the experiencing of warm and tender sexuality, the patient is now able fully and completely to be this potential, to live and exist in it, to transform into being it. If the deeper potential includes the experiencing of aggressive defiance, the patient is able to undergo the nuclear change into being the good form of this aggressive defiance.

At the same time, there is a receding or washing away of constructed worlds and behavioral means for either avoiding these former deeper potentials or experiencing them in painfully disintegrative ways. No longer must the patient be a person who avoids and denies the experiencing of warm and tender sexuality or aggressive defiance. No longer must the patient be a person who experiences warm and tender sexuality in painfully disintegrative ways or who experiences aggressive defiance in painfully disintegrative ways.

Symmetrically, the new person uses new behaviors to build new worlds in which there is a wholesome good-feelinged experiencing of the good forms of warm and tender sexuality or aggressive defiance.

Again, all of these changes occur within the therapy session and thereby constitute a third class of in-therapy outcomes which occur as consequences of therapist operations under particular patient conditions.

4) There is a consideration of actual changes in the extra-therapeutic person living and being in the extra-therapeutic world. To the extent that the patient has undergone the above three kinds of in-therapy changes, the patient is ready to consider this fourth kind of change. It is here that the changing patient has the choice and opportunity to entertain the risk of changes in the extra-therapy world.

This fourth class of in-therapy consequences includes the sheer consideration of actual changes in the extra-therapy world. This may consist of changes in the degree of welcoming such changes, in the degree to which the patient seriously considers the real possibility of changing ways of being and behaving. Or this may consist of changes in the sheer intent to undergo defined changes in the extra-therapy world. Or this may consist of actually trying out changes which are intended for occurrence in the extra-therapy world.

There are two kinds of changes. One consists of changes in bad-feelinged ways of being and behaving. To the extent that the patient has allowed substantive changes to occur in the session, the patient has moved into being a qualitatively changing person. That is, the patient has allowed himself to be a person who experiences available potentials more fully and deeply, who has more integrated relationships with deeper potentials, and who has greater freedom of movement in disengaging from his continuing identity and being the deeper potential. The question is whether the patient is ready to consider being this changing person in the real world outside therapy, and thereby leave behind the bad-feelinged ways of being which constitute the old continuing person. This is the risk and this is the new choice.

For example, the old continuing person had continuous headaches, stuttered almost all the time, trembled and shook, had back pains, heard inner voices screeching how rotten she is, smiled when she was angry, had terrible pains in the shoulders. During the session the patient joined into processes of therapeutic change so that the last half of the session was, almost for the first time, free of the headache. Speech was fluent. Head and arms were steady. The pains in the back and shoulders were gone. The head was clear; there were no voices. Being angry happened with no smiling. Now the risk is that of being the changing person who was there in the last half of the session in the real extra-therapy world.

Is the patient ready to give up the old ways of being and behaving which constructed and insured pain? Is the changing person ready to let go of that part which must construct the family into the ultimate rejecting agent, to let go of building someone into the hated enemy, to let go of constructing worlds in which the net result is that awful experiencing of being used, taken from, destroyed? Letting go means also disengaging from all the subtly effective behaviors which do the painful work in the utterly real extra-therapeutic world.

This is one class of actual changes in the extra-therapy world. It includes changes in those ways of being and behaving which are accompanied with bad (painful, disjunctive) bodily sensations and feelings. The actual consideration of such changes constitutes one class of in-therapy outcomes. The second class consists in being and behaving as the changing person, with heightened good (pleasant, exciting, alive, whole, harmonious, solid, grounded) bodily sensations and feelings.

In the session, the changing person tasted what it is like to welcome actual new ways of being and behaving. Is the patient now ready to have that same eager readiness in the extra-therapy world, to be welcoming toward the possibility of risking one's own changings in ways of being and behaving?

In the session, the patient allowed the heightened experiencing of potentials, the more integrative relationship with deeper potentials, the actual being of deeper potentials. Now the patient faces the possibility of allowing these changes to occur also in the extra-therapy world, to be a changing person whose bodily sensations and feelings are good ones.

One faces the risk of being a person who experiences a new freedom and open spontaneity, a new giving and yielding, a new closeness and intimacy, a new silliness and giddiness, a new firmness and toughness, or whatever is there for this person to experience in its good form. But this carries with it the risky possibility of meaningful and significant changes in ways of behaving. It means behaving in new ways which provide for appropriate situational contexts which accommodate such experiencings. It means the new occurrence of subtle little behaviors as well as behaviors which effect sometimes massive changes in one's family, work, interpersonal relations, style of life, surroundings, body, physical appearance. In the therapy session, the patient frequently allows some of these new behaviors to occur. The patient may, for virtually the first time, with good sensations and feelings, laugh uproariously, have powerful erections, be silly and giddy, scream out orders, cry in loving tenderness. The change consists of the in-therapy consideration of being these ways in the extra-therapy world.

Here are four kinds of in-therapy outcomes which the theory of experiential psychotherapy holds as occurring within the session itself. By a disciplined study of these in-therapy outcomes, our theory of practice can move ahead. My invitation is for other theories of psychotherapy to identify their own valuable in-therapy outcomes, whose study may contribute to the further development of their own theory of practice.

Experiential psychotherapy develops by accepting the working characteristics of a good theory of practice described in this chapter and thereby studying actual practice through the vehicle of the conditions-operations-consequences paradigm. I suggest that this is a reasonable way of further developing many of our theories of psychotherapeutic practice.

# 2

# *What Experiential Psychotherapy Is and How It Works*

The purpose of this chapter is to answer two questions. One may be phrased as follows: What is experiential psychotherapy? What are the ways in which it may be defined? The second may be phrased in these ways: How does experiential psychotherapy work? How does a therapist carry out experiential therapy? What is the sequence of steps in experiential psychotherapy? In the first chapter, my aim was to show how a theory of psychotherapeutic practice, experiential psychotherapy in particular, can grow and develop down from a parent theory of human beings and up from a careful study of the actual data of practice. My aim in this chapter is to give an overview of the experiential psychotherapy which comes about and develops from these two processes.

## WHAT IT IS

### *It Is a Theory of Psychotherapy Growing out of a Humanistic-Existential Theory of Human Beings*

Experiential psychotherapy is the child of a humanistic-existential theory of human beings, especially as given in the writings of persons such as Gordon W. Allport, Ludwig Binswanger, Martin Buber, Charlotte Buhler, F. J. Buytendijk, Henri F. Ellenberger, Viktor Frankl, Erich

Fromm, Eugene T. Gendlin, A. Giorgi, A. Gurwitsch, Martin Heidegger, Edmund Husserl, Karl Jaspers, Sören Kierkegaard, Ronald D. Laing, Abraham H. Maslow, Rollo May, M. Meerleau-Ponty, Claudio Naranjo, Jacob Needleman, P. D. Ouspensky, Jean-Paul Sartre, Erwin Straus, W. Van Dusen, R. Von Eckartsberg, D. Wyss, and others. Histories of this body of thought, viewed through the window of experiential psychotherapy, are given in the works of those such as Havens (1973), May, Angel, and Ellenberger (1958), and Wyss (1973). This particular form of experiential psychotherapy, while rooted in the conceptual bed of humanism and existentialism, is directly linked to my own version of these writings (Mahrer, 1978a).

*Humanistic-existential thought and the field of psychotherapy.* Of the philosophers and thinkers in the history of existential and phenomenological thought, I consider Edmund Husserl and his pupil, Martin Heidegger, as perhaps foremost in taking significant steps toward the field of clinical psychotherapeutics. But their work was not enough by itself. What was needed was some reaching out for such ideas from the field of psychotherapy.

Enter Ludwig Binswanger. I credit this psychiatrist with the role of the major figure who turned to existential thinking from the field of clinical psychotherapeutics. Among those who reacted strongly against the very foundations of Freud's basic theory of human beings, Binswanger may be acknowledged as the major figure who not only found existential and phenomenological thought more suitable, but also brought that body of thought into the field of psychotherapy (Havens, 1973; Holt, 1968). In my opinion, a second figure, also quite important, was Minkowsky. In concert, these two clinicians were prominent in carrying forward the ideas of existential and phenomenological thought into the field of psychotherapy.

If we look at some of the preeminent pioneers, we see Husserl and Heidegger as existential-phenomenological thinkers who moved that body of thought toward clinical psychotherapeutics, and we see Binswanger and Minkowsky as clinicians who called upon existential-phenomenological thought. Here are the beginnings of the theory of clinical practice from which experiential psychotherapy emerges. Although other existentialists and phenomenologists play significant roles in that scenario, and although other clinicians also contributed at the time, these are four of the dominant figures in the actual origins of a theory of experiential psychotherapy.

*Stirrings toward a theory of psychotherapeutic practice.* Once a theory of human beings concerns itself with psychotherapy, sooner or later there are stirrings toward generating and extracting a theory of psychotherapeutic practice. Binswanger had undertaken a momentous split from Freud's theoretical conceptions of human beings, but he remained generally faithful to the psychoanalytic method of therapy. Indeed, Binswanger and Freud ". . . shared a considerable span of working years, and the fact that psychoanalysis was a comparatively late product of Freud's life allowed Binswanger to be a contributor to the movement at a very early stage of its development . . ." (Holt, 1968, p. 241). Binswanger tried to follow a psychoanalytic method of therapy while viewing the events of psychotherapy through the eyes of an existential theory of human beings. It could not be done. If you really accept the psychoanalytic way of carrying out therapy, you must also accept the psychoanalytic theory of human beings. If you really believe the existential theory of human beings, you will have difficulty trying to carry out a psychoanalytic way of doing therapy. Binswanger had difficulty.

Out of this conceptual antimony, Binswanger took steps toward formulating a theory of psychotherapy more in line with existential than psychoanalytic thinking. He referred to what was being born as existential analysis, and spoke about "being-in-the-world," an existential concept which nudged forward a theory of psychotherapy: "The formulation 'being-in-the-world' . . . is . . . a statement about an essential condition that determines existence in general. From the discovery and presentation of this essential condition, existential analysis received its decisive stimulation, its philosophical foundation and justification, as well as its methodological directives" (Binswanger, 1958a, p. 191). Here was the possibility of a new theory of psychotherapeutic practice, generated from an existential theory of human beings. But there it essentially stopped.

No intact theory of practice has fully emerged out of the existential theory of human beings. It is my impression that many clinicians hold to an existential theory of human beings while their work with patients is essentially psychoanalytic (cf. Boss, 1963; Condrau & Boss, 1971). The stirrings are still there, but little progress seems to have been made in developing an existential theory of psychotherapy with its own methods and procedures. This struggle is exemplified in Medard Boss's attempts to separate from Freud's psychoanalytic theory of human beings while still declaring the possibility of a unique way of doing psychotherapy. "At first, it seemed as if Daseinsanalysis differed from psychoanalysis only, or mainly, on the theoretical plane; however, it has become increasingly clear that theory and practice can never be wholly separated" (Condrau & Boss, 1971, p. 508). However, we are still at the stage of stirring toward our own approach to practice: "From the standpoint of method, Freudian psychoanalysis remains the basis of this psychotherapeutic approach. Nevertheless, it is just this philosophical reorientation in our conception of man's nature that opens up new ways of approaching the patient . . ." (Condrau & Boss, 1971, p. 489). We are still waiting for our own theory of practice.

And there are voices urging us to get on with the job. Vespe is representative of such nagging complaints: ". . . as existentialists we seem so adverse to conceptualizing our knowledge and formalizing our procedures that after some 30 years the existential in psychotherapy is in need of some kind of laxative! How fertile will existential psychotherapy be and how relevant will it become if its meaning cannot be grasped or communicated?" (1969, p. 84). Havens (1973) and May (1958, p. 76) echo the same frustration in the need to articulate a theory of psychotherapeutic practice from an existential theory of human beings. Yet the first steps had been taken and there was no turning back.

The purpose of this book is to propose a theory of psychotherapeutic practice which derives from existential, humanistic, and phenomenological bodies of thought. One way of defining experiential psychotherapy, then, is by referring to its conceptual roots in an existential-humanistic theory of human beings.

*It Is a Theory of Practice Which Accepts Experiencing as Its Pivotal Axis of Psychotherapeutic Change*

Every theory of psychotherapy has one or two pivotal ways of bringing about therapeutic movement or change. Of the various axes of psychotherapeutic changes, ours is that of experiencing. A second way of defining experiential psychotherapy is that it is a theory of practice which accepts experiencing as its pivotal axis of psychotherapeutic change. There are many ways of describing the axes of change used by the various theories of psychotherapy. Of these, I shall name four axes, including that of experiencing (see Figure 2.1).

One axis consists of insight and understanding. When the patient gains the right kind and amount of insight/understanding in the right way, then personality/behavioral change occurs. Some rely on the patient's acquiring insight and understanding of the relationship between the patient and the therapist. Some therapies favor insight/understanding of unconscious material. Some rest their faith on insight and understanding of the etiological circumstances in the life history of the patient, especially those in which the target problem first came about. Some favor insight and understanding of underlying cognitive assumptions, of feelings/emotions, of the therapist's world view, of the therapist's ideas about social relationships or what life is like or how people change or the nature of personality structure. Whatever the refinement, the pivotal axis of therapeutic change is some sort of proper insight and understanding.

Some therapies rely upon modification of the cues and stimuli upon which behavior is held to be contingent (see Figure 2.1). While there are

| Theory of Human Beings | Axis of Psychotherapeutic Change | | | |
|---|---|---|---|---|
| | Experiencing | Insight, Understanding | Modification of Behavioral Contingencies | Therapist-Patient Relationship |
| Humanistic-Existential | Logotherapy Feeling-Expressive Gestalt<br><br>Humanistic Intense Feeling Emotional Flooding Provocative Encounter, etc. | Existential | Self-Disclosure | Client-Centered |
| Biopsychic | Primal Daseinsanalysis Bioenergetics | Psychoanalytic Direct Psychoanalysis Analytic Transactional Analysis | | Psychoanalytic Direct Psychoanalysis |
| Biosocial Learning | Implosive | | Behavior Cognitive Behavior Rational-Emotive Systematic Desensitization | |
| Other | | Reality | | |

Figure 2.1. Illustrative Psychotherapies Classified by Theory of Human Beings and Major Axis of Psychotherapeutic Change

differences in the definition of behavior, differences in the supposed nature of the cues and stimuli upon which behavior is held as contingent, and differences in the ways of modifying these contingencies, many therapies accept this as their pivotal axis of therapeutic change.

Some therapies rely upon the patient-therapist relationship as their pivotal axis for personality-behavioral change. The notion is that the key to therapeutic change is the proper establishment and development of whatever is regarded as the right kind of patient-therapist relationship. Within this family, some may have faith in what they term the establishment and development of a transference relationship. Others may favor one which is characterized by empathic understanding, congruence, and positive regard. Still others favor different key components such as mutual trust or love or openness. Regardless of the favorite key components, the faith is that some kind of patient-therapist relationship is a pivotal axis of psychotherapeutic change. However, experiential psychotherapy does not accept this as its pivotal axis of psychotherapeutic change.

Our family of psychotherapy accepts experiencing as its pivotal axis of therapeutic change. This is the meaning of experiencing in our approach. To my knowledge, the actual term "experiential psychotherapy" is perhaps most appropriately credited to Carl Whitaker and Thomas Malone (1953). They used that term in the sense that genuine therapeutic change occurs through processes of experiencing. Thereafter, the term was extended and solidified by Gendlin, especially in his earlier works (e.g., 1961, 1962, 1964). Today it refers to a family of psychotherapies rooted in a humanistic-existential theory of human beings and accepting experiencing as its pivotal axis of psychotherapeutic change.

*It Is a Family of Psychotherapies Rooted in a Humanistic-Existential Theory of Human Beings and Accepting Experiencing as Its Pivotal Axis of Psychotherapeutic Change*

There are many psychotherapies which are rooted in the humanistic-existential conception of human beings or which accept experiencing as their pivotal axis of change or which qualify on both counts (Figure 2.1). Experiential psychotherapy is a family which may be defined by pointing out its working family members. A listing of these family members would include at least the following: logotherapy, feeling-expressive therapy, Daseins therapy, Daseinsanalysis, Gestalt therapy, existential therapy, existential analysis, humanistic therapy, intense feeling therapy, provocative therapy, holistic therapy, encounter therapy, bioenergetics therapy, psycho-imagination therapy, cathartic therapy, crisis mobilization therapy, phenomenological therapy, emotional flooding therapy, and others, including aspects of such related approaches as client-centered therapy, implosive therapy, and primal therapy.

Psychotherapists who fall in the experiential family include at least the following: Carl A. Whitaker, Thomas P. Malone, Rollo May, Eugene T. Gendlin, Ludwig Binswanger, Medard Boss, G. Condrau, Joseph Zinker, Joen Fagan, Irmalee Shepherd, James F. T. Bugental, Ernest Keen, G. Corey, A. Esterson, Ronald D. Laing, Leida Berg, Adrian Van Kaam, J. H. Van den Berg, H. E. Lehmann, A. R. Mahrer, Neil Friedman, J. B. P. Shaffer, Sidney M. Jourard, E. Sagarin, James Simkin, Frederick S. Perls, Paul Olsen, Rahe B. Corlis, Peter Rabe, Thomas Hora, Arthur Burton, M. Eigen, Leston J. Havens, D. Wyss, Earl Brown, Magda Denes, John Warkentin, Elizabeth Valerius, W. Van Dusen, Joseph E. Shorr, G. Serban, S. Rose, Claudio Naranjo, Hugh Mullen, Iris Sangiuliano, Abraham Levitsky, Henry Holt, Robert R. Carkhuff, Bernard G. Berenson, I. A. Caruso, Henri F. Ellenberger, H. Fingarette, John Enright, D. S. Arbuckle, and others.

Experiential psychotherapy is defined by pointing to the writings of these persons, as well as by pointing to the above psychotherapies. Some of the experiential psychotherapies share both the theoretical conception of human beings and the axis of therapeutic change. Some emphasize one or the other. In Figure 2.1, I have tried to place some of the members of the experiential family within an overall schema of the several proposed axes of psychotherapeutic change, and also the major theories of human beings. With regard to the major theories of human beings, I have organized these into humanistic-existential, biopsychic, and biosocial learning. This is one of many ways of organizing theoretical conceptualizations of human beings. With regard to the axis of psychotherapeutic change, I have used the fourfold division proposed earlier.

According to this schema, there are many therapies which, on both counts, fall outside the experiential family. For example, cognitive behavior therapy and rational-emotive therapy neither share a humanistic-existential theory of human beings nor count on experiencing as their major axis of therapeutic change. While the schema is exhaustive, some illustrative therapies which fall outside the experiential family on both counts, from my perspective, are included.

There are some therapies which do not share the humanistic-existential theory of human beings, but they do count upon experiencing as a major axis of psychotherapeutic change. As illustrations, primal therapy and implosive therapy may be said to use experiencing as their major avenue of change, but the former rests upon a biopsychic theory of human beings and the latter is built upon a biosocial learning theory of human beings, according to this schema.

Similarly, there are psychotherapies which share a humanistic-existential theory of human beings but which do not count upon experiencing as the major axis of personality change. As illustrations, Jourard's self-disclosure therapy and client-centered therapy use other major axes of psychotherapeutic change, while their predominant conceptualization of human beings is humanistic-existential.

This leaves a rather large group of therapies which fall within the experiential family on both counts (Figure 2.1). The question here is which of these therapies are more closely and systematically linked to a humanistic-existential theory of human beings and more closely and systematically use experiencing as the major axis of psychotherapeutic change? Which is the true exemplar of experiential psychotherapy?

Gestalt therapy is a dominant member of the family, and it has certainly toyed with the throne. Perls allows that there are three top contenders: "Gestalt therapy is one of the . . . three types of existential therapy: Frankl's logotherapy, the Daseins therapy of Binswanger, and Gestalt therapy" (Perls, 1971, p. 16). However, it may be that the humanistic-existential roots are contaminated by other basic conceptualizations of human beings: "Gestalt has been (and still is being) developed by Frederick S. Perls out of three distinct sources and influences: psychoanalysis, particularly as modified by the early Wilhelm Reich, European phenomenology-existentialism, and Gestalt psychology" (Enright, 1970, p. 107). Nevertheless, many salute Gestalt therapy as the true exemplar of the family, both in terms of theory of human beings and in terms of the mode of psychotherapeutic practice. Denes-Radomisli puts it well: "To my mind, and as I practice it, Gestalt therapy is the direct, immediate, and authentic translation of existential theory into practice through techniques that fulfill and actualize the theory more completely than any of the other existential technical approaches currently in use" (1977, p. 26).

Gendlin's experiential psychotherapy is, to my mind, another contender. Certainly its rich explosion in the 1960s justified the promise. However, it seems to have moved into increasingly greater concentration on the development and refinement of one primary method, focusing (1978a, 1978b).

As I read the scene, there is no single experiential psychotherapy.

There is a family of experiential psychotherapies, more or less sharing a common humanistic-existential theory of human beings, and, at the same time, developing and refining various ways of using the common experiential axis of psychotherapeutic change.

Here, then, are three avenues toward answering such questions as: What is experiential psychotherapy? What are the ways in which it may be defined?

## HOW IT WORKS

The main purpose here is to answer the following questions: How does experiential psychotherapy work? What is the sequence of steps in experiential psychotherapy? The secondary purpose is to answer the following questions: What are five kinds (or classes) of therapeutic experiencing? What are the methods for bringing about each kind of experiencing? Now that there are so many kinds of methods throughout the experiential family, how may they be orchestrated into a single, integrated system of experiential psychotherapy?

The context is a session. Each session of experiential psychotherapy uses the same five ways of bringing about therapeutic change. In some sessions, we may call upon only some of the five, and in other sessions we may use all five. Nevertheless, each session follows a sequence of five steps and each step is a kind or class of therapeutic experiencing (Mahrer, 1978b). We shall consider each step (or kind of therapeutic experiencing) in turn, on the understanding that these steps occur in each session, from the first through the last session.

### Attention-Centered Bodily Experiencing

As indicated in Figure 2.2, the first step (and also the first kind of therapeutic experiencing), is attention-centered bodily experiencing. There are two coupled indications that this is occurring. One is that the preponderance of the patient's attention is centered upon some focal center, and the second is that there are at least moderate sensations and feelings occurring in the patient's body.

In preparation for this first step, the patient lies back in a reclining chair. Eyes are closed throughout the session. Likewise, the therapist lies back in a reclining chair, and the therapist's eyes are also closed throughout most of the session. Each session ends when the sequence of steps is completed and experiential work is over. The patient is the primary determiner of when work is completed for that session. Accordingly, sessions may be for one or two or three hours or so, depending upon the patient and what is occurring in this particular session.

The therapist allows, encourages, and instructs the patient on how to let bodily experiencing occur. The patient is to allow heightened sensations and feelings to occur anywhere and everywhere in the body.

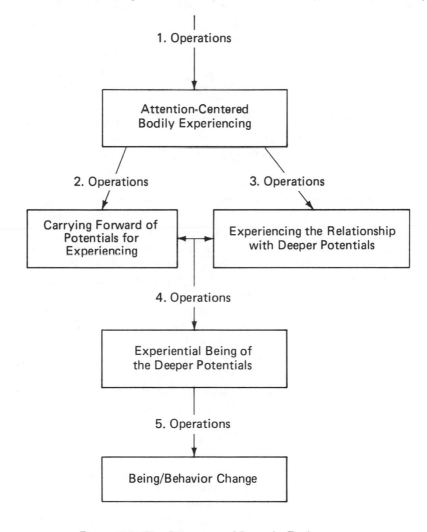

Figure 2.2. The Sequence of Steps in Each
Experiential Psychotherapy Session

The key is letting at least moderate bodily experiencing occur. Some of these bodily sensations may be pleasant and some may be unpleasant. Accordingly, the patient may undergo bodily sensations accompanying feelings of being scared, anxious, excited, pleased, gloomy, confused, happy, giddy, terrified, wondrous. There may occur a headache, butterflies in the stomach, a sense of lightness and buoyancy, hand trembling, sweaty palms, a hot ball in the chest, noise inside the head, sleepiness and drowsiness, sexual sensations in the genitals, itchy skin, pressure in the head, cold or hot sensations in the feet, blood pounding in the ears or chest or abdomen, cramping in the back muscles, sweating in the armpits. The patient may laugh, cry, yell, bellow, swear, roar, groan, whimper, stutter, or merely note that something is indeed happening in the body.

In effect, the therapist tells the patient how to let bodily sensations and feelings carry forward until they are at least moderate. This means that patients are having such bodily sensations and feelings right away, in each session, perhaps within the first minutes and typically within the first 15 minutes or so. Patients learn how to do this themselves.

These bodily sensations and feelings occur when the patient pours most of her attention upon some meaningful and significant focal center. That is, one important kind of experiencing occurs when the patient pours most of her attention into the personally meaningful core of something which has special meaning and significance to the patient right now. When the patient does this, the experiencing occurs in the form of moderate or strong bodily sensations. Here is one class of experiencing, and here is the first step of experiential psychotherapy. Although some credit must be shared by many members of the experiential family, I especially recognize the work of Gestalt therapists and the sensitive ground-breaking work of Gendlin (1966, 1968, 1969, 1972, 1978a) in developing and refining this first kind of experiencing.

The technical problem is how to identify the right attentional centers. How do therapist and patient find those centers of attention which have the richest possible yield for bodily sensations? From the work of many experientialists, a number of categories can be proposed:

1) There may be attentional centers which are immediately compelling, already accompanied with moderate or even strong bodily sensations and feelings. Essentially, the patient enters the session quite ready for this first kind of attention centering. Once the patient learns how to proceed directly to these already compelling attentional centers, the

patient allows attention to go to whatever it is, and with accompanying strong bodily sensations and feelings. In effect, the therapist says, "You know what to do; go ahead."

Right at the beginning of the session, for example, the patient may enter directly into a state of confused helplessness, attending to the awful way his mother talked to him on the telephone yesterday, and crying like a mistreated, unhappy child. Or the patient may attend to the way he just stood there, frozen and fixed, not doing anything when his friend was hinting how cold he was, and there is a heavy pressure filling the insides of his head.

This class of attentional centers has high priority. Once the patient knows how to proceed directly to this class of attentional centers, relatively little work is required of the therapist.

2) A second class of attentional centers includes the patient's deepest and most profound fears. These typically include the fears underneath all other problems, those terrible things about oneself which have been there from the very beginning of one's life, the awful core of one's basic character. These are the fear-laden fundamental parts of oneself which are really beyond all hope of ever really going away, the immutable parts with which one has been and will always be forever stuck. They constitute the ineluctable final end, the fate, the destiny from which there really is no escape. These sometimes may be approached through the catastrophically worst feelings the patient has ever had, the worst thing the patient ever did or almost did, the absolutely worst lifelong secret, the dreaded terror, or the utter certainty of the lurking ingrained craziness, lunacy, deranged state, "psychosis," insanity (e.g., Shorr, 1972, 1974). To the extent that the patient allows the preponderance of attention to be directed onto these focal centers, bodily sensations reach the working level of experiencing.

3) A third class of attentional centers includes changes in oneself and in one's personal world. The patient allows her attention to go to changes which are occurring over the past weeks or months or years. The more attention is focused on the more meaningful aspects of these changes, the more likely it is that bodily sensations will reach a working level. In this class, it is common that a measure of these changes may be accompanied by pleasant bodily sensations, though most are accompanied by painful bodily sensations.

The patient attends to changes in her body: I am losing weight; my legs are getting heavy and old; I have noticed blood in my stools. Or there are changes in feelings and ways of being: I've lost my zest and nothing means much anymore; I am starting to drink and that scares me; I am getting sexy lately. Or the patient attends to changes in the way she responds, reacts, is treated by, interacts with other persons: I have lost all my friends and just think about suicide; my husband doesn't even bother talking to me lately; I have been looking at other women and feeling curious about what it would be like to sleep with another woman; people look at me with eyes full of hate.

4) Attention may be centered on internal bodily states and events. To the extent that the patient pours sufficient attention into the right aspects, accompanying bodily sensations are at least of moderate intensity. The patient may attend to aches and pains in the head or lower back or chest, the fetus, skinny legs, the ulcer, cancer, the mysterious disease or illness, the heart valve. There may be bodily feelings such as heaviness, being split off inside, shakiness, dizziness, butterflies in the stomach, hot ball in the chest, loss of juices, energy, sudden weakness, clutching up.

5) There are compelling figures and objects. When the patient allows attention to pour into these particular figures or objects, bodily sensations become moderate or strong. This occurs when the patient's attention goes further into the compelling father, the ex-husband, the deceased grandmother, the baby who died, the menacing enemy, the hated rival at work, the son or daughter, the mean boss. Some of these figures and objects are current, and some are residuals from the past. They share a compelling quality, as if they are able to fill the patient's attentional world.

6) There are incidents in which bodily sensations rose up. The patient's attention is led to specific situations either by the avenue of the situation or the nature of the peak feeling. For example, there may be situations in which they ridiculed you, you were on top of the world, the other person hated you, or when they said that special something about you. Or, the situation is approached by naming the peak feeling. For example, it is the situation in which you felt quite embarrassed, or attacked, or filled with fear, or preciously special; your blood pounded, suddenly you were hot all over, you almost passed out.

The peak of feeling might have been private or public; it might have felt great or awful. It probably occurred very recently, but it may have occurred long ago. It might have been a conspicuous scene or a subtle little incident, it may have occurred in the real world or in one's fantasy or dreams. In any case, the patient is to place attention more and more on the details of the actual moment in that incident when the bodily sensations or feelings peaked.

This is one kind or class of experiencing. It is one way of organizing some of the contributions of many experiential therapists. The commonality is that there are heightened bodily sensations coupled with the focused centering of the patient's attention. Existential therapists contributed to this first kind of experiencing through their work on dread, terror, and the uncanny immutable destiny (cf. Binswanger, 1958a). Implosive and psycho-imagination therapists work with emotionally filled scenes and incidents (e.g., Shorr, 1972; Stampfl, 1977; Stampfl & Levis, 1967). Although many members of the experiential family contribute here, perhaps the most refined work has been done by Gestalt therapists with regard to body awareness and by Gendlin with regard to the focusing on felt meanings. Yet all of these contributions comprise one kind or class of experiencing as the major axis of therapeutic change.

My proposition is that this is the first experiential step in the sequence of steps which comprise experiential psychotherapy (Figure 2.2). Although some members of the experiential family may rely predominantly on this one kind of experiencing, I suggest that it can be more effectively used as the opening step in a sequence. If we use all the five ways of experiencing, then an effective psychotherapy can be constructed based on the work of members of this family. In any case, each session uses therapist operations (see Chapter 7) to bring the patient to a working level of experiencing; that is, the first step is achieving attention-centered bodily experiencing.

The next step is either that of carrying forward of potentials for experiencing, or the experiencing of the relationship between the patient and deeper potentials, or both. I shall describe each in turn.

*Carrying Forward Of Potentials For Experiencing*

Throughout the experiential family, there is a valuing of the sheer carrying forward of whatever the patient has available to experience. The emphasis is on what this particular person has available right now. It may consist of the potential for experiencing oozing sexuality, loving intimacy, dangerous vulnerability, explosive wildness, controlling dominance, utter worthlessness, delicate preciousness, frenzied bewilderment, comforting protection, anything. As long as the potential is there in this person, and as long as the potential is available right now, the aim is to carry that forward. The patient is to experience it more fully and deeply, with greater amplitude and saturation.

This second kind or class of experiencing is highly valued by most of the members of the experiential family. Indeed, the notion of carrying forward whatever the person has available to experience was there before psychotherapy took it over. Certainly it was a significant part of the work of Breuer and Freud (1936), and suffuses itself throughout words such as catharsis, abreaction, feeling expression, and similar words inside and outside the experiential family (Nichols & Zax, 1977). The idea is old and common.

What is new is how to orchestrate the carrying forward of potentials for experiencing. It is here that many different members of the experiential family have made contributions.

*Clarifying the focal center of attention.* The carrying forward of whatever potentials for experiencing are there is accomplished by clarifying the focal center of attention. When the patient is attending to something which is accompanied with moderate bodily sensations, the process is one of further clarification of that focal center. The main contributors here are existential phenomenologists who have refined and developed the phenomenological method (Binswanger, 1958a, 1958b; Boss, 1963; Ellenberger, 1958; Gendlin, 1969, 1978a; Havens, 1973; Wyss, 1973). Most existential phenomenologists have shown how this method can be used on any focal center of attention, while Gendlin's focusing method is especially refined in regard to the internal felt meaning aspects of attentional centering. In any case, the common theme is that potentials for experiencing are carried forward as the focal center of attention is further clarified.

*Clarifying the situational context.* The carrying forward of potentials for experiencing is accomplished by clarifying the encompassing situational context. The idea is that the patient is to be and to exist in a concrete situation, to be here rather than with the therapist. This method is again common, but it is especially refined and developed in such approaches as psycho-imagination therapy (Shorr, 1972, 1974), crisis mobilization therapy (Bar-Levav, 1976), implosive therapy (Stampfl, 1977), and primal therapy (Janov, 1970; Rose, 1976). Details of the immediate scene are filled in and brought into relief, details such as the time of day, the physical posture, the various sights and sounds which are here, the other people who are present, and so on. As the situational context is clarified, the patient increasingly exists in the situational context, and experiencing carries forward.

*Disclosing the critical moment: Kairos.* Potentials for experiencing are carried forward by disclosing (opening up, penetrating into) those precious critical moments in which the patient hovers at the edge of giving in to the verging experiencing. It is as if there is an instant in which the slightest movement in one direction will carry the patient into a full measure of that experiencing. Within existential phenomenology this is referred to as the moment of Kairos (Binswanger, 1958b; Ellenberger, 1958; Kelman, 1969; Wyss, 1973). All the right elements are here at this instant, poised to explode into the rush of experiencing. Typically these occur and pass in a brief instant, quickly suffused or covered over so that the imminent experiencing is passed by. These critical moments may occasionally be wrapped in a package of traumatic upheaval, occurring dramatically two or four times a year or so. But they also quietly come and go during every day or so, and the pulsating potential for experiencing is silently shut down almost without disturbing the patient, time after time after time. Experiencing is carried forward when the patient goes into the critical moment and allows the occurrence of the blocked-off experiencing.

*Direct interactive expression.* Experiencing is carried forward to the extent that the patient expresses the right action in a direct manner from the patient himself to the effective target in direct interaction. This method has probably been most highly refined and developed by Gestalt therapists. Indeed, this is one of the defining hallmarks of the Gestalt school. The patient is to express the concretely appropriate action, which opens up the experiencing. The patient is to express it directly to the proper target, not to some vaguely alluded to, generalized other.

*Fullness of expression.* Experiencing is carried forward by using more and more of the body in greater and greater intensity of expression. The body is to be the avenue of experiencing. Toward this end, the body is to get into appropriate postures and positions. Expression is to come from the hips, torso, arms, legs, throat, head, back—from all parts of the body and the body as a whole. Full expression is the business of the whole body, not merely words marching in lock-step out of the patient's head. Accordingly, there is to be movement of the relevant body parts and also from the body as a whole—kickings, hittings, cryings, dry heavings, twistings, shakings, wrenchings, and any other form of bodily expression. In addition, the bodily expression is to reach full heights of intensity, volume, amplitude, saturation. The patient screams, yells, louder and louder; the patient pounds harder and harder. The patient laughs or cries out with sufficient intensity to carry forward the experiencing. One of the keys here is repetition, over and over again until experiencing is carried forward.

Many of the members of the experiential family use this way of carrying forward experiencing. Yet much of the credit for refining and developing this way goes especially to such experiential therapies as bioenergetics, cathartic therapy, feeling-expressive therapy, and emotional flooding therapy.

This is a second class of experiencing. In contrast to the first, attention-centered bodily experiencing consists of the sheer carrying forward of whatever this patient has available for experiencing. This is a second part of the experiential axis of bringing about therapeutic change. It is a second way in which the work of some of the members of the experiential family may be organized. But I propose something more than that. I propose that this second class of experiencing is systematically related to the first. Carrying forward the potentials for experiencing is most effectively reached by starting with attention-centered bodily experiencing. Not only does the experiential family have five kinds or classes of experiencing, but they organize themselves into a sequence of steps (Figure 2.2). It is this sequential organization of the five kinds of experiencings which gives experiential psychotherapy its systematic therapeutic power.

*Experiencing the Relationship With Deeper Potentials.*

The sequence of steps in experiential therapy opens with attention-centered bodily experiencing. Once the patient has reached the working level of this initial kind of experiencing, the method offers an option. Either we may move to the carrying forward of potentials for experiencing, or we may move to experiencing the relationship with deeper potentials, or back and forth between these two (Figure 2.2).

This third kind of experiencing grows out of a fusion of two ideas in the history of psychotherapy. One is that therapy moves ahead when the patient gains insight and understanding into whatever is regarded as deeper personality processes (e.g., unconscious, intrapsychic dynamisms, latent tendencies, basic cognitive assumptions, the inner self). In one form or another, this idea is common to many psychotherapies outside the experiential family. The second idea has been developed mainly by such proponents of encounter therapy as Bugental (1965, 1978), Havens (1973), Hora (1959, 1960), Jourard (1968, 1976), Kovacs (1965), Malone, Whitaker, Warkentin and Felder (1961), Mullan and

Sangiuliano (1964), Schutz (1967, 1971, 1973), Warkentin and Whitaker (1965), and Whitaker, Warkentin and Malone (1969). Essentially, this second idea holds that therapy moves ahead when there is an encountering relationship between patient and therapist.

The fusion of these two ideas constitutes a powerful third kind of experiencing. It consists of the full-feelinged, encountering relationship, rather than merely insight and understanding, between the patient and the patient's deeper potentials for experiencing. Here is the encountering relationship between the patient and his own deeper potentials for experiencing, rather than between patient and therapist. Here is a two-way, interactional relationship, instead of a one-way relationship of the patient to the deeper personality process.

While existential-humanistic theorists have explored these internal relations between the person and deeper personality processes, the technical problem has been how to bring about this experiencing in actual psychotherapy. I credit Gestalt therapists with doing the most work toward solving this problem (e.g., Levitsky & Perls, 1970; Perls, 1971, 1976; Polster & Polster, 1974). Their method consists of the patient's enacting both sides of the encountering dialogue. The patient is to be himself (the continuing, substantive self) in encounter with the deeper personality process; then, next, the patient is to "be" the deeper personality process in encounter with himself, "over there," perhaps seen as sitting in the other chair. Here is one way of trying to effect a full-feelinged encountering relationship between the patient and the patient's deeper personality process. In my opinion, more work has to be done to make this method adequate. But it is one way.

There is another way. It is derived from the existential idea that one person (the therapist) is capable of merging into the identity of another (the patient), literally aligning with or sharing or "being" the deeper personality process of another (cf. Buber, 1957; Havens, 1973, 1974, 1976a, 1976b; Hora, 1959; Kohut, 1971; Mahrer, 1978d, 1980b; Whitaker, Warkentin, & Malone, 1969). Chapters 7-9 focus on this radical step in which the therapist disengages from his own identity and merges, to some degree at least, into the deeper potential of the patient. The radical proposition is that the therapist is thereby able to be the voice of the patient's deeper potential, to take on its identity.

Consider the patient who experiences being the rejected one, being hated and unloved, the awful source of father's deep-seated unhappiness and anger. Suppose that the underlying deeper potential consists of a defiant toughness, an independent firmness and singlemindedness. These words point toward something which the patient has seldom if ever experienced. To the extent that the therapist takes on or fuses with this deeper potential, the therapist is in a position to interact with the patient, to enable further experiencing of the relationship between the patient and this deeper potential.

In this encounter, the therapist-as-deeper-potential may interact with the patient along a number of lines. (a) The therapist may give expression to the deeper potential's behavioral tendencies, fantasies, wishes, impulses, feelings. In so doing, the therapist expresses the good form, the spontaneous, exuberant, good-feelinged form of that which the patient typically avoids and defends against. "Tell him to stick it up his ass." . . . "Let's get the hell out of here. They are all crazy anyhow." . . . "You're bigger and tougher than that sonuvabitch. Pick him up and smash him against the wall." (b) The therapist voices the way the deeper potential regards the patient, bathing the patient in its own insights and understandings. "Come on, baby, how about asking forgiveness and crying like a baby?" . . . "Oh, you did it now. They're going to throw you out of the family, and then what'll you do?" . . . "You are disgusting. The bad little boy. Go ahead, feel rotten. You deserve it." (c) The relationship between the deeper potential and the patient is characterized by fondness, commitment, warmth, and includes elements of playfulness, acceptance, chiding, sarcasm, good humor, loyalty. It is an integrative relationship of harmony, oneness, intactness. (d) The relationship is relentlessly encountering, giving the patient no options to get away, ameliorate, or avoid the increasing intensity of the confrontation. It grows to peaked clashes.

Following these full-feelinged clashing encounterings between the patient and his own deeper potential, there is a qualitative change in the experiential nature of the relationships. Instead of distance and separation, blocking and avoidance, there is now fusion, assimilation, closeness, mutual welcoming; there are bodily sensations and feelings of inner peacefulness, oneness, harmony. The nature of the deeper potential undergoes a qualitative shift from its perceived bad form to its perceived good form, as a desirable way of being and experiencing.

Here, then, is a third kind of experiencing, a third strand of the experiential axis of therapeutic change. It is based upon existential ideas of assimilating into the identity of the other person, upon the work of encounter therapists, and upon Gestalt methods in which the patient enacts both sides of the encountering dialogue. However, this third kind or class of experiencing is not yet common in the experiential family. It will be accorded its proper debut in this book.

Experiencing the relationship with deeper potentials is also proposed

as having its own place in the sequence of steps of experiential psychotherapy (Figure 2.2). More than just a third kind or way of experiencing, it occurs in a sequence. Following the first step, one either carries
forward potentials for experiencing, or experiences the relationship with
deeper potentials, or moves back and forth between the two. There is
an organized sequence of steps; we move now to the fourth kind of
experiencing, the fourth step in the sequence.

### Experiential Being of the Deeper Potential

In several lines of Eastern thought underlying meditation and contemplation, the aim is for the person to reach a state in which he leaves
behind or disengages from his identity or self or continuing personhood
(e.g., Byles, 1962; Chang, 1959; Deikman, 1966; Maupin, 1965; Ouspensky, 1957; Suzuki, 1956; Watts, 1961; Wilhelm, 1962). My impression is
that such a step is essentially outside the conceptual bounds of most of
our Western psychotherapies, wherein change is limited to the substantive continuing personality structure of the patient. Although
changes can occur in the patient's behavior, within the functioning personality structure, and between this continuing personality structure
and whatever is conceptualized as deeper within, the patient—the essential identity or core of the patient's I-ness—remains fixedly outside
the domain of change.

Here is where existential thinking offers a profound and exciting challenge to the field of psychotherapy. Existentialists speak of the complete
letting go of and the wholesale disengagement from one's personality
structure, from the continuing personality or self or identity, from the
being in which one has existed, from the continuing sense of who I am
and what I am, from the "conscious ego." Existentialists refer to the
final existential choice of no longer being the person I am, the final
ending of this person, the headlong plummet into the bottomless abyss
of nothingness, the state of vacuum, limbo, existential death. Existentialists speak of the wholesale metamorphosis of the very center of my
I-ness, the complete being of a whole new person, the nuclear transformation of the heart of my identity. I refer to writings of existentialists
and existential clinicians such as Angyal, 1965; Binswanger, 1958a, 1967;
Boss, 1963; Caruso, 1964; Ellenberger, 1958; Frankl, 1959, 1967; Havens,
1973; Heidegger, 1963; Holt, 1968; Jourard, 1976; Laing, 1960, 1969; May,
1958, 1964, 1967; Naranjo, 1969; Schachtel, 1959; Van Dusen, 1957.

In contrast to the first three kinds of experiencing, what is unique is that the nuclear center of the person, the sense of I-ness or Dasein, undergoes a radical wrenching out of the whole domain of personhood (self, being, identity, consciousness), and into the deeper potential. It is the being of a different, new person. What is referred to as "I" is now the deeper potential. "I" now *am* the deeper potential.

Existentialists have shown us how to conceptualize this fourth kind of experiencing, how to talk about and describe it. What we have yet to develop are the ways of bringing it about in psychotherapy. Once again we turn to members of the experiential family for beginnings of ways which can be organized into working methods of implementing the experiential being of the deeper potential.

*Succumbing into and through the catastrophic threat/state.* The monstrous disintegrative face of the deeper potential may manifest itself internally or externally. That is, it may appear internally as an inevitable madness, craziness, state of utter derangement and insanity; or the awful state of utter depression; or the ineluctable driving force toward an inevitable suicide; or any other catastrophic internal threat or state which is the bad form of the deeper potential. On the other hand, it may make its manifest appearance externally as evil forces out there, a vengeful enemy, a chaotically out of control external world. Behind all of these are the looming deeper potentials as the catastrophic threat/state against which the patient wrenchingly struggles.

The method of being the deeper potential is to succumb completely to the catastrophic threat/state. Give up the endless struggle against, the fear-laden defenses against letting it take you over. Succumb, surrender, give in to it; indeed, welcome the wholesale being of it, embrace it, fuse and merge into it. Be the craziness, the death, the out-of-control, the piece of shit, the foul slime, the rage, the evilness, the failure, sucking parasite, hated one, the dirt, the catastrophic threat/state. This method is built upon the work of experientialists such as Laing (1960, 1962) and Boss (1963), Gestalt therapists, as well as the work of Stampfl (1977), Hogan and Kirchner (1967), Rose (1976) and others.

*Doing to them what they did to you.* A second way of being the deeper potential is by reversing those crucial interactions in which you are the receiver, the victim, the passive target. In these crucial interactions, father dominates you, mother forces you to please her, the other person assaults you or has complete power over you. The cancer kills you, the insanity takes you over. For many patients, life is an endless struggle against what others do or did to the patient. In these crucial interactions, the power resides in others and what they do to the patient as helpless victim who can never really escape.

The deeper potential resides in these crucial other figures or agencies. Accordingly, disengaging from one's identity and being the deeper potential is the wholesale reversal in which the patient does it to them. I do the unthinkable. I dominate father. I force mother to please me. I assault the other person and gain complete power over that person. I kill the cancer. I take over the insanity. Gestalt therapists refer to this as the "method of reversal" (Perls, 1971). In psycho-imagination therapy it is called "accusing the accusers" (Shorr, 1972). Psychoanalytic therapists refer to this as the "method of converse consequences" (Loevinger, 1966). It is doing to them what they do to you.

*New experiencing in redivived critical moments.* Therapeutic work often uncovers moments in one's life which were paramount in setting the contours of how one is subsequently. These are the moments when subsequent ways of being were locked in, or when deeper potentials were slammed out of possibility. Typically these moments are filled with quite intense bodily sensations and feelings, and they generally occurred early in life. They are critical moments. When you were five years old, a friend of the family put his finger in your vagina and your whole body froze with scary tension. When you were seven, your mother raged about your masturbating, and your whole world was filled with a protective moat of distance and withdrawn separation.

The patient has the opportunity of reentering into these moments. This time she has the further opportunity of being the deeper potential. Instead of the rigidly austere person whom she is, cooly distant from others, secretly depressed and suicidal, she is to be the revealed deeper potential: spontaneously sexual, bodily aroused, openly lascivious and wanton. The patient enters into being this deeper potential and undergoes this new experiencing within the context of the revitalized early critical moment. She lives in the critical moment and this time experiences a bodily aroused sexual spontaneity with the family friend who puts his finger into her vagina; she experiences the wanton lasciviousness with the mother who is raging about her masturbation. In so doing, the patient undergoes the experiential being of the deeper potential.

*Self-encountering.* The roots of another method lie in the Gestalt technique of enacting both sides of the encountering dialogue, as well as in the detachment from self which occurs in meditation and contemplation. Essentially, the patient detaches from the continuing (personality, identity) and encounters that self from within the deeper potential. The patient moves into being the deeper potential of bodily aroused, spontaneous and wanton sexuality. From within this perspective, the patient encounters the person whose whole body freezes with tension when the friend of the family puts his finger into her vagina. The patient encounters the ordinary person who is filled with a protective moat of distance and withdrawn separation, who is rigidly austere, cooly distant from others, secretly depressed and suicidal. From within the deeper potential, the patient encounters that self. She sees that self in vivid detail. She talks to that self, has feelings about that self, playfully chides or forcefully attacks that self. She engages in an encountering relationship with that self and, in so doing, lives the experiential being of the deeper potential.

*Full experiential being of the deeper potential.* In carrying out each of the above methods, the key is full experiencing. The patient is to allow bodily sensations and feelings to reach high levels of intensity, amplitude, and saturation throughout the whole body (e.g., Nichols & Zax, 1977; Ouspensky, 1957; Rachman, 1969). There is to be repetition of the right behaviors within the right contexts, until full experiential being occurs (cf. Levitsky & Perls, 1970; Perls, 1971). Also from Gestalt therapy comes the importance of speaking as "I" in being the deeper potential. All in all, experiential being of the deeper potential requires fullness, intensity, completeness, and saturation.

The experiential being of the deeper potential is a fourth kind of experiencing, another way of organizing some of the work of experiential therapists. In addition, this fourth kind of experiencing has its place in a sequence of steps, for it is reached by carrying forward potentials for experiencing and/or experiencing the relationship with deeper potentials (Figure 2.2). We now turn to the fifth kind of experiencing, the final step in the sequence.

## Being/Behavioral Change in the Extra-Therapy World

The fifth kind of experiencing is that of being this changing person within the extra-therapy world. To the extent that the patient has undergone the first four steps or kinds of experiencings, substantive changes have occurred in the patient. The stage now consists of the extra-therapy world. Will the patient remain this new and changing person when he leaves the office? Will the new and changing person be and behave in new and changing ways in the extra-therapy world? Will the new and changing person construct new and changing extra-therapy worlds? The fifth kind of experiencing is the risk of being and behaving this new and changing person in a new and changing world.

Whereas many behavioral therapies seek to effect (a) problem-behavior changes (b) in the continuing, unchanging person, experiential therapy emphasizes (a) changes in the whole spectrum of being and behaviors (b) of the changing person. We offer the new and changing person the choice of existing outside the therapy room.

*New and changing ways of being/behaving.* In the therapy session, there was a new and changing person. It may have lasted five to 10 seconds; it may have lasted for a half hour or more. But here is a person whose experiencing is fuller and deeper (step 2), whose relationships among potentials are more integrative (step 3), and who is a qualitatively new person (step 4). This person behaved in new and changing ways which were accompanied by good bodily sensations and feelings. This person constructed a new and changing world in which experiencing was broader, deeper, and more integrated. Is the patient ready to confront the utterly real possibility of being this new and changing person outside the therapy room?

Being this new and changing person means risking changes in actual behavioral ways of being with oneself, with others, and in the kinds of worlds one constructs and in which one exists. These are actual and real changes in the way one is. They come from a new and changing person who may simply laugh more, or listen more attentively, or spend more time with someone. This person may behave in little ways which provide for more peacefulness and integrity, or for more vitality and excitement. This person may be and behave in ways which construct slight or major changes in the world in which the person exists. Here is a new way of being with other persons, a change in one's life situation, home, family, work, personal style, physical body, interpersonal relations, or anything else which comprises the worlds in which one exists. Here are actual being and behavioral changes coming from a new and changing person who experiences more and with greater breadth and depth, and who experiences more integrative relations among and between potentials for experiencing.

*Letting go of old ways of being/behaving.* In the therapy session, the new and changing person may have let go of old ways of being and behaving.

The person may have disengaged from the old personality who behaved in painful ways. These behaviors may be as discrete as stuttering, whining, arguing, or nose-picking. Or, these behaviors may be instrumental in constructing worlds in which the patient is painfully helpless, hurtfully rejected, aggressively assaulted. These behaviors may refer to bodily events and states and phenomena such as ulcers and cancers, headaches and backaches, bodily tremblings and shakings, heaviness and numbness (Mahrer, 1980a). While the patient had been a person who could let go of these old ways of being and behaving in the therapy session, the question is whether the new and changing person is ready to face the risk of being this new and changing person who can let go of these old ways of being and behaving outside the session in the extratherapy world.

This means confronting the utterly real possibility of letting go of old ways of being and behaving which insured pain and unhappiness, which truncated experiencing, which maintained painful and unhappy interpersonal relationships, which constructed worlds appropriate for pain and unhappiness, which insured the existence of the old person and insured against the presence of the new and changing person. The patient may let go of being cold and distant, or warm and loving, of being controlling and dominating, or controlled and dominated. One may let go of being the leader, the loyal one, the true friend, the charming one, the politician or hard worker or devoted spouse or loyal child. To the extent that these are of the old person, the risk is that of being a new and changing person who lets go of the old ways of being and behaving.

My first proposition has been that five different kinds of experiencings may be organized out of the work of the various members of the experiential family. In developing experiential psychotherapy, I am drawn toward use of all five rather than any one or two alone.

My second proposition has been that each of these five kinds of experiencings is a consequence of separate and distinct sets of therapist (and patient) operations (Figure 2.2).

(a)  When a patient pours most of his attention on a meaningful focal center, and when the patient allows bodily sensations to occur, the consequence is heightened bodily experiencing.
(b)  When the situation and the focal center of attention are clarified, when the patient lives through the critical moment, when the

patient engages in direct interactive expression, and when this occurs with fullness of expression, then the consequence is the carrying forward of whatever this patient has available for experiencing.

(c) When the therapist merges into the deeper potentials of the patient and engages in an encountering interaction with the patient, the consequence is heightened experiencing of the relationship between the patient and the deeper potential.

(d) When the patient succumbs into and through the truly catastrophic threat or state, when the patient does to the critical figures the profoundly significant thing that they have done to him, when the patient undergoes the alternative deeper experiencing in the redivived critical moment from the past, when the patient encounters and confronts the ordinary continuing person whom he is, and when this is carried out with full experiential expression, then the consequence is the momentous shift out of the operating domain and into the experiential being of the deeper potential.

(e) When the person who has undergone these experiencings considers the possibility of being and behaving as this new changing person in the actual extra-therapy world, then there is increased experiencing of being a new and changing person in a new and changing extra-therapy world.

My third proposition has been that these five kinds of experiencings can be organized into a sequence of steps, and that such an organization of steps provides the therapist and patient with a profoundly effective experiential psychotherapy.

This, then, is an overview of how experiential psychotherapy works. It is one brand of experiential psychotherapy which seeks to build upon the work of the whole experiential family.

# 3

# *The Practicalities of Experiential Psychotherapy*

An overview of experiential psychotherapy also needs to include some of the more mundane practicalities. Each approach to psychotherapy has worked out its own practical procedures for dealing with everything from outfitting the therapy room to selecting patients, from the length of the therapy session to the kinds of notes used by the therapist. In these practical matters, the theory of practice tells us very little. Instead, we have to take into account what the current professional guidelines have to say, what years of clinical practice have to offer, and what the parent theory of human beings tells us. Many of these issues, therefore, are somewhat sensitive. They require careful judgment and thinking. Yet the decisions on practical matters must be made, and we do our best to weigh everything which is relevant in arriving at decisions.

## THE THERAPY ROOM

What are some considerations in deciding where the therapy room is to be located? In order to carry out experiential psychotherapy, what facilities should the therapy room include?

### Location

The location is to convey the following to both the patient and the therapist: "If you want to undergo the work, if you are serious about learning what to do, and about undergoing the process, here is where we work. You are the important one here. I can show you how to follow the method, and I will undergo the process along with you." The question of location is largely determined by the degree to which the location conveys this message. We avoid locations which predefine that the therapist fulfills given roles, the patient fulfills complementary roles, and their relationship is such and such (see Chapters 5 and 6). Study the location of therapy rooms. Be sensitive to the messages these locations convey about the therapist and the patient and their role relationships. To the extent that the location conveys the experiential message, it is appropriate; to the extent that the location conveys predefined role relationships, it is inappropriate.

This means that experiential psychotherapy may be carried out in a room located in the therapist's home. It is possible that such a location can convey the experiential message and can minimize other predefined role relationships. This is one important consideration in my preference for locating my therapy room in my home. Clearly other predefined role relationship messages may well be conveyed by locating the therapy room in one's home, but it is easy to minimize these. It is also possible to locate the therapy room in a building or part of a building, but this is difficult to accomplish without falling into highly defined role relationships for both therapist and patient. If the therapy room is not located in the therapist's home, I prefer facilities which are designed expressly for experiential therapy and nothing else.

The serious problem is that typically both therapist and patient are caught in predefined roles in almost all locations which provide psychotherapy. Accordingly, I have grave doubts about the feasibility of carrying out experiential psychotherapy in most outpatient clinics, rehabilitation centers, private practice offices in medical centers or professional buildings, social agencies, mental health clinics, medical hospitals, penal institutions, counseling services, or any other setting typically housing psychotherapy services.

Even before the two persons meet to begin therapy, the location surrounds them in defined roles. For example, powerful role messages are conveyed by the presence of a receptionist and secretary, by the waiting room, by the forms the patient is told to fill out. Messages are screamed out by the suite of expensive offices in the exclusive building for private psychoanalysts, or by the social agency housed in a government building. There may be medical patients or psychiatric outpatients, or hallways and rooms carefully designed so that no one sees patients come or go. There are doors with names and labels on them, and personnel who carry out the business of the place. Appointments are for 50 minutes; regularly scheduled appointments are important. Someone will see you for an "intake interview." What insurance plan will cover your fees? Do you have an appointment with Dr. Sorenson or Dr. Packard? The person who uses these services is a family problem, a crisis case, a clinic referral, a group member, a court referral, a welfare case, someone trying to get something from the agency, an emergency, someone fortunate to be seen by the doctor, someone to be evaluated or assessed.

Before and after the first contact between the two parties, most locations enmesh them in highly defined role relationships which are grossly inappropriate for experiential psychotherapy. The therapist must be careful in selecting a location which minimizes these roles.

I prefer a location which is accessible to the extra-therapy worlds of both patient and therapist. It is no accident that the opening and closing steps of each session involve the patient and the external world. Accordingly, I am not drawn toward locations which contrast with daily living. Here I am referring to groups of people coming together for a few days or a week in some retreat or park. Such locations invite the participants to leave the real world, to come together with others in a sample of what life can be like; retreat with us and let us be together. In order to carry on experiential work, such locations are inappropriate. For many other delightful purposes, such locations are highly appropriate, but not for experiential work.

## Facilities

Experiential therapy requires quiet. When the patient and therapist are listening carefully to what is happening inside, there are to be no intrusive sounds from outside the room. It also requires noise. Patient and therapist may yell or cry or laugh. This means that the room should keep inside sounds inside, and outside sounds outside. The room should be sound-proofed. Use carpeting and tapestries. Surround the room with corridors of space. Use double doors. Let the patient and yourself know that the sounds are your sounds.

Since sessions may last for two or three hours or so, therapist and patient occasionally may use toilet facilities. Since experiential work calls for careful attention to immediate bodily sensations, there are times when having to urinate or defecate may interfere with otherwise ongoing bodily sensations. Accordingly, toilet facilities are to be quite accessible.

Each approach has a set of practical and theoretical reasons for the physical location of therapist and patient. For example, if the approach emphasizes a two-person relationship, face-to-face with one another, then it makes sense to use two comfortable chairs more or less facing one another. In experiential therapy, a major consideration is that the patient is to be free to move the torso, arms and legs, free to turn and twist, to assume different physical postures. Over the years I have come to favor a large reclining chair with a separate large hassock. The chair is on a swivel and it can be used to sit up, lie back, or swing around. It is comfortable enough that the patient may remain in it for hours, may curl up or move about in it, twist around in it or fall asleep in it, move all parts of the body in it.

With regard to the therapist, our theory and practice indicate that the therapist is to undergo what the patient undergoes. Furthermore, the therapist is to attend to whatever the patient is attending to. Accordingly, the therapist uses the same kind of reclining chair and hassock. The two chairs are at an acute angle to one another such that they are both "pointing" toward the same attentional center. These two chairs may be four or six feet away from each other so that patient and therapist may comfortably talk to one another or attend to a single focal center. It is as if both are attending to the same thing, only instead of a physical center such as a fireplace, in experiential therapy the focal center is whatever is the meaningful attentional center of the patient.

Although the seating arrangements are designed to facilitate the physical postures and attentional centering of both patient and therapist, one may find all sorts of other reasons to justify the seating arrangement. For example, Freud arrived at the physical arrangement of the patient on the couch in front of the seated psychotherapist because such an arrangement facilitated free associations, facilitated projections upon the neutral analyst, and suited Freud's preference for not being looked at by so many patients so many hours of the day. Haley adds a few other reasons and aims for some therapists who use that same physical arrangement: "By placing the patient on a couch, the analyst gives the patient the feeling of having his feet up in the air and the knowledge that the analyst has both feet on the ground. . . . he finds himself literally below the analyst and so his one-down position is geographically emphasized" (Haley, 1959, pp. 115-116). Although it is often inviting to think of reasons for one physical arrangement or another, whichever one the experiential therapist selects should enable attention to bodily sensations and bodily movement so as to facilitate therapeutic experiencing.

The patient is to have eyes closed throughout the session. The therapist's eyes are likewise shut throughout most of the session. Accordingly, illumination in the room is to be low and non-intrusive. Windows are to be shaded or blocked with curtains, both for illumination and sound-reduction purposes.

Additional considerations come from the person who is the therapist, rather than from experiential psychotherapy, and here there is considerable variation. Because of the person I am, I have a desk, loads of books, sculpture and paintings, a file, a typewriter, wall hangings. I occasionally have a small blanket, a heater, or a fan. Because each experiential therapist is a different person, some of the props and furnishings will differ.

## RELATIONSHIPS WITH THE PERSON WHO IS THE PATIENT

Outside of actual therapeutic work, the therapist is just another human being. When engaged in experiential therapy, the therapist is a master of the trade. Most experiential therapists will operate in very similar ways when they work. But outside of the actual therapy work the guideline is that you are the person you are, just another human being. We shall discuss the relationships between the person who is the therapist and the person who is the patient in the context of all of their interactions outside the actual therapeutic work. Basically, the question is: What are the guidelines for the way the therapist is in those situations? Basically, the answer is: The person is the person one is.

In addition, there are some principles which come from the theory of experiential psychotherapy and which apply in general to these situations. In your relationships with the person who is the patient, you are the person you are in the particular way of carrying out these general principles.

### Initiating Contact: Referrer, Referree and Self

In initiating contact, the person who is to be the patient is the one who initiates direct contact with the person who is to be the therapist. This is one guiding principle. How the therapist is in this interaction depends on the person the therapist is. This is the second guiding principle.

If someone wants to refer or make an appointment for another person, the important point is that whoever intends to be the patient is to have a free hand in initiating direct contact with the therapist. There are always two possibilities in these situations. One is that the referrer is left free to make an appointment for himself or herself. The other is that the referree is also left free to make his or her own appointment. Let us discuss the latter first. Consider the instance of a parent who calls and wishes to make an appointment for a son.

Mrs. Follette: Hello. Dr. Anderson? I would like to make an appointment for my son Louis. He is 18 and . . . mixed up about things. He's moping and . . . depressed around the house. He is getting into a little trouble and he feels depressed. Would you have time to see him? He could come just about any time. I mean, if you are busy . . .

Dr. Anderson: Sure. I think I can arrange a time. *Ask him to give me a call if he wants.* (Here is the key statement.)

Mrs. Follette: Oh . . . well I think I could set up a time with you now.

Dr. Anderson: Nope. I would prefer for him to talk with me directly, and we could work out a time. If he's interested, he can give me a call anytime.

The son called that evening, and an appointment was arranged. This guideline is followed whether the caller is a person who talks about a spouse or employee or friend or anyone. We follow this guideline also when the caller is a professional person who makes a professional referral:

Dr. Anderson: Hello, Dr. Finch, this is Dr. Anderson. I'm returning your call.

Dr. Finch: Oh, yes. I have a patient that I think needs your help. She's getting paranoid lately and her husband is getting quite upset. Maybe you ought to see him too. . . . I've been treating her epilepsy for the past four years, and it is pretty much under control, but she's been telling me about things that have been bothering her lately and they sound paranoid to me. I'd like to have her see you.

Dr. Anderson: Fine. What's her name?

Dr. Finch: Mattie Thompson.

Dr. Anderson: OK . . . I would like her to give me a call and we can make an appointment. How's that?

The person who is to be the patient is the one who has the choice of making the contact or not. There are extreme instances of, for example, the person who appears crazy or deranged. A daughter calls about her mother who is in her late sixties and is taking all her clothes off in front of people. The social worker wants to make an appointment for a client who just sits in the basement and refuses to eat. A husband calls about a brother-in-law who makes a career of psychiatric hospitals and is a menace in the neighborhood. I am no longer surprised by the high proportion of such referrees who actually make the first contact themselves when the experiential therapist is reasonably firm in granting them the right to choose whether or not to initiate the contact. On the other hand, some of these persons never call. We shall discuss more about this later.

Earlier I mentioned that the referrer is left free to make her or his own appointment. Our guideline applies both to the referrer and the referree. Accordingly, whoever makes the initiating contact may be given the choice of making an appointment for himself. Consider the husband who calls about his wife:

Mr. Wilson: Dr. Anderson? My name is Wilson. I got your name from someone who saw you in therapy. It's my wife, Ann. She's taken to drinking, and I think it's just getting out of hand. I just don't know what to do anymore. Do you see someone like that?

Dr. Anderson: Sure. How about asking her to give me a call and we can talk about an appointment.

Mr. Wilson: (Pause) I've taken her to . . . uh . . . we just came back from a vacation and that did no good. I'm just . . . I don't know what to do anymore.

Dr. Anderson: If you want to make an appointment for yourself, we can. If you would like her to, ask her to give me a call.

Mr. Wilson: Would you see me? . . . I can come anytime. When can I have an appointment?

Our guideline grants the ostensible referrer, or the referee, or both, the choice of having an appointment. In carrying out this guideline, plenty of room is given the therapist to be the person he is. For example, one therapist may be brisk and efficient, another may be friendly and responsive, while a third may be bubbling with good humor. You are the person you are in these initiating contacts.

In effect, then, all referrals are self-referrals. It may start with some other person wishing to refer a patient, but it is the patient himself or herself who undertakes direct contact.

*Office Relationships Before and After Therapeutic Work*

Therapeutic work starts when both persons are reclining, with eyes closed, and the patient is ready to attend to something meaningful. Therapeutic work finishes when the patient opens the eyes and the session is finished. Before and after therapeutic work, the therapist is to be the person that the therapist is. Clearly there are professional guidelines for responsible practice. But within such professional guidelines the experiential therapist is to be the person that he is right here and now. Once therapeutic work begins, most experiential therapists simply carry out the method, and there is a great deal of commonality in the way they are. But before and after therapeutic work, their own individual personalities predominate, and they are free to differ because they are different persons. There is no script for the behavior of the "professional experiential therapist" in these office relationships. Let us consider a few standard situations.

How do you greet the patient before going into the therapy room? What do you do when the patient has a coat, packages, an umbrella? Our guideline suggests that one therapist may be a little fatigued, somewhat grumpy. Another therapist, or the same therapist on another occasion, may be pleased and warm, or cheerful and ebullient.

Suppose a patient takes a real interest in the appointments of the therapy room. She indicates that she likes one painting and inquires if this other is new. She has been in therapy for about six months and never really noticed this painting or the books or the plants before. What do you do? Be the person you are right now with this person. Here are different therapists responding to the similar situation:

T: OK, OK. Enough chit-chat. If you're ready to start, sit down, lean back and let's get to work.

T: No it's not new! It's been there for 20 years. You're a real observer, you are!

T: Well, I have had it for a couple of years . . . I really like it. . . .

The patient may talk about the weather as he and the therapist walk into the therapy room: "I hate this weather. The wind! I have a big old elm tree. It's dead and I should have it removed. I'm afraid it will crash against the house." The therapist responds by being whoever the therapist is right there.

T: Oh? That's too bad. Another one of those big old elms. Too bad.

T: Come on in; it's nice and safe here. No wind.

What does the therapist do when the patient walks into the therapy room and hands the therapist a clipping or a book or a letter? As usual, the therapist is a person now, and not the therapist who carries out the experiential method. Accordingly, therapists will differ:

T: Oh great! Something to read. . . . Do you want me to look at this now? I'll do whatever you say.

T: (Looks at the book) Ah yes, I know this. It's a fine book. . . .

One's professional codes will have much to say about many kinds of office relationships and conduct. In addition, there are hundreds of little situations where codes of professional conduct stop, yet where the therapist must make decisions about how to be. Our guideline is for the experiential therapist to be the person he is, within all the reasonable and responsible other considerations for how to be and behave.

### Extra-office Relationships with the Patient

Codes of professional conduct likewise tell us a lot about extra-office relationships with the patient. Within these strictures, our guideline remains that the therapist is the person he is.

There often occur chance meetings. For example, therapist and patient may be at the same check-out counter in the market, or at the same social gathering, or waiting for the bus at a street corner. How does the therapist behave? One therapist may be comfortably social, another may be inclined to cut short the chance meeting as soon as possible, while a third may become tight and anxious. They are however they are.

Does the experiential therapist participate in social relationships with the patient? Far from chance meetings, these are extra-therapy relationships in which one or both actually pursue social relationships. I am referring here to social gatherings typically at the home of the therapist, the patient, or a mutual acquaintance. Our guideline does not expressly forbid such social relationships (cf. Fromm-Reichmann, 1958). I know of experiential therapists who are quite comfortable in such social relationships and whose therapeutic work is not impaired thereby. I, however, am quite uncomfortable about participating in these relationships, and I avoid them.

Much of what the experiential therapist does or does not do in these extra-office relationships is determined by the kind of person he is. Of course there are limits. This guideline is not license for selling real estate to your patients or violating your favorite commandments. The person whom you are will have more or less consideration for professional codes of conduct, and also for the kinds of role relationships you are setting up. For example, I do not call patients to get them to come for therapy. I do not buy things for my patients. I do not send gifts to my patients. I do not go out for a drink with my patients. I do not call patients to chat with them. I do not have parties comprised of patients and former patients. These activities annoy me. But they annoy me primarily as a person. I worry about the kinds of role relationships these construct, and I can become concerned about the professional ethics which are involved. Yet most of my not doing them comes from the kind of person I am.

### Responsibilities of the Experiential Therapist and Patient

When a person is considering experiential therapy, the person has a right to some information. Keeping in mind the professional codes of conduct on this issue, it is my conviction that the following list is illustrative of the information the experiential psychotherapist has a responsibility to provide the patient.

(a) Your name and degree.
(b) A professionally simple way of describing your approach to psychotherapy. For example, I describe my approach as "experiential psychotherapy."
(c) Your fee. I charge a fixed fee per hour. The patient has a right to know whether you have a sliding fee scale, whether payment is expected at the end of each session (as is my practice), whether there is a charge for missed appointments, how far in advance sessions may be cancelled.
(d) Your address and telephone number.
(e) The kinds of persons you see for therapeutic work. For example, I see only individual adults. The prospective patient is given the right to know whether you accept adolescents or children, families or couples, or whether you provide group therapy.

(f)  The length of the session. I let patients know that our sessions tend to be approximately one to four hours each. Whether the session is fixed or flexible should be indicated.

(g)  The contractual arrangements for the sessions. I work one session at a time, and contractual arrangements are made only for the next session. If you expect a patient to have regular appointments one to five days a week, or if you expect a patient to contract for a six-month block of appointments, that should be indicated.

My preference is to provide this information in writing and to have it available before the initial session. If the patient is considering the step of undergoing an initial session, I regard the provision of such information as my responsibility. In a similar way, I am the teacher of the steps in the experiential method. In the course of every session, there is a symmetrical responsibility for granting the patient the choice of taking or not taking the next step and for showing the patient how to decide. Although this will be discussed later in some detail (Chapter 7), each session consists of next steps, and the therapist, as teacher of the method, talks with the patient about the patient's readiness and willingness to undertake this immediate next step, how to proceed with the next step, and how to judge whether or not the patient is ready right now for the next step. As a responsible experiential therapist, this is accepted as my responsibility. As a practicing therapist, this is effective in the successful undertaking of the next step.

At the close of a session, there is a question about a subsequent session. Our guideline cedes to the patient the right and the responsibility for a subsequent appointment. Each session is regarded as the beginning and the end of its therapeutic work. In both explicit and implicit communication, the therapist leaves it up to the patient whether another session is desired. The patient is responsible for undertaking therapeutic work or for deciding not to undertake therapeutic work, and this applies to both specific next steps in the session and also whether or not to have a subsequent session. In this work, the therapist is the teacher of the experiential method, the one who undertakes work with the patient. In actual practice, most patients build regular appointments. Sometimes these work out to be once or twice a week, sometimes more often, occasionally less often. In any case, the patient quickly accepts the responsibility for holding the major hand in deciding whether or not to have a subsequent session.

The granting of responsible choice to the patient is rooted in our theory of human beings, and it is expressed in the actual practice of experiential therapy. I am aware that other theories of human beings and other therapeutic approaches have their own good reasons for their own guidelines on the issue of the division of responsibility for subsequent appointments. They can cite hard economic considerations, codes of professional conduct, responsibility for the welfare of the patient, legal grounds, client motivation, clinical experience, administrative planning, and other heavy domains of consideration justifying the importance of the therapist's determining subsequent appointments. The therapist determines that the patient is to have daily 50-minute sessions; this patient "needs" to be seen at least twice a week; that patient "requires" at least six to nine months of intensive therapy; appointments are to be Tuesdays at 4:30 P.M. For whatever package of reasons, most therapists reserve the right to have the larger hand in determining that a subsequent session shall occur, when it shall be, and for how long. That is not the way in experiential psychotherapy.

I am aware that this is a sensitive issue. In most therapies it is exceedingly important that the therapist have the larger hand in these decisions. Economic considerations alone would force most therapists to find good reasons to schedule regular and frequent appointments. If the decision about whether to have another session, and perhaps even when to have it, lies preponderantly in the hands of the patient, income drops. Accordingly, it is imperative to talk about client welfare, professional responsibility, and any other matter which would insure that the patient has regular appointments, and as frequently as the traffic will bear. With regard to these economic considerations, I agree. However, I would contend that the door is still open on the following question: Are considerations of patient welfare, effectiveness of therapy, and professional responsibility and ethics best served when the preponderance of responsibility for a subsequent session lies in the hands of the patient or in the hands of the therapist? The humanistic-existential theory of human beings and the experiential approach to therapy argue in favor of responsibility lying preponderantly in the hands of the patient.

These same sensitive issues arise in the matter of the patient's extra-therapeutic world. To what extent and under what conditions does the experiential psychotherapist assume professional responsibility for the patient's extra-therapy world? Does the experiential therapist assume the preponderant responsibility for having the spouse or parent or child or friend also seen in therapy? Does the experiential therapist assume preponderant responsibility for contacting an employer, a physician, an attorney, for determining where and how the patient shall live, how the patient comes to and leaves therapy, and similar matters of daily living? If we exclude the unusual extreme instances, the humanistic-existential theory of human beings and the experiential approach to psychotherapy leave the preponderant responsibility in the hands of the patient.

The whole matter of relationships with the person who is the patient is terribly serious and knotty. Decisions and choices are thrust upon the therapist in the actual daily practice of therapy, and practical matters must be resolved. I have tried to bring together considerations from a humanistic-existential theory of human beings, from an experiential approach to psychotherapy, from professional codes and guidelines, from legal and ethical and moral bodies of thought, and from the roles and role relationships of the patient and therapist. The net result is that a large measure of responsibility remains in the hands of the person who is the patient.

## THE THERAPY SESSION

With regard to the therapy session itself, there are such practical questions as: How long is the session? How frequently are sessions held? Does the patient smoke during a session? Does the therapist take notes? What sorts of notes does the therapist use during or after the session? We shall discuss some of these practicalities of the therapy session itself.

### Length of the Session

Ordinarily, experiential sessions take around two hours or so. Often they run for three hours. Occasionally they are about an hour, and sometimes a marathon four-hour session occurs. One of the reasons for both the length and the variability of length is that the patient has a large hand in determining the end of that session's therapeutic work. If we accept this guideline, it seems that most patients do not set a 50-minute hour (cf. Gendlin, 1972; Rose, 1976). They continue until they are ready to stop. The therapist may well show the patient helpful ways to gauge readiness to end or not to end the session, but the patient has the larger hand in determining that this session is over.

Another reason for the length of the session is that it seems to require a couple of hours or so to do the therapeutic work. We have a sequence of steps which are followed (see Chapter 2), and progress through these steps calls for around two hours or so. Clearly these steps can be short-circuited or modified, but in general the work of experiential therapy cannot ordinarily be done in 50 minutes, nor does every patient require the same length of time to undergo the steps of therapeutic work.

How, then, does the experiential therapist schedule patients? The dominant guideline is to leave plenty of time for each scheduled patient. This means that you may work with only one or two or three patients a day, and the therapist's day is built around this schedule. You may schedule an experiential patient at 8:00 A.M., another at 2:00 P.M., and a third at 7:00 P.M. Clearly this may well leave the therapist with considerable free time. I am well aware of the scheduling difficulties this presents to experiential therapists whose professional life mainly involves work with patients. For such persons, compromises are often made. For example, they may work experientially with only one or two patients a day, or they may work out an agreement with the patient that the next session will be no more that two hours or so. My own preference is to work with only one patient a day, and to build a professional life which includes other kinds of professional work such as teaching, research, writing, and supervision.

Ordinarily I find that most patients and therapists work out their own rather regular session lengths. After 20 or 30 sessions or so, one patient may tend to end after two to two-and-a-half hours; another may generally end after an hour-and-a-half to two hours. However, special consideration usually must be given to initial sessions. Before this session, I apprise the patient to reserve two or three hours or so, and I find that these initial sessions vary a great deal from patient to patient.

*Frequency and Number of Sessions*

Each session is the beginning and the end of therapeutic work. At the close of the session, patient and therapist may consider whether or not to have another session and when it shall be. Most patients schedule one or two sessions a week. A smaller proportion schedule sessions over three or four consecutive days, or prefer a session every couple of weeks. With regard to number of sessions, there seem to be two clusters. One group seems to carry on therapeutic work for six to nine months or so, and the second continues for about a year and a half to two years. These are the clusterings which occur when the patient has the larger hand in determining the next session. But I have my preferences also. I find that

I like intensive short-term work of about a month or so, and I prefer sessions every other day or thereabouts. For longer-term work, I prefer at least a good year of two sessions a week. But these are personal preferences. I am sure my preferences play a large part in our negotiating for the next session, but always with the major responsibility in the hands of the patient.

In the first few sessions, with many patients, there is an explicit or implicit asking of what I think. Should I have a session tomorrow? What do you think?

T: I work a couple of ways at least. Sometimes we can have a session right away. Maybe the next day. Sometimes we wait a few days, maybe more.
Pt: I can have one tomorrow?
T: (Pause) Yep. We can.

Sometimes I tell a patient what others commonly arrange, i.e., some prefer the next session in a day or so, and others seem to prefer waiting a week. I give information. I tell my preferences. But the overriding principle is that the patient has the major hand in deciding both whether to have another session and when it shall be. Even in the first few sessions, these dialogues are rather brief. I find that patients accept such responsibility quite easily. This applies to all ways of describing patients—therapeutically sophisticated and naive ones, young and old ones, those who are doing fine in their lives and those who are racked with troubles.

After a while most patients settle into a routine. They arrange an appointment on Monday and on Thursday, starting at 5:30 P.M. At the close of each session they simply note that they want the next one on Thursday at the same starting time. Once in a while a patient will want to change the routine and have another session right away, or after a longer interval. In all of these arrangements, the therapist must participate.

Ordinarily I do not schedule more than one session at a time. However, I find that occasionally I do work with persons who come from out of town for something like a weekend of therapeutic work. Typically this is a one-time affair rather than a regular set-up. I have misgivings about participating in such arrangements, and these misgivings will be discussed in Chapters 5 and 6. Nevertheless, I do accept a few such invitations. Sometimes they are with former patients who want to return for a short burst of sessions. Sometimes they are with new patients who call or write for such marathon work. Under these conditions I agree beforehand that, for example, we will start one session on Friday at 7:00 P.M., a second on Saturday at 2:00 P.M., and the third on Sunday at 10:00 A.M. We generally work for a total of seven to ten hours.

## The Physical Rules for Therapeutic Work

The patient's eyes are closed throughout the entire session. Therefore, glasses and contact lenses are to be removed before therapeutic work begins. Because there are occasionally some physical wrenchings, I ask the patient to put the glasses or contact lenses on a table at some distance from the reclining chair. There is no smoking during the sessions. In part because it is inconvenient to smoke when eyes are closed, and in part because patients have confirmed that attention to smoking interferes with attention to therapeutic work, cigarettes and pipes are placed on an ashtray at some distance from the chair.

With rare exceptions, patients are to remain in the chair. But they are free to use the chair any way they wish. Most recline with their feet on the hassock. They move about in the chair to accommodate whatever is going on. Only rarely will a patient get out of the chair in the course of therapeutic work.

For the most part, these are the rules. In the beginning of therapeutic work the therapist may mention these as follows:

T: You sit over there, and I'll be right here. . . . That's right, put your feet up. You can take your shoes off if you wish. . . . Yeah, remove your glasses. You can put them over there. You are going to have your eyes closed throughout the session. So will I, at least most of the time. It's important that you attend to whatever is happening inside, so keep your eyes closed throughout. . . . Good, now just lean back and get settled.

If patients ask for some explanation of why they are to lean back or not smoke or keep their eyes closed or whatever, I provide answers. Mainly, these rules are there to help both patient and therapist attend to what is happening inside, to bodily sensations, to feelings, thoughts, images, experiencings. It is interfering if the patient sits up, smokes, looks at the therapist. Both patient and therapist follow the same rules and for the same reasons. Occasionally, especially in the initial sessions, a patient will not want to follow these rules.

Pt: Well, I don't think I could do that. I want to see you. . . . I would get tense if I had to keep my eyes shut. . . . I'll talk to you like this.

His eyes are open, and he is sitting up in the chair. The guideline is that therapeutic work begins when the patient is ready to lean back, close the eyes, and so on. The way of carrying out this guideline will vary with the person who is the therapist:

T: We can chat as long as you wish (therapist is reclined, but with eyes still open), but whenever you are ready to start work, just lean back and close your eyes.
Pt: I don't think I've ever talked with anyone with my eyes closed like that. Dr. Stillman referred me to you because he thinks that I . . . I talked with him about this drinking that's starting . . .
T: (Grinning) Uh-huh, ready to start work?
Pt: Do you make all your patients close their eyes? . . . And you close yours too?
T: Yes, and yes mine are closed too . . . most of the time. . . . It's the best way to really pay attention to what's important, to what you want to say, to what's going on inside.
Pt: (Sighs, leans back, closes his eyes) I'm embarrassed. . . . I have sexual problems. . . . I don't know. . . . It's so hard to say. . . . My wife and I want to have a baby. She wants to. And I have never had an orgasm. I've been lying to her for almost two years now and we are going to doctors to think about getting pregnant and I don't know what to do. I've lied and pretended all my life but I've agonized about this all the time, and I never told anyone what it's like. I think something is really wrong with me and I'm afraid. God, I'm really terrified that something is really wrong with me. . . .

I chose this excerpt because I have found it is common that more and better experiential material comes out easier when both therapist and patient follow these rules. But even when the initial dialogue is less blurted out, experiential work calls for following these rules.

There are some special rules which apply to the therapist rather than to the patient. When the therapist is especially upset or in turmoil or anguished, experiential work cannot proceed. When the therapist's body is filled with some temporary compelling sensation or feeling, experiential work cannot proceed. It is the responsibility of the therapist not to have a session under these conditions. Experiential work cannot proceed if the therapist has a bad cold or a nagging toothache or a pounding headache or a broken finger which throbs. To the extent that these are compelling, the therapist will be unable to attend to bodily sensations and feelings. It is wisest not to undertake therapeutic work under these conditions.

## The Therapist's Notes

I use notes for three reasons. One is to help in work with this patient. The second is for my own writing and research and thinking about experiential psychotherapy. The third reason is that notes are useful for administrative matters. We shall discuss each of these in turn, starting with the use of notes in the work with patients.

There are two kinds of notes which are helpful in working with particular patients. One set answers this question: What potentials for experiencing were revealed in this session? The second answers a related question: What were the circumstances or settings or conditions under which that potential for experiencing came closest to full occurrence?

During the session itself, the therapist may write a few words about the nature of something which occurred with high intensity, and also about the circumstances or settings or conditions under which it occurred. For example, if the peak of experiencing consists of the patient being helplessly bewildered and confused, the therapist may mark down the words "helplessly bewildered and confused." If this occurs when the patient is living in a scene in which he is being yelled at by his wife, the therapist may write down "yelled at by wife." The therapist writes down these words after the experiencing subsides, and the therapist is once again the teacher of the method.

As soon as the session is over, the therapist expands upon these notes. The first aim is to set down the very best words which describe the nature of the strong experiencings which were revealed during the session. What were the peaks of experiencing during this session? How may the nature of the experiencing be best described? "Helplessly bewildered, chaotic, confused, losing grip on things." Then the therapist adds this to the cumulative record of this patient's potentials for experiencing. Over the course of the sessions, there may be three or four, or eight or ten, constellations of words describing this patient's potentials for experiencing. As we reveal more and more from session after session, these constellations of words change. They reflect what therapeutic work has accomplished. They become more and more accurate. The notes may look like this:

> (a) Helplessly bewildered, chaotic, confused, losing grip on things, falling apart. (b) Cool and distant, removed, keeping others away, separation. (c) Warm and loving tenderness, holding and being held, closeness, oneness, softness. (d) Fighting, competition, being better than, pushing out ahead, rivaling, winning, outdoing.

Some of these potentials for experiencing are accompanied by good and wonderful bodily sensations and feelings. Some are accompanied by bad and awful ones. Some refer to the way the patient is, the way he behaves and operates in his life. Others seem to be deeper potentials, possibilities which are there within the person. Some are related to one or two other ones. For example, whenever there is a heightened experiencing of warm and loving tenderness, closeness, oneness, there is the imminent awful beginning of a deeper experiencing of falling apart, of chaos, of helpless bewilderment.

In essence, the therapist builds a constantly changing picture of the potentials for experiencing in this changing person, their relationships with one another, and their relative depth or availability within the person. This is what we learn and know about this person. The data consist of those moments in the session when the level of experiencing peaks, and we ask what the nature is of the immediate experiencing.

After the session, the therapist also studies these moments of peak experiencing to get some information about the circumstances or settings or conditions under which that potential for experiencing came closest to full occurrence. Suppose, for example, that we consider the experiencing of utter chaos, of losing one's grip on things, of falling apart. During the session, this experiencing is quite strong when the patient seems to be falling headlong into darkness and when there is a piercing sound like a siren or angry screaming. Although there is no clear memory of anything like this, when the patient hears that same piercing sound and his body lurches forward and straight down, the awful experiencing occurs. Suppose also that the experiencing of competitive rivalry started to occur most prominently when the patient was seven years old, and the family was invited to the home of a wealthy distant relative. The patient was playing with the son of that relative and the son ridiculed the way the patient threw a ball. In that moment, the patient was filled with a raging competitiveness, but he managed instead to freeze up and become tight and locked. From such data, the therapist keeps a running account of specific circumstances or settings or conditions under which the experiencings started to occur, or occurred in either a truncated or twisted way.

These are the two complementary kinds of notes which are useful for work with each patient. By means of these notes, the therapist builds an increasingly changing and increasingly more apt set of answers to questions such as the following: How would you describe this person? What are the salient features of this person's external world? What is the nature of the operating potentials and the deeper potentials? What are the prominent behaviors used to build the external world and to provide for experiencing? What are the relationships among potentials? What is this person like? All of this is what the experiential therapist does while some other therapists are doing "psychodiagnosis." Or, put differently, where some other therapists do psychological evaluation or assessment or psychodiagnosis, the experiential therapist answers these questions.

Very few notes are taken during the session. I usually jot down a few key words during those interludes when I am the teacher of the method. However, when the patient reports a dream, I take down the dream verbatim. Dreams are the one exception to the general rule of very sparse notes (Mahrer, 1971, 1975a). Following the session, then, the therapist reviews what occurred in those precious moments of higher levels of experiencing. It is during this time that I also take notes for myself. That is, I try to learn something about psychotherapy from the session. This is my second reason for taking notes.

In some sessions I find that something has gone quite well. The patient, or the patient and I, did something that strikes me as exciting. It may be the discovery of something new, or finding something that worked in a way I had never thought about. I learn something good and new by studying such rare occurrences. More often I find myself puzzling over problems, over traps and enigmas, over old problems in psychotherapy or my way of doing psychotherapy. I try to solve these problems. Occasionally there will be an event which is striking. It is unusual and compelling, although it is not some sort of exciting break-through or nagging problem. For example, I had a pronounced ringing in my ears which suddenly and unaccountably became the raucous screeching voice of someone who was about to die. Or, when the patient and I opened our eyes at the end of a session, for the first time we both had "tunnel vision," and everything seemed very small and far away. Out of such study and rumination, I find myself writing notes about psychotherapy, all generated by what happened in the session.

A third reason for notes is administrative. I have in mind a bookkeeper or secretary at an agency, an insurance company, and, rarely, an attorney. The notes consist of a running account of the dates of the sessions and the payments, or any other business or professional matters such as calls from other persons inquiring about the patient.

All in all, then, there are three sets of notes, each for different aims and purposes. You may observe that these three sets of notes do not include statements about the way the patient looked and dressed and acted that day, what the patient talked about that day, what sort of progress was made that session. There are no statements about treatment goals or plans of action or treatment programs. What is more, notes about the patient are not kept from the patient. Descriptions of the potentials for experiencing and the circumstances or settings or conditions under which they occur are just as known by the patient as the therapist. They are discussed and described in virtually each step of the session.

We now turn to a most important practical matter for both the person who may undertake experiential therapy and the therapist. This is the question of the appropriateness or inappropriateness of this therapy for this person at this time.

## PERSONS FOR WHOM EXPERIENTIAL PSYCHOTHERAPY IS APPROPRIATE

This therapy is not for everyone. It is appropriate for those persons who are able to carry out the experiential method. This means, in regard to the first step for example, that the person is able to place most of his attention on some meaningful center (not on the therapist) so as to allow moderate to strong bodily sensations to occur. It is not appropriate for those persons who are not able to carry out the experiential method, e.g., the person who places most of his attention on the therapist and the therapeutic relationship or the person whose bodily sensations fail to reach at least a moderate level.

The other considerations used in most other approaches are either irrelevant for us or relevant only insofar as they make sense in terms of the actual carrying out of the experiential method. Accordingly, we are not concerned with such matters as the person's intelligence, social class, psychological sophistication, presenting complaint or problem, motivation for psychotherapy, external resources, psychodiagnosis, nature or degree of psychopathology, personality traits, psychodynamics, ego strength, object cathexes, verbal abilities, degree of personal stress, overall adjustment, degree of sociopathy, ability to relate to others, or any of the other matters which are often assessed and weighed and evaluated in most other approaches. If any of these play any part in the patient's actual carrying out of the experiential method, we prefer going directly to the practical issue of whether or not the patient is ready now to do what the experiential method calls for. If the person can follow the method, this therapy is appropriate; if the person cannot, this therapy is not appropriate.

From our perspective, then, the question is not what patient characteristics are appropriate for experiential therapy. Nor is the question what kinds of problems in what kinds of patients are successfully treated with experiential psychotherapy. Our question is simply whether or not the patient is now ready and capable of following the experiential method.

As indicated in the prologue, this book relates to psychotherapy with adults, not children or infants. At the upper end, for persons in their sixties, seventies, even eighties, the therapy is appropriate; persons in these age groups can follow the experiential method. The actual method described in this book is appropriate for children and adolescents as young as 12-14 years of age. It is my impression that younger children and infants can also follow the principles underlying the experiential method, but the actual procedures must be modified (Mahrer, 1970a, 1978a; Mahrer, Levinson, & Fine, 1976). Thus, the principles behind the method allow this therapy to be appropriate for children and infants, though the actual procedures comprising the experiential method described in this book are inappropriate for these younger persons.

Our single criterion may be complemented by some further considerations about those persons for whom experiential therapy is appropriate.

*It Is Appropriate for Some Persons Who Eschew the Ordinary Patient Roles*

There are many persons who are sensitive to the ordinary role of patient and to the ordinary role relationships between doctor and patient. These persons seldom enter psychotherapy. For some of these persons, the idea of being a patient is itself bothersome. The fact of placing themselves in that role is itself significant, and loads of changes have already occurred should they step into the office for the first session. Others engage in methods of self-change. Still others regard psychiatrists and psychotherapists in general as incompetents, as self-declared professionals who prey upon the public, as plying a trade which is ineffective at best, immoral generally, and occasionally dangerous. If they should somehow try a session or two with some therapist or other, they frequently bolt from the patient role, reinforced in their convictions about the whole enterprise.

Experiential psychotherapy is appropriate for a large proportion of these persons. In hearing or reading about the method, or in an initial session or two, these persons find that they are the boss, the responsible one. The therapist is merely the teacher of a method, and their relationship is predominantly with their own work rather than that of patient to therapist. Not only do many of these persons find therapy palatable, but they are able to carry out the method and follow the procedures rather effectively. This brings to experiential psychotherapy many persons who would ordinarily avoid a fair number of typical psychotherapies. This therapy is appropriate for such persons.

## The Nature of the "Problem" Has Little Bearing on Appropriateness

Regardless of how the patient's "problem" is described, the so-called problem seems to have little to do with the appropriateness or inappropriateness of experiential psychotherapy. If the patient puts her attention on her stealing from stores or her secret drinking, and bodily sensations are at least moderate, the chances are that experiential therapy is appropriate for this person. If, on the other hand, she preponderantly attends to the therapist in a relationship of bad little girl to strong parental authority, then this therapy is generally not appropriate.

It does not matter how therapies go about defining the patient's "problems." Some may concentrate on verbalized initial complaints: She says that she steals from stores; she complains that she drinks too much; she voices suicidal preoccupations; she complains that she is unassertive. Some therapies define the patient's problems from the perspective of the therapist, often assisted with a battery of psychological tests. Accordingly, the patient's problem consists of a depressive reaction, repressed hostility, certain cognitive ideas, being the rejected child, weak ego, ambulatory schizophrenia, overdependence upon her mother. Even though experiential psychotherapy does not use such descriptions, the practical guideline is that the appropriateness of this therapy has little to do with the nature of patient "problems."

Suppose we consider the nature of the meaningful centers upon which the patient's attention is focused, with moderate or strong bodily sensations. These centers may vary within and between sessions. It may include attention to the cancer, the scary feeling in the stomach, the sense of being inadequate, the look on the spouse's face, key words which the significant person says, being scared to be alone. When "problems" are described in this way, the same conclusion is in order. That is, to the extent that the patient is able to dedicate the preponderance of attention so that bodily sensations and feelings are at least moderate, this therapy is appropriate.

It may appear somewhat surprising that experiential psychotherapy is appropriate for persons with deadened feelings, those who talk about having no feelings or being depressed or numb or dead. Whether the patient describes himself in these ways or someone else describes him in these ways, the experiential method appears to be relatively appropriate. What is surprising is how common it is that bodily sensations occur even when the patient is being that way or attending to aspects of being that way. As the patient focuses upon being frozen or unfeelinged, something generally occurs in the body. There is a felt heaviness, or tears happen, or tension occurs in the stomach. All in all, the specified nature of the "problem" has little to do with whether experiential psychotherapy is appropriate or inappropriate.

## The Question of "Psychosis," "Emotional Illness," "Severe Psychopathology"

Experiential psychotherapy does not include such technical terms or constructs or phrases. But these words have meaning in many other approaches. The question may be phrased as follows: To what extent is experiential psychotherapy appropriate for patients whom other approaches would tend to describe as psychotic or emotionally ill or having a serious disorder or severe psychopathology? If there is a measure of communication in such a question, then I would answer in two ways. One is that experiential psychotherapy is somewhat appropriate for such persons in general. The second is that experiential psychotherapy is appropriate or inappropriate for such persons depending upon three further considerations.

I am talking about persons who, either for a short or long time, act in ways which professionals and nonprofessionals would regard as weird, as strange and bizarre, as deranged, as looney, as indicating that the person is being crazy. This is the person who is not all there, who makes people feel that something is wrong with him. When such persons initiate their own appointments, my impression is that experiential psychotherapy is generally appropriate.

The "generally" in that phrase brings us to the three further considerations. If the consideration applies to the person, this therapy is not appropriate; if the consideration does not apply, then this therapy may be quite appropriate:

1) If the deeper potentials are completely barricaded, this therapy is inappropriate; if the deeper potentials are not completely barricaded, this therapy may be quite appropriate. Humanistic theory (Mahrer, 1978a) gives us the picture of some persons as having won the struggle against some deeper potentials by achieving such incredible distance and separation that the deeper potential is virtually sealed off. After struggling against a deeper imminence of the experiencing of lusty sexuality or murderous assaultiveness, often for their whole lives, the battle is won. These deeper potentials no longer are a bother. They are essentially completely barricaded, so pushed down and suffocated that they offer no further problems.

To the extent that the person has achieved this, experiential therapy is inappropriate. Such persons will seldom seek psychotherapy. If they elect experiential psychotherapy, they would almost certainly not be able to follow the method.

Some persons are like this. Of the persons who are like this, some are in the group we are talking about, i.e., persons whom other approaches would describe as psychotic, or with severe psychopathology, or emotionally ill. However, many persons are like this who may be described as quite well-adjusted, as the ordinary "normal" persons. They have likewise succeeded in the final sealing off of deeper potentials. No longer bothered by these deeper potentials, they fulfill many of the common meanings of well-adjusted and normal. Regardless of whether they appear crazy or well-adjusted, normal persons or deranged lunatics, such persons are inappropriate for experiential psychotherapy.

What this means is that experiential therapy is appropriate for all those persons who are still in some sort of contact with their deeper potentials, still able to feel scared or depressed or anxious or whatever signals the working presence of deeper potentials. As Gendlin (1972) indicates, experiential therapy is appropriate even with long-hospitalized persons in whom the deeper personality processes are still capable of some life. Nor does it matter how bizarre or weird the person seems to be. Many persons behave in deranged and "psychotic" ways in their extra-therapy life, but within the session are able to follow the experiential method. If the deeper potentials are not completely sealed off and barricaded, this therapy may be quite appropriate; if the deeper potentials are completely sealed off and barricaded, this therapy is not appropriate—and this applies to the person who is regarded as psychotic or normal, to the long-hospitalized "schizophrenic" or the mental health professional.

2) Experiential psychotherapy is inappropriate for those "psychotic" (deranged, emotionally ill, disordered, severely psychopathological) persons for whom it is necessary to establish therapist-patient role relationships characterized by extreme distance and separation. On the other hand, this therapy is rather appropriate for those persons, described as "psychotic," who can set aside their extreme distancing tendencies while following the experiential method.

Many persons who are called psychotic tend to keep a lot of distance between themselves and others. They may live within their own worlds and use peculiar ways to keep others at a safe distance. No one is to get near them. They respond to internal voices, but not to external persons. They are dramatically withdrawn. Experiential psychotherapy is perhaps somewhat cordial for such persons because the usual therapist-patient relationships are minimized. Relationships are with whatever the patient attends to, and not with the therapist. Whether or not the patient wishes to undertake a session or the next step within the session is up to the patient. All in all, the therapist offers a method which gives the patient the opportunity to be the way he is and which does not push any sort of interpersonal relationship onto the patient. Many of these persons are thereby able to follow the experiential method, and this therapy is appropriate for them. Indeed, once these patients are free of imminent role relationships being pushed onto them, it is interesting how easily the relationship-avoiding behaviors are left at the therapy door and taken up again when the session is over.

More often, the problem lies with the therapist and not the patient. It is the therapist who regards the patient as psychotic and thereby establishes a therapist-patient role relationship characterized by distance and separation (Condrau & Boss, 1971). Across this distancing relationship, the therapist regards the patient as psychotic, as alien. To the extent that the therapist engineers such a role relationship, experiential therapy is inappropriate. On the other hand, if the therapist is free of such distancing role relationships, this therapy is appropriate for both parties.

3) Experiential psychotherapy is appropriate for persons whose centers of attention may be described as psychotic, crazy, deranged, weird, bizarre, severely pathological. The patient may be attending to the strange voices which no one else hears, to the snakes or the blood, the enemies who are plotting to poison her or control the world, the bugs inside the liver and intestines, to all sorts of weird and bizarre phenomena. Indeed, many experiential patients sooner or later pour their attention onto such centers. Even for persons whose extra-therapy lives are filled with such phenomena, experiential therapy is quite appropriate.

In summary, experiential psychotherapy seems to be appropriate for those persons whom other approaches may describe as "psychotic" (or emotionally ill or severely psychopathological) to the extent that (a) deeper potentials are not completely barricaded and sealed off, (b) relationship-avoiding ways of being can be set aside in following the experiential method, and (c) they put the preponderance of attention on centers, even though these centers may be described as psychotic, deranged, unusual, or bizarre. All in all, I find that experiential therapy is appropriate for a large proportion of such persons called psychotic or emotionally ill or severely psychopathological.

## Some Special Considerations for Appropriateness

There are other special considerations which indicate that experiential psychotherapy is appropriate. One has to do with crisis. This therapy is quite appropriate for persons in crisis. Clearly there may be exceptions here and there, but in general the state of being in crisis is extremely suited to the experiential method, because the patient is typically in a state of strong bodily sensations and a great deal of the patient's attention is focused on some highly meaningful center. The patient is already experiencing. Indeed, the experiential method virtually calls for the patient's allowing himself to enter into what is ordinarily meant by a state of crisis.

For persons in crisis states, initial sessions should occur as soon as possible after the patient makes the initiating overture. As with each session, we go directly into therapeutic work. Whether for initial sessions or at any time during the patient's therapeutic career, the therapist should be available as much as possible and as soon as possible.

Therapies vary in their attitude toward the appropriateness of work with patients in crisis states. Where experiential therapy regards crisis as aiding therapeutic work, psychoanalytic therapy sees crisis as a real block (Freud, 1953).

Another special consideration has to do with immediate and compelling bodily aches and pains. Suppose the patient has a pounding headache or backache or swirling nausea. Suppose that there is a physical hurt of one kind or another. Is therapeutic work appropriate? Is the patient ordinarily able to carry on experiential work? I find that ordinarily the answer is yes. Typically these serve as the compelling centers of attention, and therapeutic work starts from there. The same is true when the compelling center of attention is some external person or event, or an internal thought or idea. The person may be plagued by his dominant wife or his competitive colleague or the persistent fear of death. The patient can talk about nothing else. In these instances also, experiential work is appropriate. There is a defined and compelling focal center of attention and the experiential method can be followed.

A final set of special considerations involves the personal preferences of the therapist. When I look back over my own personal reactions toward starting work with patients, I can identify five considerations which lead me to start work with patients. One is that I am quite inclined to undergo experiential work with persons who are about to have babies. For me, the key time is about a year or so before conception and a few years or so after birth, or a few years before and after adopting a baby. Second, I am drawn toward work with professional therapists and to those who are in training for our profession. Third, I am inclined to work with patients who seem genuinely ready for serious nuclear personality change, wholesale and radical changes in the very core of personality. Fourth, I have found myself quite drawn toward patients with cancer and other life-threatening body states. Finally, I have found it exciting to work with persons in their sixties, seventies, and eighties. Each experiential therapist is entitled to an acknowledged set of personal preferences.

## PERSONS FOR WHOM EXPERIENTIAL PSYCHOTHERAPY IS NOT APPROPRIATE

This therapy is not universal. Perhaps the simplest criterion of appropriateness or inappropriateness is whether or not the person follows the experiential method. If the person does not or will not or can not, this therapy is not appropriate. At the practical working level, this is the criterion, and it is the responsibility of the therapist to work with the person in deciding whether or not this therapy is appropriate. At the close of an initial session, we take up the issue of another appointment, and it is here that the degree to which the patient was able to carry out or not carry out the method is to be considered seriously.

For whatever reasons, many persons do not carry out the experiential method. There has been no careful study of those who do and do not carry out the method. However, it is my impression that somewhat under half of the persons who may well be appropriate for all other therapies are not appropriate for experiential psychotherapy. The reasons will be discussed below.

*Persons for Whom a Relation with the Therapist Is Paramount*

Experiential psychotherapy is not appropriate with persons for whom it is of paramount importance to engage in a role relationship with the therapist. For these persons, psychotherapy provides the opportunity to engage in some highly important, extremely significant relationship in which the patient fulfills one role and the therapist fulfills a complementary role. These persons need, want, seek such a role relationship. The therapist must be their one and only best friend, or the all-powerful one who will fix them, the understanding and compassionate one, or the one who represents all the authority of society, their hated enemy against which they fight the final battle, their magical helper who will make everything better, the one with whom they can achieve some sense of meaning and value and connectedness, the one whom they can manipulate to get what they want, the one upon whom they can place demands. Under these circumstances, experiential psychotherapy will not work; it is inappropriate.

For these persons, there is practically no way that they will place most of their attention on anything other than the therapist. However, we must differentiate these patients from the far larger group of patients who must construct role relationships with someone, but that someone is not restricted to the therapist. For example, the patient is geared to make someone into her best friend, but she is quite prepared to allow her attention to go to the best friend who died recently, the best friend who never was, the best friend who was there when the patient was a child, the brief encounter with the special person who might have become the best friend, and so on. For this larger group, the experiential method can be followed. But for those patients who must engage in a role relationship with the therapist per se, experiential therapy is inappropriate.

There are at least two reasons why this therapy will not be appropriate under such conditions. One is that the experiential therapist either is the teacher of the method or undergoes the experiential process along with the patient, but never (or practically never) does the therapist engage in the fulfillment of role relationships. The therapist does not fulfill a role of the patient's best friend or the understanding one or any other role relationship.

The second reason is that the patient who engages in a role relationship with the therapist is thereby not able to carry out the experiential method. The first step in each session requires that the patient place the preponderance of attention on some meaningful focal center and little or no attention on the therapist or the relationship with the therapist. The patient who must defy the therapist, or be understood by the therapist, or engage in any kind of relationship with the therapist, cannot carry out the experiential method.

Some patients must engage in a certain kind of role relationship with the therapist now. They may be ready for experiential therapy in a few days or months or never. I may try experiential work with such persons for an hour or so. Sometimes we may even decide to give it another try in another session. But my overriding tendency is to honor and respect what they need and want and are asking for. I may refer these persons to other therapists who are likely to be much more fitting.

What proportion of patients must have a role relationship with the therapist, must place most of their attention on the therapist to the exclusion of allowing their attention to go to any other center? My impression is that a small proportion of patients, perhaps ten percent or so, must do this. For such persons, this therapy is inappropriate.

Are there any characteristics or qualities common to these patients? I find that being this way cuts across virtually all ways of categorizing patients. It is not especially common in patients who are old or young, psychologically sophisticated or naive, full of problems or with very few, smart or dumb, patients in this or that "psychodiagnostic" category or whatever. It is simply a pragmatic consideration that experiential psychotherapy is inappropriate with persons for whom the relationship with the therapist is paramount.

*Letting the Person Be; Experiential Psychotherapy Is Not Imposed on Persons*

This therapy is inappropriate for persons who are pushed or pulled into the therapist's office, who are there because of the pressure of some other person or agency. When therapy is imposed upon the person, experiential psychotherapy is inappropriate.

There are at least two reasons why therapy is inappropriate under these conditions, and both concern the consequent difficulty in carrying out the experiential method. One reason is that persons on whom therapy is imposed simply are unable or unwilling to carry out the steps of the method. It is hard enough for the person who is really "let be," who takes up this therapy on his own initiative. Each step of this therapy depends upon the patient's seeking it, being ready and willing to work. For persons on whom therapy is imposed, the actual steps of the method simply cannot be negotiated.

The second reason is that when therapy is imposed upon the person, the preponderance of therapy generally consists of the establishment and working out of some specific role relationships. It becomes a game of the one who imposes therapy and the willing victim or resister or distant one. It becomes a game of strong one and weak one, the representative of a powerful society and the little person, the social helper and the designated helpee, the one who is going to do it and the one who is going to have it done to her, the two together against the big external agency that imposes it on both of them, the specialist and the one who is imposed upon, the therapist cog of society and the patient cog of society—and dozens of other role relationships expressing the underlying commonality that somehow being in therapy has been imposed upon the patient.

To the extent that therapy is the working out of these role relationships, the patient is in no position to carry out the experiential method. Nor is the therapist. It simply will not work.

As a group, psychotherapists have eagerly participated in the construction and maintenance of a professional-social world in which therapy is imposed upon all sorts of persons. We impose therapy on children through their parents, through the legal system, through social workers in agencies with legal and quasi-legal powers to impose therapy (casework, counseling, treatment, "help"). The school system is given enormous power to impose therapy on children. All the mental health professions have power to impose therapy on children. The medical profession has enormous power to impose therapy on children. We create conditions, give them labels, train professionals to exert pressure on children who are labeled retarded, delinquent, emotionally ill, autistic, slow learners, learning disabled, and so on and on and on. The net result is that we have thousands upon thousands of children upon whom therapy is imposed.

The system of hospitals and outpatient clinics, agencies and community centers, allows enormous professional-social pressure on persons to be in therapy. These institutions are there in part to do therapy on persons who are pressured by judges and physicians, probation officers and personnel officers, school teachers and school psychologists, nurses and police officers, dozens upon dozens of professionals who exert pressure on persons to go there for treatment.

Therapists are taught how to ensnare patients and to impose therapy upon them. We learn how to "motivate" patients, to convince them that they "need help." You have an emotional illness. You need treatment. You have a psychiatric condition. You need "help." You should see a psychotherapist. See the problems and conflicts and difficulties you have; if you do not get help you will lose your job, be alcoholic, fall apart, become suicidal, never "get better." The circular reasoning goes on and on, entrapping the person into imposed therapy. Therapists are taught how to keep patients in therapy, how to keep them coming, how to expand the patient to include the child, the spouse, the friend, an acquaintance, the other parent. We learn how to evaluate and assess, to diagnose and write reports on the basis of which we "recommend" psychotherapy. All in all, our professions give us the justification, the value system, the ethics, the tools, and the stature to use soft and hard means of imposing therapy on whole segments of the population.

Instead of imposing therapy on persons, experiential psychotherapy takes the position of letting the person be. Not only is this in accord with the humanistic-existential perspective on human beings, but this position maximizes the chances that the patient will be able to carry on the experiential method. However, we have thereby identified a large group of persons for whom experiential therapy is not appropriate. If we put together persons on whom therapy is imposed and persons for whom a relation with the therapist is paramount, we have a large class of persons for whom experiential psychotherapy is inappropriate. Indeed, a very substantial proportion of these persons undergoing other kinds of psychotherapy is considered inappropriate for experiential psychotherapy.

*Patients Who Are "High" on Drugs or Alcohol*

In general, the patient who is high on drugs or alcohol will be unable to focus attention upon a meaningful center. The patient is much less able to carry out this or any other step in the experiential method. Accordingly, experiential therapy is not appropriate while the patient is in this state, and it holds for patients who occasionally show up in such a state. It holds for strong doses, and it holds for moderate amounts.

It is easy to think of drugs and alcohol as opening the person up to more experiencing. It might loosen me up, unfreeze me a bit. But that is not the issue. Instead, the issue is whether or not the patient will be able to carry out the experiential method. With rare exception, the answer is that his ability is impaired. The patient often becomes looser and more unfrozen, more opened up and free. He will coast and roam about, blabber and slide every which way, but he cannot carry on the experiential method.

The same holds true for most medications. Too many medications only serve to interfere with the work of experiential therapy. The question is typically how much. If the kind and amount of medication interfere with therapeutic work, then this therapy is simply not appropriate for this patient at this time.

# 4

# An Illustrative Session

This chapter provides a concrete illustration of the sequence of steps in experiential psychotherapy (see Chapter 2). Here is how experiential therapy works. It is the 34th session of 56 with a patient who had about two sessions a week for 10 months. I regard this session as representative of relatively good sessions with relatively proficient patients.

The aim is to provide a script which is illustrative of what patients say and what the experiential psychotherapist does. Accordingly, the script is based upon an actual session, but every statement by patient and therapist was significantly altered both to protect the identity of the patient and to better illustrate the steps and methods of experiential psychotherapy. Proper names and sexes were changed. General situations and incidents were replaced with others, either invented or taken from other patients. Some part or parts of every statement was either deleted, significantly modified, or replaced by another.

The final product would seem rather familiar to perhaps many patients in experiential psychotherapy, though the actual content of the words would not fit. All in all, this is to be taken as an invented script designed to illustrate both the overall process and the specific interchanges of a single session.

Figure 4.1 provides both an introduction and an overview of the external world, the operating and deeper potentials, and their relationships—all occurring in this session. In the first step, the patient's attention is on a friend, Peter, and she moves into the experiencing of being needed, caring, providing, tender (Figure 4.1). Related to this is another operating potential, referred to by words such as capable, smart, competent. In this session, another operating potential is also brought into play. It is the experiencing of being useless, a failure, a nothing. There is some carrying forward of these three operating potentials (step 2, Figure 2.2), and the relationship between these and a deeper potential (Figure 4.1; step 3, Figure 2.2). After this work results in some integrative softening of the relationships, the next step involves the patient's disengagement from the whole operating domain and entrance into being the deeper potential (step 4, Figure 2.2). This occurs within the context of scenes from her early life. Finally, the session ends with the consideration of actual risked changes in her way of being and behaving in her extra-therapy world (step 5, Figure 2.2).

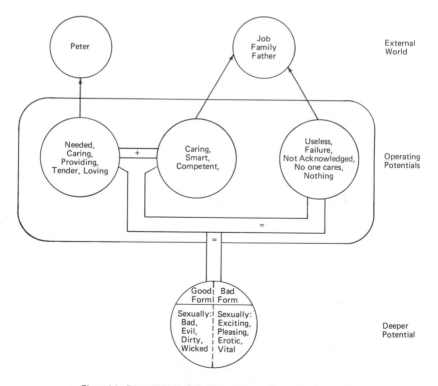

Figure 4.1. External World, Operating and Deeper Potentials
of Patient in Illustrative Session

Tied to each step, a number of changes occurred in this session. Disintegrative relationships among the operating potentials and between operating and deeper potentials softened and became more integrative. With this came a washing away of bad feelings of tension and disharmony, and a companion heightening of integrative feelings of oneness and inner peacefulness. For some time in the session, there occurred a change in the form of the deeper potential, so that the patient lived the experiencing of the good form of the deeper potential, a wonderful and exciting good sexuality. Not only has the relationship with the deeper potential become more integrative, and not only has the form of the deeper potential shifted from bad to good, but the deeper potential has at least momentarily become a part of the operating domain.

These changes in turn open the way for further changes in the operating domain and the nature of her constructed external world. There is less of a tendency to experience being useless and a failure, less of a tendency to avoid this by a bad-feelinged sense of being needed and caring or capable and smart, and less of a tendency to construct external worlds accommodating these painful experiencings. One risk is the dropping away of these three operating potentials; another risk is the construction of changing external worlds to accommodate the experiencing of these operating potentials in new ways accompanied by good feelings. There is also the heightened tendency of constructing changing external worlds accommodating the experiencing of the good form of the former deeper potential, the warm and exciting sexuality. Finally, with these internal changes and changing readinesses to build changing external worlds, the patient has undergone changes in the therapy session itself and, in the last step, considers the possibility of risking actual changes in her self and her life outside the therapy session proper.

T1: (We are in the office, both seated. I have leaned back and closed my eyes after having chatted with her for a couple of minutes as we entered the office.) I'm ready.

P1: (Quietly, after a short pause.) Yes.

T2: (I begin by inviting the patient to describe her bodily sensations so that I can have similar ones.) OK. I want to have the same body sensations you do. I'm ready. Take 10 or 20 seconds. Just listen. Wait. Take your time. Where are they? Where are they mainly? (Sometimes we start with the attention directed onto some center. Sometimes we start by the therapist allowing himself to have the same bodily sensations as the patient. If we take this route, the first step is for the patient to locate where they are.)

P2: (After about 15-20 seconds.) Here, my stomach. Uh . . . mainly here. I feel it all over the stomach here.

T3: Stomach. (The therapist allows attention to proceed to the stomach.)

P3: And legs. (Pause. Often the sheer attending to prominent bodily sensations will start a progression of bodily sensations.) But . . . no, mainly here in the stomach.

T4: OK. (Now the therapist is attending primarily to the stomach.) Hmmm . . . wait . . . stomach . . . here . . . OK.

P4: Right here.

T5: OK. Now just describe what they're like. I want to have the same thing you do. The same thing. Just right . . . let me have them too. Just the same. (She frequently starts with bodily sensations mainly in the stomach or chest or legs. My aim is to have her guide me so that I can indeed have the same sensations as she does.)

P5: Like butterflies. Kind of strong. I can feel them. Kind of strong. Butterflies. It feels hot, apprehensive . . . hollow. (The therapist is now to have the same kind of sensation as the patient is describing. The therapist lets himself have those physical sensations here in the stomach.)

T6: Oh . . . tensed up. Tight. Scared. (That was bad. These bodily sensations should be described in physical terms as the patient is doing. Perhaps I was excited at starting to have the same sensations. I am often surprised at the ease with which I can have the same bodily sensations as the patient describes.)

P6: Yes, that's right . . . I feel not so tight . . . sensitive, vulnerable. (Now the patient is doing what I did, i.e., using words that tell very little of what the bodily sensations are like. We are off track.)

T7: Hot . . . hollow . . . like empty? The whole area? (I am trying to have it the way the patient is having it.)

P7: It's warm all over here, like inside and . . . hot . . . more like I'm scared.

T8: All right . . . wait . . . OK . . . Now I feel the blood beating . . . boom, boom . . . and it is butterflies . . . Yes. (I was now aware of the blood beating in my stomach area, and the butterflies were present.)

P8: But only delicately. (It is helpful when the patient corrects your version of the bodily sensations, adds a little here and there in order for you to have quite similar bodily sensations.)

T9: (Pause.) OK. (I try to allow the sensation to be delicate and not strong.)

P9: A little tight and tense and the blood is beating. And it is butterflies and I feel vulnerable. (As she describes, I am aware that I have sensations like this. I am pleased. Sometimes, even with this skilled patient, it takes much longer for me to share her bodily sensations.)

T10: Yeah . . . yeah . . . I have it . . . it's like this. (Now that I have similar bodily sensations, the next step is for the patient to let her attention go to whatever is there and accompanied by moderate bodily sensations. Right now our sensations are moderate. Either these will increase somewhat or they will be replaced with some other kind, but of at least moderate intensity. She is quiet now, and I turn to the instructions for this next step. I have given these instructions at least once or twice in each previous session, so she is quite familiar with them.) . . . Now just let your mind go to whatever is there when you let it come. Something there now when you let yourself attend to it. Something that . . . and let the sensations in the body happen, get strong. Let things in the body happen. Whatever. Let the sensations in the body be strong, very strong . . . when you put all your attention on it . . . I will too. Now we'll both attend to it. We'll see whatever it is. You talk about it and I'll talk about it . . . (The general idea is there in the jumbled and choppy sentences, namely that the patient is invited to let attention go to whatever is there already. This is one way to approach the first step as indicated in Figure 2.2.)

P10: Something did happen, just a few days ago. Last evening.

T11: I'm ready. (I posture myself so as to receive whatever her words connote. I want to see whatever is brought forth from her words. My attention is distributed all around, with very little on her directly.)

P11: I felt funny when I think of two things. Yes . . . lately Peter called from Montreal and oh I just get a million feelings. Peter calls and I feel so screwed up inside. (My attention is on Peter on the phone. I am letting myself feel screwed up inside. As I start to do this, my attention is pulled by a sensation in my mouth. It is suddenly quite dry. Somewhere there was a far off hint of a thought that I have no idea who Peter is, but then the dryness is here again.) Sometimes he just calls . . . I don't see him for a while and then he calls.

T12: My mouth is dry. (I say this sort of in general, not especially to her. When bodily sensations are compelling, I just mention them. In the background is Peter, and some of my attention is on him.)

P12: I am pleased to hear from him. The way he talks. Friendly. Seductive. Friendly. Feel maternal and caring and feeling this. And the other is oh no, I can't still be like this. Back and forth. It is frustrating. . . . I'm thinking of the past when I was little. . . . I still feel vulnerable. . . . My husband . . . and I want to see him. I want to see him. But all those traps. (She is talking as if not to me, but more just letting the attention go. I am free to see what her words connote, and I allow all the images to flow as she talks. But when she says "all those traps" the tension and the butterflies in my stomach become much stronger.)

T13: "All those traps" . . . "those traps" . . . my stomach and the butterflies. (I am using increases in my bodily sensations to guide us in the centering of attention.)

P13: All those years. Those years. I don't want to see him. . . . I feel so sorry for him and I do things to help him and then he'll do crazy things and he'll lean on me and he'll expect all those things from me. He'll do crazy things and I'll get mad and then I'll get so apologetic. It's a trap. I can't keep stable. (Here is where she shows how quickly she allows the preponderance of her attention to be on something meaningful and not on me. It is as if most of her attention is directed onto the other person and on what that brings forth from her. Most patients take much longer to reach this point. At the same time, the accompanying bodily sensations in me are of at least moderate proportions. This is the working level of experiencing. Now that she is at this level, I am free to allow my attention likewise to be on whatever she is building, and to allow my own sensations to be likewise at the moderate level. When I do this, I sense something inside, a clearer version of what is being experienced. At first this is blurry. Then I sense it more accurately. It is a caring for the other person, a tenderness for Peter. As I allow this to come forth, and as I allow myself to experience this, there is an easing of the butterflies, and now there is a warmth in my whole chest region. This is new and it is of moderate intensity.)

T14: Tender . . . it's all right. It's OK. (I describe this inner experiencing, and do so as if I am saying this to Peter, directly.)

P14: He was slender, and thin, with a big dark, wonderful head of hair. So trusting. Yes. Long limbs, large. Peter is large but not fat. Slight. Must have been a slight child. There is such a serious air about him. Sensitive inside. Even frightened by noises, like thunder and lighting. . . . Some voices now. Yelling and screaming voices. (I hear the voices. They change the bodily sensations. Everything tightens up inside instantly, and the stomach especially tenses up.)

T15: Loud voices. Loud. I hear loud voices.

P15: Yes.

T16: Oh!

P16: Loud. (She says this evenly, in modulated tone.)

T17: Like people yelling, arguing. (My attention is on the voices.)

P17: But it all just fell apart. It ended. I don't know what happened. . . .
I hurt him! (I had been attending to the voices. She wasn't. My attention goes to what her words are building: A meanness, a cruelty, a doing something hurtful to Peter.)

T18: Yes.

P18: (Pause.) I shouldn't have hurt him! (This is said with rather strong feeling. I sensed something deeper, something which was devilishly pleased at hurting him. It felt tough and nasty.)

T19: He is going to have the scars from this for years! You are bad! (This was said almost in good spirits, as if it was wicked good fun to have done this to him. I am being the voice of this deeper potential, relating directly to her from within this potential.)

P19: (Soft crying.) I don't know. (She pulls back from the deeper wickedness.)

T20: (Gently, but sarcastically.) Awwww . . .

P20: (Soft tears.) He's so tender and vulnerable. (We are now well past the first step in the session, the aligning of our bodily sensations, the letting attention go to something accompanied by moderate bodily sensations. Only about a third of the patients can come to this point so quickly. Because she does this, and thereby allows the therapist to join with her, the therapist can begin having some of the experiencings occurring in the patient. In P13 there is a sensing of a tenderness, a being caring. This is in relation to Peter. In P18 there is a sensing of something related yet different, an inner hurting of others, a tough and nasty deeper experiencing which enjoys doing harm, and again this is in relation to Peter. Here are hints of two coupled experiencings, mere suggestions to be held with low confidence.)

T21: You did a bad thing! (In being filled with this meanness and nastiness, the therapist can scold her for what she has done to him.)

P21: (Softly crying.) It wasn't my fault. No! (Now we are engaging one another. She is interacting with a deeper part of her which she ordinarily avoids and denies.)

T22: Oh, come on! Look what you did!

P22: (Pause.) It just didn't work out. (Pause.) I always felt like it was my fault. (She is quiet, after having essentially allowed that she had been responsible for hurting Peter. The silence continues for about a minute. Then I am no longer inside the patient. Slowly I am me again, outside the patient, aware of my own thoughts. The sensations in my body are now neutral. She and I have both withdrawn from the beginnings of a little encounter between her and the deeper experiencing which may consist of being mean and nasty to Peter. I am no longer experiencing that, and no longer seeing Peter.)

T23: It's all vague now. Where are we? What is there?

P23: I don't know.

T24: Just look. (I am counting on the patient to stay there, to see whatever is there, to remain with attention on something meaningful. Otherwise, we have a choice of either returning to where we stopped or starting over.)

P24: (Pause.) He's at my apartment. My father . . . he's sitting in the chair near the window. Maybe 10 years ago. Longer. He's not even looking at me. I did something wrong. (Here is a skilled patient. Our work with Peter had brought forward another scene. I attend to what her words invoke.)

T25: Seeing him. Looking at him.

P25: Can't remember . . .

T26: Something's bothering him . . . sitting . . . glasses, he has glasses. (This is what my attention is drawn toward. I describe what I see.)

P26: He doesn't have glasses. He has a bad leg. An accident on the railroad before he married Mom. He said, "Haven't you learned right from wrong?" Something about my job, or the way I was with the family. . . . I don't know. . . . Maybe I did something wrong. . . .

T27: Haven't you learned right from wrong?

P27: I can hear it. Always that same way. The voice. (She is quite fixed about the voice, the words. I too am compelled by what is coming from father.)

T28: Critical, a critical voice, the whole tone.

P28: I haven't done a good job. I did something wrong. He talks to me like he is lecturing me. He comments on the passing scene. Just talks. Not really to me. Just about me. Like, "I told you so." He is so judgmental. Oh my God, he's so judgmental! Everything is bad. He is the one who says it is bad. I never really . . . (Now the patient is in such direct interaction with him that she is just about talking directly to him. This is described in Chapter 2 as carrying forward the experiencing potential by direct interactive expression. The therapist may carry this forward by saying it directly to the father.)

T29: Don't! Don't do this! You're so damned judgmental! You are! You always are! (The patient is not ready for such direct interaction. She waffles a bit, but remains there.)

P29: It's all going on in my head. It's all happening. I could never find any peace with him. . . . He never acknowledged me.

T30: No.

P30: It's like I never existed. (She is almost saying this directly to him, with the preponderance of her attention on him. I too am attending to him, and I again venture a direct statement to him.)

T31: Look at me! Talk to me! Acknowledge me, dammit! (But again I fail. She does not speak directly to him.)

P31: I wanted so much to be acknowledged! Just know me a little! (Here she comes quite close to direct speech to him.) . . . I tried so hard. (The last few words constructed something new, the sense of failure. Now the therapist is pulled by this, and allows himself to fall into being the voice of this experiencing.)

T32: (In a hard, flat tone of voice.) Well, forget it, baby. You'll never be acknowledged and you know it!

P32: (Tight and anxious.) No! He'd talk about me. He regarded me. He always talked about me. I know it. The trouble was he would talk about me with someone else all the time. Mom told me. It was like it was always deflected and never to me. He was cold and harsh with me. To someone else. Like it was about me. He did talk about me. But never to me! I could never get the pleasure. . . . I wanted it. . . . I never could win. . . . (She is defending, arguing, giving evidence against the awful certainty that he never really acknowledged her and never would. She was assembling evidence that he really did think highly of her. As given in Figure 4.1, we are working the relationship between the experiencing of being a failure, unacknowledged, and, on the other hand, the experiencing of being capable and being caring. It is an encounter.)

T33: (Laughing.) What bullshit!

P33: What?

T34: Keep it up baby! Try to convince yourself. (Mocking.) He really did acknowledge me! He really did! Oh my God what bullshit! (Lightly and playfully.)

P34: He did!

T35: Sure!

P35: (Now she joins my side.) I was never supposed to talk back to him. Nothing I did was ever right, not enough. I was not supposed to be cheeky . . . never. . . . Hell! I wasn't even supposed to think it! I was supposed to be nice! He always lectured me. Lectured about me and everything about me. This and that. A whole childhood. Talked about me and never talked *to* me. I don't think he *ever* talked to me! I was supposed to be good for them, for the family! The Jacksons were the one. For the family. The Jacksons were the important ones. You see, I'm the youngest of the bunch. So I was supposed to be the nice one, the good one for the family! I'm supposed to be the one who excelled at everything. Oh God, what an ultimate put-down! (The level of bodily sensations is rather high, and the feelings are good ones. I am drawn into this, and I increase the feeling level one notch while saying all of this directly with quite good spirits.)

T36: Are you listening everybody? That's what you all did to me! I'm supposed to be the great one in this fucking family! That's the rule. But no one ever sat down and said it to me directly. Listen Hortense or Grace or whatever your name is . . . what's the kid's name anyhow? I forget with all these damned kids around. . . . Well, here's what you gotta do . . . be great! Be a great Jackson. And be good. Do not be bad. Be good. (Changing roles and speaking from within the patient.) You never told me! Do I have it right? Is that it? Huh! Say something, dammit! (I am carrying forward the experiencing which she began in P35, which she hinted at in P31, and which I voiced in T32, T33, T34, and T35. This consists of an angry certainty that I never was acknowledged, that I know this, and that I am angry about being so mistreated. All of this is the carrying forward of experiencing at the operating level.)

P36: I get years of lectures, years! (She is loudly complaining.) I'm told how women are supposed to be, and how little girls are supposed to grow up. That I get a bellyful. Years of that, over and over. (We are together in the carrying forward of this experiencing.)

T37: Right.

P37: It never stopped. (In the therapist there is a sense of anger. It is directed at father and the family who are right there.)

T38: (With strong feeling.) I've had it! No more lectures! (The therapist speaks with the grammar of the patient, referring to oneself as "I." Now the patient joins the therapist in speaking directly to father and the family. Experiencing is brought forward efficiently when nearly all of the patient's attention is directed toward the other person.)

P38: (Forcefully.) You just lecture me! You don't listen! You never listened, never! I can't ever remember when you listened, ever listened. Other people did. Not you. Never. You don't even know that I exist. (Pause. Now there occurs a shift. The forceful complaining washes away.) You lectured at me like I was supposed to listen or something . . . I don't know. (She is now dejected, talking in a slow and confused way.)

T39: I feel funny. (My bodily sensations have shifted. Now I am almost ready to cry.)

P39: (Pause.) What was wrong? (Slow and confused. In the therapist there is a sense of being bad. I am unwanted and dumb.)

T40: Well, here I am, the idiot. Dumb. Yep, just dumb . . . I don't think I want to hear any of this. What am I doing in this family anyway?

P40: (Sighs.)

T41: (Almost whispering.) I don't belong here. (The therapist has been talking as a dumb child who is only dimly aware of being a dumb kid. Now the patient switches. She becomes the one who defends against this experiencing by being the good girl, the smart achiever. Here is the rattling back and forth between these two operating potentials as indicated in Figure 4.1.)

P41: I got an award. . . . I won the certificate in junior high . . . (She speaks as a little girl who is defending herself against what the therapist voices in T40 and T41. The therapist is now the other side in interaction with her. The aim is to open up these coupled experiencings and their relationship.)

T42: Well, what do you know!

P42: The certificate . . .

T43: Well, that doesn't matter.

P43: It was a special award . . .

T44: You don't say?

P44: (Starts to sob a little.) I was on stage. (She is beginning to exist in a scene from childhood, a scene which will later become an important element in this session.)

T45: That doesn't count.

P45: (She cries softly.)

T46: Aw, listen to her crying.

P46: (Crying.) My father was there. (She is having strong bodily sensations, and so is the therapist. The blood is pounding and tension is high throughout the body. The therapist now shifts attention onto father who is dimly there in some scene involving the granting of a special award.)

T47: Father, there . . . there he is. (The therapist's attention is on a vague image of father.)

P47: Sitting there. (Bodily sensations are now tight in the therapist.)

T48: Oh! Oh!

P48: He's sitting right there. (She sees him vividly.)

T49: Lots of others, and he is there with lots of others.

P49: Yeah . . . and when I . . . they handed me the certificate, the award . . . (This is now quite intense. Something new is heading toward experiencing.)

T50: It's happening.

P50: It was a special award!

T51: Yes.

P51: He made a face at me! (She bursts into hard tears.) He laughed at me! He made . . . oh God, how could he do that? (This last is hurled out with hard tears. In the therapist, there had been that warm filling up of tears around the eyes. When she cried hard, the therapist's eyes filled with tears and they rolled down his cheeks. The sense was that of a baby who is shocked and terribly hurt by the sudden meanness of a parent who simply should not be that way. Now the crying filled the whole face and nose and throat. The patient bawled hard for about three minutes. Both therapist and patient said a few words, but they were obscured by the crying. We had been experiencing more and more of the sense of being useless, not recognized or acknowledged, of the utter fruitlessness of countering that by achieving and getting signs of being special. After three minutes or so she is again the one who is special, who does well.)

P52: . . . I did well! It was something special!

T53: Hummmm.

P53: It was a special award. (The therapist drifts into the other side, the sense of failure, being useless.)

T54: He doesn't care! What the hell does he care? It's nothing.

P54: (Cries hard again.) Nooo!

T55: He knows it's nothing. (Now the patient's attention moves to father and how he seems, what he does. She sees the awful gesture which says so much and opens up so much in her.)

P55: It's like thumbs down . . . like he didn't want to acknowledge me. . . . He put his thumbs in his ears and he wiggled his hands and he made a crazy face!! He looked crazy!! Mocking me! I couldn't take it!

T56: What?

P56: (Screeching with tears.) I can't take it! (The therapist is now with her, seeing him and experiencing the shock.)

T57: He's ridiculing me!

P57: He just made a crazy face! Why? (She is crying hard through all of this.) He's sitting right there. So close.

T58: Up close, real close.

P58: That face!

T59: Awful!

P59: I see Dad and he makes a crazy face! What an awful put-down! How rotten! That crazy face . . . terrible. . . . It just squashed me completely. I don't know. It ended me. (I am looking at father. Now her words construct a person who is powerful, huge, menacing, with power to do this to her. This is new.)

T60: He's got power! Look what he can do! (She also attends more pointedly at him.)

P60: I hope she doesn't get a swelled head. He makes sure that I don't get a swelled head. Like he's supposed to do that. (The therapist sees this coming from the father, and furthers it just a bit.)

T61: Gotta keep the kid in line there.

P61: No!

T62: Keep her swelled head . . .

P62: (With pleading hurt.) I looked at him for pleasure, like he'd be pleased. There should be . . . he should be proud of me, proud of me . . . and . . . no, he makes a crazy mocking face at me! He squashed me. For no reason. Just wasn't proud. He made that crazy face . . . (It is as if these words are being said to him. The therapist gives voice to these words directly to him.)

T63: Look what I did! Be pleased with me!

P63: (Big sigh, almost a shudder in the whole body. It also occurs pointedly in the therapist's body.)

T64: What are you doing? (This is said to father.)

P64: I felt . . . dirty. . . . It was awful. . . . I was so . . . so ashamed. . . . Other people probably saw him. . . . He was so conspicuous. . . . Something awful about me . . . (With father still there, the attention shifts to what is occurring within the patient. This is what the therapist tries to let happen to him. Here is the first presence of a deeper experiencing. See Figure 4.1.)

T65: Bad, real bad.

P65: Something awful . . . about me . . . (She says this almost dreamily, quietly. Here is something deeper than the experiencing of not being acknowledged, of being useless, not special. Here is a dirtiness, an awfulness which deserves to be mocked and ridiculed. Father knows this in her. The therapist sinks into being the voice of this. We are now entering into the third step of experiential therapy. See Figure 2.2.)

T66: (In a wicked tone of voice.) He knows all about you.

P66: (She sighs, a kind of hurtful sigh, as if this is all too true.)

T67: He sure does. He knows it all!

P67: (In a state of dreamy floatiness, as if she is deeper in that moment, expressing what perhaps had been contained in that instant. She is dreamy, loose.) He made that awful face . . . yeah. . . . There's a lot of noise all over. . . . It hurts. Too loud. And he wiggles the fingers. And that look on his face . . . that awful look! Why? Why would he do something so awful like that? (The therapist is the voice of that deeper part, the part that is dirty and bad.)

T68: Because he knows. (She is still quite within this scene, and she speaks to the deeper experiencing.)

P68: But I was the star student. I won . . . they acknowledged me. I was a good student.

T69: That doesn't matter. (It is as if the operating and deeper potentials are talking together.)

P69: They acknowledged me.

T70: Yeah. (Here is the confrontation starting to take place. She is talking as a little girl who is being faced by the deeper truth. She struggles to avoid the deeper part which is wicked and bad, the part that father is mocking and ridiculing. Her voice is that of a little girl, plaintive and hurt, whining and defensive.)

P70: I was selected on the panel. They asked me to . . . Mrs. Lambert selected me . . . I was good . . . I told them only the best students were invited to go . . . I had the good grades. I had all A's. They only named three to go . . . I wasn't boasting. No, they gave me the certificate. It was a ceremony. (The therapist continues in the encounter, remains the voice of the deeper part.)

T71: Listen to her! Poor little me. See how good I am?

P71: I was!

T72: What drivel! We know what you're really like, right? (This must have resonated from both the deeper part and also from the father. She now sees the father again.)

P72: He's just sitting there, in the audience, and he mocked me!

T73: Right!

P73: He mocked me! (Her attention is riveted on father. The therapist likewise attends to him. We follow the path of higher experiencing, and this means alternating between steps 2 and 3 as required. See Figure 2.2.)

T74: Look at that face!

P74: Yes!

T75: What a look!

P75: I heard him! . . . Others must have seen him. They must have.

Everyone could have seen him. It just stood out! . . . (These words are being said as if directly to him. Accordingly, the therapist expresses the words directly to him and heightens the experiential level by expressing it with heightened intensity.)

T76: What the hell are you doing? You idiot! You're making an asshole out of yourself—and me!

P76: (Soft tears. Pause.) You never were direct . . . (She began talking, almost whispering. She was thoroughly in this scene with father, saying to him what was there to be said, but which had never been said. It was halfway between being the hurt and shocked good little girl and the wicked little bad one which the therapist had voiced. Her tone was hushed, and there were long pauses. Tears were on her face, and she spoke in a hushed voice which could barely be heard. From what little could be heard, the gist was: You didn't have to do that; was I that awful? Bodily sensations in the therapist were quite strong. There was a warmth throughout the skin and face and in the throat and chest. She spoke in this manner for nearly 10 minutes. After a while, I felt quite heavy, sluggish, sleepy. Time had evaporated. I "woke up" from having fallen into a sleep-like state guided by her words to him. When I "awoke," she was evidently in a different scene with father, and her voice was loud enough so I could hear what she was saying.) . . .I think it only happened once and it was in the kitchen. Or maybe in the patio. He had been arguing with mother about something. . . . I don't remember what it was about. We all felt bad. I did . . . I know I did something wrong and I went out to apologize to him. I can't remember where it was, what I did. (I was still sluggish and lost.)

T77: I'm a little lost. (She continues without a break, without hearing me.)

P77: He was angry, and I know I should have apologized. But I don't think I did. . . . (I am aware of being outside, attending to her from a distance. I am external, aware of myself. My head is clearing, and I am aware of her as the patient. My body sensations are low. She may have been working, but I am not. Under these conditions, we have the choice of returning or not. I give her the instructions for this.)

T78: Something was happening, something in that instant when we are seeing him . . . that face . . . the face he makes. Tears are there, and really something more . . . something started . . . just was ready to begin.

P78: Yes.

T79: I got lost somewhere. Take me back there. Or anywhere else?

P79: Yes.

T80: If you're ready, I am. This time . . . if you're ready, take me back in that instant? I know it was just . . . a split second and everything was all sudden. But with the tears something starts to happen. To be ready . . . or, is this where we go?

P80: Yes.

T81: Take me back there. With him.

P81: (Pause.) I felt so exposed . . . exposed. (I position myself to feel what it is like to say this, to feel so exposed. I describe what it is like for me.)

T82: Naked . . . singled out.

P82: Stuck . . . exposed . . .

T83: Yeah.

P83: I'm getting the award and I am on the stage and I see them all out there. (We are now back there. I am seeing them.)

T84: All of them, and noise.

P84: I'm getting the award.

T85: Yes.

P85: The award.

T86: Like a sea. And they are . . . they are sitting there.

P86: Yeah. I see my parents over there. Close. And I looked for them to share it with me. (Now the electric sensations of tightness are there in me.)

T87: Oh!

P87: And then! (At this point she starts hard crying.) He does it! He makes that fiendish face! (This is the point we had reached. She had bolted at that instant before. I want to stay here and not bolt, not drift away.)

T88: There it is! The look! The look!

P88: Yes.

T89: More! Again! More!

P89: That face! That awful face! (There is a sudden chill down the therapist's back. Because it is prominent, it is described.)

T90: Oh! I gotta chill down my back! (But her attention is rapt on the face.)

P90: That look is awful. It's devastating . . . it's terrible. (I see that look vividly again. It compels me.)

T91: The eyes look awful. It's terrible.

P91: It's like being stabbed. It's so sudden! (This seems to be said directly to father. I go further in saying it directly to him.)

T92: What are you doing to me?

P92: Everything feels so . . . empty . . . like everything's gone. Nothing's there . . . the whole bottom falls out of me. . . . I don't know. . . . (Moans. Her tone is changed. Here is something new which is occurring in her in relationship to father in this instant. It seems like something deeper which is starting to be experienced more.)

T93: I'm feeling something more . . . (It is sensed, not quite present yet.)

P93: He's doing something. He's . . . he's not letting me be proud. He's stopping it. He's cutting me short, cutting me from being . . . the glow of me. (This is new. I don't know what it is yet. As I let whatever it is affect me, I have a painful sense, a hurting.)

T94: Hurting me. I hurt.

P94: No, he won't let me have a swelled head. (Her tone is final, sharp, authoritative. I become flustered and confused.)

T95: Why? (I have no idea where that came from. But she lets that go and continues with him and what is occurring in her.)

P95: He can't deal with it. It's just wrong. Too much. It is a prize. They are praising me. I am getting a compliment. . . . He's got to push it off. . . . He can't let it be good. No swelled head. (I return to him and the experiencing in me. Mainly there is rising tension in me. My head becomes a little dizzy and tears fill my eyes.)

T96: It's too much.

P96: Yes.

T97: It's getting too much.

P97: Yes. (I am trembling in my hands and I am aware of the tears which are filling me.)

T98: The tears . . . let them happen.

P98: (She cries.)

T99: Tears! Crying! More! (She lurches forward and extends her arms and hands. Tears are streaming down her face. This is the beginning of what had been there but which did not yet come forth. As described in Chapter 2, it is the carrying forward of potentials for experiencing by disclosing the critical moment.)

P99: I wanted so much to please you! Anything! Anything at all! Just to please you! Ooooh! Aaah! (She is howling with tears.)

T100: But . . . but . . . there is more! More!

P100: (She moans and makes groaning sounds as she yowls in tears.)

T101: More! (The therapist is screaming this.)

P101: I wasn't bad! (This is screamed out, very loud. As indicated in Figure 4.1, she is now in close engagement with the deeper potential.)

T102: I wasn't bad! (I scream this with even more volume.)

P102: (long pause, filled with hard crying.) Yeah! . . . I *was* too!!! . . . I was . . . I was . . . I was . . . (She is howling. I am letting the badness affect me, feeling what it is like to be bad.)

T103: Oh yes. I damn well was!

P103: (She continues the hard crying.) . . . I was! . . . I was! . . . I know I was! . . . (This is like a confession. My attention is drawn toward father as I speak from the part which is truly bad.)

T104: And he knows too!

P104: Yes. (Deep and profound crying.)

T105: He knows. (I am wicked. I am being the deeper potential, and relating directly to her.)

P105: He knows that I am . . . oh God, he knows. But he could never acknowledge me. Oh God. (Her arms continue to be rigidly outstretched, and her body tightly packed, leaning far forward. She continues crying for a minute or two.)

T106: He knows. (Quiet, with certainty.)

P106: Yes.

T107: That face . . . his eyes are almost wild! (That was there for me. But not for her. I had deflected her. She was starting to be filled with the nature of the badness, especially in relation to father. She had approached this several times and pulled back. Now she would pull back again. In the following, the level of experiencing drops.)

P107: Well, he was grumpy. An irascible old man. He was just an eccentric, and . . . well, that's the way he was. Everything about him . . . everyone thought of him that way. He grew up there, and they knew him as an eccentric. I guess he was.

T108: Well, there's my idiot father. There he is. (This was feeble. The level of bodily sensations was far too low to warrant having said anything along those lines. It was a mistake.)

P108: He was always that way. (Pause. Nothing. Everything has been shut down.)

T109: Yeah. (We are way off now. Back where we started. We were talking to each other. There is a long pause. I have private thoughts about what to do now that I am separated from her and relating to her. While I am drifting in ruminations, she carries on with therapeutic work. In almost a whisper she says:)

P109: I am bad. (I position myself to be with her, and to allow both the badness and father to be there. She is a competent patient, and she works hard.)

T110: I am bad.

P110: I was bad. There is something wrong with me. (I am having tension in my body. But it is the badness which fills me and compels me.)

T111: Yes. Yes, there is.

P111: I'm rotten inside. Rotten. God, I know it. I know it. (I see father and now he is thinking that. I am practically confessing this to him.)

T112: Yes! He's thinking something like that. Something. Like something inside him is saying something to me!

P112: Yes, I know! (She is breathing quite hard as she blurts this out.)

T113: There's more!

P113: I can take it away from you any time I want to! Any time I feel like it! You are *nothing*! Nothing! You have no power! No power! Only what I make you! That's all you are! I can rip it away any time I want! (Tears have come and she is screaming. There are blasts of loathing and rage. I speak with the same volume, but she has gone ahead of me. Where she can express what is coming from him, I stay safely away. She is more prepared than I am for what is starting to come forth.)

T114: And he can! It's true!

P114: YES! (This is screamed out. I stay with her, at least in level of amplitude, but I am less a part of the experiencing than she.)

T115: RIGHT.

P115: Any time he wants. (Something about these words have the effect of my being a seductive woman teasing my father. The whole relationship is now sexual. This was a swift switch. Something in her words changed the whole scene and my whole identity. Here we are sliding into being the deeper potential. It happens easily. This is important, for a significant shift is taking place.)

T116: Right.

P116: He knows he can do it. (I am getting sensuous sensations throughout my body.)

T117: Yeah.

P117: Don't get too cocky. I can show you how slow you are. I have your number. (Between me and my father is a sexual teasing. The tone is playful. I like this.)

T118: Ooooh. And you are vulnerable. He's right. (I speak to her from this sexuality, this teasing. I am dripping with seductiveness.)

P118: He's right . . . as long as I want him to love me, he can destroy me. (In one sense, here is an insightful statement. In another sense, however, she constructs a vivid and powerful scene in which she is full of pleading love for him, and he powerfully destroys her entreaties. I begin to describe this.)

T119: How? I see . . . (But she interrupts and then builds a fully sexual scene. She indicated this scene with her father in P41, and now what was deeper is being opened up. That early critical moment contained a highly erotic deeper experiencing which is now starting to occur.)

P119: He is so big. Strong. And he knows more. . . . He made me feel . . . hollow. Yeah, hollow. Like there's nothing inside me. I feel hollow inside. All empty. . . . He's so big. . . . It's hot. All over. It comes up hot, inside. I'm so hot. What's happening? (There is eroticism and sexuality oozing all over as she says this. Here is a half-formed scene in which she is hollow, hot, passive, sexual, and the man is big, strong.)

T120: Ooooh. So vulnerable . . . (This is said in a silkily sexual manner. But she quickly runs.)

P120: Yeah. (With this she uses her usual way out. She cries and feels hurt and anguished. There is sobbing.)

T121: Yeah.

P121: I want to hide . . . but there's no place to hide. (The hard crying continues. Then it winds down and finally stops. In the therapist, the sexual scene evaporates. The bodily sensations come to a close. We are both below the working level of experiencing. Soon the therapist is outside the patient. We had both experienced the sexuality and then we both ended it. At this point we move to the next step. After a deeper experiencing is brought forth, we are to look for another, usually earlier situation in which such an experiencing was even more present. We do this by describing the experiencing and the nature of the situation in which it may have occurred. I am now the teacher who explains the next step.)

T122: If you are ready, we can move to the next . . . I will describe something, and you just listen. Listen. Just be passive, and let whatever memories come to you. Just listen. Let yourself remember, even brief flashes when I describe.

P122: Yes.

T123: If you are ready?

P123: Yes.

T124: Is this all right? Shall we wait?

P124: OK.

T125: OK. Just listen. Passive. Be passive. Try to remember. Let memories come to you. Feel whatever starts up. Try to remember. Just see whatever is there.

P125: Hmmm.

T126: I'll describe. Just listen, and let me know if you see whatever. From any time, or anything. You might be two or five or eight or 11 or 15, whenever.

P126: Hmmm.

T127: You are little. A little girl. Being little. A man is there. Someone older. With you. A man. Someone older. Father, Or someone else. Older.

P127: Yes . . .

T128: He's getting at you. Going to get at you. Feelings in you. You feel helpless and vulnerable. . . .

P128: Hmmm. Yes.

T129: Hot, you are hot. Feels hot. (I use the main characteristics of what we had just been through.)

P129: Aaah. (Her body starts to move. She slides down in the chair and moves her body.)

T130: Someone here with you. Hot . . .

P130: (Low moan. She puts her hands to her hips and moves her body.)

T131: Hollow . . . all hollow . . . and warm, hot . . . very hot.

P131: Aaaah. Aaaah!

T132: It's happening. (The therapist positions himself to be aligned with the patient. He slides further down in the chair and allows the same bodily sensations to occur in him. At the same time, he lets himself be with and see the dim outlines of a man who is there.)

P132: He is sticking . . . he is sticking his finger in me . . . ooooh! Yes . . . he's doing something to me . . . he's . . . the finger is in me. (The therapist experiences this. It occurs as a pushing into, an intrusion.)

T133: Touching . . . pushing . . .

P133: Warm, all warm all over. (She is living in this scene now).

T134: Feels good.

P134: I'm just five or six . . . yes, the same feelings . . . he's . . . I feel just so helpless. A man I met . . . he did it to me . . . smelled . . . funny smell . . . he's putting his finger into me. Has a part of the finger missing on one hand . . . putting the finger deep in me and . . .

T135: It's in. (My whole body is undergoing this).

P135: Pushing it in.

T136: Hot.

P136: I'm helpless . . . helpless . . . but . . . (She is writhing and breathing hard, short hard gasps).

T137: Can't move.

P137: Helpless . . . but, but . . . (This time, when she says "but," there is suddenly a chill down the therapist's back and down into the legs.)

T138: Something . . . (She continues, cutting these words short.)

P138: It's so . . . public! It's public! (There is panic in the way she says this. The therapist is frozen.)

T139: I'm scared!

P139: It's out in the open!

T140: Somebody'll know!

P140: I'd go to Denny's garage and my friends could see, and I didn't do anything. I didn't even run away. And I'd go to the woods and the man would be there and maybe someone'd see us! I would go to places. . . . Oh I'd go all the time everywhere. Everywhere! Somebody'd see me. My friends would know. (The deeper experiencing was quite close by. She was bothered by the deeper sexuality. It was bad and would lead to trouble. But it was here now, and the therapist could play with it. In the following set of statements, the therapist is the wicked bad aspect of the deeper sexuality. Throughout the following exchanges the patient stays there, close to and involved with the deeper eroticism.)

T141: Bad! Oh how bad you are. Tsk. (This is said almost lightly, playfully. But she wallows in the badness. She cries again and blurts out:)

P141: Something's wrong with me! . . . Something was always wrong with me! I know it. (Tears and crying.)

T142: That's because you are really bad.

P142: (Crying still.) Something's wrong . . . I know.

T143: That's right. You are fundamentally bad, and you've always been. We know.

P143: I have something wrong with me. Nobody knew.

T144: Nobody knew? Maybe they did!

P144: Oh! . . . (She twists her head from side to side, crying.)

T145: Maybe everyone knew!

P145: I feel so gross. So fucking embarrassed! I am just awful. (Pause.) It stuck out all over the place! They all knew!

T146: Right! Your friends . . . and more! The family! They knew! (That evokes the image of father.)

P146: He must know how bad I am.

T147: He knows maybe everything.

P147: (Pause.) Yes.

T148: (Sonorously.) He knows all the badness in you. All of it.

P148: It's like I want to get a totally black picture! (Then the words spill out rushed, hurried.) I see flash after flash of how bad I am. Oh my God. Yes . . . yes . . . oh yes! Oh my God. It's . . . awful. It's awful. They did things to me . . . I did things! Oh my God! (This is one way in which the deeper potential first reveals itself in its good form. The patient steps back and witnesses her self enacting the good form of the deeper potential. Essentially, she sees it being, in this instance, a sexual eroticism which is accompanied by good feelings. The work has been that of carrying forward the process of experiencing, and also that of working the relationship between the patient and the deeper process. The consequence is that the deeper potential can come forth accompanied by better feelings, and it emerges in its good form. At this point, the bodily sensations in the therapist are now light and eased. I see the patient doing all sorts of delightful sexual things with older men and other children.)

T149: Hey, this is great! I'm watching a pornographic . . . (But this emergence of the good form of the deeper experiencing was not to last. The patient interrupts the therapist and returns to being the cute one, the smart little girl who is acknowledged by them. It is one of the last-ditch attempts to avoid being the deeper erotic sexuality, and to do so by being a capable little girl, appealing and smart, as given in Figure 4.1.)

P149: I see little Cassie (referring to herself) sitting on the lawn. Sunshine. She's so cute. Playing. The apple of their eye. Hey! They're taking her picture. I think she is smiling and waiting. The picture. She's wonderful, and the lawn is so green and the sunshine. She's so little and so cute. (The therapist sees two scenes, side by side. In one, there is little Cassie, about six years old, playing sexually with an older man. In the other is cute little baby Cassie.)

T150: (Cooing.) Yeah.

P150: In a green dress. With white . . . (The therapist remains within the deeper eroticism, disgusted with this backing away.)

T151: (Oozing with sarcasm.) I think you got them all fooled, cute little baby Cassie.

P151: Just a little girl . . .

T152: (Laughing.) Yeah, but inside. Ho, ho, ho. Inside . . .

P152: God! I don't think he knew about the men! The men! God there were so many men! Oh no, he didn't. No, he didn't. (This is virtually being said directly to father. The therapist gives voice to this.)

T153: Hey Pop! I got something to tell you. Just a wee surprise . . . (She quickly interrupts.)

P153: Oh no! I'm not going to upset him. (Instead of saying this directly to father, she pulls back and talks about him. For a while, in P152, she was close to being the bad little girl.)

T154: (Quickly and lightly.) And that would really upset him. Wow! It'd explode all over him!

P154: (In rising tension, but not far from good feelings.) It would!

T155: Damned right!

P155: Yeah! It would be more proof of how bad I am. (The interchanges are fast throughout all of this.)

T156: *More* proof?

P156: Yeah! . . . that's funny . . . that's real funny! . . . If they told him it would just be *more* proof. Yeah!

T157: (Laughing.) He already . . . even before all this . . . (Hard laughing.)

P157: God! It *is* all my fault! All my fault! It *is* all because of me!

T158: You're bad from the very beginning!

P158: I know. (She says this in a matter-of-fact manner, and then pauses. Suddenly she says:) I'm *not* bad! I'm not! That's not true! (The therapist is the deeper part which is bad, is evil, and knows it.)

T159: Go ahead. Try to impress him how you're not bad. Impress him.

P159: (She speaks in a little girl tone of voice. She does not like being treated this way.) I'm not really bad.

T160: (Mocking her.) I'm not really bad. . . . Listen to her.

P160: Daddy, I'm not bad. (She bursts into hard crying. Over and over again she works to avoid experiencing the deeper potential. While it gradually becomes illuminated as an erotic sexuality, she continues avoiding the experiencing of it. However, it is much closer now, and she is much closer to experiencing it. Her attempts to avoid this experiencing are becoming brittle and ineffective as she moves closer and closer to it, and as the therapist voices the deeper potential's relationship toward her.)

T161: Nice try.

P161: (Cries hard. Now she is undergoing hard racking crying.)

T162: Well, none of this does any good . . . none of this little shit will work. (The therapist is removed, cool, somewhat disdainful. It is as if the deeper sexuality is not taken in by what she is.)

P162: (Hard crying.)

T163: All you wanna do is fuck.

P163: NO!!! SHUT UP!!! (She screams this out. Her voice is powerful.)

T164: Tsk tsk tsk.

P164: I'LL JUST WALK AWAY!

T165: Oh my, isn't that dramatic? (The therapist is wholly unaffected by all this. There is a pause, and then she shifts toward being the deeper sexuality.)

P165: I'm rotten inside. Filth. Sick. Garbage rotten. (She says these words, but they come as if from another person, another part of her. She is now entering into being the deeper personality process, the erotic, sexual experiencing. All of the work of the session thus far has brought her to the point where she is being the deeper potential. This is described in Chapter 2 as the experiential being of the deeper personality process. However, she is only beginning at this point. As she continues, however, she moves increasingly into being this deeper erotic sexuality—we will be able to describe it more accurately later on—and, furthermore, into the pleasant-feelinged good form of this deeper potential.)

T166: (Lightly and with good feelings.) Sexual dirt. Oozing sexual dirt. Filthy and rotten. (Laughs.) Little Cassie, the baby whore! (Then she talks, and the feelings are likewise light and pleasant. She does indeed sound like a different person.)

P166: Bad. Garbage, Ugly.

T167: Awful juices . . . shit.

P167: Everything inside . . . everything. (We are playing with all the dirty sex stuff inside.)

T168: Green and brown. Dirty. Garbage.

P168: Oh bad . . . I feel . . .

T169: Yeah.

P169: Sticky. All over my body. (The therapist lets that happen.)

T170: Wet. All wet.

P170: I don't have a head . . . gone . . . empty. Nothing there. (Now in a dreamlike way:) All hot. Whole body is . . . hot! Sticky. Oh the whole skin all over is hot. I am hot.

T171: All over . . . and inside too. (How vivid these bodily sensations are!)

P171: Yeah. Real hot. It's hot!

T172: Oh wow!

P172: And I'm going to catch him. So hot and sticky. All over my body. (In front of the therapist is "the man.")

T173: Yeah. There he is! (I see some man, an unclear image of a sexual man.)

P173: That's all of me. Me. (It is as if she is displaying herself to him.)

T174: He knows. He sees.

P174: Yeah. He knows. (Bodily sensations are strong.)

T175: Everything else was all sham and lies. (Now she cries and laughs. The tears are overridden by the laughing and the good feelings.)

P175: I'm just dirty . . . inside my body is dirty!

T176: And you never really tried to get away. (The lighthearted laughing continues. But now there is an added quality, a lilting teasing tone.)

P176: A lady did. She told him. She told my Daddy about sex, and he said that's what I never got from your mother. (Giggles.) Sex. (It is common that when the patient enters into being the deeper potential, a new stream of early memories comes forth.)

T177: (Singing this.) Oh he never got sex from my mommy ta tum de tum . . .

P177: (Laughing). I like sex!

T178: Well here, Daddy. How about this! Rum de dum . . . boom de boom!

P178: He never got the kind of sex he wanted from her. Well, no, I suspect that she is kind of . . . fastidious! (With this there is a short hard jab of laughter.)

T179: But I'm kind of sexy!

P179: Yeah!

T180: Hey Daddy! (The therapist is feeling great. Delightfully open sexuality is pouring forth, and there is Daddy—sharing, vividly right there.)

P180: Yeah. (She giggles.)

T181: Yeah.

P181: (Laughs a kind of belly laugh. Suddenly, the therapist sees him naked, stark naked.)

T182: He never saw me naked.

P182: (Laughing.) He might have! (The therapist is a little girl, openly and enjoyably wicked and sexual.)

T183: I am not good or smart or a leader or nice. Really, I mean down there where there are really . . . inside where all the stuff is. Inside where I am not good. Definitely not good. I am bad. Wicked and naked and sexual and bad. Take a look! Hmmmmm! (Now the patient has disengaged from her continuing identity, and she enters into being the deeper potential, as described in Chapter 2. She is genuinely a different person, at least for a while. What is atypical with this patient is the ease with which she disengages from the continuing identity and enters into being the deeper potential and, what is more, the good-feelinged form of this deeper potential. Most patients require more work as described in Chapter 2 under "Experiential Being of the Deeper Potentials.")

P183: I loved their touch. The old man touched me and I loved it. Hell, I even played with girls. I mean "played," I touched their genitals. Wiggled and fondled them. (Laughs lightly.) They are probably . . . (she laughs fully) . . . I'm the one who . . . got them into trouble! I mean there are loads of women telling therapists about how they started sex and (we both get the picture and laugh delightfully) . . . I'm the one who got them . . . I did it! . . . I got into all their dark secrets . . . their sex . . . and I was just a child. A wicked child! (Laughing.)

T184: What? Are you that great wonderful sexy kid?

P184: Yeah, that's me! (We are laughing.)

T185: Bad!!

P185: Oh I did love the man's touch. That was the center of my whole childhood! I loved the touching. Loved it! I cared about men. Not boys. Men! I was fascinated by men. Aha! Men! And . . . there was always a mystery to it. A real mystery. (The therapist enjoys the mystery, and senses the fascinating presence of the man.)

T186: Exciting . . . mysterious.

P186: I could never see his penis. (But there it is, down there, fascinating and wonderful.)

T187: Well there it is, down there. Want to touch it? (She is a little girl, wholly here with the man, and her voice is that of the little girl in this scene.)

P187: What was it anyway? What's it? Huh? I don't know what it's like. Huh? I don't know what it's like. (Her voice is that of a little girl; she is being the little girl. From within the context of the good-feelinged open sexuality, there are scenes which are present. Typically these are early scenes, open to further and to deeper experiencing. To get into these scenes, one must be the little girl who is the deeper potential. Such experiencings are unavailable to the ordinary adult person whom she was up to this phase of the session.)

T188: Except there it is. It's right there. See it?

P188: (Giggles.) Yeah.

T189: Aw, let's go ahead.

P189: We're in the kitchen and you always walked around. It's open in the fly, Daddy. You have those dirty white things on and you always walked around in your underwear. It's there. I can't quite see . . . quite. (The therapist is peeking at it.)

T190: But sometimes . . . sometimes I see a little.

P190: (Laughs.) He had that privilege.

T191: C'mon, let's open his fly and . . . look!

P191: (Laughs.) I want to! It could be something, eh!

T192: C'mon!

P192: Well, there always seemed some great and wonderful mystery. Who knows? Something . . . wow! A thing or two . . . (Now the therapist's attention is compelled by father walking around, offering provocative little peeks at the genitals.)

T193: That guy is provocative. Look at him sexing up the family! Show us your big balls, great man! (This is as far as she will go. From this point, the very center of her withdraws back from within the deeper potential, and she heads back into being the ordinary identity. But that takes some time, and she is not yet completely withdrawn back into the ordinary identity.)

P193: I'm mixed up between . . . (But the therapist is still here, lagging behind.)

T194: Daddy.

P194: (Pause.) I don't know. I want to take a look!

T195: And he wants to show them off!

P195: (Confused.) Who's bad?

T196: You are. Right?

P196: Well, no . . . (At this point the whole scene becomes real and vivid, in a new way. My attention is pulled to a sense of someone missing.)

T197: I see! I see! Here's the kitchen. But someone's missing. (It seems she is sensing the same thing. My body loses the good sensations, and rising tension starts to occupy the chest and face.)

P197: I know . . .

T198: Hey! Where's Mom?

P198: I don't know. (Pause.) I think she is moving about somewhere. . . . I don't know. (Pause.) Oh . . . (She sighs. This was a side track. What compelled me was not there for her. Instead, she was attending to father, while the center of her I-ness was gradually moving back into her ordinary identity within whose perspective the erotic sexuality was bad. The rising tension in me accompanies this change in her. Now it becomes a pronounced dizziness.)

T199: I'm dizzy! (But she attends only to Father.)

P199: I want to know what's there!!! I WANT TO KNOW!!! (This is blasted out to him with powerful authority and yet with a fearfulness. I am swept along this same tide.)

T200: SHOW ME!!! I HAVE A RIGHT TO SEE!! I WANT TO KNOW. TELL ME!! SHOW ME!!!

P200: I want to know. I want to know!! . . . Do it! I do have a right to know!! (My heart is beating very rapidly, and the skin all over my upper torso is tight and tingling. But my attention is focused on him there, almost transfixed.) Oh! Oh! Oh! (She lurches forward and her arms and legs are almost locked tight. Her arms are outstretched, and her fingers splayed out. The whole body is tight. Arms are reaching as far as they can go. It is as if the deeper experiencing is engaging in erotic sexuality with father. It is being this way with him in a kind of open co-participation. She, however, is retreating back from this and into her ordinary identity. She is unable to go through this experiencing in the good-feelinged way the deeper potential offers. She is being carried along, and shortly she will use even more dramatic bodily means to divert and deflect the open sexuality which is occurring. She begins coughing and has difficulty breathing. Her face starts to turn red, and she makes low gutteral noises.) Ughhh . . . uuuuugh . . . haagh . . . haaagh. (The therapist's attention is still on father, and the therapist is much more filled with the good feelings of open and shared sexuality. I speak to him from within this.)

T201: Let me see! . . . You damned dirty old man!

P201: (Gagging and coughing. Body is still in the same position.)

T202: Well then, put on your pants!

P202: Uuuuuugh! (She continues the gagging. She is barely able to breathe, and now her head is trembling while her face is quite red. This is her way of retreating from the experiencing which the therapist still continues.)

T203: I'm surprised that he didn't shove it in your mouth and then smash you for being bad!

P203: (Gagging noises. Her body is still in the same position.)

T204: He should have diddled you. . . . Aw, he should have shown it to you and let you play with it and then stuck it in you.

P204: (She is still coughing, but the intensity is much less, and her body relaxes somewhat. The gagging stops.) He didn't do that. (These words are whispered.)

T205: Aw! (The therapist is playfully mocking her. But the bodily sensations are now reducing. The scene is slowly fading.)

P205: (Sighs. Yawns. Stretches. For the therapist, the image of father is gone. I am now out of that scene and am external. There is a pause.

I am aware of the patient and what we have done. I address the patient and talk to her.)

T206: My head is warm.

P206: Yes, mine too. (Pause. She is exhausted.)

T207: (Yawns.)

P207: Something's different. I feel different. (I misinterpret this as referring to bodily sensations. I check mine out and report to her.)

T208: Kind of tingly in my hands mainly. (That is not what she meant at all. She continues, tolerant of my mistakes.)

P208: Something happened. I don't know quite . . . I don't know. It feels different somehow. (Pause. I let my attention go, and I see flashes of this and that.)

T209: Loads of things are flashing quickly.

P209: Yeah. I ran away. I just ran away . . . oh, I don't know. It's so complicated. (It is common that periods of new understandings follow from having been the deeper potential. It is as if the patient has been another, deeper person, and that experience is talked about after having come back to the person they had been. Because of that experiencing, they are now somewhat a different person, not quite the same one they had been at the beginning of the session.)

T210: Yeah. Bye Daddy. It's all fading. (That was inert at best. At these times, I picture myself as hurrying to catch up with the progress of the patient. Patients proceed generally in the right direction, and I scurry over here and over there, but usually returning to where they are going.)

P210: There's no reason . . . I just run. All the time. How silly. How really silly. I do it now, I do it all the time I guess. (Here is more of the patient seeing what the deeper process is and how she copes with it. But I settle into the deeper process and sense the sexual experiencing.)

T211: *You* run! I got more to do than that!

P211: Today there's just no sex. (Laughs.) None. I really ran from that. Oh dear. (But sex is stirring in the therapist. Body sensations are rumbling.)

T212: What a waste.

P212: Yeah, I think it's dumb. I ran here and I run everywhere.

T213: I'm getting real sexy. Right here in the loins.

P213: I masturbate sometimes. And I love doing that. And I have my memories. (What pulls the therapist now is the sadness of some dry old memories and a little masturbation. In general, we are in the stage where the patient has been the deeper potential, has emerged out of it after a good measure of experiencing the being of it, and is now reassembling, coming together. This is when statements of insight and understanding are common. We are heading toward the final step in which the patient allows herself to consider personal and life changes. But we are not there yet.)

T214: Wow, those sexy memories. How sad. Sad. Heavy feelings. No sex. Too bad. (She is still light and somewhat laughing, as if "at" herself.)

P214: I keep it all away. Under wraps or something. Gone. It's really gone. I did a job on that. Nothing. Just empty. I don't have it any-where in my life . . . Oh Jeez! When I get involved . . . huh! . . . Then I get too involved. I get too sexual.

T215: Watch out. Overwhelming sex. You'll sweep all over someone. Too much for them. Bad. Very bad. You're too strong. Too much. Watch out! (Playfully kidding the patient.)

P215: But not in the last years. Oh no. Not then. No, I run away like I did here. Bolt. I run away. Still do (Here we are, attending to the patient's real world. We are moving rapidly into the fifth stage. In Chapter 2 this is labeled, "Experiential Being/Behaving Change in the Extra-Therapy World." Ordinarily it takes work on the part of the therapist to bring the patient's attention to her actual extra-therapy world and to the consideration of changes in her and in this world. With her, however, in this session, she moves easily and gracefully into this final step.)

T216: What a life you have! Tell me. I'm interested. How do you manage to live so there's no sex? (I started with the consideration of how she constructs pain and unhappiness in her world. To the extent that this can be identified, we can then consider the possibility of dropping these situations which she builds.)

P216: (Laughs.) I don't know.

T217: It's probably so effective . . . (She interrupts and then proceeds, with good feelings, to see what she does.)

P217: I've been living and capable. I've been . . . the one they count on for . . . for everything! I know what I do! I have men and women who are tender and they need me, and they are frail. (Yes, she is right. She builds all of this into her life. It crowds out even the pos-sibility of sex. She is good and needed and—acknowledged. After the patient identifies how and what she does to crowd out the deeper potential or to arrange for pain and unhappiness, then she is to con-sider simply leaving go of these ways of being.)

T218: That'll do it.

P218: It's all over my life! Everywhere! I surround myself with people like that. (Now it pops into my mind that this is where we began the session. She started with Peter, from P11 to P22, and the way she was to him and he was to her.)

T219: Peter.

P219: Right, Peter . . . he . . . traps me. I make all of them too much for me and I feel overwhelmed by them. Sure! There's no room for sex in my life. Nowhere!

T220: What a pity!

P220: And it was just starting to come alive. That's when I started seeing you. I think I scared myself! It can come alive. It really can! It will be! (I am talking with a part of her which experiences sexuality, a part which had come forward in the work of the session. This is the major portion of the person who now looks out upon her actual life and begins considering the kind of life it wants for itself. Again, she has moved easily and gracefully into this state, whereas it typically requires work to move into this state.)

T221: You sound like there are things you really want in *your* life.

P221: It's time. It's about time . . . (Laughs.) There's so much to do. I feel good. Oh, I *really* feel good . . . yeah!

T222: Oh! Oh! The juices are stirring and there's a partner there somewhere. (She is excited and almost giddy. Yet her attention is on the life outside therapy. We are moving to this final step in the sequence.)

P222: I feel like I've been drugged . . . like sleeping. Sort of just awake. Like I've been asleep. What a waste! I mean a real waste! I feel like I've been having a rest for about 20 years or so. Even through a marriage . . . hmmm. I know that. Silly I think. Hmmmm. But I don't want a rest anymore. (This sense of awakening is common after the fourth step, i.e., after being the deeper potential.)

T223: So? (We face the possibility of actual changes in the person she is and in ways of being and behaving. Ordinarily this requires a fair measure of work. She does this easily. What follows is a rush of ideas.)

P223: I never saw it like this before. I feel . . . whole, and sexual. You know, I feel like a kid, like an adolescent sort of and like sexual is good. Those people around me. I pick them, and I get them to be so damned leaning on me. Damned, I'm so seductive. Lean on me. Be frail and loving and tender, and be too much for me. Lean on big competent me. I'll take care of you. I'll do everything. And then I'll feel like a dead one cause you're all over me, and I'll be big and fat and heavy and I'll drink too much and I'll be overwhelmed by booze and fat and people and all my damned responsibilities that I put on me like 40 extra pounds. Oh that's some life for me I'll tell you, some life. Well, maybe I can say goodbye to all of that. Bye-bye. It's over. Let's see. I've got to arrange to feel somehow bad about all of this. Well, I really don't. She's been a stupid idiot all her life. And she needs someone to have sex with. I want sunshine and sex and . . . Do you know what I'm gonna do? Well, I'll tell you. I'm going to quit my job.

T224: What?

P224: I am tired of being the one who . . . and that's the end of booze. (Laughs.) I think I've had enough. My weight is going to shed, down about 60 pounds. I don't need all that extra stuff. That's the end of that. And Peter. Wonderful Peter. You've got a surprise in store for you. Oh you do. Get yourself ready, kid. It's time we straightened it all out, and I mean everything. It's time we made it stiff. I'm going to let you be whatever you are, my friend, and if that means sex, then that's the way it's going to be. Listen to me! I even sound different. *Her* voice was soft and serious. *I'm* different. Hello Peter! Come over, and stay the night. We are going to be grownup children who can sex it up, and I won't let you lean on me, and I won't be big babe, the heavy one, and I won't even be boozed up for you. Come on over, it's about time I think.

T225: It sure feels good. I'm all tingly.

P225: I feel like I want to crawl out of all this blubber and wiggle around and leave the drunken fat old lady just be there. Jeez it seems different now. And the job, what a crazy thing I've been doing. It's killing me. All the time. It's like it . . . I just don't need it. I don't know what I'm going to do, but not that anymore. I've been suffocating myself. Being the responsible one. For what? Cause she has to be good, that's what! Well, I have no idea what I am gonna do, and I damned well am going to think hard, I mean real hard about it. No more getting myself into these corners anymore. That's the end of that. Whee! Yeah!

T226: (Laughing.) I can't keep up with you.

P226: You don't have to 'cause I feel light and . . . free, and that's not something I've ever felt before. (Pause.)

T227: (Pause.) You're serious.

P227: I am. I really am. (Pause.)

T228: It sounds . . . great. I feel happy.

P228: What a different feeling. New. Like I can do things! I can do all these things. Like living a different life. Like being me sort of. Like being the kind . . . sort of being the me I never was. Oh that sounds wrong. Maybe though. I think you know what I mean. I never felt like this before. Like doing all these things is easy. (Perhaps going through the five steps has allowed a new and changing person to be present.)

T229: Great!

P229: I just have to remember it's possible. (She has outlined changes in her and in her life. Is she ready to make these changes?)

T230: What's possible?

P230: (Laughs.) I love being different. That's what's possible. And I can do things. I feel different. Like . . . I think I want to start with the booze. I'm giving it away. I don't need it. Let's see . . . all of the stuff. I'll give it to Jan. Yeah. She'd love it. (Laughs.) Yeah, and that's the end of the booze . . . and then. Hmmm. I have things to do with Peter, and Maurice.

T231: Who?

P231: Maurice.

T232: Maurice?

P232: OK, you don't know him. I got things to do with Maurice. (Long sigh.)

T233: What. What things?

P233: I want to masturbate with him. Let's see. I think I'll call him. We kidded about that. Once. He . . . (Laughs) . . . I don't know. Yeah. I think I'll call him and tell him to come over. Yeah. I think I'd shock him. Maybe. Oh I don't know. I think I want to masturbate with him. (Laughs hard.) He'd love that.

T234: Delightful!

P234: Sure will be. Enough of that. Ha! I'll . . . I want to be with him! I think I will be with him. Why not. I've wasted enough time. Hello Maurice. Come on over. Come on, and plan to spend the whole evening. I want to get you to masturbate me. Oh that'd be just wonderful. You should be good. Ha!

T235: Are you really going to do that?

P235: I don't know. (Screeches excitedly.) But I think so.

T236: Think so! C'mon. Yes or no. You stinker.

P236: (Laughs.) Right! Ok, yes. Yes. Yes I will. I gotta lot to do. I really can do them! I can! Why not!

T237: Why not? Well, let's see, why not! Hmmm. I should be able to think of at least three reasons why not. Let's see.

P237: No, dammit. You will think of some. I don't want to hear them. I gotta lot to do anyhow. You keep your reasons. I have things to do.

I'll start with sex and booze and Peter and Maurice, and it all seems so easy. Why the hell have I waited so fucking long?

T238: Well because . . .

P238: (Interrupts.) 'Cause I've been asleep, that's why! (Laughs.)

T239: I feel great.

P239: (Laughs.) I gotta feel light all over. Younger like, and my insides are shaking but nice. All inside. There's a lightness and a . . . what do you call it . . . a sort of . . . I don't know . . . there's a word. Oh, I don't care. I just feel good all over. I like bodies . . . (Long yawn.)

T240: Well, what's next?

P240: I think I'm ready to stop now.

T241: OK. Take your time. Open your eyes. Slowly . . .

P241: Hello. (Grins.)

T242: Oh, hello! (Work is over.)

P242: (Grins.) Has it been that long? I feel so good! Two and a half hours!

T243: I see.

P243: (Stretches.) Oh! That feels good. (Pause.) OK, there. Here. (Puts a check on the table.)

T244: (Stretches.) Thanks.

P244: Is tomorrow convenient? No, wait, I can't tomorrow. How about Wednesday?

T245: Wednesday. Wednesday . . . that's all right. Let's see. When?

P245: Same time? (Looks at watch.) Almost two and a half hours? Seemed like an hour . . .

T246: Same time . . .

P246: Is six all right?

T247: Good. Yes, that's fine.

P247: (She gets up.) I can't get over how fast it goes. I'm ready to lose 60 pounds.

T248: By Wednesday? Sonuvagun!

P248: Well maybe!

T249: How about Thursday?

P249: Funny. I feel lighter, and sexier. I never felt like this. What a potion. . . . I think I'm taller. (Laughs.)

T250: You look taller!

P250: Oh it's cold out there. Me for a fire. I hate driving . . . this damned weather.

T251: Yeah. I hate it.

P251: Brrr. Have a good evening. I will too. (Laughs.)

(We leave the office.)

# II

# Requiem for Therapist-Patient Relationships

# 5

# *Therapist-Patient Relationships: Critique*

The purpose of Part I (Chapters 1 through 4) was to provide an overview of the theoretical framework of experiential psychotherapy and the way it works. In both its theory and method of pratice, this therapy introduces a locus and function of the therapist which distinguishes it from many other therapies. In a radical shift toward the phenomenological paradigm of humanistic-existential theory, we have moved away from a fundamental pillar of most therapies, namely, the therapist-patient relationship. The purpose of Part II is to establish the basis for the requiem of the traditional therapist-patient relationship, and thereby to invite a few therapists to consider the possibility of our alternate paradigm. Toward this end, the present chapter offers two propositions. One is that virtually all psychotherapies may be described as expressions of four paradigms of therapist-patient relationships. The second is that, as a consequence, virtually all psychotherapies are constrained to the playing out of role relationships conjointly constructed by therapist and patient. On the basis of these two propositions, it will be argued that most psychotherapies are inevitably caught in serious and unresolvable problems, and that one way out consists of a radical shift to the phenomenological paradigm of experiential psychotherapy.

Portions of Chapters 5 and 6 are based upon my article titled, "The Therapist-Patient Relationship: Conceptual Analysis and a Proposal for a Paradigm-Shift," published in *Psychotherapy: Theory, Research and Practice*, 1978, 15, 201-215.

## PARADIGMS OF THE THERAPIST-PATIENT RELATIONSHIP

Experiential psychotherapy uses a phenomenological paradigm of the therapist-patient relationship (II, Figure 5.1). It is based upon one set of assumptions. In this section I am proposing that virtually all other psychotherapies use four paradigms which are based upon a second set of assumptions. You make your choice. Either you accept the assumptions underlying the phenomenological paradigm, or you accept assumptions which give rise to other paradigms of the relationship between therapist and patient (Mahrer, 1962). These other paradigms are identified as the subject-object paradigm, the interpersonal paradigm, the patient's frame-of-reference paradigm, and the encounter paradigm (Figure 5.1). Your choice may be explicit or implicit. In any case, the choice pertains to at least the following assumptions:

1) Most therapies are based upon an assumption that therapist and patient are two fundamentally separated entities. Each is its own organized entity. Each has its own identity, with its own definition, its own continuity and substantiality. There is a therapist-person and a patient-person. This is assumed in the paradigms labeled subject-object, interpersonal, patient's frame-of-reference, and encounter (Figure 5.1). With the exception of the humanistic-existential theory of experiential therapy, virtually all theories of human beings and virtually all therapies accept this assumption.

In contrast, experiential therapy rests on the assumption that altered states are available wherein the therapist and patient can integrate with one another. The personhood or identity of one can assimilate or fuse with that of the other. The therapist can become a part of the personality of the patient. The two are not assumed to be two fundamentally separated entities.

2) Most therapies are based on the assumption that these two fundamentally separated entities are limited to a relationship with one another. They are capable of interacting with, responding and reacting to, affecting and influencing each other. In contrast, experiential therapy accepts the assumption that the person who is the therapist can assimilate into and fuse with the person who is the patient. In this state, the therapist can exist within the world of the patient and can experience what is occurring within the patient. The therapist is capable of sharing the external and internal domains of the patient.

3) Most therapies are based on the assumption that therapist and

patient exist within an encompassing world of objective reality. Therapist and patient may perceive it differently, may respond and react to different aspects of it, but the assumption is that it exists, it is objectively real, and it encompasses both therapist and patient. In contrast, the assumption accepted by a humanistic-existential theory of human beings is that each person constructs one's own phenomenal worlds. These phenomenological worlds may be constructed by the person (therapist or patient) alone or, generally, in conjoint work with other persons. In place of a single world, we accept multiple phenomenal worlds. In place of a world of objective reality, we accept phenomenological worlds which may or may not use building blocks with "real" qualities. Instead of a separate world encompassing therapist and patient, we assume phenomenal worlds constructed by these persons.

If you accept our assumptions, you will likely use a phenomenological paradigm of therapist and patient (Figure 5.1). If you accept the other assumptions, I suggest that you are constrained to using one or more of the following paradigms of the therapist-patient relationship.

## The Subject-Object Paradigm

The therapist is an objective observer of the patient, and the patient is the subject or object of the therapist's observations. Their relationship is that of observer and observed.

In this paradigm, the hallmark is the objectivity of the therapist's observations of the patient. Accordingly, the therapist is to be a carefully trained scientist in the natural sciences tradition laid down by Descartes and Locke. Students are to learn how to be objective scientific observers armed with objective tests, scales, instruments, and devices rigorously honed to contribute to an organized package of observations about the subject as the object of their study. This is the relationship of the careful scientific experimenter to the object of his experimentation, and it is the relationship of the objective therapist to the patient as object of his observations and carefully programmed interventions. (It is fitting that psychotherapy be regarded as "intervention" in this paradigm.) The objective scientist-observer-intervenor ". . . shall attempt to grasp and explain the observable behavior of the other, conceived as an object of nature, passively receiving and responding to stimuli emitted by the real world. These stimuli, as well as the responses thereto, shall be conceptualized in terms of the procedures and constructs of physical science and the experimenter shall take for granted the validity of his own perceptions" (Fischer, 1970, p. 62).

As an objective observer, the therapist is to be free of any deeper personality processes (signified as Y in Figure 5.1). Such deeper per-

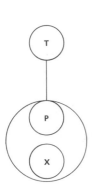

IA. Subject-Object
Paradigm

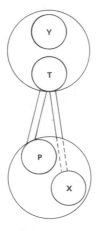

IB. Interpersonal
Paradigm

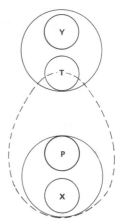

IC. Patient's Frame-of-
Reference Paradigm

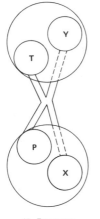

ID. Encounter
Paradigm

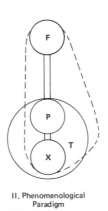

II. Phenomenological
Paradigm

T — Therapist
P — Patient
Y — Therapist's Deeper
    Personality Processes
X — Patient's Deeper
    Personality Processes
F — Meaningful Attentional
    Center

Figure 5.1.  Paradigms of the Therapist-Patient Relationship

sonality processes in the objective therapist are regarded as confounding intrusions (e.g., Fromm-Reichmann, 1958; Hartmann, 1959), or as noise in the objective processing of observational information (e.g., Fiske, 1970; Hathaway, 1956; Meehl, 1954). Likewise, the subject is either described as having no (subjective, mysterious, unobservable) deeper personality processes, as in many extreme behavioral approaches, or as comprised of deeper personality processes which are open to the carefully objective observation of the therapist, as in many psychoanalytic approaches. In its ideal form, here is pure objective observation, unsullied by the deeper personality processes of the therapist. The scientifically observing therapist accurately assesses what is occurring in the patient, with or without deeper personality processes. Such a relationship is signified by a thin line (Figure 5.1).

Those who use a subject-object relationship will observe anything their theories of psychotherapy deem important. These therapists do not all look for the same thing in their patients, even though they use the same paradigm. Some may observe cognitive slippages where others will observe regressive symptoms. Some accurately assess slight mood shifts, while others note subtle foot movements. By means of tests and all sorts of assessment devices to complement the observing therapist's powers, one can measure hundreds of things which are considered important in many different approaches.

Although theories differ on what is to be observed, the therapists share a subject-object paradigm resting on the same three assumptions:

(a) Therapist and patient are two fundamentally separated entities, with the therapist as the carefully objective observer and intervenor, and the patient as the object of the therapist's objective observations.
(b) Their relationship is constrained to that of observer and observed, removed scientist and the subject of the objective observation.
(c) The therapist has contact with and use of the objectively real world which encompasses both therapist and patient.

*The Interpersonal Paradigm*

A second paradigm has been constructed on the same three underlying assumptions. Instead of the relationship of observing therapist and patient as the subject of these observations, the relationship itself is elevated to a two-way interaction, a distinctively interpersonal relationship. Proponents of this paradigm regarded this interpersonal relationship as a goldmine of therapeutic data and therapeutic change. Indeed, the interpersonal relationship was virtually apotheosized as the definition of psychotherapy itself (e.g., Bordin, 1959; Ellis, 1959; Goldstein, Heller, & Sechrest, 1966; Hobbs, 1962).

In this paradigm, one may highlight some particular aspect or component of the interpersonal relationship. For example, the important aspect may be the relationship between the patient's deeper personality processes (X in 1B, Figure 5.1) and the therapist (T in 1B, Figure 5.1). This has been especially developed within classical psychoanalysis. Within the psychoanalytic family itself, other members emphasized the more interactional relationship of the therapist as a person (rather than a projected construction of the patient's deeper personality processes) with the patient as a person (e.g., Alexander, 1963; Alexander & French, 1946; Sullivan, 1953a, 1953b). Other therapists may emphasize the communication and linguistic component of the interpersonal relationship (e.g., Gottschalk, 1961; Scheflen, 1960, 1966). Some emphasize the interpersonal relationship as a model, or as possessing reinforcement value, or as offering a corrective therapeutic experience, or as an anxiety-free context in which learnings can take place. In perhaps more subtle ways, the interpersonal relationship offers a rich source of data concerning the deeper effects of the patient on the therapist (e.g., Bachrach, 1968; Greenson, 1960; Reik, 1948; Schaffer, 1958) and, through the therapist, to others in the patient's world (Benedek, 1946; Fromm-Reichmann, 1958; Rado, 1956, 1962).

In all of this, the commonality is that:

(a)   Therapist and patient remain two separate, intact entities, each with a continuing, substantive identity.

(b)   There is a relationship between these two fundamentally separate entities. In this paradigm, the relationship is an interpersonal one which occurs between the therapist and the patient, including the patient's deeper personality processes. It is noteworthy that the therapist's own deeper personality processes (Y in IB, Figure 5.1) are typically excluded from direct participation in the interpersonal relationship.

(c)   Both participants in this interpersonal relationship are taken as existing within an encompassing world of objective reality.

Out of the same three assumptions comes this second paradigm of therapist-patient relationships.

## The Patient's Frame-of-Reference Paradigm

A third paradigm may well be credited to Carl Rogers. He emphasized the added element of the patient's frame of reference, a sensitive acknowledgment of the patient's highly personal frame of reference on the encompassing world of reality (e.g., Rogers, 1951).

The patient's own frame of reference is indicated, in Figure 5.1, by the dotted oval around the patient and a part of the therapist. As in the previous two paradigms, the therapist remains a separate entity, distinct and intact from the patient. While the therapist knows and appreciates the patient's frame of reference, it is the therapist's own separate intactness which is required for effective therapeutic use of the patient's frame of reference. The therapist must be solidly reliant upon his own distinct separateness, and must guard against becoming stuck or engulfed in the patient's frame of reference (Rogers, 1951, 1962):

> Am I strong enough in my own separateness that I will not be downcast by his depression, frightened by his fear, nor engulfed by his dependency? Is my inner self hardy enough to realize that I am not destroyed by his anger, taken over by his need for dependence, nor enslaved by his love, but that I can exist separate from him with feelings and rights of my own? When I can freely feel this strength of being a separate person, then I can let myself go much more in understanding or accepting him (Rogers, 1958, p. 15).

The separate therapist and the separate patient are held in this paradigm, as in the previous two, as existing within an encompassing world of objective reality. In the typical disparity between the patient's frame of reference and a more accurate, objective, realistic frame of reference ". . . the therapist's goal is to help the client to clear up or modify the distortions in his communication . . . the therapist must enable the client to explore fully the client's expression of his distortions in order to assist in their modification. . . . To hear and bring to bear the more appropriate frame of reference is the preeminent task of therapy" (Carkhuff & Berenson, 1967, p. 56).

In this third paradigm:

(a) Therapist and patient are assumed to be two fundamentally separate and intact entities.
(b) Their relationship is predominated by the patient's frame of refer-

ence. The patient has this frame of reference, and the therapist acknowledges and uses the patient's frame of reference.
(c) Both therapist and patient are assumed to exist within an encompassing world of objective reality upon which the patient's frame of reference is but one perspective.

## The Encounter Paradigm

In the fourth paradigm, the distinguishing characteristic is the direct participation of the deeper personality processes of the therapist (Y in ID, Figure 5.1) and the deeper personality processes of the patient (X in ID). Everything in the therapist relates with everything in the patient, and herein lies the encounter.

Such a relationship is characterized by mutual sharing, openness, self-disclosure, honesty, authenticity, a real meeting, a confrontation, and, in pure form, "the unconscious-to-unconscious affective relationship between therapist and patient . . ." (Whitaker, Warkentin, & Malone, 1969, p. 255). Depending upon the therapeutic approach which uses this paradigm, the deeper processes of therapist and patient include bodily sensations, feelings, impulses, fears, discomforts, fantasies, thoughts, dreams, behavioral tendencies, incipient actions, affects, imagery, memories, weaknesses.

Yet this fourth paradigm rests upon the same three assumptions as the previous paradigms:

(a) It is assumed that the therapist and patient exist as two basically intact entities, separate from one another, each with substantive identities.
(b) These two separate entities engage in a relationship with one another. In this paradigm, the relationship is that of an encounter which includes the deeper personality processes of both relating entities.
(c) The two relating participants exist within an encompassing world of objective reality.

## Conclusions

Sharing the same bedrock assumptions, these paradigms include fundamentally separated therapist and patient who exist within an encompassing world of objective reality. They occur as four paradigms because each is distinguished by its own version of the relationship which inevitably must occur between these two persons. Some therapies use one paradigm exclusively; some may use two or more. Yet comparisons between and among these four paradigms occur on a fixed base of shared underlying assumptions.

These four paradigms differ basically and radically from the phenomenological paradigm (see Chapters 7-9). In our paradigm, it is assumed that the personhood or identity of the therapist can assimilate into or fuse with the personhood or identity of the patient. Accordingly, the locus of the therapist can occur internally within the patient (T in II, Figure 5.1). In this state, the therapist is assumed to be able to share both the internal and external domains of the patient. When the patient attends to a meaningful focal center (F in II), the therapist can likewise share the same attentional center. The locus of relationships radically shifts from that of external, separated therapist and external, separated patient (as in IA, IB, IC, and ID), to either the relationship of patient (and therapist) with the meaningful attentional center (F in II), or to the relationship between patient (P in II) and deeper personality process (and therapist) (X in II). Finally, in our paradigm it is assumed that patient and therapist exist in multiple phenomenal worlds constructed by the patient, the therapist, and both conjointly.

## PSYCHOTHERAPY AS ROLE RELATIONSHIPS

When therapist and patient are separate entities who engage in a relationship with one another, each will construct some role for himself and a complementary role for the other. "I am the therapist. My role is that of the good father, the doctor, the kindly and understanding old man. You are to be the patient, the one with troubles. You are to need and value a knowledgeable and kindly old doctor like me. I will make things all better, and you must look upon me with warmth and affection, as I do you." Of course the patient will bring along the role he builds for himself, the complementary role he builds onto the therapist, and the relationship between the two. In its blunt form, the thesis of this section is: Because most therapies assume therapist and patient as separate entities, relating together within an encompassing world of objective reality, psychotherapy is fittingly described as the working out of role relationships conjointly constructed by therapist and patient.

Indeed, the thesis is that the dominant characteristic of most psychotherapy is the working out of conjointly constructed role relationships. From this perspective, psychotherapy is little else. Most of the techniques and methods, the tools and the procedures, just about everything which comprises what therapists do and why they do it—all of this is in the service of the role relationships which therapist and patient work out.

In a more careful form, the thesis is: To the extent that the preponderant attentional center of the therapist is the patient, and of the patient is the therapist, these two relating persons will tend conjointly to construct sets of interactional roles around each other; accordingly, psychotherapy will be comprised, at least in part, of the working out of these role relationships. When I speak of a relationship, I am referring to a condition in which most of the therapist's attention is on the patient, and most of the patient's attention is on the therapist. This is not the condition in the phenomenological paradigm. But it is the predominant condition in all other paradigms.

In actual practice it works this way. The patient talks to the therapist about something. This something might be her problem, her childhood, what happened a few days ago, how she feels about this or that. It could be anything. As the patient talks to the therapist, how much of the patient's attention in on whatever she talks about, and how much of her attention is on the therapist? What proportion of her attention is on the therapist, on their relationship, their interaction, even as the patient tells about her inner feelings or the way her older sister used to scratch herself at the table? If most of the patient's attention (say 70 to 90 percent) is on the therapist, then my thesis is that it is inevitable that the patient will construct some role for herself and for the therapist, and that the two will be engaging in some kind of relationship between these two roles. (In experiential therapy, these percentages are reversed. Most of the patient's attention, say 70 to 90 percent, is on some meaningful focal center, and only very little is left to be aware of and with the therapist. Accordingly, these therapist and patient roles do not occur.)

Symmetrically, the therapist listens to the patient and talks to the patient. The therapists in any of the four paradigms described earlier—that is, most therapists—are external to the patient and in some sort of relationship. Accordingly, whenever the patient or the therapist talks, most of the therapist's attention (say 70 to 90 percent) will be on the patient. The therapist will address the patient, will talk to the patient. Most of the therapist's awareness and attention are centered directly on the patient. This holds whether the patient is talking or whether the therapist is talking. Accordingly, it is inevitable that the therapist will be constructing some role for herself, will be building some role around the patient, and psychotherapy will reduce to relationships between these complementary roles. When most (it need not be all) of the therapist's and patient's awareness and attention are on one another, then psychotherapy consists of relationships between the roles they conjointly work out with one another.

Do changes occur? Will there be "effects" of "psychotherapy"? Will something happen as these two persons work out their mutual role relationships? Of course. If I (as patient) fulfill the role of the little boy who wants a strong parent, and if you (as therapist) fulfill the role of strong parent to a little boy, then changes will occur over 10 or 50 or 200 hours of our being together. But . . . and this is the rub . . . the changes or effects which occur are virtually all a function of what happens between a strong parent and a little boy, or whatever roles we work out and develop as our particular role relationship. All in all, most psychotherapy is constrained to be relationships between mutual roles constructed by therapists and patients, and this I propose as accounting for nearly everything which occurs in what is called psychotherapy.

*The Therapist and Patient Build Role Relationships Without Really Knowing*

The therapeutic literature is familiar with role relationships. We know that many patients try to get us to fulfill certain roles (e.g., Haley, 1961, 1963, Halpern, 1965; Mullan & Sangiuliano, 1964; Perls, 1971). Perls tells us to watch for patients who try to get us to be their god or their wailing wall or their scoundrel against whom they can rail. Psychoanalytic therapists are keenly alert to patients who try to entrap them in role relationships: He treats me as the father he never had; she competes with me as her preferred older sister; she wants me to be her seducer. Unfortunately, these are the deceptive tip of a monstrous iceberg in which most psychotherapists are caught while priding themselves on their cleverness. Therapists know all about a few of the most blatant roles which patients try to throw around therapists. What therapists seldom see are the roles they build for themselves and their patients, and the complementary role relationships in which they unwittingly co-participate.

"I am quite astute at seeing the role relationship traps in which you get yourself caught. Because I am not caught in them, I must be role-free." Thus the rational-emotive therapist observes the client-centered therapist who is busy observing the psychoanalytic therapist, and the whole group of players are rather blind to their own constructed role relationships—which, of course, are easily visible to everyone else. Because I do not play the role of the dogmatic authority, I must be free of role relationships: "I have not found it satisfying or helpful to intervene in the client's experience with diagnostic or interpretative explanations, nor with suggestions and guidance. Hence the trends which I see appear to me to come from the client himself, rather than emanating from me" (Rogers, 1970, p. 167). I do not get caught in your role relation traps, and you may not get caught in the ones you see me caught in. The problem is that our assumptions and the paradigms of therapist-patient relationships insure that we are all caught in role relationship games—even if we are not caught in the few in which we see our neighbors caught.

We may be aware of some of the roles our patients try to get us to fulfill. We may be aware of some of the roles our colleagues fulfill. We may even be aware of one or two favorite roles we ourselves play. But what we have yet to accomplish is the radical shift to a phenomenological perspective from which virtually all psychotherapy is seen as the subtle working out of complementary role relationships conjointly constructed by therapists and patients. Once we can escape from the assumptions underlying our four paradigms, then most psychotherapies are illuminated as a grand enterprise of conjointly constructed role relationships.

Some of these are so evident that a concerned and sensitive colleague (teacher, supervisor) may become aware. We may see in our fellow therapist how she gains in therapy the significant role relationships which are missing in her daily life. Only with her patients does she fulfill the role of the close and intimate one, or the one who is needed and valued, or the one who engages in safe sexuality, or the one who is a model of mental health, or the true and loyal friend (cf. Bugental, 1964; Lawton, 1958; Mullan & Sangiuliano, 1964). Or, we may see how the therapist slowly shapes and moulds the patient into expressions of the therapist's own problems. Some therapists work patients into states of depressed futility at being unable to solve problems, just as the therapist is depressed and futile about really having failed at resolving her own problems. Therapists who are basically distrustful of others slowly work their patients into similar states of a basic distrust of others. Therapists who must cling to a solid piece of security gradually force their patients likewise to find and cling to their anchored piers of security. Or, the therapist may slowly entwine around patients the role of carrying out what the therapist is unwilling or unable to carry out. Thus some patients are led to break away from parental control, to act out spontaneously, to wallow in sexuality—by the therapist who is under parental control, who is frozen and tight, or whose sexual life is barren.

All in all, therapist and patient are constrained to construct and play out role relationships in an enterprise called psychotherapy. Starting with the assumptions behind the paradigms which necessitate these role relationships, the therapist and patient are caught in a subtle network of forces essentially beyond the awareness of both participants. Once they meet and begin their relationships with one another, their own personal determinants develop and refine the particular role relationships befitting their conjoint personalities. But even before they start to work on one another, both parties are already caught in role relationships which are ingrained in the profession of psychotherapy and in particular schools of psychotherapy.

*Role relationships are ingrained within the profession of psychotherapy.* There are at least three reasons why professional role relationships are largely invisible to most therapists and patients alike. One is that the profession of psychotherapy has ingrained these role relationships within the ground of our profession. They are folded inside our professional values, our codes of conduct and ethics, our traditions of what we are to do as professionals, our statutes and laws, the training and education of our psychologists, psychiatrists, social workers, and counselors. They are so ingrained that they are invisible. The second reason is that our profession offers a set of role relationships, perhaps five or ten or so. If we were to offer just one, this role relationship would be more visible. When a set of role relationships is ingrained within our profession, they are less visible. The third reason is that these role relationships cut across most approaches to psychotherapy. They are thereby hidden behind more public differences among our various theories and schools of psychotherapy. Nevertheless, our profession provides a number of ingrained role relationships for therapist and patient.

One role relationship invests the therapist with a healthy measure of an intent to change the patient. In pure form, the therapist in this role sets out to get the patient to be different. My aim is to change the patient, to get the patient to be the way I think he should be. My intention is for the patient to get a job, learn to communicate with his wife, not be afraid of crowds, be more assertive, be less pushy, be heterosexual, be more angry, be less angry, be more independent, be less defiant. Sometimes the intent to change the patient is more general. I intend for the patient to be more social, more adjusted, more normal, more mature, more authentic. For example, client-centered therapy consists of ". . . a relationship in which at least one of the parties has the intent of promoting the growth, development, maturity, improved functioning, improved coping with life of the other . . . in which one of the participants intends that there should come about, in one or both parties, more appreciation of, more expression of, more functional use of the latent inner resources of the individual" (Rogers, 1958, p. 7).

Sometimes the intent to change the patient is explicit and sometimes implicit. It may refer to concrete changes or to more diffuse changes. It may be defined in terms of an individualized treatment plan based upon diagnostic assessment, or it may consist of a general set of goals for all patients. But the very profession of psychotherapy offers this role to therapists.

Once the therapist assumes this role, the patient is thereby invited to assume some sort of complementary role. Either the patient is invited to be acquiescent, cooperative, accommodating, or the patient is invited to be resistant and uncooperative (cf. Wheelis, 1969). By assuming the role of the one who intends to change the patient, the therapist constructs the complementary role in which the patient is a willing object of the change or an unwilling resister of the change. The patient, then, is confronted with the therapist's intent to change him, and this generates the counter intent to resist (Haley, 1963; Heidegger, 1963; Laing, 1960; Ouspensky, 1949). Here is one set of role relationships ingrained into the very profession of psychotherapy.

But this is only one set of role relationships. The profession also offers the therapist the role of confidant, the close friend who accepts and understands, the one who provides a sense of intimacy and oneness. "Confide in me. Tell me your secrets. You can be close and intimate here with me. Confess your secrets to me. Tell me very personal things about yourself. Let me know your most private thoughts, your most personal feelings. Trust me with your heartfelt hopes. Let me be your best friend." The trouble is that this complementary set of role relationships is ingrained within the profession of psychotherapy. It is grounded into our training and education. It is present whether the therapist is using Gestalt techniques or psychoanalytic techniques, whether the therapist describes the patient in terms of transactional analysis or personal construct theory. Here is a second set of role relationships ingrained into the very profession of psychotherapy.

If you become a psychotherapist, our profession might outfit you with the role of authority. Here is a third role for the therapist. You know about the patient's psychodynamics. You know about the darkly mysterious forces which lurk within the patient's unconscious. You are the authority in knowing what causes the patient's problems. You are the expert in psychic problems, psychodynamics, the laws of human functioning. You know what it means when the patient has this symptom, that quirk in his history, that score on the test. Our profession will train and groom you to fulfill the role of authority.

When you are the authority, your patient must fulfill some complementary role. For example, your patient may be the seeker of knowledge, someone who needs and values your special wisdom. Or your patient may be the passive one who does what you say, is the weakness to your strength. Or the patient plays with you, touches your inner uncertainty and confusion, attacks your having to be the authority. Or the patient may fight with you in a struggle for domination. In any case, the profession quietly and silently offers some therapists the role of the authority, and that includes complementary roles for the patient.

This is only one way of describing a few of the roles which are interwoven into the very fabric of our profession. But the roles are there, ingrained into our tools and our theories, our research and our procedures, our codes and axioms, our methods and our techniques, and we are largely unaware of the roles and role relationships which are thereby invisibly played out with our patients. From out of the profession itself come role relationships which constitute the larger part of what occurs between therapist and patient. Psychotherapy is little more than role relationships, some of which are bestowed by the profession itself.

*Ingrained within the school of psychotherapy.* Each school of psychotherapy has its own roles for its therapists, and complementary roles for its patients, quietly ingrained in its own way of making sense of patients, its own notions about what accounts for the way the patient is and what the patient can be, its own ideas about how change occurs. I propose that virtually all things which distinguish each school serve as props for particular role relationships between its therapists and its patients.

In one school of therapy, the therapist fulfills the role of the model, the exemplar, the one who is competent in transcending human problems (cf. Jourard, 1976). With the therapist in this role, the patient is to be in the role of the one who follows the model, who learns from the exemplar. Within this school, the methods and techniques serve to enhance these role relationships. For example, the therapist is to open himself up, to self-disclose. "The master learns to liberate himself from dehumanising forces, freeing himself thus to lead a life that he has chosen. He is then in a position to show others how he did it so that they might do it too. His technique, if he has any, is to serve as a model, to show off, to make himself transparent" (Jourard, 1976, p. 37). Methods and techniques are appropriate or inappropriate to the extent that they contribute to the therapist role of the model or exemplar. This school's theory of human beings and theory of change make sense because they justify and explain the role of exemplar and the patient as the follower of the therapist as model. Patients are regarded as progressing to the extent that they start thinking and behaving as the therapist. Ingrained within this school is the role relationship of the therapist as model or exemplar, and the patient as the follower of that model.

Classical psychoanalysis feeds the role of the therapist as the removed authority, with superior knowledge about the patient's deep-seated problems. The complementary role of the patient is that of the inferior child who passively acquiesces to the superior knowledge and wisdom of the therapist. Psychoanalytic techniques are designed to build these role relationships for both therapist and patient. In order for the therapist to be the removed authority, the techniques include sitting behind the patient, observing the patient's free associations, interpreting to the patient what the patient is really like, using superior knowledge about psychopathology, psychodynamics, symptoms, and symbolic meanings. Notions about change and improvement likewise serve this role relationship. For example, the patient is regarded by the therapist as getting better when the patient embraces the therapist's way of understanding the patient (i.e., gains "insight"). The patient is understood as having some condition or other because of the dynamic interplay of mysterious psychic forces to which only the therapist is privy. Everything feeds the role relationship of the therapist as the removed authority and the patient as the passive child, and all of this is ingrained into the very fabric of the psychoanalytic school of psychotherapy.

In many of the behavior therapies, the therapist fulfills the role of the behavior expert. "I know what makes behavior tick, and I can do things to modify behavior. The role of patient is to be the object upon which I do my work." Virtually everything about the school feeds into the construction of these two complementary roles. The behavior therapist has learned the principles and laws of human behavior. His training bestows upon him the mantle of the science of psychology. The behavior therapist gathers the technical information necessary to diagnose the problem and to frame a behavior change program. Within the perspective of behavior theory, patients are regarded as complex organisms who operate on the basis of responses to internal and external stimuli; change occurs on the basis of modifying the cues and stimuli upon which the patient's behavior is contingent. Ingrained within the very fabric of most behavior therapies are the role of the therapist as behavior expert and the role of patient as the object of the therapist's behavior modification.

The same story unfolds for nearly all of our therapies. Each outfits its practitioners with a major role or two, and its patients with complementary roles. These role relationships are ingrained into the very fabric of each therapy. The methods and techniques, the procedures and the operations of each therapy serve to feed these role relationships. Explanations of how the patient got to be this way and how the patient can change to be some other way all fit rather neatly into justifying the role relationships of each school. The content of the training and education programs favored by each school slowly outfit the adherents to fulfill defined role relationships. Each school's attitude toward research, as well as the kind of research it fosters, feed into and support its ingrained role relationships.

*Conclusions.* Virtually all psychotherapies rest upon assumptions in which therapist and patient are two separated entities who relate to one another within an encompassing world of objective reality. As a consequence, it is necessarily inevitable that therapists and patients fulfill role relationships with one another. These role relationships are conjointly constructed by therapist and patient, and they dominate this enterprise we call psychotherapy. Indeed, psychotherapy lends itself to description as little more than the working out of role relationships. These are largely outside the awareness of both therapist and patient because these role relationships are ingrained into our profession and into the fabric of each school and approach to psychotherapy. In an extreme form of the conclusion, then, psychotherapy is preponderantly a relationship between the therapist, in one role, and the patient in a complementary role, with both being essentially unaware of their roles and role relationships. Therapists and patients differ primarily in the actual roles and role relationships, but nearly all are engaged in the same chimerical game which we dignify as psychotherapy.

*Some Common Role Relationships*

I am going to describe three role relationships which I regard as common. One is the therapist as parent and the patient as child. A second is the therapist as saint and the patient as supplicant. The third involves the therapist as scientist-god and the patient as the one who seeks transformation. My point is that there are common role relationships, and that these common role relationships virtually characterize what we call psychotherapy.

I propose that most of the psychotherapeutic literature merely describes common role relationships. The common roles of therapists and patients are presented in the literature on how the therapist is to be and what the therapist is to do, on both the process and the outcome of therapy, on effective therapists, on the characteristics of patients who are regarded as improving or not improving in this or that kind of therapy. All in all, I suggest that our psychotherapy literature gives support to the following common therapist and patient role relationships.

*Parent and child.* Therapists who fulfill this role relationship say in effect to their patients, "I am the parent, and you are the child. I shall relate to you as if you are a child, and you are to relate to me as if I am your parent." This role relationship works to the extent that the patient brings to therapy a cordial and complementary role relationship in which the patient says in effect to the therapist, "I am the child, and you are the parent. I shall relate to you as if you are the parent, and you are to relate to me as if I am a child." When the two parties approach one another with these sets of role relationships, there is a mutual goodness-of-fit, and they settle into the roles of parent and child.

Some therapists are very apt parents. They fulfill the role quite well. Some patients truly need and value therapists as parents. Under these circumstances, the parent-child role relationship works well. What happens in the course of therapy depends upon the particular kind of parent-child relationship important to the two parties, and also it depends upon the deeper personality processes of the two. Here are five kinds of parent-child relationships worked out and conjointly pursued by particular therapists and patients:

1) The parent/therapist is strong and firm, and unquestionably the dominant force in the patient's life. In this role, the therapist exerts a

lot of power in the managerial decisions in the patient's life. Changing jobs, having a baby, getting a divorce—important decisions are to be made after consultation with the parent/therapist. If the patient/child gets into trouble, the strong therapist is there to bail the patient out, or the therapist uses that to teach the patient a lesson. The child/parent slides into a state of regression onto the parent (cf. Rado, 1956, 1962). Nothing can be done without the therapist knowing all about it. The patient is dependent upon, made secure by, and a little fearful of the parent/therapist. They usually have a relationship extending over years.

2) The parent/therapist and the child/patient fight with one another. The therapist tries to make the patient grow up, and the patient resists the therapist's efforts. The therapist considers the patient childish, is bothered by the patient's demandingness, lack of responsibility, refusal to grow up like the therapist wants. The therapist nags and scolds the patient for not doing what the therapist says, becomes frustrated and angry with the patient. The patient has mixed feelings about the therapist. Often the patient tries to do what the therapist wants, and seeks the therapist's approval and acknowledgment. But they always return to the same old fight between the resisting child and the parent who tries to get the patient to grow up. Their career is marked by testings of one another, love and hate, and occasional explosions.

3) The parent/therapist is the boundless provider of archetypal mothering, and the child/patient is the sucking infant. Glover speaks of "the eagerness of some therapists to give suck" (Lawton, 1958, p. 29), usually in order ". . . to allow the patient to make up for the loss of the indispensable mother love" (Condrau & Boss, 1971, p. 514). The therapist provides what the patient's parents failed to provide. and justifies this as a kind of "corrective emotional experience" (cf. Alexander, 1963; Alexander & French, 1946; Boss, 1963; Hobbs, 1962). Accordingly, the good parent/therapist offers the patient the infantile care, love, nurturance, devotion, and unflagging protection which the original parents failed to provide. The patient is to be in the role of the needy one, the baby who soaks up all the mother's archetypal milk. Their career ends when the patient is no longer appreciatively sucking or the therapist's milk dries up for that patient.

4) The therapist is the model of adulthood, the role model, the exemplar of an adult who has successfully made it, the teacher of grownup skills. Sex-role identification and sociological factors come into play in this relationship. Accordingly, the female patient needs a female therapist, the Catholic patient needs a Catholic therapist, the black patient

needs a black therapist. The therapist has an adult outlook on life, has achieved something in the adult world, has managed to overcome the obstacles in becoming an adult. In this relationship, the patient is a child who seeks to become like the therapist, to be shown the way by the parent. The patient becomes the junior version of the therapist, takes on the outlook and philosophy of the parent, benefits and grows from the relationship with the parent. Their career ends when the patient becomes an adult like the therapist, or when the patient no longer seeks a role model in the therapist.

5) The patient becomes the child who is and does what the therapist dare not be or do. Between the two is a bond in which the therapist gets the patient to be some way and then half-scolds and half-condones the child for being that way. Accordingly, the patient is shaped into being tough or defiant, impulsive or spontaneous, irresponsible or lazy. Because the therapist cannot be that way, the patient is scolded; because the therapist uses the patient to be that way, the patient is condoned. Typically they have a close relationship in which therapist and patient just continue on as parent and child.

In order to bring about any of the parent-child relationships, both therapist and patient must have ways of parentifying and childifying each other. Fortunately, psychotherapy offers many ways to accomplish this. For example, the parent knows the adult world of reality far better than the child. Is something real? Is this the way the world works? Clearly it is the therapist/parent who knows, and the patient/child who must find out from the parent. The therapist is unquestionably the one who decides what is real, what the world is really like, and the child's degree of reality contact. "What you think is understandable because you are not yet a mature adult like me. When you are grown up (cured, free of your problems), then you will see things the way we parents do." There are other ways of parentifying and childifying:

The parent/therapist knows the child/patient far better than the child/patient does. "We know what you are really like. We know your hopes and your fears. We know what makes you tick, and you do not." We talk about the patient's psychodynamics or deeper personality proc- esses or "unconscious." We of course know all about them, and the child/patient does not. Accordingly, we know what the child's real inner feelings and reactions are. You do not hate your mother; you love her. You do not love your father; you hate him. We invent the rules of the game by which we know all about you, and you do not know all about you.

Parent/therapists have ways of inserting doubt and uncertainty whenever the child tries to know himself. By means of our knowing all about your psychodynamics and unconscious, you can never be sure about yourself. Whatever you think about yourself must be confirmed by us or come from us. "Analytic maneuvers designed to arouse doubt in a patient are instituted early in analysis. . . . Doubt is related to the 'unconscious ploy.' . . . This ploy is often considered the heart of analysis since it is the most effective way of making the patient unsure of himself. Early in an analysis the skilled analyst points out to the patient that he (the patient) has unconscious processes operating and is deluding himself if he thinks he really knows what he is saying" (Haley, 1959, p. 117). By these means the child is forced into doubt and uncertainty of his own notions about himself, and into increasing dependence upon the therapist's notions about what the patient is really like.

In order to be the parent, the therapist uses hard-sell and soft-sell methods to force the patient to have complete trust in the therapist as the most potent figure in the patient's life. I am to be the most significant person in your life; have complete trust in me (cf. Shaffer, 1978). Make no one more important than me; never waiver in your complete trust in me. Therapy with me must be the most important thing in your life (Haley, 1959, 1961; Lawton, 1958). Do not have any other therapists. Do not consider anything more important than me. Trust only your therapist. If you stray or falter I will punish you. I have the power. "He may, for example, determinedly proceed to get the patient to break up a courtship, a marriage, or an extramarital affair in order to prove his (the therapist's) power" (Lawton, 1958, p. 29).

The therapist childifies the patient with sweet promises of the archaic parent. I shall give you love, care, concern, knowledge, learnings, understanding, counsel. I shall soothe your hurts and anguishes, make it all better, wash away your tears and problems. I will help you grow and develop, become beautiful and strong, happy and at peace with yourself—and I shall always be proud of you and love you, and be here if you should ever need me. And when, much later, it becomes clearer that the archaic promises are unfilled, the parent/therapist's ways of coping with the patient's wails, hurt, despair, and anger only serve to drive the patient further into the child's role.

Psychotherapeutic lore and traditions, theories and ethics, methods and techniques all combine to enable the ready therapist and patient to fulfill the role relationships of parent and child. Stripped of its professional garments, much of what is called psychotherapy stands as role relationships between the parental therapist and the childlike patient.

It is inviting to think of certain psychotherapies as befitting the parent-child relationship. I think a case can be made that this or that therapy lends itself to such a role relationship. I think also that a case can be made that one or two therapist-patient paradigms are especially appropriate for the parent-child role relationship. For example, one may easily think of many psychoanalytic therapists, using the subject-object paradigm and the interpersonal paradigm, as exemplifying the parent role to the patient's child role. That may be. But, regardless of especially cordial psychotherapies and therapist-patient paradigms, the parent-child role relationship stands as one common way in which many therapists and many patients play out their version of what we call psychotherapy.

*Saint and supplicant.* The second common role relationship is one in which the therapist says in effect to the patient: "I am a special human being, a saintly person. I shall let you have a personal relationship with me. I shall accept you and bestow personal attention upon you." This relationship comes to life to the extent that the patient says in effect to the therapist: "I am a supplicant who needs and wants and values a relationship in which you are a saintly person who offers me a personal relationship in which you accept me and bestow personal attention upon me." When such persons come together in a mutual goodness-of-fit, they settle into a career of saint and supplicant.

What must the therapist be like in order to fulfill the role of the saintly one? To begin with, the therapist must exemplify that little bit of magic which is the special human being. The therapist must be preeminent in goodness, piety and virtue. The therapist must be so much of a human being that the therapist rises above human beings. The therapist is to be humble and modest, open and sharing, honest and disclosing. The therapist is to be wise and experienced, yet with that special quality of growing and becoming. The therapist is to be internally harmonious and congruent, integrated and whole, even with regard to personal insufficiencies and as-yet incomplete developments. The therapist must be able to give of himself, to love and accept, to enter fully into relationships. In short, the therapist is to be a very special human being whose human qualities are developed to the level of saintliness (cf. Rogers, 1957, 1963, 1965, 1967, 1970; Schofield, 1964).

In addition to being this special kind of person, the therapist must enter into a special kind of relationship with the patient. The gift which the saintly therapist bestows upon the patient is that of an intoxicatingly precious relationship with the saintly one. The therapist is with the patient, spends time with the patient, anoints the patient with special attention and concern. The therapist knows the patient, sees into him, into his thoughts and feelings, his inner loveliness and possibilities, frailities and wonderfulness. The therapist has unwavering trust and confidence in the patient. What is more, the therapist accepts the patient, prizes him as of worth and value, sees qualities and potentialities which are good and fine, perhaps even touched with a wisp of his own saintliness. These are special qualities of a special relationship with the special person who is the therapist (cf. Alexander, 1963; Alexander & French, 1946; Rogers, 1957, 1963, 1965, 1967, 1970; Schofield, 1964; Shoben, 1949; Truax, 1963).

Although this role has been especially refined within the client-centered school of therapy, it is open to therapists of other approaches. The saintly therapist may exemplify a value system and philosophy which is humanistic or Christian or psychoanalytic or behavioristic—as long as the therapist is a special saintly person who can engage in the special saintly relationship.

It is important to note that this therapist role demands a complementary role for the patient. The patient who is lonely and needs a friend will not be cordial to the saintly therapist. Nor will the patient who is weak and confused, and who needs a strong authoritarian parent. In order to be the saintly one, there are complementary role definitions and demands for the patient. To begin with, it must be clear that there is only one saintly person, and that is the therapist. This is not a relationship between two saints. Indeed, it is demanded that the patient be a most ordinary human being. Specifically, the patient must lack the special qualities of the saintly therapist. The patient is to have problems, be hurting, be plagued with human anxieties and worries, out of touch with his insides.

In addition, the patient is to be a supplicant who craves the special relationship offered by the saintly therapist. He must need and value that little slice of heaven when such a saintly person gives undivided attention. There must be some magic in the idea of a saintly person. Being in the saintly one's presence must be elevating and purifying. The patient must have a little spark of perhaps wanting to be saintly oneself. It must be important to be the object of the therapist's concern and attention, the chosen one given the gift of a personal audience. To be thoroughly known and understood by the saintly one must be precious. To be accepted and prized, seen to be of worth and value—all of this must be excitingly uplifting.

All in all, the role of the saintly one defines such a complementary role for the patient. Each role requires the other. The goodness-of-fit occurs when therapist and patient fulfill these two roles for oneself and for the other. Then there will be a good bonding between these two persons.

To the extent that there is a goodness-of-fit, changes will occur. These changes are determined by the relationship, and they are the consequences of a career in which the patient is supplicant to the saintly therapist. For example, the patient may feel special, acknowledged, singled out. The patient may become a little like the saintly therapist: open and honest, in tune with one's insides, internally together and integrated. The patient may feel like a special person who is understood and prized by another even more special person. These may well be regarded as important and desirable changes, highly valued especially by persons who fulfill the role of the supplicant to a saintly therapist.

In this relationship, one of the most powerful agents of change is that of acceptance. But acceptance is a double-edged sword which exerts effects which are good and bad. Let us consider two such effects: (a) Acceptance by the saintly therapist is highly controlling and defining of the supplicant patient. The therapist who intends to accept the patient, whose way of being emphasizes accepting the patient, thereby controls and defines the patient into being the one who is accepted. The patient is forced to be the accepted one, to be in the role of the one who cherishes being accepted (Hora, 1959). If the saintly therapist were fully accepting, the therapist would have to let go of every shred of intention to be accepting, letting go of all the accepting methods and techniques, the entire role of being the accepting one—but that would violate and destroy the essence of the saintly role and the saint-supplicant relationship. (b) The act of acceptance exerts a powerful influence by redefining the patient's behavior as positive (good, of value and worth, acceptable), and redefines that which underlies the patient's behavior as also positive (good, of value and worth, acceptable). By massive implication, this defines a shadow side of the patient as unacceptable, bad, negative. Once this shadow side is created, it is either shoved into the dark and never mentioned, or it is made to appear positive in the light of acceptance. In an extreme form, the intent and attitude of acceptance are effective in taking over the patient's behavior through such influence and control. "This influence and control occurs when the therapist accepts the patient's behavior and defines it as cooperation rather than opposition . . . it is necessary to acknowledge and accept his behavior and thereby 'take it over' " (Haley, 1963, p. 63).

Here, then, is a second common role relationship between therapist and patient. What the therapist does and how the therapist operates are ways of fulfilling the role of the saintly one and working out the appropriate relationship with the supplicant patient. What transpires over the course of psychotherapy is determined by this role relationship. We may dignify this enterprise as psychotherapy, but it lends itself to apt description as a role relationship between therapist as saint and patient as supplicant.

*Scientist-god and the transformed*. Frank (1961) documents the distinguished history of the third common role relationship. It is the long history of the healer and the sufferer, the physician and the patient, the change agent and the seeker of change, the modifier of behavior and the one whose behavior is to be modified, the guru and the seeker of truth, the scientist-god and the transformed. The therapist says in effect, "I have the knowledge and the skill to bring about change in you. Believe in what I can do and you shall be changed." The patient says in effect, "I seek change in me. I am ready to believe in your superior knowledge and skill to effect change in me." When such persons come together, they mutually co-construct one another into the roles of scientist-god and the seeker of transformation.

What is to be transformed can vary from a distal behavior to one's innermost soul, from a localized anxiety to innermost anguish. The therapist can reduce nail-biting and bring about assertive behavior. The illness can be cured. The problem can be alleviated. The hurt and the pain can be eliminated or assuaged. The therapist can bring about growth and development, metamorphosis and the actualization of human potentials, self-cleansing and redemption. "In his search for a redeemer, the neurotic meets his therapist. It is by no means wholly neurotic to long for a healer who could assume the burden of guilt, descend into the neurotic hell in order to redeem finally the neurotic through his triumph over guilt" (Caruso, 1964, p. 162). In her search for behavior change, she meets her behavior therapist. Finally she has found the therapist who can assume control over her behavior, use scientific knowledge of behavioral programs, and triumph over the target behavior on her behalf.

No matter whether the transformation is to occur in a concrete little observable behavior or a whole new authentic personality, the therapist must produce results. For the saintly therapist and the supplicant, and for the parental therapist and the child, all the therapist has to do is play the role and enact the relationship. Changes occur when the therapist fulfills the proper role and the proper role relationship. But for the scientist-god, things are much tougher. This therapist must produce results. While the saintly therapist is being saintly and the parental therapist is being parental, the scientist-god must have some way of reducing nail-biting or freeing the patient of guilt.

In other words, the scientist-god must have some trick up his sleeve. There must be some way of transforming the patient into an assertively behaving person or into someone who is no longer afraid of crowds. There has to be some god-like powers to produce miracles so that the patient is transformed into a healed person, a mature adult. There must be a way of producing results. So we have the patient carry out this regimen, follow this treatment procedure, undergo this cure, accept this way toward transformation.

This means that the scientist-god must have proof of his powers to effect transformation. He demands objective rules for proving that he has indeed brought about the transformation. There must be criteria that the miracle has been produced, that the behavior change has been brought about. Science requires proof of its technical effects, and religion requires proof of miracles. Accordingly, scientist-gods work out criteria of their powers to effect transformation. For example, we must have criteria that the transformations are observable, demonstrable, repeatable, consensually validatable, reliable, confirmable, objectively measurable. There are two sides to these criteria. One is that the scientist-god can then prove that he indeed has effected the transformation; the patient is to be convinced, and so is the scientist-god. The other side to these criteria is that other therapists are shown to be false scientists, gods who are not to be believed. Accordingly, scientist-gods coerce other therapists to use these criteria in the name of science-truth-godliness. Then it can be shown that these other therapists are false, are deceivers, charlatans, sloppy, unscientific. Just try to prove that you can achieve our transformations, our outcomes; adopt our criteria and you shall see that only the scientist-gods can produce transformations.

All of this requires that the scientist-god must have a distinctive relationship with the patient. The therapist must have the patient fulfill a distinctive role and relate to the therapist in a particular manner:

(a)   The reservoir of transformation lies in the power of the therapist; it does not lie in the patient. Transformation occurs because of the special powers held by the therapist, in the therapist's special knowledge and technical scientific know-how. Their relationships must confirm that the therapist is scientist-god, with knowledge and powers to effect the transformation.

(b) The patient is to have faith in the knowledge and power of the scientist-god. The patient must have faith that drinking this potion, carrying out this regimen, following this procedure will result in the transformation. Much of the role-relationship games of the therapist are geared to instill and to insure this faith in the canons of the scientist-god. If the patient dares to doubt or lose faith, then the therapist thunders the wrath of the vengeful scientist-god; the heavens roar and the gigantic pillars of science quake, ". . . I, your therapist, am Jehovah. Do unquestionably what I say and have no other gods before me" (Lawton, 1958, p. 29).

(c) The patient must surrender that part of himself which is to be transformed. In effect, the patient must relate to the therapist so as to say, "I hand over this part of me to you. You take it over. You do things to transform it. It is yours." There is always some ritual act in which the patient defines what the part is, and then hands it over to the therapist on a platter. The patient reaches that point in his life when some behavior is to be changed, and the patient must undergo the act of surrendering that behavior to the scientist-god. "It is at such critical points of anxiety and despair where man, having reached the limits of his endurance, becomes ready to surrender himself to God in the Spirit of Fiat voluntas Tua, or seek psychotherapy in a serious and accepting way" (Hora, 1962, p. 79). During the therapeutic process, the therapist accepts ownership over whatever aspect of the patient is to be transformed.

(d) Because the therapist is the manifest representative of Science or God, the major identity of the scientist-god is that of being the purveyor of the power of transformation. Accordingly, the therapist is faceless. The therapist is the healer, the technician, the change agent, the behavior control machine, the effective computer, the guru, the physician. It matters very little whether the Scientist-God is interested in camping or bowling, has an ulcer or menstrual cramps. What is important is the power, the knowledge, the technical skill.

This relationship is different from the relationship between the therapist/parent and the patient/child, and between the therapist/saint and the supplicant. I suggest that the question of the relative importance of techniques versus a therapeutic relationship (e.g., Lambert & Bergin, 1976) be replaced by a question such as: What roles do therapists and patients conjointly construct, and what is the place of techniques in each role relationship? Depending on the particular roles, I suspect that technical considerations assume more or less importance.

## Conclusions

With the notable exception of humanistic-existential theories of human beings, it is argued that virtually all theories of human beings and their psychotherapies assume that therapist and patient are two separated, intact entities who are constrained to relationships with one another within an encompassing world of objective reality. Accordingly, these psychotherapies must use one or more paradigms in which therapist and patient relate to one another on the basis of a subject-object paradigm, an interpersonal paradigm, a patient's frame-of-reference paradigm, or an encounter paradigm. As a result, it is proposed that virtually all psychotherapies are aptly described as the playing out of role relationships mutually constructed by therapist and patient. The changes which occur are a function of these role relationships and are limited to the playing out of the particular role relationship of the given therapist and the given patient. These role relationships are essentially outside the awareness of both therapist and patient. They are ingrained within the profession of psychotherapy and the particular school of therapy, and they take a specific form and shape as a result of the personality makeup of the given therapist and patient.

I am building a case for an indictment against all psychotherapies which accept these assumptions, and for the eventual requiem of therapist-patient role relationships. I am suggesting that a way out of this dilemma consists of a radical shift away from such assumptions and toward those which are represented by the humanistic-existential theory of human beings and an experiential psychotherapy. In short, I am inviting psychotherapists to consider abandoning a theoretical framework in which psychotherapy is little more than a grand game of mutually constructed role relationships, and in which whatever changes occur are mostly a function of these role relationships. I am inviting psychotherapists to adopt a framework in which psychotherapy can be considerably more than mere playing out of role relationships. Experiential psychotherapy is one such alternative framework.

# 6

# *Therapist-Patient Relationships: Problems*

Whenever psychotherapy is predominantly a matter of relationships between therapist and patient in their mutually constructed roles, there will be problems. Since most psychotherapies assume a therapist and a patient as separate entities who relate to one another within an encompassing world of reality, since these assumptions constrain psychotherapy to relationships between therapist roles and patient roles, since most psychotherapies are constrained to role relationships in which the predominance of attention is directed onto one another, then most psychotherapies are constrained largely to the playing out of role relationships—and the inevitable consequence is a set of very serious problems. The purpose of this chapter is to describe these problems. In addition, the purpose of this chapter and the previous chapter is to invite therapists to let go of the entire assumptive system to which these problems are yoked, and to consider the alternative approach offered by a humanistic-existential theory of human beings and experiential psychotherapy.

## THE RELATIONSHIP PRECLUDES AND
## DELIMITS INTERNAL RELATIONS

Many psychotherapies include notions about internal or deeper personality processes, and these psychotherapies commonly aim at helping

165

to bring about some sort of therapeutic change in the relationships among these internal personality processes, and between the patient and these internal personality processes. Whether these internal personality processes are called unconscious processes, psychodynamics, the inner self, or whatever, one of the serious and inescapable consequences of therapist-patient role relationships is that these psychotherapies are essentially unable to accomplish what they want to accomplish. That is, the therapist-patient role relationship seriously precludes and delimits the promotion of therapeutic internal relations.

## The Truncation of Attention Upon Internal Personality Processes

The therapist-patient role relationship sharply truncates the amount of sheer attention the patient can place upon internal personality processes. Many therapies want the patient to focus all or most of one's attention on internal personality processes such as thoughts and ideas, the flow of associations, the feeling of hurt or shame or confusion or anger, the personal meaning and significance of the clutching up in the stomach or the hot sensation in the chest, the feeling of love or competition or being rejected or being the loyal one. The problem is that very little of the patient's attention can be deployed onto such internal personality processes when most of the patient's attention is on the therapist. Because the therapist-patient relationship anchors most of the patient's attention, very little is freed for the internal processes.

Accordingly, therapists can never really use methods which call for a great deal of attention on internal processes. Furthermore, we know very little of what occurs when all or most of the patient's attention is centered on some internal process.

*"Talking about it" truncates the relation with it.* "Talking about it" occurs when the patient talks to the therapist about something personal. Our paradigms of therapist-patient relationships (Figure 5.1) practically insure that this is what occurs most of the time in most psychotherapy. Therapist and patient talk to each other about the patient's feeling of uncertainty, the way the patient avoids pushy people, the peculiar fantasy life, the unconscious death wish, the meaning of the patient's anxiety, or any other personal matter.

The problem is that to the extent therapist and patient talk to one another about it, the patient is unable to have a relation with it. The patient is thereby unable to see it fully, confront or engage it, perceive and grasp it, encounter it, feel it, experience it (Enright, 1970). In short, the relationship is truncated. In many therapies, it is desirable that the patient's relation toward the internal personality process be strong, and that emotions and feelings likewise be strong. But the necessity of talking about it insures that the relation has to be muted and mild and truncated (Halpern, 1965; Havens, 1973).

The very grammar of talking about it contributes to the truncation. The predominant channel of communication has to be between patient and therapist rather than between patient and whatever is internal. Instead of talking directly to his cancer or his dependency or his fear, the patient has to talk to the therapist about the internal process. In every way, the therapist-patient relationship forces these persons to talk to one another about it, and that insures that the patient's relation with it is sharply truncated.

*External Acceptance Fails to Lead to Internal Acceptance*

Many therapies hold to the proposition that the offering of acceptance (love, trust, understanding, positive regard, care) by the therapist will be followed by the patient's heightened acceptance of what is presumed to lie within. "The patient is at last able to love himself because he has experienced complete acceptance from the therapist . . ." (Shaffer, 1978, p. 77). If the therapist accepts the patient, the patient will accept himself. Here is a grand justification for the therapist patient relationship. The proper relationship is supposed to facilitate internal relations.

The trouble is that it does not work. An external relation tends to preclude and delimit an internal relation. When the therapist accepts the patient, there is no such acceptance by the patient of her unconscious sexual wishes or deeper hatred of others. There is no substantial increase in the patient's acceptance of whatever may be said to lie deeper within the patient's personality (Naranjo, 1969). "This point must be emphasized because of the common error in many circles of assuming that the experience of one's being will take place automatically if only one is accepted by someone else. This is the basic error of some forms of 'relationship therapy' " (May, 1958, p. 45). If anything, acceptance (or love or positive regard) by the therapist toward the patient will tend to emphasize the patient-therapist relationship, and thereby the relationship between the patient and genuinely internal personality processes will be deemphasized.

For some patient-therapist couples, acceptance by the therapist may be followed by all sorts of consequences other than acceptance by the patient of internal personality processes. For example, the patient may refer more to herself, tell more about her thoughts and ideas and feelings. The patient may talk to the therapist about all kinds of things, especially now that the therapist is and will probably continue to be accepting. But such consequences have little if anything to do with actual acceptance by the patient of her own internal personality processes.

For many other patients, on the other hand, the offer of acceptance by the therapist only serves to validate and heighten the already negative and distanced relation between the patient and internal personality processes. These are the patients for whom it is quite important to construct and maintain separation and safe distance between themselves and others, and also between themselves and internal personality processes. Laing (1962) describes such persons as having to maintain such a safe distance, and he reiterates the enormous technical error of attempting to violate this protective barrier by onslaughts of therapist love and closeness and acceptance. This only mobilizes heightened distance and vigilant avoidances both between patient and therapist and also between patient and deeper personality processes. All in all, acceptance by the therapist generally fails to lead to heightened acceptance between the patient and internal personality processes. Again, the external relation acts to preclude and delimit internal relations.

### Distancing and Deadening the Internal Relationship

Regardless of the nature of the therapist-patient relationship, its net effect upon the patient's internal relationship is that of widening the internal gap, instituting greater distance, objectifying and deadening what lies internally.

*The impenetrable gap.* An impenetrable gap exists between the separate and intact entity who is the therapist and the separate and intact entity who is the patient. The therapist can never feel the actual feeling occurring right now in the patient. The therapist can never experience what the patient is experiencing. The therapist will never see what the patient sees in the exact way the patient sees it. The therapist will not share the world in which the patient exists and feels and sees and experiences—as long as the therapist interacts with the patient over an external relationship between two separate entities.

Of course the two will relate and interact. They can affect and influence one another, love and hate one another. The therapist can observe and evaluate, encounter and confront, explain and interpret, empathize and disclose, accept and understand. But they can never cross the impenetrable gap between the two separated entities.

The problem is that the impenetrable gap between patient and externally relating therapist maintains an impenetrable gap between patient and internal personality processes. This problem is no problem for therapies in which no internal personality processes are presumed. Nor is it a problem for therapies in which an impenetrable gap does not interfere with their technical procedures. But it is a problem for therapies which consider it important for patients to blend with their insides, to fuse and assimilate with them, to be them, to feel and undergo them, to no longer maintain the separating gap. These therapies are not satisfied with patients' seeing their insides, knowing about them, trying to live with them, always across a moat. These therapies want a genuine meeting of patient and internal personality processes. The problem, however, is that the external impenetrable gap means that there will be an internal impenetrable gap. If anything, the external relationship will insure this gap, reinforce it.

*The deadening of internal relations.* The relationship between patient and therapist has the net effect of deadening (pushing down further, blocking and sealing off) internal personality processes. All too often, the nature of the patient-therapist relationship serves to avoid (deflect, polarize, hide) the deeper personality process so that the growth of the relationship between patient and therapist acts to widen the relationship between the patient and what is deeper. Even therapies which aim at exploring what lies deep within the patient are vulnerable to this problem. Transference and countertransference relations are viewed as occurring within an encompassing role relationship which serves to deaden the relationship between the patient and whatever deeper process gives rise to (and is thereby hidden by) the manifest transference and countertransference relationship.

If the internal personality process relates to being autonomous and independent, the patient may well be led to seek a role relationship in which the therapist is a close and loving friend. If the internal personality process involves a chaotic madness, the patient may be led to seek a role relationship in which the therapist is a secret lover. Virtually any patient-therapist relation, including those of a "transference" variety, has the net effect of deadening the patient's relation with some internal personality process. Accordingly, the internal personality process which inspired the role relationship is further and further deadened.

All in all, role relationships between therapist and patient tend to preclude and delimit relationships between the patient and the patient's deeper personality processes no matter how these internal processes are construed. Attention to these internal processes is diluted. Talking about these processes tends to truncate the patient's relationships with them. The common proposition that acceptance by the therapist leads to patient acceptance of internal processes may be challenged. The impenetrable gap between external and separate patient and therapist insures a similar impenetrable gap between patient and internal processes, and the role relationships themselves lead to the progressive sealing over and deadening of the internal personality process. The precluding and delimiting of the patient's relationship with deeper personality processes are necessary consequences of role relationships. There is no escaping these consequences by therapies which are vulnerable to such role relationships, and virtually all psychotherapies are vulnerable to these role relationships.

### THE RELATIONSHIP LOCKS IN
### THE THERAPIST AND THE PATIENT

Therapist and patient work with one another to build role relationships. The problem comes about as these role relationships gradually become firmer and more entrenched. As these role relationships grow, the therapist and patient who were the conjoint architects now become the victims of those very role relationships. Sooner or later a point is reached where they are locked into these role relationships.

*The Therapist Cannot Get Out of the Role Relationship*

In many therapies there are times when the therapist is to talk to the patient about the kind of relationship the patient has toward the therapist. It is important that the therapist help the patient understand that right now he is trying to resist the therapist, or seduce the therapist, or treat the therapist in this or that way. The relationship from patient to therapist contains important therapeutic material for the patient to see, to understand, to have insight into, to learn from. The problem is that the mutually constructed role relationship grows to a point where the therapist is essentially unable to get out of the role relationship in order to talk to the patient about it. It becomes increasingly difficult to extract oneself from such role relationships. Accordingly, it becomes harder and harder for the therapist to carry out therapeutic strategies which require that the therapist get out of the relationship in order to talk to the patient about it.

Indeed, the therapist's attempts to squirm out of the role relationship are increasingly like struggling in quicksand, with the net result that the therapist is more and more imprisoned in the very role relationship from which he struggles to emerge. Suppose that the patient and therapist work out a relationship in which the patient never really gets what he wants; he tries, but in the end he is always squashed. The therapist is the elusive seducer, always promising but never really coming through. Each attempt by the therapist to step out of this role relationship serves to lock the therapist further into that role relationship. To the patient, each attempt by the therapist to step out of the relationship only proves that the therapist is indeed elusive, always promising but never really coming through. It proves that the patient never really gets what he wants; see how elusively seductive the therapist is. Many role relationships are all-consuming and lock the therapist in so that every attempt by the therapist to step away from the role insidiously locks the therapist in even further.

To the extent that this occurs, therapist and patient become locked into their respective role relationships, and therapy becomes little more than the playing out of these role relationships. It is the career of the poor patient who never gets what he wants and the seductive therapist who promises but never comes through. Or it is the career of the saintly therapist and the patient who seeks to be bathed in the light of the saint. As the players become locked into the very role relationships they created, they are enjoined to play out the script to its end.

## The Patient Cannot Get Out of the Role Relationship

As therapist and patient are successful in constructing mutual role relationships, one of the consequences is that the patient becomes increasingly locked into that role. This leads to problems.

One of these problems is that the patient is essentially unable to get out of the role relationship in order to see (understand, feel) himself in this role relationship. The patient cannot see that he is baiting the therapist, or that he is being the seductive little boy, or that he is being the one who is overlooked and misunderstood. Many therapeutic operations require that the patient get out of the role relationship with the therapist. These operations are effectively blocked to the extent that the patient is locked into the role relationship. The patient is unable to see how he is being in the relationship because the patient is too locked into the relationship to get out of it.

Another problem is that the therapist-patient relationships pull so much of the patient's attention that too little is available for other material. For example, some therapist operations call for a fair measure of the patient's attention to go to past incidents and events. The trouble is that the patient cannot get out of the immediate therapist-patient role relationship to do this successfully. Talking about the past is incorporated into the immediately ongoing role relationship so that the patient is caught even more in the role as he looks at past material. The patient who is in the role of the slavish follower of the therapist will be further enacting this role as he discusses incidents and situations from his past. Fenichel (1953) shows how the therapist-patient relationship functions as an effective barrier and trap against the possibility of the patient's seeing or discussing his past. The very act of turning to the past entrenches the patient further into the role relationship.

In the same way, methods which require the patient's directed attention will be subverted because the patient simply cannot get out of the role relationship. Instead of attending to the description of the feeling of helplessness, the patient will be constrained to playing out a particular role in talking about her feeling. The method will not work very much. Nor will methods which call for the patient's attending to the way her sister was with her when they were living in the house before father died, or really seeing the look on her baby's face when the patient twisted the baby's arm in a crazy fit of rage. It simply is difficult for the patient to get out of the immediate role relationship enough to carry out these methods. Instead, the patient is caught in the role relationship which dominates everything the patient does, and the consequence is that any method is short-circuited which requires that the patient get out of the role relationship in order to carry it out.

Finally, the role relationship tends to grow to a point where it dominates even the extra-therapeutic life of the patient. Many of the roles which the patient brings into the relationship gain their importance from what is occurring, or not occurring, in the patient's world. With no one who cares in the patient's world, the patient invites the therapist to be the important one who really cares. Lacking a strong authority in his world, the patient turns to the therapist as the strong authority. Symmetrically, many therapist roles have powerful implications for the patient's extra-therapy world. If the therapist is to be the great healer, no one else in the patient's world is to try to supplant the therapist. If the therapist is to be the wonderful model whom the patient is to emulate, no one else is to fulfill that role in the patient's life. Accordingly, not only is the patient unable to get out of the role relationship, it assumes an increasingly central focus in the life of the patient outside therapy. Whatever the nature of the role relationship, it becomes superior and unrivaled in relation to much if not all in the patient's world, more important than family, children, one's work and play, one's entire extra-therapy world. The patient is progressively unable to get out of a role relationship which tends to dominate the patient's whole world.

## Feeling and Experiencing Are Truncated

Once the therapist and patient are locked into a role relationship, one consequence is a truncation of the depth and breadth of the patient's feelings and experiencings. Most psychotherapy consists of the patient's talking to the therapist about something. The problem is that the patient's role relationship keeps the patient from high levels of feeling in relation to whatever the patient talks about. If the patient is in the role of the secretly loved and prized one, the strong feelings will be incorporated within that role. Telling the therapist about the way her mother used to hide money in the house will be carried out within the role of the secretly loved and prized patient. Strong feelings will not occur in regard to the mother's hiding the money, or father's belching at the table, or jealousy about the spouse's relationships. Instead, there is a truncation of feelings, a reduction in the immediacy of feeling, a depersonalizing (Polster & Polster, 1974).

This curtailing of feeling and experiencing occurs regardless of what the patient is talking about. The referent might be something which happened in a recent dream, or an incident which occurred yesterday. The referent might be an ongoing fantasy or thought or notion the patient has about something. It might be some event which occurred a few months or years ago, one which was highly significant in the patient's life. It might be an incident or a scene from the patient's early childhood. To the extent that the patient is fulfilling a role relationship with the therapist, the feeling which can occur is truncated.

The patient may be undergoing strong feelings as he talks with the therapist about his sexual feelings toward his sister. In the course of therapy, the patient may come to have strong feelings as he sees the extent of his hidden sexual feelings toward his mother. Carnal feelings, incestuous feelings, all sorts of taboo sexual thoughts and wishes may be talked about with strong feelings. But the ceiling on the feelings is truncated by the role relationships. The technical question is this: Will the sheer intensity of feeling be higher in the actual, lived, vividly real interaction with the key figure, or, on the other hand, as the patient fulfills a role relationship in talking to the therapist about sexual feelings toward the key figure? My clinical conviction is that the height of feelings is far greater under the former conditions than under the latter. Many patients talk freely and easily about incestuous feelings toward a parent, but feelings soar to extreme peaks when these patients are freed of role relationships with the therapist and, instead, live out the vivid sexual encounters with the parent.

What about feelings which occur in the role relationship with the therapist? Many therapies rely on the therapeutic value of such feelings. I would level the same charge against such feelings. That is, I suggest that the depth and breadth of such feelings are greater with key other figures than in role relationships with the therapist. When the patient fulfills the role of the one who is used and manipulated by the therapist, feelings may become strong. I suggest that feelings are far more intense when the patient undergoes the wholesale sense of being used and manipulated in relation to the critically key figure in the patient's world. Transference feelings may be high; these feelings are higher in interaction with the key figure from which they are transferred; the feelings are diluted and altered by the role relationship encompassing the so-called transference: "The original neurosis of the patient, which is based on his childhood experiences, is thus transformed in an artificial 'transference neurosis' which is a less intensive repetition . . ." (Alexander, 1963, p. 441). When, in addition, these feelings must be filtered through a particular role relationship in which the transference occurs, the ceiling on the patient's feelings is even lower.

Not only does the role relationship reduce the height of the patient's feelings toward the therapist, but there is also a truncation of the breadth of feelings. Each role relationship means that certain feelings toward the therapist will likely occur, while other feelings toward the therapist are less likely to occur. If therapist and patient construct a role relationship in which the patient is used and manipulated by the therapist, then the patient may feel hurt, helplessness, rage and rejection. It may come as a surprise when the patient is later working with a different therapist with whom he feels intense jealousy or love or competitiveness or any other kind of feeling outside the bounds of those pulled by the particular role relationship built with the former therapist. Each role relationship will tend to truncate the breadth of feelings to those appropriate for that role relationship. When the role relationship is that of supplicant to the saintly therapist who surrounds the patient in acceptance, positive regard, and empathic understanding, it is less likely that patients will undergo gales of rollicking bellylaughs, or that the patient will be filled with lusty sexual feelings. Each role relationship tends to truncate the patient's feelings to those which are appropriate for the particular role relationship.

All in all, the role relationship grows and grows until it tends to lock in both therapist and patient. The therapist is increasingly stuck in that role relationship and has increasing difficulty getting out of it. So too is the patient increasingly stuck in the role relationship. The net result is that many operations cannot be carried out effectively, the role relationships assume superiority in the patient's world, feeling and experiencing are truncated both in depth and breadth, and therapy consists more and more of the mere playing out of the role relationships in which both participants are increasingly locked.

## THE RELATIONSHIP LOSES AND DISTORTS THERAPEUTIC DATA

Every therapy has its own version of valuable therapeutic data. These may include early childhood memories, a recurring fantasy, a feeling of lost hope, a chill down the back, the situation in which the symptom first occurred, or any of hundreds of bits of information, cues and stimuli, reactions and cognitions, feelings and experiencings. The problem is that the inevitable role relationship enjoins the loss and systematic distortion of whole domains of data, all essentially outside the awareness of the therapist who is functioning within some role relationship.

### The Relationship Loses Therapeutic Data

Regardless of the nature of the role relationship co-constructed by therapist and patient, data will be admitted which are cordial to that role relationship, and there will be a loss of data which are not cordial.

*The relationship systematically loses domains of personal history data.* Consider the therapist who fulfills the role of the earnest helper, caring and concerned, and the patient who fulfills the role of the needy one, ready to trust and depend upon the therapist. In the course of their fulfilling this role relationship, the patient may disclose all sorts of childhood incidents which make sense within their particular role relationship. But other incidents will tend not to come to light because they fall outside the role relationship. Anamnesic material is a function of the particular role relationship. Even so-called factual case history information varies with the nature of the role relationship constructed by the therapist/interviewer and the patient. Indeed, summarizing the determinants of such information-gathering, Bucklew (1960, 1968) concludes that the collection of even apparently factual case history material is more aptly described as a highly idiosyncratic ". . . creation of the patient in social interaction with his therapist . . ." (1968, p. 158).

What the patient is led to remember is partially determined by the role the patient is fulfilling and the nature of the role relationship with the therapist. Out of 20 or 30 years of growing up, two or 20 or 30 hours of recollection will disclose those memories which feed a relationship of, for example, a trusting and dependent patient toward a caring and concerned therapist. Freud (1924) was meticulous in acknowledging that a transference relationship systematically admitted only selected chains of historical data while excluding whole other realms whose potential therapeutic usefulness could not be assessed. With little or no awareness of the nature of the role relationships, the danger is that the therapist is led to a seriously biased picture of the patient's personal history.

*The relationship loses the patient's phenomenological reality.* There are two ways in which the role relationship insures the loss of data from the patient's phenomenological world. One is that the sheer external relationship insures that the therapist can never undergo what is occurring in the patient's phenomenological world. The second is that what the patient reports to the therapist about that phenomenological world is not only determined by the role relationship, but is also a further step away from the actual data. The net result is that most therapies operate with the loss of this whole realm of potentially therapeutic data.

The therapist who is external can never know or share the phenomenological reality of the patient's world. While the patient may be seeing that very special look on her mother's face, the external therapist cannot. The therapist can never hear the way mother says those key words, the tone of voice, the soft lilt over here and the jagged edge over there. The therapist will not see the look on the patient's child, that wondrous and trusting look when the patient grins at her child and holds her close. The therapist will never see the garage where the patient played as a child, the tree in front of the house, the steps of the school, the picture hanging in her room, the bicycle she had, the pet pigeon, the collection of elephants near her bed. The therapist will never hear the bark of the dog or the call of her mother or the eager whispers of her younger sister or the voice of her childhood boyfriend. Some of these things are immediate, some recent, and some very old. Some are mundane, and some may be dramatic and unusual. But all these data are lost to the therapist who can never see or hear what the patient sees and hears. Indeed, much of what the patient sees and hears the therapist may not even know about.

The externally relating therapist is unable to know (share, have) the particularly alive interaction between the patient and her world. The therapist cannot share what it is like to walk along the street with her best friend, to wait after class for the teacher to say what she wanted to say, to watch her husband sitting depressed at the table. The therapist is unable to be there with those other persons, to know what it is like to live in this particular interaction. Such data are lost to the separate external therapist who is constrained within some kind of relationship with the patient.

Nor will the external therapist share the feelings, emotions, bodily sensations, and experiencings which are occurring right now in the patient. Typically, the therapist will be essentially unaware of their occurrence. Even if the patient happens to talk about them or undergo them, the therapist would not likely have them. The therapist does not share the patient's feeling of helplessness or joy, cannot grasp the feeling the way it is happening right now in the patient. The patient may be feeling scared, but the therapist is unable to have that feeling of being scared. The therapist is unable to have that momentary panic, or that sense of bewilderment, or that state of being cut off. The therapist is unable to have that chill down the back, or the hot hollowness in the chest, or the pounding ache in the temples. All of these data are lost to the external therapist, who may never know of their immediate existence and who must operate without knowing or grasping what they are like in this patient right now.

While the patient is talking, or while the patient is being silent, all sorts of images and fantasies may occur. The patient is talking about the car she has, and there are images and fantasies of an accident, or of her brother wrecking the car, or of tap-dancing on the roof of the car. The therapist may never know about these images and fantasies. Even if the patient were to talk about them, the therapist would never have them the way the patient has them. Some of these are fleeting and some are persistent, some are blurred and some are concrete. Some are unimportant and others are therapeutically valuable. But none are grasped by the external relating therapist in the way they occur in the patient.

In the same way, the patient will have all kinds of private thoughts, cognitions and ideas. The patient may think thoughts such as, "I'm getting tired. . . . My head hurts. . . . I always get mixed up. . . . I don't think I want to tell him about that. . . . He seems sort of disinterested in this. . . ." Generally such thoughts are simply outside the therapist's awareness. Even if the patient tells the therapist about such thoughts, the therapist cannot grasp them or have them the way the patient does.

The problem is perhaps best exemplified in the patient who is silent or who is forcibly withdrawn. Consider the patient who suddenly stops talking and is silent for ten seconds or so. Consider the patient whose style is that of being quite withdrawn, saying very little. Consider the patient whose words seem far afield from bodily gestures and movements. With such patients the therapist is challenged to know what is occurring, to share the feelings and thoughts, the inner experiencings and emotions which are going on inside (cf. Gendlin, 1972). The external therapist has little chance of sharing the phenomenological world of such patients.

Even when the patient tries to tell about everything which is occuring, the therapist who is external is simply not able to grasp or share or have it the way the patient does. The therapist is not able to share or know the external world in which the patient lives, or the nature of the patient's interaction in that world, or the feelings and emotions and bodily sensations and images and fantasies and private thoughts occurring in the patient. Telling about it does not mean that the therapist has it the way the patient does. Nor can the therapist grasp or know the phenomenal reality which is occurring as the patient is telling about something. But this problem is magnified even more with regard to the myriads of things of which the patient is only slightly aware or dimly senses. If the theory of psychotherapy admits of phenomena beyond the patient's awareness, this whole realm is even further outside the externally relating therapist's phenomenological sharing.

The net result is that the therapist loses entire domains of data whose potential therapeutic usefulness cannot be gauged by the external therapist. This therapist is unable to share or grasp or have these data, unable to undergo the phenomenal reality of the patient. The culprit consists of assumptions of two separate entities consigned to interpersonal relationships within an encompassing world of objective reality. Because of these assumptions, the therapist loses whole domains of data which fall outside the delimiting boundaries of the assumptions themselves. As a consequence, Needleman (1967a) argues that little progress toward a science of psychotherapy ". . . is possible unless joined to a method of description that is free from the metaphysical and epistemological presuppositions of contemporary natural science. It is argued that these presuppositions are historically such as to rule out the reality of the very phenomena to be explained. Thus, a psychology which attempts to stay totally within the fold of Western science is an unproductively circular enterprise that can never be entirely sure it is addressing its proper subject matter" (p. viii). Some therapies may find it valuable to use the patient's phenomenal data and much broader realms of the patient's personal life. As long as these therapies rest upon such assumptions and are constrained to role relationships, such domains of data are essentially lost.

## The Relationship Distorts Therapeutic Data

The role relationship systematically distorts therapeutic data to fit in with the particular nature of the role relationship. What is more, to the extent that the role relationships lie outside the awareness of therapist and patient, the participants have little or no idea of the nature or extent of the distortion. Consider a patient who is geared to be a little girl with a strong mother who can direct her into the adult world, and consider a therapist who plays out the complementary role of the competent woman. Their relationship will systematically distort the data which are obtained.

This role relationship will invest its own particular significance to much of what the patient talks about. If the patient talks about her mother, the role relationship will systematically distort the meaning to fit in with the patient as little girl with the competent mother/therapist. Accordingly, material about her mother will be regarded as indicating how needy the patient was, or how deficient the mother was as a model, or how good the therapist is at understanding what the patient is saying, or as indirect messages about how the patient feels about the therapist. When the patient talks about her childhood, the role relationship will lead the therapist to hear the patient being secure enough to regress, or the patient is trusting the therapist with personal incidents from her past, or the patient is symbolically being a little girl with the strong mother/therapist. Whatever the patient talks about will be processed through the role relationship encompassing both therapist and patient.

Because the therapist operates out of the role of the competent woman with this little girl, whatever occurs is given significance in terms of this role. The patient will be regarded as changing or not changing in terms of the changes open to the little girl in relation to the competent mother. Accordingly, the patient will be seen as changing in terms of growing up, or becoming competent, or identifying with the therapist, or giving up little girl characteristics, or gaining in adult competencies. In other words, the avenues along which change can occur are already determined by the particular role relationship. One role relationship may allow for changes in increasing or decreasing intimacy. Another may pull for changes in normal adjustment. A third may see changes in terms of dependence-independence. A fourth may pull for changes in terms of increasing expressiveness. The nature of the role relationship distorts the data so that those changes are highlighted which are cordial to that particular role relationship.

With one therapist, the patient constructs a relationship in which it is important to share everything, to pour it all out, to confess it all finally to such a person. The patient tells every little secret. The patient has memories which he had never remembered before. The patient opens up everything. In this relationship the very sharing of such material invests it with special meaning. Most of what occurs in months of therapy is in the service of feeding this very special relationship with this very special therapist. With a new therapist, the patient and therapist co-construct a relationship which is different. Now the patient is on the verge of making frightening major changes in his life. He is in the role of the scared person who needs a strong and capable guide, a therapist with stable strength to guide him through the potential major changes. The patient spends months telling about the same material. Only now what the patient talks about is used to feed a relationship of the insecure patient to the stable therapist. The point is that the relationship between therapist and patient invests ostensibly the same data with its own meaning and significance. The relationship distorts virtually everything the patient says to fit in with the particular nature of this relationship.

From within one role the therapist sees and hears one set of data; from within another role the therapist sees and hears another set of data. Each role relationship systematically distorts data in its own distinctive way.

Every word uttered by the patient, every gesture and expression are received differently by therapists in different roles. The therapist who is the competent mother will receive data differently than the therapist who is the god-like omniscient one, or the therapist who is the seductive center of the patient's world, or the removed observer who will bring about profound changes in this emotionally ill patient. When the patient tells about her husband's lack of understanding, the competent mother-therapist may hear a little girl who is going to become, later, a more competent woman in heterosexual relations. The therapist who is the seductive center of the patient's world will hear a woman becoming increasingly involved in a relationship with the therapist. The therapist who is the removed observer will spot various psychopathological indicators of deep-seated psychic conditions which will become cured in the process of therapy. Each role relationship determines the way in which the therapist receives and makes sense of virtually everything the patient says and does.

All of this means that essentially the whole realm of the patient's inner world is beyond the therapist. At best, data about the patient's inner world are distorted as they pass through a circuitous role relationship between patient and therapist. No matter how experienced and sensitive the therapist, there can be no direct contact between the therapist and the patient's inner world. The patient's inner feelings and thoughts, fantasies and experiencings, emotions and cognitions—the whole realm of the inner world—are around the corner from the therapist who is told about them by a patient in one role relating to a therapist in another role. Little wonder that the data about the patient's inner world must be treated as distorted.

But the problem of distorted data only starts here. Ordinarily the therapist undertakes three giant steps backward from direct and undistorted understanding of the data of the patient's inner world. The first giant step is to organize the already distorted data into a sketch of the patient. This is called a psychodiagnostic evaluation or assessment or clinical picture or psychodynamic summary. On the basis of distorted data about the patient's inner world, an even more distorted description of the patient is constructed. She is an anxiety reaction. The problem is that she is frigid and sexually repressed, with fears of submission. This patient has a pre-psychotic personality. She is in a bereavement process. We build elaborate descriptions of what her insides are like based upon distorted data. The second giant backward step is to construct a treatment program on the basis of a distorted clinical evaluation which is based upon distorted data. These are the objectives to be pursued for this patient, the way we want this person to be. We will aim at getting her to be more sexual, or to communicate better with her husband, or to find another sex partner, or to be less dependent, or to be more assertive. Finally, the third giant step is to use some methods to reach these treatment objectives. We use assertiveness training or desensitization or bereavement therapy or communication programs or dozens of other ways to try to get her to be the way we think she should be based on our notion of the way we think her insides are. By means of these three giant steps, psychotherapists move further and further from the initially distorted data about the patient's inner world as seen across a distorting role relationship.

What makes matters even more troublesome is that the methods used to obtain data about the patient's inner world are devised and used by an external therapist constrained to some role relationship with this particular patient. Instead of directly grasping the patient's inner feeling, the therapist in one role asks the patient, in another role, to talk about something internal. Or the therapist gives tests to the patient so that the patient gives information about the inner world. The role relationship sharply limits the methods to those which involve a role relationship which distorts the very data the methods are designed to provide.

All in all, the role relationship between therapist and patient loses and distorts large realms of data whose therapeutic usefulness lies generally outside the awareness of the therapist. Again, the role relationship virtually insures the loss and distortion of all these data. For many therapies, this is a most serious problem indeed.

## THE RELATIONSHIP GENERATES
## RESISTANCE AND FRUSTRATION

The role relationship between therapist and patient generates a considerable amount of patient resistance and frustration. Indeed, I suggest that a large proportion of what is generally referred to as patient resistance to and frustration with therapy is brought about by the role relationship itself. We tend to blame the patient, in large measure, for losing faith in therapy or becoming despondent about therapy or fighting the therapeutic process or being uncooperative or losing motivation or defending against what we call the therapeutic process. Nearly every therapy recognizes patient resistance and has ways of dealing with this phenomenon. I suggest, however, that the role relationship generates its own resistance and frustration. Here again, this problem is an essentially serious and unresolvable consequence of the therapist-patient role relationship.

## By Forcing a Role Relationship onto the Patient

Almost without exception, each therapist fulfills some therapeutic role which is yoked to some complementary role for the patient. Before the patient even steps into the room for the first appointment, there is some encompassing role waiting for the patient. Certainly, after one or two sessions or so, the initial jockeying around leads to a rather well-defined role into which the patient is to fit. The patient is to be the beholden one who is going to be made wondrously different by the fine therapist. Or the patient is to be the person with the problem which the therapist will fix. Or the patient is to be the one who appreciates the therapist's understanding friendliness. Or the patient is told in effect, "I am the doctor, the one who must be seen as important and special in your life. You must see me this way. You must look up to me and respect me." Every therapist role has a complementary patient role, and the person who is the patient is confronted by the challenge of acceding or not acceding, giving in to the role or resisting it. When the patient does not accede, there is resistance. Accordingly, the role relationship is responsible for generating its own resistance and frustration, right from the beginning of therapy.

Generally there are a few phases in the unfolding of the role offered by the therapist to the patient. In the first few sessions, for example, the patient may be invited to be open, feeling, hurting, disclosing. This is the complementary way the patient is to be with the therapist who, in the first phase, is present, listening, understanding. After 10 or 30 sessions or so, the therapist may in effect say the following to the patient: "Now that you have disclosed yourself to me and felt a lot of hurt, in this next phase you are to be beholden to me for being such a fine person with you. You are to notice me, acknowledge me. Ask about me or try to be like me or have a little crush on me." After another 20 or 60 sessions, the patient is told to fulfill another unfolding phase. The therapist says in effect to the patient: "Now you are to feel good and leave therapy. I needed this little affair with you, but you are now to leave. And you are to leave in friendly admiration of me." With each phase in the role the patient is to be, there is a strong likelihood of a fresh wave of resistance and frustration on the part of the patient. Accordingly, throughout the course of psychotherapy, whether that means five or 500 sessions, the patient is forced to deal with changing role pressures. The net result is a series of generated phases of resistance and frustration.

Because of the pressure to fulfill the complementary role, patients are led to undertake at least three options. One is to resist. The second is to give in or acquiesce or accommodate, i.e., fulfill the complementary role to that fulfilled by the therapist. The third option is to dance together with the therapist, to work out a smooth routine in which both partners co-construct the kind of complementary role relationship which has high goodness-of-fit for both partners. Resistance is high under the first option. Resistance is quite low under the third option. The second option leads to a few consequences. Sometimes therapy lasts only a few sessions, largely because therapy does not provide the kind of role relationship the patient seeks. Sometimes therapy lasts longer, but the patient suffers the effects of acquiescing or accommodating to the role forced upon him by the therapist. When this occurs, therapy is predominantly for the therapist and the role relationship is important to the therapist, not the patient. To the extent that the patient is forced to accede to role relationships imposed by the therapist, I am of the conviction that we therapists might well consider the deep-seated and long-range effects upon the welfare of the patient. I believe these are serious, are subtly powerful, and are counter to the value system of such theories of human beings as the existential-humanistic theory. These are serious value considerations, with serious professional, ethical, and moral issues which deserve careful study (cf. Mahrer, 1980c).

In many therapies, there is an indirect acknowledgment of the opening skirmish in which the patient is forced to accede to the role complementary to that fulfilled by the therapist. Using smooth phrases, this enterprise is referred to as establishing a good rapport, or developing the patient's motivation for therapy, or building an effective working relationship, or gaining the patient's cooperation. Dreikurs (1956) is representative of the hundreds of ways of winning this opening skirmish: "Winning the patient's cooperation for the common task is a prerequisite for any therapy" (p. 112). Whatever words are used, one large part of what occurs is that the patient is pressured to fulfill a particular role relationship complementary to that fulfilled by the therapist. The counter pressure is some kind of resistance, generated by the therapist's efforts.

If the patient starts therapy from within the role of the helpless child, resistance and frustration are generated when the therapist pressures the patient to fulfill some other role, e.g., the sexually intimate partner. If the patient is ready to engage in a sexually intimate affair with the therapist for whom it is important that the patient instead fulfill a role of a helpless child, resistance and frustration are likely to be generated. In effect, the poor fitting of roles leads the patient to say, "I want to be in this role, and you are pressuring me to be in that role." The consequence is resistance, generated by the rules and games of role relationships.

Many of the roles imposed upon patients involve acceding to the way the therapist wants the patient to become. That is, many therapist roles include a heavy component of an intention to change the patient in particular ways. Sometimes these ways are general, and sometimes these ways are fitted to the specific patient. The commonality lies in the therapist's intention to change the patient, and in the patient's accommodation to being someone who is changed in that way. One therapist may have the intention of having the patient become a good and responsible mother; stay in the family and be happy. Another therapist may have the intention of having the patient leave the family; throw off the bonds and be autonomous and independent. These are forceful challenges to the patient, and they invite the patient to resist. Do not give in to someone who wants to change you. Do not give in to someone who wants you to stay in the family or to get out of the family. When the intention to get the patient to change is a significant part of the therapist's role, that generates its own measure of resistance. In so many ways, the therapist's forcing the patient to fulfill some complementary role generates a good measure of resistance and frustration.

### By Engaging in the Role Relationship

It is virtually assured that patient resistance and frustration are generated by means of the therapist's sheer engagement in any role relationship. This almost damns the bulk of therapies to problems brought about by role relationships and prevented from solution by the role relationships themselves.

*Filling in the missing part in the patient's life.* Some patients build worlds in which they sorely lack a figure such as a parent or a lover or an anchor to reality or a true and loyal friend. This is the way they live, namely, with that important part missing. Their lives consist of wonderful brief interludes in which they finally manage to locate the right person, and then they systematically destroy the relationship. Having located the good parent, they kick and scream and fight and resist and are frustrated. The relationship ends, and the patient sets out on another search for the missing parent or lover or whatever. Quite often, the patient's search for the perpetually missing part brings him to his therapist. Such a role is irresistible to many therapists. The therapist is to be the loved parent the patient has never really had. Therapists are real suckers for such role relationships. But the scenario plays itself out, and soon the patient is kicking and screaming in frustrated resistance. The therapist is accused of not being a real parent, or the therapist failed as an anchor to reality, or the true and loyal therapist/friend did not meet the tests. As a result, there is considerable resistance and frustration generated by the therapist's acceding to the role of the missing part in the patient's life (cf. Mahrer, 1970c, 1978c).

The first phase of the role relationship sought by the patient is that of finding the therapist and binding the therapist to the patient in a wedding. Accordingly, the patient says in effect, "See how needy I am for a good poppa? Would you like to be my good poppa which I have sorely missed my whole life?" This is courtship and wedding. After the therapist eagerly plays the role of the good poppa, or whatever is sorely missing in the patient's life, the second phase is instituted, in which the patient sets about resisting and fighting the good poppa who is shown to be not really a good poppa. This is one trap in the therapist's fulfilling of the sorely needed and missing part in the patient's life, a trap with built-in resistance and frustration.

A second trap consists of the therapist's stepping into the role which was recently vacated. Here is the patient who has had a good poppa or lover or anchor to reality or true and loyal friend throughout long stretches of the patient's life. Then, in some way, the role was vacated. Poppa died; the lover had babies and turned into a mother; the true and loyal friend traumatically became a snake in the grass. In steps the therapist, brimming with eagerness to replace the missing part. For a few months or a year or so everything is fine. Then the problems start to arise. The therapist is not a real lover; he talks a lot but there is no action; he starts putting up all sorts of barriers which he had hidden in his professional closet; he will not make love with me. As the problems grow, the whole relationship starts to unravel, and the net result is resistance and frustration generated by the therapist's having stepped into the role of the recently missing part.

Many therapists are quite vulnerable to accepting patient's invitations to step into the missing role. Therapists love to do this. But the trap is set for the subsequent phases which are fraught with often considerable resistance and frustration.

*Contracting to deliver the change.* Some therapist roles include a contract in which the therapist explicitly or implicitly promises to deliver the change. That is fine as long as the contract specifies a change which is deliverable. But if the therapist is unable to deliver, or if the change is not specified, or if the agreed upon change is not a concrete thing which can be delivered, there is trouble.

Sometimes the therapist simply fails to fulfill his part of the contract. He promised to get rid of the back pain or the stutter, and he simply did not deliver the product. He agreed to transform the patient into a hero or a success, and he failed. Many therapists promise to deliver changes which they fail to deliver. When that occurs, it is not surprising that considerable resistance and frustration are generated.

Sometimes therapists get themselves caught in role relationships in which they lead patients to expect changes which are impossible. The patient is led to expect that she will receive endless love. But now she sees that it is not endless at all. The patient is led to expect that he will be the most loved baby, but reality intrudes and confronts him with the fact that he is 38 years old, and there are other real babies who are loved more than he is loved. The patient is promised that lifelong dreams will finally be realized; only much later does it emerge that the lifelong dreams must remain dreams and cannot be realized. The patient is promised perpetual cuteness or strength or charisma or life or security, and then the reality of creeping age and menacing end of one's life erodes the promises. The patient is promised that he will be accepted no matter what, and then the patient faces the inevitable conditions and limitations and disclaimer clauses. The net result is the generation of resistance and frustration.

The therapist explicitly or implicitly promises the patient that he will offer a particular change and then the patient will be happy or a new person or secure or charming. After months of therapy it turns out that the change might have been delivered by the therapist but the consequence never materialized. The patient is no longer afraid of anal intercourse or being alone at night. The patient can now engage in assertive behavior or tell somebody no. The patient can now spend more time with the kids or drive a car by herself. However, the patient is not significantly more happy, nor is the patient a new person or secure and charming. Consequently, there is generated resistance and frustration.

Often, there are hidden conditions in the contract. For example, the patient is led to expect that she will feel secure or happy, or that she will be an assertive person or a less frightened individual. When it slowly dawns on the patient that this is not occurring, the therapist points to a hidden clause which says that the change will occur only if the patient does this or that. She must first embrace the therapist's life philosophy, or she must do everything the therapist says, or she must give up her whole relationship with her parents. Resistance and frustration occur over whether the patient really tried hard enough, or fully embraced the therapist's philosophy, or completely gave up her relationship with her parents.

It is common that the hidden clause is precisely what the therapist tells the patient the consequent change hinges upon. In effect, the therapist promises that if the patient does this, the result will be sheer delight: The back pain will go away, the patient will be happy and healthy, everything will be fine. But to obtain this wonderful change the patient must do much more and much better. This time try to really trust the therapist completely; until now you have only sort of trusted. This time have a giant whopper of an insight; until now you have only had little ones. This time, really do what I have been telling you to do; until now you have only tried half-heartedly. This time be a fine patient and carry out this procedure really well. Resistance and frustration ooze from every pore of such a dialogue. The therapist is scolding the patient for not being a good enough patient, and the implied warning is that if the patient does not do better the contract is voided. This is an excellent way to promote resistance and frustration in the patient. All in all, when the therapist contracts to deliver the change, the scene is built for eventual resistance and frustration.

*Accepting the patient's resistance invitation.* There are at least three kinds of patient roles which are eminently designed to insure plenty of resistance and frustration. One is the relationship-avoiding, person-distancing patient who exists behind a safe moat of separation. Everyone within distance is an intruder to be resisted. Unfortunately, many therapists place themselves in positions in which they are here with such persons who really never wanted to be here in the first place. Unfortunately also, many of these therapists love the challenge of such withdrawn patients who are regarded by such therapists as fair game for therapeutic love, understanding, and friendship or, on the other hand, masterful control, forceful intervention, and therapeutic stratagems. Almost always, the net result is screeching resistance and frustration in the fight between these two armored antagonists. They deserve one another.

Another warring pair is the therapist who simply cannot resist the challenge of the patient who says in effect, "I am going to resist you at every turn. I need someone who enjoys trying to overcome me. This is how I live. Will you accept my invitation? I can resist any therapist on the block." This is war from the very outset. There are always therapists whose nostrils flare and whose muscles are set on edge by such a challenge. Therapy becomes a tug-of-war.

The third kind of invitation to resistance is more subtle. Here is the patient who is caught between two ways of being or two dynamic systems or two operating potentials or however it is described. Perls (1976) is representative of those therapists who are keenly sensitive to such traps, and who refuse to engage in such invitations. If the patient is caught and stuck, if the patient merely rattles back and forth between the two sides, the therapist is in danger of getting trapped in the web of resistance and frustration. For example, the patient is caught between either giving in to others, being painfully dependent and used by others, always failing to meet the expectations of others or, on the other side, being painfully autonomous, removed, cut off, separated, lost. Both sides are painful, and the rattling back and forth is equally painful. The trap is that the therapist is in danger of failing to budge the patient out of the state of being stuck, and failing to derail the patient off of the rattling back and forth between the two horns of the dilemma. The net result is heightened resistance and frustration.

*Erosion of the therapist role.* Resistance and frustration are generated by the gradual erosion of the therapist's roles over the course of two or three decades of practice. Resistance and frustration are a part of a progressive state of failure and depression, worthlessness and "burnout" in the therapist who finds his own therapist role slowly falling apart. Now it is the therapist who contributes to the resistance and frustration.

The therapist gradually reaches an age in which it is getting clearer and clearer that he is not a god in his therapeutic work. The implied promise in his twenties and thirties has gradually become frayed and threadbare in his fifties and sixties. The therapist slowly senses that she is not the great wise woman. Or the therapist slowly awakes to a sense of no longer being a strong and solid base for patients to cling to. Or it dawns on the therapist that he has not been able to bring about major changes in his patients; he is not a therapeutic miracle worker as he had hoped to be. Therapists enact roles for three to five decades, and that is plenty of time for it to become clear that the role one has been playing is tattered and ineffective. The net result is heightened resistance and frustration in the therapist who has engaged in these role relationships for so many years—without much real success.

## CONCLUSION AND INVITATION

Almost without exception, psychotherapies are built upon a conceptual foundation which insures that psychotherapy is predominantly a grand game of role relationships between therapist and patient, conjointly constructed by the two participants. As a result, these psychotherapies are caught in serious and essentially unresolvable problems. One set of problems is that the relationship precludes and delimits the patient's internal relations. A second set consists of the locking in of both therapist and patient into these role relationships. A third set includes the loss and distortion of otherwise useful therapeutic data. A fourth set of problems involves the generation of resistance and frustration. These problems are yoked to the conceptual foundation of virtually all of our psychotherapies.

Humanistic-existential theories of human beings, and the experiential psychotherapy based upon those theories, represent a conceptual foundation which is essentially free of these problems. Experiential psychotherapy is not a grand game of role relationships, nor is it yoked to such serious and unresolvable problems. The invitation is to consider experiential psychotherapy; the invitation to theorists and practitioners is to consider letting go of their therapist-patient assumptions and paradigms and to consider those of an experiential psychotherapy which is essentially free of such role relationships and role relationship problems.

In short, I am inviting psychotherapies to a requiem for therapist-patient role relationships. I know that it is important for many therapists and many patients to play out such role relationships with one another. But this enterprise is not psychotherapy, at least as defined in Chapter 1. It is the carrying out of role relationships. Such an enterprise of mutual role relationships can be improved by more effectively getting the right patient and therapist roles together with one another, and by refining the ways of fulfilling the roles which patients call for and need in their therapists. Then we shall have more effective role relationships.

But for those who are interested in the carrying forward of psycho-therapy, at least as defined in Chapter 1, I suggest that it is time to study the assumptions and conceptual restraints under which virtually all of our psychotherapies stumble along, and to consider alternatives to the paradigms under which we are forced to operate (Chapter 5). I suggest that we can do more than free ourselves of the serious and unresolvable problems described in the present chapter. I suggest that by letting go of the assumptions which force us to use paradigms yoked to such incapacitating problems, we will be free to consider exciting alternatives, and to develop genuine and effective theories of psychotherapeutic prac-tice. Humanistic-existential theories of human beings and their exper-iential psychotherapy comprise but one of these alternatives. The invitation is for theorists and practitioners of psychotherapy to do what experiential patients are invited to do, namely, to disengage from the assumptive system (operating domain) in which they exist and to allow themselves to try out other available systems. The balance of this book stands as an invitation to adopt the phenomenological paradigm of pa-tient and experiential therapist.

# III

*The Basic Practices
of the Experiential
Psychotherapist*

# 7

# *Therapist/Teacher and the Focusing of Attention*

We are now ready to discuss the phenomenological paradigm of the experiential therapist. The basic practices open with the first step (Figure 2.2) in which the patient's attention is focused on a meaningful center and bodily sensations are at least of moderate strength. The purpose of this chapter is to answer three questions: What are the aims and reasons for focusing attention in this way? What are the various kinds of centers into which the patient's attention may be focused? What are the methods and procedures by which the therapist focuses attention so as to reach the first step in the experiential sequence?

## THE AIMS AND REASONS FOR FOCUSING ATTENTION

There are three aims and reasons for focusing attention upon a meaningful center:

(a)  Role-relationship problems are minimized.
(b)  The patient's sense of choice and responsibility is enhanced.
(c)  The subsequent steps of therapeutic work depend upon the proper focusing of attention.

*Minimizing Role-Relationship Problems*

From the beginning of the session, most of the patient's attention is on a meaningful center and not on the therapist. In Figure 5.1, this focal center is indicated as F in the phenomenological paradigm. This means that the patient is not talking to the therapist. The patient is attending to and interacting predominantly with his cancer, or his being the perpetual loser, or the way his father looks at him, or any other meaningful attentional center. Because the preponderance of the patient's attention is not upon the therapist and the interaction with the therapist, and because the preponderance of the therapist's attention is not upon the patient and the interaction with the patient, role-relationship problems are virtually eliminated.

The focusing of attention begins right off. Even in the beginning of the initial session, the patient is shown how to do this. There is no "intake interview," no standard evaluation or assessment. Attention is centered in the first session, the second session, the middle session, and the final session. During the session itself, work proceeds on each step only after the patient's attention is centered.

By beginning with attentional focusing, there are at least two ways in which a patient's tendency or readiness to construct role relationships with the therapist is minimized. One is that the patient is enabled to build that important role relationship with some meaningfully attended-to figure other than the therapist. If the patient is geared to be the bad one who is going to be pushed around by the scolding authority, the patient's attention proceeds to the more veridical center. Soon the patient is attending to his scolding father or to the grandmother with whom he is always the bad one. The important role relationship is constructed around a significant figure in the patient's life—not around the therapist.

The second reason is that the way is now open to undergo experiencing rather than playing out role relationships. If the therapist does not engage in working out role-relationship games, then the patient is free to focus attention upon experiential centers. The patient may be geared to be the bad one who is pushed around by the scolding authority. But the invitation to attend to whatever centers are meaningful may well lead the patient to his girlfriend and to the experiencing of a sense of solid security with her. Consequently, the patient who is geared toward constructing role relationships with the therapist can undergo experiential work without becoming swept into therapist-patient role relationships.

Even with patients who are geared to start therapy by instituting patient-therapist role relationships, the centering of attention generally works. Most patients engage in attention centering quite easily. Patients are not the problem. Therapists are the problem. Therapists have a harder time than patients in giving up role relationships. If a patient is concerned about her increased drinking or her attraction to her brother-in-law or her cancer, she can rather easily place the preponderance of her attention on these centers. She has something important (and easy) to do. But the poor therapist often feels lost. She hesitates to place the preponderance of her attention on the patient's cancer or attraction to the brother-in-law. Instead, therapists often need and want to talk to the patient, to place most of their attention on the patient, to have the goodies of role relationships. For those therapists who are ready to do what patients are typically ready to do, role-relationship problems can be essentially left behind.

In order for the patient to learn how to focus attention, the therapist must provide instructions. The therapist is teacher of the method. The therapist guides and instructs the patient on how to let attention go, how to focus attention properly. When the therapist is teaching the patient how to do this, the therapist is outside, external to the patient. Is the therapist fulfilling some role and co-constructing with the patient some role relationship? Is the therapist who is teacher of the method not just as caught in role-relationship games as other therapists? My answer is no. Here are some reasons:

1) Ordinarily, about 80 to 90 percent of an experiential session is spent with the therapist sharing the patient's attentional center. During all this time, the therapist is internal to the patient, aligned and fused with the patient, and is not the external teacher of the method. The therapist is teacher of the method only a small proportion of the time. This may be somewhat higher in the first few sessions or so, and much less in subsequent sessions. In an ordinary two-hour session, the therapist may be teacher of the method, showing the patient how to center attention, for only 10 or 20 minutes or so. If the providing of instructional guidelines risks role relationships, which I doubt, this occupies a very small proportion of the session. Accordingly, role relationships are minimal, if they exist at all.

2) The instructions are paradoxical. That is, by attending to the instructions, the patient attends less and less to the instructions. To the extent that the patient follows the instructions, the patient will be at-

tending to some center other than the therapist who gives the instructions. Each sentence of the instructions tends to direct the patient's attention away from the instructor. For example, if the therapist says, "Put your attention on your grandfather's face as he lies there in the hospital bed. See the face and describe everything you see. . . .," then a certain measure of attention will be directed onto the grandfather and symmetrically less in relationship to the therapist. In an important sense, the more the patient attends to the words of the teacher, the less the patient attends to the words of the teacher.

3) When the therapist is not aligned with the patient, sharing the patient's attentional center, the therapist is external and, in this location, most of what the therapist does is provide instructions. In being the teacher, the therapist just gives instructions. There is no mutual discussion of the goals of psychotherapy, no exploration of the philosophy of placing attention on a meaningful center, no attempts to convince the patient of the efficacy of doing this. The therapist shows the patient what to do and how to do it; the therapist is a working teacher and not a discursive educator, a coach and not a philosopher, an instructor and not a therapist who engages in mutually constructed role relationships with the patient.

4) The instructions are designed to allow the therapist to join with the patient in attending to the attentional center. While the therapist is giving the instructions, the therapist is attending to the patient, relating to the patient. However, as soon as the therapist finishes giving the instructions, after the last words are spoken, the therapist shifts perspective. The therapist shifts over to being with the patient and attending to whatever the patient is going to attend to. It is as if the therapist moves right over to the patient, and the two of them now look at whatever the patient is attending to.

### Enhancing the Patient's Choice and Responsibility

The patient's sense of having choices, of being the one with the responsibility, of being the person who has both the choice and responsibility—all of those are enhanced in the initial step of placing attention on some meaningful focal center. Perhaps the first point is that the patient really does have the choice and the responsibility to undertake the centering of attention. Literally, the therapist says, "If you want to carry out each step in this method, it is up to you. You are quite free to say no or yes or wait a while. If you are ready to let your attention go to a meaningful center, then we can do this, but the decision, the choice, the responsibility are yours." For each step in the experiential method, proceeding or not proceeding is the choice of the patient (cf. Keen, 1970; Mahrer, 1967a, 1975a; Shaffer, 1978).

This holds even when the therapist's attention is grabbed by something about the patient. For example, the patient may be in a wheelchair, or the patient weighs over 300 pounds, or the patient stutters on almost every word, or the patient is under four feet tall. The patient's entire family may have been killed recently in an airplane accident, or the patient was just told by the fourth oncologist in three months that she has cancer and will likely be dead within a year or so, or the patient has recently been honored with the offer of an unusual position which must be accepted or declined within the next two weeks. None of these matter, for they come from the conspicuous attention of the therapist, not the patient. Even when the therapist's attention is grabbed, the choice of attentional center belongs to the patient. Responsibility for selecting this or that attentional center lies with the patient.

Each step of the experiential method requires that the patient have a full measure of choice and responsibility in undertaking and carrying out the step (Mahrer, 1967a, 1970b, 1978b). Accordingly, each step works only when the patient chooses to do it; reciprocally, undertaking each step contributes to the enhancement of the patient's sense of responsibility.

Enhancing the patient's sense of choice and responsibility is also important because it constitutes one of the goals of experiential therapy as laid down by the humanistic-existential theory of human beings (Mahrer, 1967b, 1978a, 1978b). The very process of experiential therapy provides training and opportunity for the patient to gain enhanced choice and responsibility. Somewhat paradoxically, the patient becomes increasingly able and free to choose a direction of change in which the patient becomes a more responsible person or a less responsible person. But the responsibility for the choice becomes increasingly a part of what the patient becomes as the process itself proceeds along. Perls puts this in a rather blunt form:

> . . . if you want to go crazy, commit suicide, get "turned on," or get an experience that will change your life, that's up to you. I do my thing and you do your thing. Anybody who does not want to take the responsibility for this, please do not attend this seminar. You came here out of your own free will. I don't know how grown up you are, but the essence of a grownup person is to be able to

take responsibility for himself—his thoughts, feelings, and so on. Any objections? (1971, p. 79).

There is yet another way in which ceding choice and responsibility to the patient is important. I submit that this is instrumental in resolving the problem of avoidances or defensive barriers in accord with Kubie's thesis that ". . . every technical advance in psychotherapy has been in the direction of finding ways around . . . defensive barriers" (1943, p. 192). The technical advance is to leave the method in the hands of the patient. Most of what is referred to as defensive barriers washes away when the patient is given full choice and full responsibility. Instead of treating a patient, intervening in the patient, influencing or modifying the patient, and thereby arousing defensive barriers (see Chapter 6), the patient is merely instructed on how to use a method. All real choice and all responsibility lie in the hands of the patient, and the net result is the minimizing of problems of avoidances and defensive barriers.

## Opening the Way for Therapeutic Experiencing

The major aim and reason for focusing attention are to carry on with the work of experiential psychotherapy. As indicated in Figure 2.2, the first step is to attain attention-centered bodily experiencing. Focusing attention is the heart of this first step. Only after this first step is reached can work proceed to the carrying forward of potentials for experiencing, and to experiencing the relationship with deeper potentials. Accordingly, the proper focusing of attention is essential to open the way for therapeutic experiencing (Gendlin, 1969, 1978a).

*The meaning of focused attention.* Attention is focused when two conditions occur. One is that most of the patient's attention is on some center. For example, most of the patient's attention is on that awful sense of never doing things right, or on the way others seem to stay away from her, or on the nasty and cutting remark her friend leveled at her, or on the persistent thoughts about dying, or on the fears behind the gnawing pains in her stomach. Symmetrically, less than half of the patient's attention is on the therapist. Although the patient may be aware of the therapist, the preponderance of attention is on the center of attention and not on the therapist.

The second condition is that physical/bodily sensations are at least moderate. Indeed, the definition of an appropriate center of attention is that it is accompanied by physical/bodily sensations which reach or exceed moderate strength. Clearly this depends upon the specific patient in this specific session, and upon the kinds of physical/bodily sensations which constitute a sort of running baseline for this patient. However, for each patient, an appropriate attentional center is accompanied by such physical/bodily sensations as the following: There is a concrete sensation of warmth or heat in the face; the patient is now on the verge of crying or tears are present; there is a sinking sensation in the chest or pit of the stomach; the whole body feels light or floating; arms or legs start to tremble or feel quite heavy; there is a tension or clutching up in the chest and arms; the head aches or becomes dizzy. These bodily sensations may feel bad and bothersome or pleasant and good. They need not be powerful, but they have to be at least moderate enough to signify that something is indeed happening as the patient attends to that center.

*Opening the way for the therapist to join the patient.* When the patient's attention is predominantly on some center, the therapist is thereby enabled to do the same. If most of the patient's attention is on the nasty and cutting remark made by the friend, so too can the therapist place most of her attention on the nasty and cutting remark. When both patient and therapist have most of their attention on the same meaningful center, the therapist has fulfilled one of the two conditions for joining with or aligning with the patient (the other, sharing the patient's physical/bodily sensations, will be discussed later).

In this sense, it is a tactical step for the patient to attend predominantly to the friend's nasty and cutting remark. It is a tactical step in that the interaction between patient and therapist is reduced enough to allow the therapist to share the patient's attentional center. When both patient and therapist are seeing the friend, are there with the friend, are hearing the nasty and cutting remark, are having the impacts of the nasty and cutting remark, are interacting largely with the friend, are talking to and about the friend and the nasty and cutting remark, then patient and therapist are said to be joined to that extent. This is important, for all the steps of therapeutic work require that the therapist operate from a position of being joined with the patient. This is the phenomenological paradigm as indicated in Figure 5.1.

*Necessary conditions for therapeutic experiencing.* As given in Figure 2.2, there are five steps in the sequence of therapeutic work. Each step involves its own kind of experiencing. In order to reach and carry out each of these steps, three conditions are necessary:

(a)  The patient must have a predominance of attention on some mean-
      ingful center, other than the therapist. At least half of the patient's
      attention should be on that center—the more the better.
(b)  The attentional centering must be accompanied by at least moder-
      ately strong physical/bodily sensations. Something must be going
      on in the body, something linked with that attentional center.
(c)  The therapist must be joined with the patient.

Accordingly, the focusing of attention opens the way for each step and each kind of therapeutic experiencing which comprise the work of experiential psychotherapy.

   *Attention-centering, world construction, and therapeutic experiencing.* The more the patient focuses attention, the more the patient is constructing his own immediate world. As the patient constructs his own world, experiencing carries forward. The opening instructions enable the patient to place a great deal of attention on whatever is accompanied by at least moderately strong bodily sensations, and this enables the patient to build his own personal world, which includes that center of attention accompanied by heightened bodily sensations. Therapeutic experiencing automatically and regularly occurs to the extent that the patient does this (Eigen, 1973; Gendlin, 1961, 1962; Mahrer, 1972, 1978b; Mahrer & Pearson, 1971; Naranjo, 1969).
   In effect, by instructing the patient to let attention go to whatever is accompanied by heightened bodily sensations, we are saying the following to the patient: "Let yourself live in whatever parts of your own personal world are filled with experiencing. Start with whatever centers of attention are accompanied by heightened bodily sensations. As you construct and exist in your own personal world in this way, experiencing will carry forward."
   When the patient constructs his world and starts experiencing in it, the therapist knows what he needs to know in order to carry on the work. First, the therapist knows the nature of the operating and deeper potentials. Second, the therapist knows the nature of the phenomeno-logical world in which this experiencing occurs. And it all starts with the centering of attention. Accordingly, everything we need to carry on therapeutic work occurs to the extent that the patient directs more and

more attention toward centers which are accompanied by heightened bodily sensations. As the patient lets attention go to attentional centers that are accompanied by heightened bodily sensations, the patient exists more and more in a world of his own personal construction, and the consequence is the carrying forward of experiencing. This is how and why the centering of attention opens the way for therapeutic experiencing.

What are the aims and reasons for focusing the patient's attention? There are three:

(a)  When the patient's attention is on meaningful centers, and not on the therapist, there is a minimizing of patient-therapist role relationships and the problems yoked to those role relationships.
(b)  There is an enhancement of the patient's sense of personal choice and responsibility. The instructions and guidelines for focusing attention offer the patient a full measure of choice and responsibility. If the patient chooses to undertake the procedure, the very process of focusing attention enhances the patient's sense of choice and responsibility.
(c)  Focusing attention opens the way for therapeutic experiencing. To the extent that attention is focused upon a meaningful center, accompanied with heightened bodily sensations, experiencing is carried forward. When attention is focused upon a meaningful center, the therapist is enabled to join with the patient.

All subsequent steps of the experiential process require that the therapist be joined with the patient whose attention is centered and in whom experiencing is occurring. Accordingly, it is exceedingly important that therapy opens with the proper focusing of the patient's attention.

## THE NATURE OF EXPERIENTIAL
## CENTERS OF ATTENTION

In order to carry forward experiencing, what are the more effective attentional centers? What may the patient attend to in order to maximize experiencing?

We have excluded the interactional relationship with the therapist. As discussed in Chapters 5 and 6, when the patient attends to the therapist and talks predominantly with the therapist about something, we are plunged into role relationships and the serious problems coupled with such role relationships. Furthermore, the relationship with the therapist does not open the way for therapeutic experiencing. If we exclude those experiencings which can occur in relationships with the therapist, we are on somewhat uncharted and unexplored territory.

Our question emphasizes that whatever the patient attends to is to maximize the patient's own experiencings. This means that we have also excluded attentional centers which provide the kinds of data which many therapists want for themselves in order to know or understand the patient. In many therapies, the patient is to attend to developmental history, to case material, to anamnesic data, to biographical information. Or the patient is to talk about feelings and emotions, or what is occurring in the patient's current life, or what the patient wants from therapy, or ongoing stresses and difficulties, or dozens of other topics which provide the therapist with the kinds of data many external therapists wish to have about the patient. If we are looking for attentional centers with a high experiential yield, none of these topics will do.

Even when the patient is asked to talk about the problem or trouble, experiencing is seldom carried forward in any systematic way. The technical question here is this: How may the patient attend to "the problem" so as to maximize the carrying forward of experiencing? All too frequently, talking about the problem is accompanied by truncated experiencing. The patient identifies her problem as being unsure whether or not to remain with her husband, or as being depressed and moody much of the time. Yet, whatever words are used to define the problem, the accompanying experiencing process is typically low. We have yet to devise a way in which the patient identifies the problem so that experiencing is systematically carried forward. A second consideration is that the patient's identifying of the problem occupies a tiny proportion of what occurs in most psychotherapy. After the patient names something as the trouble or the difficulty, attention goes to other topics. If our aim is to find something which opens the way for experiencing, identifying and talking about the problem do not seem to be the answer.

Nor is experiencing carried forward in any effective way by means of the external therapist's clinical intuitiveness, sophistication, sensitivity, expertise, or ability to be loving, caring, understanding, kindly, warm, and so on. No matter how prized the characteristics of the therapist are, it does not follow that the patient's experiencing will thereby be carried forward. How, then, may the patient carry forward experiencing so as to reach the aims and objectives described earlier?

The answer is to guide the patient's attention into topics which have a high experiential yield. If the patient allows most of his attention to go to these topics, the likelihood is that experiencing will be carried forward. If the patient is ready and willing to place most of his attention on some center, and to do so in such a way that bodily sensations will be at least moderate, I propose seven topics which work. I invite the reader to try it out. Let your attention go to each of the topics described below. If you are willing to attend fully, and with heightened bodily sensations, then the chances are quite high that you will start to experience a sense of loneliness or controlling others or loving intimacy, or whatever experiencing is within you, right now, as you begin to exist in the phenomenological world encompassing the attentional center.

## Immediately Compelling Attentional Centers

Many patients will begin a session with attention already centered upon something which is accompanied by heightened experiencing. They are ready. All the therapist has to do is not interfere. Let the patient attend to whatever is already there. Sometimes it may be necessary to help the patient a bit by enabling the patient to put attention on it and not on the therapist, to allow bodily sensations to be strong, to go ahead no matter what. The therapist may simply say, for example:

T: Go ahead. If there is something right now, just go ahead. Let your attention go to whatever it is. Just let yourself go. Let anything happen in your body. Let the feelings happen. Whatever it is, see it. Talk about it. Talk to it. Let it happen.

If the patient is ready, then the patient may very well go right to whatever it is so that experiencing starts to occur right away. This happens in the first session or in the tenth or fiftieth session:

Pt: (Starts to cry and to breathe rapidly.) I just feel like crying. . . . I don't know. . . . (Sobbing.) Nothing is going right. Everything seems all wrong. . . .
Pt: Sometimes I think that I am crazy. Or if I don't fight against it I

just . . . my whole life is screwed up. I want to just give up, but I'm scared. . . . Something is wrong with me. Something has always been wrong. I don't know what it is. (He is talking in a loud voice, shaking and trembling.)

Pt: I am a good wife. I've been married for 22 years. But I am thinking more and more about what a waste. . . . My mother died a couple of months ago. I don't think I got over it. . . . All I think about is dying . . . that's all that's on my mind. (She starts to cry.) . . . I want to die! I don't want to live anymore! What's the use!

Quite often, there is something available, some center on which attention can focus so that experiencing starts to occur. Simply enable the patient to focus attention upon it. In the first few sessions, it is relatively easy. Do not get in the way. The patient who is starting the first few sessions or so generally has something on her mind, something pressing. The question is what is on the patient's mind, and the method is that of showing the patient how to go to whatever it is right away. However, the story is different in later sessions. While most patients, in the initial sessions, are already attending to some compelling attentional center, generally that does not seem to hold in later sessions. It takes some explicit reminders to attend to whatever may already be there.

T: OK. Now something may be there already. Something there in your mind. Something ready for you to attend to or to be. Just take five or ten seconds and let yourself float. See. Just wait and look. Is there something?
Pt: (Pause.) No . . . well I think of just letting myself. . . . Yes! I am sitting last night at Wallers' and they are leaving in a couple of days for Australia. I know that I won't see them again, and I know that I am glad to see them go because I can't ever cope. He is a bully and she is blind to him. I am sitting here with this damned smile plastered all over my face! God! I hate this! I hate being a damned smiling nothing. I want to tell you both what I think of you but no, not me! Good old Gloria just sits here. See my smile? I am nice, right? See my smile all over my lying face. . . . I don't have the guts to be honest with you, so I am glad that you are getting the hell out of the country. . . !

Sometimes, after a number of sessions, what is compelling is a feeling which has to do with therapy itself, with dashed hopes or a sense of depression or failure:

Pt: When will this be over? I've been coming here for almost two years. Nothing's happening. . . . I'm no different than when I started.

Pt: I don't know . . . I don't think this is going to work . . . I've been thinking that maybe . . . maybe I should stop . . . I'm not getting any better.

Pt: (Long pause.) My life is worse now than when I started. (Long pause.) I don't think I want to have any more therapy . . . nothing is any better.

Typically these words are accompanied with anger, depression, hurt and failure. Experiencing is already heightened.

Give the patient an opportunity to attend to whatever is there right now. Experiencing is ready to occur. Generally, it takes relatively little work to find these immediately compelling attentional centers. Others require more guided searching by patient and therapist. Each of the following topics calls for some explicit instructions and some explicit work to get experiencing going.

## The Greatest Fears About Oneself

There is a category of fears which comes from the most personal core of the individual. When attention goes to these greatest fears about oneself, experiencing pours forth (cf. Rose, 1976; Shorr, 1972, 1974). Typically these fears have characteristics such as the following:

(a) The fear refers to something deeply ingrained into the very heart and core of the patient. It is a part of one's central character from the very beginning of life. The patient has been this way, or has sensed being this way, throughout his entire life.
(b) It is so deeply rooted that it is absolutely immutable. The patient may learn to live with it or cope with it, but it will never go away. It is too deeply ingrained, too much a part of the way the patient really is. Therapy will never affect it.
(c) Often the fear takes the form of some unavoidable destiny, an inner

certainty that the patient will end up in some way, an inflexible
fate waiting to occur. Now, in one's adult life, that deepest fear
is moving inexorably toward the fixed destiny (Binswanger,
1967).

(d)  There is an utter truth to the fear. The patient really is that way.
No matter how one tries to hide it or how successful one is in
denying it, it is always the lingering truth about the way one is
and has always been.

Experiencing occurs as the patient attends to the greatest fear of this
nature:

Pt: I am a little boy. I don't really belong in the adult world. I'm not
ready. I'll never be ready. I was always behind. Always . . . I don't
fit. It's like something is missing in me. Having a job scares me. Being
married and having children scares me. Sex scares me. I feel like a
little boy. . . .

Pt: I don't know what I am. It's getting worse lately. . . . I just fit in to
what they want from me. I don't know . . . what I am. . . . Sometimes
I think that I'm no one at all. I feel like a shadow . . . like I am already
dead and nothing. I excuse myself for . . . I'm not a person.

Pt: There's no place for me. Nothing seems right. Maybe I've been here
before. I don't know. It isn't really for me. The place is never quite
right. I search for the place. I have no roots, no home. I don't know
what I am. . . .

Pt: Something's there. In me. Always. A thing. Like an inertia. It won't
let anything happen. Pulls me back. There's something that keeps me
in place. . . .

Pt: I am going to kill myself. Sooner or later. There is no escaping
that. . . . Why not (blows air, as if "peugh")? . . . It's going to happen. Just a matter of time.

Pt: I am 36. I study my body. Hours. I am aging. My skin. It is going
to age. I look at it and see it aging. I study it carefully. I spend hours
looking at the wrinkles and the creases. Sometimes I think of taking
a razor to my wrists. I cannot get older. Do you know what I mean?

I must do something, anything, to stop it. I'll never be an old lady. I'd rather die! I think for hours about how I can die and be buried and never rot. That is the worst hell for me. The idea of rotting. I can't abide rotting in the ground. That drives me wild! I'll do anything. . . .

When most of the patient's attention goes to the accurate identifying of this deep-seated, lifelong fear about oneself, experiencing starts to carry forward.

*The worst feeling.* One way of letting attention go to a part of the deep-seated lifelong fear about oneself is to frame out the nature of the worst feeling: "In your life today, what is the worst feeling that grips you? Try to let yourself have that same worst feeling, the one that is most painful, the one that tears you apart the most, the one you never want to have again. Of all the bad feelings, this is the worst. It may be one of feeling absolutely terrified, terribly chaotic and mixed up, or like everything is numb and unreal, or being thoroughly helpless. Try to let it come over you now. Give in to it a little so that it is here again." Here are some examples of what patients say when they use this way of attending to the worst feeling so as to reach a state of heightened experiencing:

Pt: There is nothing of mine. Nothing I got. Nothing to me. I have nothing of my own. . . . I am lonely. Like I am nothing . . . I own nothing. It's like I fill a little space and I don't make any real difference to anyone. People like me . . . but I'm not really anything. Like there's some reason why I have nothing of my own.

Pt: I am afraid. . . . I think something's happening to me. . . . When I talk to people, I feel like I'm right on the verge of doing something crazy, and I feel trapped. I got to get away. They are going to get too close and hurt me. I start to shake and shake inside. I never screamed. I feel like hurting someone or maybe I am going to go crazy or run away. But it is all inside and I feel this.

In order to open the way for experiencing, useful "worst feelings" are those in which the patient senses the imminence of falling apart. Of one's intact self crumbling and caving in. Existentialists find this state in a particular kind of awful anxiety: ". . . Dasein is anxious in the face of the collapse of its world, the gradual dissolution into insignificance of the totality of its involvements. . . . Those ways in which Dasein had previously grasped itself, even taken itself for granted, no longer make sense" (Fischer, 1970, p. 95). This brings us to the next way of getting at the greatest fears.

*Craziness.* A large proportion of patients have at least a speaking acquaintance with states in which they dip into craziness. They know their own personal lunacy or derangement or psychosis. "Let your attention go to the way you get when you become a little crazy, when you become like a maniac, a real psychotic. What are the signs that you have something in you that is crazy? What is it like when you start to lose your mind? How do you get? What is it like? It might take you over for a few minutes, or much longer. Or it might just come very close. There are times when you know that there is something really wrong with you, that there is a craziness in you. What are those times?" The more a patient allows himself to attend to this, the more experiencing carries forward.

Sometimes the patient will describe a kind of crazy state which occurs in the current life:

Pt: Well, it happens sometimes when I am listening to someone talk to me. I listen and then . . . like I don't really listen and, and then something happens. I . . . this is hard to say. I see their face like it is putty or something, and the words don't make sense anymore. I see them like that and I hear funny. I see insects and bugs and worms in the head. But I really see them! There they are . . . they are moving and slimy and dozens of them. The words just fade out and act like sounds. Words. But I don't know what is there 'cause I don't even know who is there. It is weird. . . . Something happens to me. I say nothing. . . . I know that something is wrong.

Pt: I catch myself sometimes. Yes, it's scary. I think that . . . like being crazy. Well, I am reading or something. Maybe eating alone. In a restaurant or at home. I almost think . . . I'll just stay like this. Nothing will happen. Like stopping. Staying there. Not doing anything. Like becoming frozen or like concrete or something. I have no thoughts. Just stay . . . not move. It feels like it, it's not bad. Just . . . like everything stops. It shuts down and I stay here sitting and not listening or moving ever again. There is something peaceful about it. Maybe like dying. . . .

Sometimes patients will describe incidents or states which occurred a few years ago, or when they were children. In any case, when attention goes to such centers of attention, experiencing carries forward.

*The worst behavior.* Another way of getting at these deep-seated fears is to attend to those behaviors about which the patient feels the worst. "Let your attention go to something you do that bothers you the most, something you do that when you think about it, when you look at it, you feel terrified, scared to death, terrible! You shouldn't do it. Doing it makes you feel rotten, maybe afterwards. It is something you do or some way you get when things are too much for you. Maybe others know about it and maybe they don't. But you do it!"

Pt: Right off I am thinking that . . . I do mean things to my son. He is six. I twist his leg. So it hurts him. I twist his leg almost off. I feel like something comes over me when he is bad. I go into his room and I grab his leg or his arm, and I twist it, I make welts on his skin. I am afraid that I might kill him. He hates me. He is scared of me. I bruise him.

Pt: My daughter is 13. She's very ripe for her age . . . she's mature all right. My old lady knows about this. I have had Kelly and maybe five or ten of her girlfriends. Jesus I shouldn't do that. I told the priest about it, and I don't know what comes over me. They are delicious, they are. Round and curvy, and . . . oh, Lord, I think sometimes I'll hang myself before I'll ever get over it. No one can come over to our house anymore. They want to kill me, they do. The parents. I ain't got anyone pregnant . . . but I know that I want to go to some other place where they don't know me and have me some of them little girls, young and eager. I am so mixed up about this. It's like the devil gets into me, and I think the parents are going to lynch me. I'd give anything . . . but then again I get so damned excited like there's nothing else on my mind. Those little ones, oh those little asses. Oh my God!

*The secret.* The greatest fears about oneself can be illuminated through carefully guarded secrets. "Let your attention go to the secrets about you, the things about you that no one knows. No one knows the real truth, not your family, not your friends. Only you. It may be the truth behind the lie about you. The lie you have kept for so many years. No one really knows what really happened. No one really knows that you were the one. No one knows the secret thing you do even now. You hide it from everybody. If they found out . . . oh, it would be awful . . . your secret . . . for maybe years and years."

Pt: (Long sigh.) I don't know what's stranger. I was in therapy for two years and I never . . . it never came up . . . I (laughs hard) . . . I can't say it. Wait! OK. Here is confession! Well, I have a closet in my office. There is a mechanical pencil in it. They don't even make them like that anymore. You see . . . I am a kleptomaniac. Whew! (Long sigh.) I have been stealing things since I was 12! I have a safe in my closet. Just an old safe. I moved it around. I have things in them . . . (screeching laughter).

Pt: Ummm. I hear voices. . . . (Gasps.) I know how that sounds! I hear two voices, one older woman and a younger woman. I have been hearing them for almost three years. I have no idea when it started. They cackle and they talk to me. I know that sounds crazy, but I hear them! I really hear them! They are here now, screeching at me! (He breaks into sobs.)

*Changes in Oneself and One's World*

Experiencing is carried forward when the patient's attention goes to changes which are taking place in the current life. "Let your attention go to changes which are happening. Changes in you and the way you are, the way you feel lately, the way you respond to things. There may be changes that you are noticing inside your body, things changing inside. There may be changes in the way you feel and the way you think. You may be doing something new now, or doing it much more lately, or you may be doing something a lot less. You may notice changes in the way you are with close friends or other people, or the way others seem to be with you, the way they treat you and react to you. Some of these changes may be very bothersome, scary maybe. And some might be delightful, really pleasing. Some might be little ones, you would hardly notice. Others might be big changes, really large changes in you and your life lately." When the patient's attention goes to these, here are some examples of statements accompanied by the carrying forward of experiencing:

Pt: I don't know what's doing it to me. I'm not nice anymore! I wonder why . . . I don't smile like I used to. And I don't spend that much time with my friends. Friends! I don't have as many friends anymore. I stay at home most of the time now and . . . I am starting to feel annoyed inside. Sometimes I think after that I should . . . I think mean things! Vicious . . .

Pt: When I walk along, I think that I am me, in this body. But it all seems strange. Like who am I? What am I doing, being this person, in this body? Walking along here . . . I look in the mirror . . . maybe the last couple of weeks, and I get nervous. I look at my body, my shoulders and legs and everywhere, and I . . . well, it doesn't seem to belong to me!

Pt: I listen. I mean, I shut up now. How to say? It's strange. I look into their eyes now. I don't think I ever realized. I never really listened to someone. I can't say. It's different. I see that I love talking to, no, listening to, someone talk. I look at them when they talk. Betty told me about her vacation, and she said that I was the only one who . . . why, I felt great. I was really wanting to know. Like I'm being closer. It's so . . . it's so different.

Pt: I am more consistent with the feelings. The ones I have. I am being more consistent. I say things now, and what I say is more consistent with what I . . . well I feel things. Like if I don't agree, if I disagree with something that someone says, well now I can. (Laughs.) I level more. It is fine too! I can level more when I don't agree, when I really disagree! I am truer. I say things that are truer. That's it!

Pt: (Quite upset and starting to cry.) I don't know. Things are just getting out of hand. Piling up. I can't get anything done. It's like the world is getting too much for me. I can't keep up with anything anymore. It seems that people are talking faster and everything is getting speeded up. Noises are getting faster and louder. I think I am getting something wrong with me!

## Physical/Bodily Phenomena

Attention may be directed toward the body so that experiencing starts to carry forward. These phenomena include the more physical aspects of the body, emotional and feeling states which are present, and other phenomena taking place inside the body. "Let your attention go to your body, to good things or bad things that are happening there, things that pull your attention, that make you feel good or bad. Does it feel like something is happening in your body? Is something growing or changing inside? Are there feelings that are there? Is there something very precious and wonderful in the body? Are there thoughts or voices inside the head? Just let your attention go to your body, to things happening inside." When sufficient attention pours onto physical/bodily phenomena, experiencing carries forward.

Pt: My mind is never off of the cancer. (Pause.) Sometimes when I wake up, it's like I don't remember maybe for a minute or so. Then it comes back to me. I always feel like it yells at me. I'm bad. I'm bad . . . I'm supposed to feel bad. I am bad somehow. If it isn't there I won't remember. It's like a hideous guard or something, a devil. It hates me. It screams at me that I am bad. I don't think I'll ever get rid of it. My life is over. . . .

Pt: The sweating again. It's awful. Like a big red nose or something. I figure out afterward that I am uncomfortable. Sometimes I try to exert my will, if I have any left. I try to not let the sweating get bad. But it is now getting over my face too. It's worse, I think. Now I just stand there and . . . all I can think of is getting away, getting home, and taking off all my clothes and lying on the bed, and then sometimes it stops. The sweating, oh that damn awful sweating!

Pt: There is this thing. In my head. Again. Always there. I feel like it's alive . . . a sort of moving mass of stuff. Like a phantom inside my head. . . . It reacts to things. It's like God. It has a distinct mind of its own and it sometimes wants to hurt me. It makes noises like little purrings or gurglings. If I turn my head to the side, it is heavier on the left side. I don't know whether it is a friend or if it's something to plague me.

### Significant Figures and Objects

Experiencing carries forward when the patient's attention is focused on significant persons and significant objects. Many patients have one or two such figures or objects. The key is showing the patient how to locate the right one.

*The lifelong significant other.* Here is that person who is at the very center of one's world, who has always been the key figure. "Let your attention go to someone who has always been the central one in your life. A father or mother or brother or sister or grandparent or someone. There are always strong feelings about that person. You hate them or love them or need them or struggle to please them. Your whole world is around them. They affect you like no one else. That person may still be living, or maybe died some time ago. Let that person fill your mind."

Pt: I don't know why you hate me! I have always been different because of you. I think I should have killed you! Yes! I should have taken a knife to you. I got married and I got divorced because of you. I hate you! There's no pleasing you at all. I could never do what you want. I could never please you. I spend ten years in a marriage trying to be the nice girl I thought you wanted me to be! What a joke! What a terrible joke. You don't really care, do you?

Pt: My grandfather died, and I never got to say goodbye. I didn't even know. They never told me. He was the only one who listened to me and he liked me. No one in the family . . . (Crying.) You used to tell me stories and you loved me! (More tears.) You shouldn't have died. . . . Why did you die? Why?

*Significant childhood objects.* "There were very special things when you were a child. Just let your attention go to them. Special things. Your things. Things you treasured maybe, or things that made you have feelings. A picture or a gift or something in your room, or things you collected, hidden things."

Pt: I had a gold ball. Metal. Used to keep it in my pocket. Never told anyone about it. I used to touch it all the time. . . . I don't know what happened to it! . . . For years it was . . . I kept it secret. It was little but it fit into my hand. Always kept it in my left pocket. I hid it under my pillow all the time, and I looked at it all the time. It was magic. It could make everything all right. It's the only thing that I ever had.

Pt: There was a picture in my room. My sister broke the glass. A little picture of a woman in a gown. Sort of shadowy. She was beautiful. I think I was in love with her all my life. I don't know where it came from. She didn't look anything like my mother or my aunts. She was slender and so lovely. Each lover sort of reminded me of her. Don was built like her. I had that picture until I went to college. But I always think of her. . . .

*Current significant figures and objects.* "Let your attention go to those special people in your life today. Or things, objects. They are special. When you let your attention go to them, something happens. Feelings start up in you. It happens when you look directly at your wife or your father-in-law or your child or the boat you are building or the gun you just bought." In each of the following, experiencing moves ahead as the patient attends to this figure or object:

Pt: I am looking at Alex (*her five-year-old son*). Poor little guy . . . I shouldn't have kept him. I shouldn't have had him. Jack hates him (*Jack is the man with whom she is living*) and I am afraid that I do too. He is an unhappy child already. I don't want him. If I were really honest . . . well . . . I am afraid that I am stuck with him. Poor little bugger. He really doesn't have a chance. I sometimes think of someone telling me that something awful has happened to him. . . .

Pt: There is this girl next door. I can't get her out of my mind. God, there is something about her. She is so appealing to me. I'm old enough to be her father, but her body is so great. I masturbate all the time about her. I think of her at night when I am in bed. All the time. I shouldn't be thinking about her but I can't get her out of my mind. Her body drives me wild. I will never ever do anything of course. Never. Oh that would be awful. . . .

Pt: I keep a gun. . . . I don't think I'll ever use it. . . . I play with it all the time. It is hidden. (Long sigh.) At night I take walks downtown. With it. Some day I might even . . . I walk around with it, and I have it handy. I keep it. I will never use it. I will never take it out. But I have to go on the walks. At night. I always pretend . . .

## Moments of Heightened Feelings

Experiencing can carry forward by letting attention go to those moments when feelings rose up. Here is a rather full set of instructions for letting attention go to such moments:

T: Let your attention go to moments when feelings in you were quite strong. These are the moments when your whole body got weak and you were about to collapse, or you had a chill down your back, or your throat got tight and you could hardly talk. The feeling in you might have been bad. You felt scared or suffocated or jealous or terribly hurt. Or the feeling was really good, like giddy or very pleased and happy or on top of the world.

The feeling was strong, and it probably lasted just a short time, like a few seconds or so when it reached a peak. Sometimes it could have showed to others, like when you screamed or laughed or your face got red. Other times it was all inside, and only you knew, like suddenly feeling very sexy inside, or your stomach clutched up.

It happened in some situation, some place, when someone did something or something almost happened or started to happen. It may have been when you were crossing the street and the car almost hit you, or you were talking with someone and certain words that they said started feelings in you. But they were very special moments that happened in some situation.

Some of these moments happened very recently. Just a day or so ago. But others may come to mind, times from long ago when the feeling was very strong in you, very strong. It may have happened several years ago, or even when you were little, long ago. It may have happened in a dream you had recently, or one that repeats itself every so often. Maybe it is a moment in a scene that is going to happen in a few weeks or years from now. But in any case, it is a moment when the feeling is very strong. Even for a few seconds or so, very strong.

It is important to include both good and bad feelings. Accordingly, going to moments of joy and happiness is useful, and, for some patients some of the time, locating the right attentional center is accompanied with laughing and smiling and generally good humor. In this sense, therapists lose a whole domain of useful data when they regard starting with good feelings as improper therapeutic material, masking of some more legitimate material, evidence of a "flight into health," or resistance to the therapeutic process. Most of the moments are filled with bad feelings. But those which are filled with good feelings are also quite useful in the carrying forward of experiencing.

Feelings of both kinds occur in dreams, and dreams are regarded, in experiential therapy, as instances in which heightened feelings occur in special moments (Mahrer, 1966, 1971, 1975a). Indeed, dreams are regarded as quite precious starting material. The actual work with dreams is outside the scope of this book. But dreams are warmly invited as extremely important centers of attention, and they fall under the topic of moments of heightened feeling.

Here are examples of such moments wherein experiencing is carried forward:

Pt: The phone rang. Sallie and I were in bed, just talking. And it rang. I didn't want to answer it. I got scared. I thought . . . maybe something from . . . I thought that something bad had happened! Like some . . . I know I didn't want to answer it. . . . It was bad!

Pt: Jack saw me in the hall. He told me that he is going to have to have his eye taken out. He and his wife have been having a bad time. She's been giving him a hard time. Jack doesn't do anything bad. He never really had a break. He looked at me and there were tears in . . . (He puts his hand to his face and cries.)

Pt: I am maybe six. I am sitting on the front porch and my Mom ain't home. I don't know where she was. My Dad lived somewhere far away, across town. My Mom ain't home, and I felt crazy. I thought the whole place was going to open up and I'd fall inside, into some cave or something. I had no place to go and . . . it's like she never really wanted me, and I don't know why she had me at all. I didn't want to be with her. I almost didn't want her home.

Pt: I am at home. Uh, at home. Something about the floor and the dishes. I don't want to start them. I feel pushed. By Manny . . . like he expects me to do them. Something bad. To do all the housework. Can't remember exactly. I didn't want to . . .

*Attentional Centers Disclosed by the Work of Previous Sessions*

Each session begins with the patient's attention going to one or more of these six areas or topics. As a group, they cover just about all the general areas or topics where the patient's attention can go so that experiencing can move ahead. But the therapist has a gold mine of additional data. During the course of a session, the therapist notes those moments when the patient's level of experiencing reaches a peak. Once or twice or maybe six or eight times during the session there is a rising up of the experiential level. These are the moments which are described in the therapist's ongoing notes (see Chapter 3). Accordingly, from the previous sessions, the therapist can provide the patient with very important examples of each of the six categories given above. The examples tell as much as was learned in the previous sessions about the nature of the experiencing and about the nature of the scene in which it occurred. Let us suppose that the therapist is sketching out the greatest fears the patient may have about himself. From a few previous sessions, a very particular fear had been illuminated, one which is very powerful and very long-term. The therapist includes it as a possible attentional center:

T: . . . For example, it may be that terror of missing something, like not having what it takes to be one of them. The other kids are playing together in the snow and you start to feel . . . different, like different than all of them, like there is something missing in you . . .

From previous sessions, the therapist and patient may have found some specific kind of change in the patient or in the patient's world, one which occurred with strong experiencing during the previous sessions:

T: . . . With the family. They are getting mad at you 'cause you are pulling away from them. You don't join them at grandma's on Sunday afternoon, and they are talking about you. Something is starting inside—"I don't give a damn about them!"—and they are going to make you pay for that . . .

The specific example may fall under the class of physical/bodily phenomena, or significant figures and objects, or moments of heightened feelings. During the prior sessions, experiencing may have peaked when some recent moment of heightened feeling was present:

T: . . . There may be a recent one, like the kind of lusty wildness, just crazy, and it happens when you're lying in bed at night, just starting to masturbate, and then you see her, clearly . . . she is about 50, lots of wild hair, made up, painted, hard stomach, long slender muscular legs, full breasts . . . yes . . . and she has the body and the look . . . she is going to drive you wild the whole night . . .

Or the moment of heightened feeling may have occurred when the patient was a child. From a previous session the therapist knows something about the nature of the experiencing and the situational context:

T: . . . or, for example, you are a little girl, and you are being scolded by grandmother. She heard you talking to your friend, the squirrel. About Daddy. And it starts to happen here. The giving in, the giving up of fighting. It starts to happen, and you feel it.

T: . . . or there is something that just wants to scream "leave me alone . . . get off my back! . . . I've had it . . . get away from me. Stop pushing me!" And it has something to do with the whole family, and you are three or four, somewhere. A gathering, and someone wanted to get you into something. Lots of people. All you are aware of is the pressure around you, and the bodies and the voices all vague.

T: Remember when you are very little, and in bed. Not in your house. And the main thing is how wonderful it feels. You talk to her about your sister and your toe and what it feels like to be holding her. You feel wonderful holding her and pushing way into her belly, and having her arms around you. So nice and so secure. Somewhere, hard to say, and with someone, a big woman, she doesn't say much. But it feels, oh, so good. You don't know who she is—an aunt maybe, or a good friend maybe, or a neighbor, or someone.

In the beginning of each session, the patient's attention goes to some center. By studying the work of experiential therapists, we can propose a number of areas or topics which seem to have a rich experiential yield. The above seven areas or topics are one way of describing the nature of the experiential centers of attention. If we ask, "In the beginning of the session, where or on what is the patient's attention to be focused?" our answer is given in these seven areas or topics.

## HOW TO FOCUS ATTENTION

The therapist shows the patient how to focus attention into one or more of the above areas or topics so that most of the patient's attention is poured onto the focal center, so that accompanying bodily sensations are at least of moderate strength, and so that the level of experiencing rises. The purpose of this section is to show how the therapist actually does all this.

## Therapist as Teacher of the Method

As the teacher of the method, the therapist must be skilled in showing the patient how to deploy more and more attention into the various areas or topics, how and when to undertake this step, how to negotiate the details from the beginning to that point where attention is focused, body sensations are occurring, and experiencing is ongoing. As teacher of the method, the therapist should be very competent, an expert. How does the therapist gain this expertise? I believe that there are two avenues for acquiring this skill:

One is that the therapist should use the method herself. She should become quite competent in carrying out the instructions which she is asking the patient to carry out (Jourard, 1976; Jung, 1933; Mahrer, 1975a, 1978e). This can be accomplished by being a patient herself in experiential psychotherapy, by undergoing experiential self-change, and by undertaking special training programs. In these programs the therapist takes each of the attentional topics described above, and practices letting attention go to each kind of center so that most of her attention is there, so that at least moderate bodily sensations start to occur, and so that experiencing starts to carry forward. One by one, the therapist uses each of the above topics until she has gained genuine expertise in focusing attention. I suggest a minimum of approximately 50 hours of such training, under the supervision of an expert in this procedure, in order to acquire the requisite level of competence.

The second avenue for acquiring this skill is by observing and listening to experts using the method, and by supervised use of the method in her own work with patients. I suggest a minimum of approximately 50 hours of observing and listening, and approximately 100 hours of supervised practice in this skill.

## The First Step of Each Session

Every session starts by inviting the patient to allow attention to go to some appropriate center. In effect, the instructions are always the same. Here is a modest invitation for the patient who has had many sessions:

T: OK . . . now let your attention go to whatever is there. Something
you fear, an awful feeling, something that's changing, something in
the body, someone who is just there, some moment when feelings
rose up, something on your mind . . . and let yourself feel. Let feelings happen in your body. Good feelings happen in your body. Good
feelings or bad feelings. Just let them happen more and more.

After some sessions, the patient learns how to start right out. For a
few minutes, he chats with you until he gets himself settled in the chair.
Then he closes his eyes and goes right to attentional centers. The important point is that we start the centering of attention at the beginning
of each session. Once the patient is settled in the chair with eyes closed,
the therapist gives the instructions. Chit-chat is over, and work begins.

*Each session starts fresh.* From the work done in the first session, the
therapist's notes will have a few words about an experiencing or two,
and the context in which the experiencing occurred. The second session
just might start out from there. After 50 sessions, the therapist's notes
will have a number of these potential starting places. Yet the second
session and the fifty-first session start fresh. The patient is quite free to
attend to a current center, an old one, a new one. Each session starts
fresh in terms of the nature of the attentional center.

Almost always, the specific nature of the attentional center will change
from session to session, and over the course of sessions. One reason is
that therapeutic work over one or several sessions will open up new
attentional centers linked to other potentials for experiencing. There may
be some sort of general theme to a series of attentional centers, but their
nature should change with therapeutic work. A patient may start most
sessions by attending to competitors or early memories around father
or sexual events or something happening in the body. But therapeutic
work will almost always insure that the specific nature of the center will
change. A second reason for changes in the specific focal centers is that
patients learn how to proceed to more useful attentional centers accompanied with stronger bodily sensations and with deeper, and perhaps
stronger, experiencing. As patients undergo change and as they learn
the method, the attentional centers will change. Third, the bases for the
initial attentional centers generally wash away after a number of sessions. After a few sessions, patients are not so involved in establishing
patient-therapist role relationships, and what they attend to will automatically change. For at least these reasons, it is quite understandable

that the nature of the attentional center will change over the course of sessions. Indeed, it is especially interesting to note the regularity with which initial and early attentional centers are replaced with others as therapeutic work proceeds from session to session.

In experiential therapy, the important part of attentional centers is the nature of the experiencing which carries forward. Because we use the attentional centers to carry forward experiencing, and because we have several reasons for expecting the early attentional centers to be replaced by more useful and changing ones, we do not assess therapeutic change by means of the initial attentional centers. Yet that is what some other approaches study in relation to outcome (cf. Chapter 1). If the patient was concerned initially about being overweight or unsatisfied at work, then progress and outcome typically are assessed later by studying the patient's weight change or current state of work satisfaction. In experiential therapy, all the initial attentional centers mean is that they are the attentional centers in the first few sessions. That is all. But in other approaches, they are the baselines against which outcome, change, and progress are to be gauged. There are sober therapeutic and research consequences in the way you view and use the attentional centers in the first few sessions and in the allowing of each session to begin fresh.

*The initial session.* Almost always, some sort of compelling attentional center is available in the first session. In this sense, the initial session is easy. The patient already is concerned about something. The therapist's task is to show the patient how to attend to whatever it is, how to use that material so as to allow experiencing to carry forward. Accordingly, instructions in the first few sessions generally emphasize this particular way of attending to the material, which typically is right there. Here are two examples:

T: Something is there. Something is there now. There is something on your mind, something that concerns you. . . . Go right to it. Put all your attention on whatever it is so I can see it and feel it just the way you do. And let yourself feel. Let feelings happen in your body.

T: There is something on your mind right now, something that is the reason why you are here. Try to put all your attention on it, and not on me. Try to talk about it, try to let it happen so that I can know it and see it and feel it just the way you do. Go right to whatever it is that concerns you, whatever it is. And let yourself have feelings in your body. The more feelings the better, either bad or good ones. Just let things happen in your body. Now, go right to it and let all the feelings happen.

In a standard initial interview, the patient goes directly to some attentional center accompanied with at least moderate bodily sensations. Experiencing occurs right away, and the patient is attending largely to some meaningful attentional center rather than preponderantly to the therapist. In other words, attention is focused in the very beginning of the initial interview. Every approach faces the question of what to do in the first session, and whether the first session is to be handled differently than subsequent sessions. In many approaches, the first session is regarded as distinctive, and it is used to gather whatever kinds of information is considered useful. Typically, it is an informational and get-acquainted session. In experiential psychotherapy, we start right out, and we do not gather the usual intake information in a get-acquainted context, because of the following reasons:

(a)   Our aim is to take advantage of whatever kind of experiential state or readiness is there for the patient. To the extent that initial sessions may be a little more charged with experiential readiness, we want to take advantage of this experiential state. "According to the Gestalt therapist, the kind of discursive presentation of symptomatic complaints that is encouraged in the usual intake therapy session distances the patient emotionally (both from his immediate feelings and from the interviewer/therapist) and encourages him to escape from the stressfulness of his here-and-now experience through a focusing on the there-and-then (i.e., in this context, a narration of his problem's history)" (Shaffer, 1978, p. 93).
(b)   Our aim is to minimize role-relationship problems. By starting right out with the focusing of attention, these problems are essentially minimized. On the other hand, by following an alternative approach in which patient and therapist gather informational data within a get-acquainted context, role-relationship problems are ripened to their fullest.

*The Parts of the Instructional Package*

There are four parts to the instructions: 1) Whenever the patient is ready, 2) the patient is to allow himself to go into a state in which the preponderance of attention is on some meaningful center, and 3) the patient is to allow himself to have at least moderate bodily sensations while 4) interacting preponderantly with the attentional center, and not with the therapist.

1) *Readiness of the patient*. The patient is the one who does the work. Accordingly, the therapist always must ask for and obtain the patient's readiness. The purpose of the instructions is to enable the patient to do the work, and if the patient is not ready right now, then the work waits. Accordingly, the therapist says: "If you are ready . . . if you feel that you want to start now . . . do you want to try it out and see if you are ready? . . . Since you are the one to do the work—I will show you what to do—you might be ready or maybe you're not yet ready. What do you think?"

2) *Letting the preponderance of attention go to a proper center*. The therapist keeps in mind the seven topics described earlier. If there seems to be some attentional center already present, then the therapist invites the patient to attend to that. If not, the therapist may generally refer to some or all of the topics, and allow the patient to choose. Or the therapist may name one and see what happens when the patient's attention goes to it. In so doing, the therapist may well mention specific attentional centers discovered from work in previous sessions.

Whichever option is selected, the therapist tells the patient to allow as much attention as possible to go to the attentional center. The patient is to understand that he is to enter into a kind of state, to leave the context here in the office and to be with whatever is there, whatever is the proper center of attention.

T: Now just let your attention go. Let yourself start to feel something in your body. Instead of being here in the office, let yourself go into some other place, a place where you feel, where feelings start to happen in your body. . . . Now you are somewhere, and you are attending to the way Shelly is, the thing you fear most about the way Shelly is . . . the worst feeling you have . . . the way you are crazy . . . the worst thing you do . . . the secret thing about you . . . yes . . . now let yourself think about nothing but that. Put all your attention on it. All your attention, and that is all you see, all you have in mind. Concentrate on it . . . put all your attention on it.

In the above instructions, the therapist selected the second topic alone (greatest fears about oneself). The aim is to show the patient how to let the preponderance of attention go to this general topic. If nothing is there, if there is no workable attentional center here, then the therapist may provide a specific center which was obtained from previous therapeutic work. That is one option. Another option is to proceed to another topic or two. Sometimes the therapist may leave the nature of the topic up to the patient:

T: Let all of your attention go. Let it go to what seems to be there. To anything. But look at something. Let yourself go into a state where things start up in your body. Think about something that pulls all of your attention, all of your attention, every bit. You are thinking about something, seeing something . . .

Sometimes the therapist may start with a center discovered from work in a previous session:

T: I am going to describe something. Try to let yourself see and feel what I describe. If you let yourself attend to this fully, and if something starts to happen inside your body, we can continue. If not, we can look for another place to start . . . OK? . . . All right. You are a little boy. You are nine years old. And you are staying with your Uncle Stan. He is telling you about your Daddy, how your Daddy used to hit your mother and he was mean, and that is why your mother took you away from him. He is walking along with you in the park, and you are looking at the cracks in the sidewalk as you walk along. And there are feelings inside you. It is hot inside your chest. You are warm in your chest. But Uncle Stan just keeps talking. He says, "Your Daddy never wanted to have you." And these words seem to get louder and louder inside your head . . . here you are now with Uncle Stan . . .

3) *Letting bodily sensations occur.* Show the patient how to allow bodily sensations to occur. These are to be at least moderate, preferably stronger. Something tangible and palpable is to occur in the body. As Gendlin (1969, 1978a) emphasizes, there is a careful and deliberate quality to this. Take plenty of time, and allow both yourself and the patient to take a welcoming attitude toward the having of moderate bodily sensations. Most patients start to have moderate bodily sensations and

then they stop, or they divert themselves to something else in order to keep bodily sensations truncated. In this part of the instructions, the aim is to go past this point and to allow the bodily sensations to happen with at least moderate strength:

T: . . . The important thing is to let feelings happen in your body. You must allow sensations to happen in your body. This is your job. . . . They can feel bad or they can feel good. Let your arms and legs start to tremble a little. Let your heart start to pound all over your chest. Let pressure happen anywhere in your body, or in your head. Let tears start to happen. Cry. Let yourself cry. Let your body be scared. Let your body get weak all over. Your legs may start to feel heavy. Your whole body may feel like it weighs a thousand pounds. Your arms or legs may start to feel huge. Let yourself feel dizzy or swirling. Or your body may start to feel good, really good. You may start laughing. Your body may feel peaceful all over. You may feel so relaxed and good. You start to feel sexy in your legs or your genitals or all over your body. Let yourself start to float and your body is light and it feels good.

4) *Interacting with the attentional center.* The words spoken by the patient are to be in relation to the focal center, and not in relation to the therapist. Not only is the preponderance of attention to be on the focal center, but everything the patient now does is to be in interaction with it, and not with the therapist:

T: Put all of your attention on whatever is there, on whatever you see. Talk to it. Say words to it. Tell it what is happening. Describe what it is like, and say the words to it. There is only you and it. I am going to be right with you, right next to you, seeing what you see, saying the words right along with you. I will be undergoing what you are undergoing. If you are looking at your father, talk to him, say words to him, describe things to him. Be here with him, not with me. If you let yourself get dizzy, and you see a gravestone, then describe what is happening as if there is just you and this gravestone, nothing else. No matter what happens in you, no matter what you see or where you are, be here only with it. Talk to it and address it. Talk to yourself about it. Think about it by yourself. Describe it to yourself. There is only you and it. You are alone with it.

*Further Instructions as Needed*

After the therapist gives the instructions, the preponderance of the patient's attention will generally go to some attentional center, and not to the therapist. If, however, the patient talks to the therapist, with most of his attention on the therapist, it is important that the therapist simply remain the teacher of the method. That is, the therapist goes over the instructions. Modify whatever parts should be modified. Repeat the parts that should be repeated. Explain the parts which should be explained. The therapist is to remain the teacher, the one who provides the right kind of instructions for this patient in this session. No matter how often the instructions are either repeated or revised or carefully fitted to the patient, the therapist remains the teacher.

If the patient works to maintain most of his attention on the therapist, the therapist may repeat the salient part of the instructions. For example, in the fifteenth session, following standard instructions, the patient says:

Pt: I am getting better with my wife. She wanted me to tell you. . . . I am staying home more, and I like that. . . . Remember, you said that I might be seeing these changes right away? You were right. I am starting to be home more, and it doesn't even seem so bad. I guess I know that you like that. (Sigh.) I like being home now. I want to thank you for that.

The therapist is being locked into a role relationship. If the therapist senses that the patient is not yet ready to start, then that can be emphasized, and the patient can be instructed to begin work whenever he is ready:

T: Well, that's nice. If you want to talk about that, fine. But if you are ready to start, then, just let your attention go, let it go to whatever is there, with real feelings in your body. What would you like to do?
Pt: OK. (Pause.) I see my daughter. I feel good . . . she is handing me the pencil, and she is starting to make all kinds of sounds. I love her. I am starting to do things with you, baby. I am feeding you now. How do you like that, huh? I'm your Daddy! Hello, baby! God, I love you!

The patient may have some business to talk over with the therapist, something to do with payment or writing a letter on behalf of the patient, or talking about a referral. After the usual instructions, the patient pursues one of these topics with the therapist:

Pt: Dr. Nagi, I have a friend, Suzanne. She wants to see you. Can I give her your name? I know you're busy. Could you see her maybe?

T: Wow! You surprised me! I was all set to attend to something and then you got me all mixed up . . . uh, sure. How about asking her to give me a call? OK? Anything else? Or do you want to start? Anything else?

Pt: (Laughs.) You get mixed up easily. . . . Her last name is Landers, and I had a big fight with her last night. Yes, the fight. I want to get down to that. It was a great fight. I threw a pillow at her. Suzanne called me a whore, and I screamed at her. "You are right! I am a whore! I've been a whore all my life and never knew it! (Hard laughing.) And so are you, you whore! We both are!" (Laughs heartily.)

The patient may ask questions of a simple clarification nature. The therapist answers accordingly. Following the instructions in the third session, the patient says:

Pt: I don't think I have to talk about orgasms anymore. I am starting to have them. We masturbate together now, and I had more orgasms last night then in my whole life. I never thought . . . but there is something else. I can talk about other things? I can talk about my mother?

T: Yes. Just let your attention go to her, or to whatever you want.

Pt: Anything I want.

T: Yes. Just let your attention go to whatever. Anything—as long as you let feelings start in your body.

Pt: (Pause.) I remember something that happened when I was little. Something I started crying about last night. My mother . . . she . . . (starts to cry) . . . my mother did something with my Uncle Don. I know she did and she hit me . . . she slapped me. . . . (Hard tears.)

Or the patient may ask clarification questions about other aspects of the instructions:

Pt: I see something sometimes like now. The look on Madge's face. But I don't have strong feelings. I just see it. And then, like now, I just see something else. The new film that I got yesterday. Should I just talk about them? Even if the feelings aren't strong?

T: Yes, if you see her face, Madge's, and then the new film, just let your attention go to them. The face, the film. Let the feelings happen. Drift around, that's fine. As long as you let bodily sensations start to happen whenever. Just try. See.

Pt: I see things without trying. I feel sort of loose. I see a woman's ring. Green. Old finger. Mrs. Kelly's ring. Oh. Yes, I am with her. Yes. She is asking me about the rent in the building. I can't look at her face. I don't want to see her. I talk to her by trying to pick out something about her and not to look at her face. . . .

By serving as the teacher of the method, the therapist has shown the patient how to place the preponderance of attention on some meaningful focal center, with at least moderate bodily sensations. In other words, we have arrived at the working level of experiencing. This is the first and fundamental aim of experiential psychotherapy, the gateway to the subsequent steps in the method. Without attaining this first kind of experiencing, the experiential method cannot get started. A working level of attention-centered bodily experiencing is essential. Now we turn to the therapist and make the momentous shift from teacher of the method to the one who enters into the patient's phenomenological world.

# 8

# Entering the Patient's Phenomenological World

In Chapter 7, the therapist is outside the patient, giving instructions on how to focus attention. The purpose of the present chapter is to describe how the therapist shares the bodily sensations occurring right now in the patient, how the therapist shares the patient's attentional center, and how the therapist shares whatever experiencing is occurring. In other words, the purpose of this chapter is to describe how the therapist enters into the phenomenological world of the patient.

## THE LOCUS OF THE EXPERIENTIAL PSYCHOTHERAPIST

When the therapist gives instructions, the therapist is external to the patient, talking to the patient, with most of the therapist's attention on the patient. As soon as the instructions are given, the therapist begins entering the patient's phenomenological world. This means that the therapist is sharing the patient's attentional center, is sharing the bodily sensations going on in the patient, and is sharing the experiencing which is occurring in the patient. Mainly, the therapist is attending to whatever the patient is attending. This is the locus of the therapist throughout most of the session. With the exception of the time when the therapist is giving instructions, the therapist may be said to be within the phenomenological world of the patient. I shall refer to this locus as being aligned or fused with the patient.

How much of the patient's attention is to be on a focal center, and how much stays on the therapist? In general, perhaps 50 to 80 percent of the patient's attention is on the focal center, and the balance on the therapist. In the same way, about 50 to 80 percent of the therapist's attention is on the patient's attentional center. Most of the time, most of the patient's and therapist's attention is on that attentional center. The therapist is not totally focused upon that center. The therapist may sense approximately what time it is, how the session is going, who the therapist is, and what the patient said a few minutes ago. But the predominance of attention is on the patient's attentional center.

### When Does the Therapist Shift into This Locus?

When the therapist is external, the therapist gives instructions. The moment the instructions are completed, the therapist shifts into this locus. Suppose that the therapist is giving instructions on how to focus attention, and the final words are: ". . . Describe it to yourself. There is only you and it. You are alone with it. Go ahead." The moment these words are spoken, even before the patient starts to speak, the therapist shifts location. It is as if the therapist now moves alongside the patient, and the therapist's attention is deployed "out there," ready to attend to something the instant the patient says words.

In many therapies, the therapist is enjoined to shift from one (external) locus to another. The technical problem is that of specifying precisely when the therapist shifts from one locus to another. In discussing this problem, Kiesler (1966) illustrates how psychoanalytic therapy has yet to define when the therapist shifts from one (external) locus to another:

> The therapist must present himself as a neutral and ambiguous stimulus to the patient in order not to distort the patient's task of free association and dream production or hamper the appearance of transference phenomena. Yet, at subsequent stages of the interaction the analyst apparently becomes quite nonambiguous, offering interpretations of childhood experiences and the transference relationship. Where does the one attitude (or complex of attitudes) end, and the other begin? What are the behavioral cues which determine the shift of set? What is the interrelationship of the various attitudes (inaction, ambiguity and/or neutrality) prevailing in the earlier stages of therapy? (pp. 121-122).

*How Does the Therapist Enter into This Locus?*

This is a key question underlying the work of phenomenological clinicians (e.g., Ellenberger, 1958; Havens, 1976a). Although phenomenological clinicians have urged that we aim at knowing and grasping the patient's subjective experiencings, we lack effective technical procedures for doing so. As discussed in Chapters 5 and 6, Rogers sought to know and grasp the patient's subjective experiencings by means of an empathic attitude complemented by conditions of warmth, acceptance, and emotional responsiveness. But these methods, I believe, maintained the therapist as distinctly external and plunged both participants into the problems of role relationships. In an attempt to draw upon phenomenological thinking to enable the empathic therapist to share the patient's phenomenological world, Havens (1973) suggests that we bracket or set aside the contents of our own head in the effort to get inside the patient's world:

> Empathy is a state of being where the patient is and therefore feeling what the patient feels. Therapists arrive where the patients are only when they abandon all those contents of their own heads which preceded that arrival and let themselves learn from within the patient's experience . . . not only the specific analytically discovered countertransferences of the analyst are to be "worked through," or the projective fantasies between doctor and patient, but the whole categorizing, reflective, thinking, and investigating attitude of the therapist must be set aside (1973, pp. 298-299).

Havens and Rogers are representative of therapists who value getting inside the phenomenological world of the patient. Yet the effective ways of accomplishing this are far more valued than they are available. In this chapter I propose how this may be accomplished.

*How Does the Therapist Learn the Skills of Entering the Phenomenological World of the Patient?*

One skill is that of sharing the patient's bodily sensations. Another is sharing the patient's attentional center. These are simple skills which can be learned through direct training. For example, in a small group of therapists, if one describes her immediate bodily sensations, others in the group can practice allowing themselves to have similar bodily sensations. If one person describes a focal center of attention, the others can train themselves to attend to the same focal center. It is a matter of training and of practice. Some persons, including some therapists, already have these skills with a rare loved partner. When the partner describes the pain in the stomach or the pressure in the chest, the person can have it too. When the partner attends fixedly on the way someone looked or spoke to her, and describes it in sufficient detail, the person can see it and hear it in just that same way. It is a matter of letting oneself carry out these skills, and it is a matter of training and practice.

### SHARING THE PATIENT'S
### BODILY SENSATIONS

The therapist goes through two operations in order to enter into the phenomenological world of the patient. One is to share the patient's meaningful center of attention. The other is to share the patient's immediate bodily sensations. First I shall describe how the therapist goes about the task of sharing the patient's bodily sensations. Then I shall discuss when the therapist does this.

*The Instructions*

There are three parts to the instructions:

(a)   The instructions give the patient the task of enabling the therapist to have the same bodily sensations as are occurring right now in the patient. If the patient is successful, the therapist will indeed share the same, or very similar, bodily sensations.
(b)   The patient accomplishes this by identifying where the predominant bodily sensations are right now.
(c)   Then the patient describes them in sufficient detail so that the therapist can have them also.

(a) *The task.* In the initial sessions especially, the therapist carefully explains that the patient is to enable the therapist to have the same bodily sensations as are occurring in the patient. Here is a standard way of doing this:

T: Something is happening in your body right now. It may be in your throat or your chest or head or legs or somewhere. I want to have the same thing in my body. I want to have the same feelings, the same sensations that are going on in your body right now. Describe where the feelings are and what they are like so that I can have them too, no matter where they are or what they are like. Then we can move ahead. Are you ready to do this?

In general, patients are ready and willing; many therapists are much less cordial because of at least two considerations. One is that the therapist who is learning experiential psychotherapy finds that sharing the patient's bodily sensations confounds such other tactics as receiving the patient's complaints, inquiring about the patient's problems, or getting clinical impressions about the patient. The therapist must really mean what is said in the above instructions.

The second consideration is that therapists must learn how surprisingly flexible are the boundaries of the bodily sensations which two persons can share. My impression is that nearly all of the immediate bodily sensations of patients can occur in the therapist, regardless of the physical differences between the two. The therapist may be a young woman, in reasonably good health, a little over five feet tall, somewhat slender. The patient may be an old man, with pains in his arms and legs, over six feet tall, and obese. The more the therapist must preserve intact separation and distance, the more the therapist will insist that she can share precious few of her patient's bodily sensations. Is she able to share her patient's sense of heaviness and tiredness in the legs, or the tightness and hurt in the joints, or the sensation of bulk and sheer girth in the protruding belly? If the therapist is ready and willing, even these kinds of bodily sensations really can be shared. If the therapist is not ready and willing, there is little or no sharing of even bodily sensations which are easy to share, e.g., the feeling of butterflies in the stomach, the awareness of blood beating in the chest, warmth in the hands, cold in the feet, pressure in the head.

It is important to note that the aim is merely to share whatever bodily sensations are there. The aim is not to relax the body, to gain a sense of awareness of the body, or to figure out the meaning of the bodily sensation.

(b) *Locating the predominant bodily sensations.* In the second part of the instructions, the therapist shows the patient how to locate where the predominant bodily sensations are right now. Here is one typical version of the instructions:

T: . . . Now just take your time. Let yourself know where the sensations
are mainly in your body. If you take your time and just wait, listen
a while, the sensations will be mainly some place in your body. They
may be mainly in your chest or your back or your head or your legs.
They may be outside, like on the skin of your face, or inside, like
deep inside the chest. Take 10 or 15 seconds and just wait, listen.

Ordinarily, the patient will locate where they are. "They are in my
chest, all over the chest . . . I got a headache, a little headache . . . my
arms and legs, both. They are like tension in them . . . I can feel it in
my shoulder, my left shoulder." In order to begin sharing the same
bodily sensations, the therapist gets ready by trying to prepare that part
of the body. Accordingly, the therapist may ask a few questions to
identify the location a bit more:

Pt: They are in my chest, all over the chest.
T: All over the chest. The whole chest . . . all over? (The therapist attends to her chest area.)
Pt: Well, maybe higher up, like below the throat here . . . and . . . yeah,
across the whole top of my chest.
T: OK . . . below the throat . . . and across the whole top of the
chest . . . OK. Inside? Is it inside? (The therapist attends to the whole
top of the chest, inside or outside.)

Pt: Yeah, inside and outside too, on the skin, and inside. Both.

The therapist attends to that area, and prepares to let some kind of
bodily sensations occur there.

(c) *Describing the predominant bodily sensations*. In the third part of the
instructions, the patient is to describe these bodily sensations in sufficient detail so that the therapist can have them too. Generally this involves therapist and patient checking and counter checking with one
another until the therapist actually has similar bodily sensations. Let us
continue with the patient who reports the predominant sensations in
the upper chest:

T: Yes, all right, inside and outside too. . . . Now describe what they
are like. I want to have them just like you do now. Same way, here
in the chest. So describe what they are like so I can have them too,
same way.

Pt: Well, I'm aware of it. Like it's energy . . . like scared? Sort of moving . . . like it's alive there . . . like there's a pressure inside. Pushing
out a little. It doesn't hurt.

The therapist tries to let that same bodily sensation occur. In so doing,
the therapist may seek clarification, especially when the therapist starts
to let the same sensation occur there.

T: I got a throbbing, like I can feel the blood beating.
Pt: No. Just a light pressure. Constant. Like I am holding my breath.
Like something scary is going to happen. Just a little pressure from
inside.
T: All right. Yes. And energy, moving very lightly and quickly all over
my chest?
Pt: Yes. . . . I can really feel it now.
T: Yeah. I have it. Yeah.

Here is another common dialogue starting with the ache in the back
of the head:

Pt: In the back of the neck. Hurts, but not terribly. The whole back of
my head. Nothing happens if I turn my head one way or the other.
T: It stays here in the back of the head . . . like the muscles are all
clenched. Tight here.
Pt: You know, if I try to relax it wants to pull my head back. But it still
hurts.
T: I'll let it go, pull my head back. Yeah, it's an effort to pull or shove
my head forward.
Pt: Like a fist. It's like a fist. Hard, and tight like a fist. And it hurts sort
of, not awful.
T: It's starting. I have it now . . . let's see. Right at the base of the head.
Pt: Uh huh.
T: A real headache. I got a headache!
Pt: Well, yes, a headache. I don't like having it.

Sometimes the sheer description of one predominant bodily sensation
will lead to its washing away, especially when it is hurtful or painful
(Mahrer, 1970b, 1975b). Headaches and backaches, butterflies in the
stomach, tension feelings in the chest and similar bodily sensations will
frequently ease and reduce when description proceeds. Let us pick up
with the above patient and therapist:

Pt: . . . Uh . . . it's changing. Feels like it's twisting a little to the . . . down. Feels like things are breaking up in here . . . breaking up. Swelling now, and softer. Swelling. Easing inside . . . it's gone. It's not there!

If this occurs, simply start over again:

T: OK. Wait . . . OK . . . now take your time again and wait. Wait, and just listen and attend to where the main feeling is now in your body. Somewhere . . .
Pt: My hands feel cold. Both hands. Cold. Not my feet. My hands are cold.

Sometimes the description of one prominent bodily sensation will lead to the appearance of another, and then perhaps another. When this occurs, the therapist tells the patient to just let all of this happen until one seems to be here now, one that remains stable for a while:

Pt: Well, it's my legs. They are shaking. Strange. I feel my legs shaking a little, both legs I mean. All the way down.
T: Legs. Shaking. Quivering. Feet too? Feet?
Pt: No, just the legs. It feels like there's a little electric current in them, not in the feet. They are shaking! They're jerking, by themselves . . . oh . . . my prick is moving now . . . getting smaller. Pulling back. I feel it. And in my balls. I can feel my balls. . . .
T: Pulling in too?
Pt: Yeah, just like they're cold a little. My prick and my balls . . . and my face now. It is like the skin is stretching across my forehead. That's the main thing now. The skin across my forehead. Tighter. A little little tighter.
T: Just describe wherever they are mainly. Take your time. Just describe.
Pt: (Pause.) . . . My God! My arms and legs feel big. Real big. I feel drugged. Like I can't move them! They feel heavy, like they weigh a thousand pounds. Heavy. This is weird. I never felt anything like this . . . real heavy. I can't move them.
T: Sort of like concrete? Mine feel like concrete.
Pt: Uh huh. Pulling down. I can't move them. They are heavy. I really can't move them. They feel huge. Big, real big. Like they are a thousand pounds and real big.

The process continues until the patient has a stable bodily sensation, and the therapist has a similar bodily sensation.

*When Does the Therapist Give the Instructions?*

If the patient starts a session with attention already on some compelling focal center, the therapist lets her own attention go to that same focal center. The therapist does not interrupt the patient by giving instructions on how to start looking for prominent bodily sensations. Quite often the patient's attention will be on the incident with the man next door, or the dismal prospects for getting a pay raise, or the incessant fighting at home. The patient's immediate attentional center takes precedence over the sharing of bodily sensations. The working guideline is that the therapist turns to the instructions for sharing bodily sensations only if it is clear that the patient is not already attending to some focal center. In actual practice, this means that roughly half of the sessions start with the therapist deciding that it is reasonable to turn to the sharing of bodily sensations. At least four considerations help in this decision:

1) In initial sessions, the therapist seldom starts with these instructions because most patients have some compelling center of attention. In general, the first two or three sessions or so are ones in which the patient goes to some compelling attentional center. Only later is it appropriate to begin with the instructions for sharing bodily sensations.

2) On the other hand, in initial sessions with some patients, there may be no compelling attentional center. Or, instructions to allow the attention to go to some center have produced nothing. For whatever reason, the patient is unable or unwilling to let attention go to anything at all. Under these conditions, it is helpful to turn to what is happening in the body right now. Here is a typical example in which the patient had been instructed to allow attention to go to several topics, and nothing happens. This is after about 20 minutes of the initial session:

Pt: (Continuing.) . . . she is getting better I think. And so I am coping all right with that. I can take care of things and we are proceeding along. . . . I really don't know what to talk about much. (So far, the patient has been talking in bits and pieces, with short frequent pauses. There seems to be little feeling, few if any bodily sensations.) But I know that I should be here. I do want to help her as much as I can, and my life hasn't been easy these past months.

T: Well, nothing much is happening in my body as I listen to you. I hear the words. But nothing inside my body . . .

When attention does not go to any focal topic, and when bodily sensations are low, it is timely to turn to bodily sensations. It is noted that bodily sensations are both a category of attentional centering and a means for the therapist to share what is occurring in the patient's body. In any case, if attention is light, we may turn to the sharing of bodily sensations. Accordingly, the therapist continues:

T: . . . so now let's turn to something else. Let your attention go to where the sensations are in your body. Somewhere in your body, right now, there are sensations. Some kind. Your feet might be cold, or you might have a slight stiffness in your neck, or your throat might be dry. Do you see what I mean? . . . OK. Take about ten seconds or so, and just decide where the sensations are mainly in your body. Start listening . . . now. (Pause of about ten seconds.) OK, now where are they mainly?

Pt: I can feel my heart beating.

T: Where? Where do you feel it?

Pt: Strange. I feel it beating in my fingers.

T: Fingers. Fingers. All right. Now I want to have the same sensations in my fingers. Just like yours. Take your time and describe what that is like. Show me so that I can have it just the way it is in your fingers.

Pt: Well, more than beating . . . it feels there. They are shaking somewhat. Shaking and I feel the blood in them. Yes. My whole hand, hands, both of them. They are shaking and I want to, it's like they want to make a fist. There. Yes, I still feel the blood beating. When I squeeze my hands into a fist, they feel like steel. Very hard. And the quivering stops now. But my hands feel like fists, hard fists. (Laughs.) My fists seem aggressive. (Laughs hard, very quickly.) My hands are aggressive! Yes, I want to make them into fists! (Laughs very hard.) I am not aggressive! I never make fists! I am such a nice guy! (He is shaking both hands rapidly, his hands clenched into fists.)

3) In subsequent sessions, if none of the other attentional topics seems to work, then it is appropriate to turn to the topic of physical/bodily centers, and to combine this attentional topic with the instructions for sharing bodily sensations with the patient. Sometimes the patient is in a low key. Sometimes the patient just skitters from one thing to another with little or no feeling. Under these conditions, it is appropriate to turn to what is happening right now in the body.

4) The therapist may begin with the sharing of ongoing bodily sensations when some kind of bodily sensation is prominent in the therapist.

For example, as soon as work begins, the therapist notes that there is a pounding in her heart, or her attention is drawn toward muscular tension in her lower back. In order to work, the therapist is to have bodily sensations similar to those in the patient, so the two should align.

T: Well, my feet are cold. I mean very cold. But that's what's happening in my body, and I want to have the same sensations that are here right now in yours. So let's start there. OK? . . . Take your time, just take 10 or 20 seconds. Where are they mainly in your body?

Except for these considerations, the therapist is free to start either with the centering of attention or the sharing of bodily sensations. Either beginning is all right, for they both lead in the direction of the first step (i.e., attention-centered bodily experiencing), and enable the therapist to enter the patient's phenomenological world.

## SHARING THE PATIENT'S
## ATTENTIONAL CENTER

The more the therapist shares the physical sensations which are occurring in the patient's body, the more the therapist may be said to be entering into the phenomenological world of the patient. This is one step. The second is for the therapist to share the patient's attentional center. The more the therapist attends to that to which the patient is attending, the more the therapist is also entering into the phenomenological world of the patient.

*The Passively Receiving Therapist and the Construction of Attentional Centers*

The therapist shares the patient's attentional center by following some simple guidelines.

*The guidelines.* Immediately after the instructions are given, the therapist takes a specific stance. It consists of being right next to the patient, figuratively, so that the behavior and words of the patient seem also to be coming from the therapist. It is as if a part of the therapist is saying the words and carrying out the behavior. The stance consists of passively allowing one's attention to be ready to go wherever the patient's attention goes. It consists of passively letting the patient's behavior and words construct something in the world of the passively attending therapist.

The therapist hears the words the patient says: "The window was open." The therapist receives the way in which these words are said, the quality of the voice, the tone and amplitude. Everything about the words and the way in which the words are spoken plays upon the therapist who is passively listening and receiving. The passively receiving therapist is affected by key pauses, meaningful words which are not spoken, short bursts of nervous laughter. Even though the therapist's eyes are generally closed, whatever comes from the patient can affect the attentional field of the therapist.

But the therapist does not attend to the behavior and the words of the patient. Instead, the therapist does exactly what the patient is asked to do. That is, the therapist's attention is loosely and evenly distributed all around, out there and in here. Out in the world and inside the body and thoughts and feelings and the whole inner realm. As the behavior and words of the patient are received by the therapist, they construct something in the general attentional field of the therapist. Or, put differently, the behavior and words of the patient have the effect of defining something in the attentional field of the therapist.

The words, "The window was open," may have the effect of placing the therapist near a window which is seen as open a foot or so. Or the words may define a window which is open just an inch or so. One therapist may see the open window vaguely while another may see it in some detail. The way in which the words are spoken also defines the therapist's attentional field. The quality of the speech, the tone, loudness, and other aspects of the way in which words are spoken have a hand in constructing the therapist's attentional field. One way of saying these words may construct a whining, petulant child who is a bother to some person who is enjoined to shut the window. Another way of saying these words may construct a fearful scene in which something ominous and menacing is outside the open window, ready to come in and do something frightening.

The more the therapist is right with the patient, allowing the patient's behavior and words to construct the attentional center, the more the therapist will tend to share that attentional center. The more the therapist allows himself to be passive, with attention ready to go somewhere, the more the therapist will share the patient's attentional center. It is remarkable how similar the constructed attentional center in the passive therapist is to that occurring in the patient. When several therapists take this position and listen in this way, it is remarkable how similar are their constructed attentional centers, both to one another and also to that which is occurring in the patient (Mahrer, 1980b). There will be differences. If five therapists listen to the patient attending to something, each may have a somewhat different constructed attentional center. But the commonalities typically outweigh the differences.

The state of passive reception means that the therapist's attention goes to whatever the patient's behavior and words construct. That is all the therapist does. There are no clinical inferences, no hypotheses arrived at by the thinking, reflecting, observing therapist. There are no private thoughts. Instead, the therapist is merely comprised of attention, passively ready to go to whatever the behavior and the words of the patient construct.

The therapist who is doing this tends to let go of notions about the patient. As the therapist attends to the threatening looking man in the elevator, the therapist does not hold conceptions of whether this is the third or the fifty-third session, whether the patient is 65 or 25 years old, whether the patient is a psychotherapist or a bus driver or a crazy nut. Once the therapist shares the attentional center, all that matters is the nature of the immediate center. Even with persons who act in bizarre ways, who have weird thoughts, and whose way of speaking is confusing and hard to follow, the main thing which is occurring is that the therapist is attending to that threatening man in the elevator.

If the patient says, "My husband came in the door and he had a nose bleed," the preponderance of the experiential therapist's attention is on the attentional field constructed by these words, while the preponderant attention of other therapists may be on the patient and notions about the patient. It is quite difficult for the preponderance of the therapist's attention to be on both the attentional field constructed by the patient's words and also on the patient himself:

> No therapist can attend fully to two things at the same time. Therefore, if he begins to conceptualize the client's experience in terms of concepts unfamiliar to the client, or to connect the client's current feelings with hypothetical childhood events far from the client's immediate awareness and perhaps at no point available to his recall, he will remove himself from his client's experience rather than enter it more deeply (Shaffer, 1978, pp. 81-82).

Sharing the patient's attentional center means that most of the therapist's attention is dedicated to that attentional field—and not to the patient.

*Some examples.* Here are some examples of what patients say after the therapist gives the instructions for focusing attention. In each of the examples, the patient's attention goes to something. Once the therapist is passively receiving, the therapist may see that something in a world of mental imagery. The therapist may see in color or black and white. The therapist may sense something near or far away. It may be a specific image or a force or agency. It may be sound, or it may be something the therapist feels and touches. It may be warm or cold. The more passively the therapist receives whatever is constructed, the more concrete and specific it will be, the more vivid and detailed it will be—whether the attentional center is the face of a person or an imminent force, a carrot or an ulcer, a statue or an idea.

Pt: . . . and then I got up during the night because the room was freezing. The window was open, and snow was coming in. . . . I got to get up. Why me all the time? She's like a little kid and I have to do all the worrying!

The therapist is cold, in a bedroom. I just closed the window. I see a little snow here on the window sill. It is quite cold. It is as if "she" is sleeping in the bed. I am attending mainly to her. I am looking at her, and I am also aware of something else: thoughts which are here in my head, "I got to get up. Why me all the time? She's a little kid and I have to do all the worrying." She is asleep all this time, and I am attending mainly to her, there on the bed.

Pt: I remember my aunt was in the hospital and I visited her. She had something wrong. Not serious. Can't remember. But she asked me things. She had that same attitude toward me. Like I don't mean anything to her.

It is hard to say whether I am sitting on a chair near her bed, or maybe I am standing. I am aware of her on the bed, about five to eight feet away, and she isn't looking at me much. She has just asked me some questions. It is vague as to what they are about, but somehow it seems to have to do with me. Although she doesn't say anything directly, even though I am attending to her, I also am aware of an attitude she is conveying and I am feeling in me. I am not much cared for; she tends to look down on me; she has little respect for me, like she always does.

Pt: . . . there are touches of it in my wrist and . . . my left wrist. And in my scalp. My head . . . I go back for tests all the time. But the cancer . . . it seems to . . . they tell me the chances are good. But I don't know. Something is so awful about it. . . .

The therapist is attending to cancer. It is vague. It is like a thing, a bad thing. The patient continues:

Pt: They do chemotherapy and it spreads anyhow. It used to be . . . it just won't go away. It just moves around. . . .

Now the therapist attends to the cancer as a resistant, virulent thing. It is still vague, but the cancer is a thing that just won't go away. It has evil characteristics, like being able to spread around. I am aware of the cancer.

Pt: Mainly I wanted to get some counseling. I would like to feel less afraid about pushing on with what I am doing. With me . . . my possibilities I mean. I don't know what they are. Not really, I mean. In whatever area. The trouble is that I feel very much held back by myself, somehow. Like somehow I can't ever have what I want. Something stops me. I'm held back by myself.

The therapist attends to a separated, other self. It is separate from me, from the patient. This other self stops me, holds me back, will never let me have what I want. It is vague, but it has substance. It is a thing with these characteristics and intentionalities.

Pt: I am at home. Uh, at home. Something about the floor and the dishes. I don't want to start them. I feel pushed. By Manny . . . like he expects me to do them. Something bad. To do all the housework. Can't remember exactly.

The therapist is in the kitchen, and is attending to the dishes in the sink, and to the floor which is not very clean. Manny is not there, but the idea of his presence is here. I should do the dishes and the floor, and Manny's presence is just about here telling me to do them.

Pt: So I wrote another letter about it to Bill, but he won't answer. . . .
(These words construct Bill, and the therapist sees a man with his
whole manner set on not answering.) I have been worried all week
about that. I thought that I should maybe call him . . . (I am standing
by the phone. Hesitant. I don't really want to call him.) But, I don't
know. He always gets so funny on the phone. He doesn't talk. . . .
(I am on the phone, and here is a long silence. Bill is irritated about
"it," and won't come out and say that he is irritated. I feel it though.)
I don't think he likes me. Sometimes . . . sometimes I think he just
doesn't like me. . . . (Bill is now quite present. He is looking at me
and has a look of real dislike on his face. This is clear. He is almost
glaring at me and not saying anything.)

Pt: Well, it is this headache. Right behind the eyes, and in the forehead.
It hurts. That's all I can say. It hurts me. (The therapist attends to a
kind of force or thing. It is located in the forehead region behind the
eyes, but its most prominent characteristic is that it has a kind of
intention to hurt; it wants to hurt me.) . . . like squeezing or pushing
at me from inside. (This makes the intention even more definite; a
thing or force that is getting at my head, squeezing and pushing hard
at the stuff in my head, behind the eyes.)

Pt: It's getting worse lately. I feel like I'm shattering. I am falling apart.
I just can't do anything right. . . . Nothing is working out. . . . (Light
tears.) I feel so useless. Like I'm no good to anybody. I am rotten and
useless. . . . (Harder crying.)

The therapist is attending to what is constructed by the words "rotten,
useless, no good to anybody." I see the insides, what I am like within.
There is filth, dirt, slime. It is ugly.

Occasionally a patient will begin a session in a kind of feelinged word-
less state. The patient may cry softly, or breathe deeply and slowly, or
put his hands on his chest or head and hurt. The few words which are
said tell very little and are separated by long feelinged silences. Yet
feelings are clearly occurring. Under these conditions, the therapist follows the same procedures. Suppose that the patient crosses his arms
across the chest, rocks back and forth, and breathes hard. This goes on
for a few minutes right in the beginning of the session. If the therapist
aligns with the patient, she will take up the same bodily position, likewise rock, and breathe hard, all along with the patient. The therapist

allows her attentional field to form. Something is there. It may be the wife gone, and the children gone. She has just taken too much, and now she is gone; it is finally all over. Or it may be that the tests are all in, and the oncologist is saying that the patient has maybe up to six months to live. Then the patient says a few words:

Pt: I've lost them! (And he starts to cry hard. Now the attentional field is defined. Christine is gone, and so are the children.) Please! Let's please try again . . . please! (I am with Chris. But I am hurting terribly, and she is different, firmer and more sure of herself; it is all over.)

*Phenomenological reality vs. therapist-patient reality.* When the therapist is predominantly attending to that center which the patient's behavior and words construct, the therapist may be described as existing in a state of phenomenological reality. That is, the therapist is attending to a meaningful attentional center within the phenomenal world of the patient and, to that extent, the therapist is sharing the phenomenological reality of the patient.

When the patient says "I," the reference is shared by both patient and therapist. With her attention on the wife who is threatening to leave, the therapist hears the patient's words as if they are coming both from the patient and also from the therapist. "If I quit my wife'll leave." The "I" in that statement comes as if from both the patient and from the therapist. Sometimes the therapist receives these words as if the therapist is really saying them along with the patient, or as if the patient is giving voice to something emanating from the therapist. There is a kind of blending or sharing. This is one of the meanings of sharing the patient's phenomenological reality.

Now that the patient has described the attentional center, it is easier for the therapist to allow most of her attention to go to that defined center. Now that the patient is attending to some focal center, the therapist is enabled to allow most of her attention to go to that center. Again, all that is necessary is about 50 to 80 percent of the therapist's attention to focus on the patient's defined center. Sharing the patient's phenomenological reality requires only that most of the therapist's attention be there, not all of it.

Once the therapist attends predominantly to the patient's attentional center, the center has a vividness, a concrete presence. It occurs with phenomenological reality. Suppose that the patient is attending to people who are following her around, who spy on her. She describes them, and thereby constructs them so that the therapist can attend to them. They are on black motorcycles. There are four of them. They are dressed in black and wear black helmets. Wherever she goes in the city, one or two of them are somewhere nearby. As the therapist attends to these motorcycling spies, they take on a phenomenological reality. "It would be quite futile for us to maintain that this table before us is more real than your motorcycling spies merely because they elude my perception and are perceptible only to you. Why don't we let both of them stand as the phenomena they reveal themselves to be?" (Boss, 1963, p. 13).

From outside the patient, from any vantage point in which the therapist regards the patient from across the therapist-patient relationship, there is another reality. It is the reality of the so-called objective world in which both therapist and patient are assumed to exist (cf. Chapter 5). From that perspective, the motorcycling spies are generally considered as not real. They are delusional. They are evidence of paranoid schizophrenia. They are signs of a loss of contact with reality. The phenomenological reality of the patient's world stands in distinct contrast to the therapist-patient reality of the therapist's world (Boss, 1963; Bugental, 1979; Havens, 1973; Mahrer, 1970b, 1978b, 1978d, 1980b). In the work of experiential psychotherapy, we choose the phenomenological reality of the patient's world.

Here is a rather dramatic way in which the difference between the perspective of phenomenological reality and the perspective of therapist-patient reality makes a real difference. Consider patient statements such as: "Do you know what I mean? . . . I spent so much of my life looking for answers from someone who understands. . . . I've always wanted to pour my heart out to someone, tell 'em my side of the whole damned story. . . ." When the therapist joins with the patient, when such statements come from both patient and therapist, then who and what is the attentional center? Who is the "you" in "Do you know what I mean?" From the perspective of phenomenological reality, the attentional center is some figure who is there to answer the question, to provide the understanding, to hear his side of the story. This figure may or may not be a therapist, or parent, or some special other person. On the other hand, from the perspective of the "objective reality" of the therapist-patient relationship, the above three statements are directly or indirectly addressed to the therapist and nothing more. There are at least two realities, two perspectives which yield and reveal rather different kinds of data.

*The Externalized Therapist: Further Instructions*

The therapist begins with instructions on how to center attention, and, immediately after finishing the instructions, the therapist aligns with the patient and allows his attentional field to go to whatever is constructed by the patient's behavior and words. A problem occurs when the therapist finds himself externalized once again. No longer aligned with the patient, no longer attending to what the patient's behavior and words construct in the attentional field, the externalized therapist is now attending predominantly to the patient.

Generally this occurs under two conditions. In one, the patient never really allows the therapist to share an attentional center. The therapist completes the instructions, moves next to the patient, gets ready to let attention go to whatever is constructed—and the patient talks to the therapist, places most of his attention on the therapist. The therapist is quickly externalized. This is the patient who says in effect, "Get away from me. I will not permit you to share my attentional field. Stay external like you were." As soon as the therapist completes the instructions, is positioned right next to the patient, and is ready to let the patient's words and behaviors define something in the attentional field, the patient says: "Do you want me to talk about Sarah? She's my girlfriend. I think you ought to know about her 'cause she is important now. I got problems on what to do with her. . . ."

The second condition is where the therapist has been sharing the patient's attentional center for some time. Then a rather curious phenomenon occurs in which the therapist always seems to wake up. Now, in the awakened state, the therapist finds himself attending to the patient, thinking about the patient, aware of the patient. It is as if the therapist had been in some altered state of sharing the patient's attentional center, and now the therapist is external to the patient, relating to and interacting with the patient. The therapist seems to wake up with an awareness of thoughts about the patient: "She has been silent for some time now; I wonder what is going on in her." "He certainly moves from topic to topic without having strong feelings." "She is feeling hurt and rejected now, and this is just the way she felt with her mother as a little girl." In any case, once the therapist is externalized, the next step is to provide further instructions once again.

*With emphasis upon the attentional center.* If the patient is talking mainly to the therapist about something, if less than half of the patient's attention is on the attentional field, then the whole process cannot proceed. Technically, what this means is that the preponderance of the therapist's attention must be on whatever is constructed by the patient in the attentional field; if only a part of the therapist's attention is on that attentional field, and if most of the therapist's attention is on being addressed, on the patient and their interaction, then the therapist is externalized and the problem must be corrected.

It is the job of the teacher to show the patient how to do it correctly, provided that the patient is ready and willing. Sometimes this may mean going over the instructions again and again. Sometimes it may mean repeated work on the more specific steps where the patient has difficulty (Gendlin, 1969, 1978a). But once the therapist is external, it is the therapist's responsibility to enable the patient to know the correct and effective ways of centering attention so that bodily sensations reach at least moderate proportions.

It is the eighteenth session, and the therapist has finished the instructions for defining an attentional center:

Pt: This guy at work, Peter . . . he is moving into my work. I don't like that. I mean he is OK in a way, but I don't like him intruding. He is a lot younger. Pushy . . . (The therapist is seeing this fellow in his late twenties. He seems to be physically close. Bodily sensations are the way they were at the very beginning of the session, i.e., a little muscular tightening across the shoulders.) But I guess he really isn't much to worry about. Thelma tells me that I am always paranoid about someone at work. (Now Thelma is there, and she is almost kidding me about this.) . . . and I think she is probably right. I remember when I worked at Templeton. . . . I was always bitching about this new guy that they hired. I guess I am just insecure about my competency. I have a right to think that way cause I move from job to job too much. . . . (At this point my attentional center is the patient himself. Along with my attention being fully on him, I am aware that my bodily sensations are neutral. We start over again.)
T: Jack, I'm attending mostly to you now. I'm not with you anymore, not attending to anything. And the feelings in my body are low. So maybe this isn't it. Maybe there's nothing here that can get anything started in our bodies. Or maybe we aren't in the right part of it. Where should we go so that most of our attention is on something and feelings start up in our bodies? (The patient continues, and we both share the same attentional center; I am no longer externalized.)

Pt: (Pause.) I want to talk about a woman I met. (Long pause.) Her name is Gloria. She is a secretary in our section. I went to lunch with her. I held her hand. . . . I touched her fingers. She's almost 10 years younger than I am. And she's married. And I think that I really like her. I think we like each other. She has red hair and a real nice voice, and she is always laughing. I think I am in love with her and she really likes me. We have . . . I told her that I wanted to touch her fingers. (The therapist is attending to Gloria, to being here at the table with her, to the touch and the feel of her fingers. I am touching them gently.)

For some patients it is important to emphasize the one to whom the patient is to talk. Talk to the person who is the center of attention, and not to the therapist. Talk to oneself, not the therapist. The following is from an initial session in which the patient's attention was centered by emphasizing his talking expressly to himself, and not to the therapist:

Pt: I think that what it is, is that if I could . . . I know you think I'm being illogical, but I recognize the state I'm in, depression. I know. But you know, I need help from you about what to do to get out of it. Am I being clear? I don't think I am, not usually. I just can't seem to get on with it. You understand, sometimes I think I just rattle on and I think I want to give you all the information you need to understand me. Maybe I can tell you more about it. I've been afraid of starting therapy. . . . I've thought about it for almost a year . . . going over all the information I supposed you wanted to know.
T: I was being afraid, and going over information. Then bam you talked to me! Suddenly I am here being talked to. If you are afraid, talk to the afraid, or talk to yourself about it. If you are going over information, then talk to yourself about what that's like. I want to be with you. We both can be afraid or go over information, or put attention on anything. Talk to yourself, not to me. OK?
Pt: OK. (Pause.) I am worried lately. About getting more and more depressed. (Pause.) I sound like a boring person. I think I am boring. I wonder if being depressed is so bad. But I've never had anyone to help me. I've never been married and never trusted any woman enough to talk with her. Oh, that sounds like something. Hell, I wonder if I pride myself on never trusting anyone ever. I am getting depressed. Let's see, how am I depressed? My head is getting dizzy. I don't think I ever talked like this before. I am thinking about my

older brother Donald. I haven't thought about him like this. Donald, what are you doing here? This is like a seance! Donald, you just left the family, didn't you? Well, Donald, I stayed with the family, and now I'm getting depressed. You know why I think I'm getting depressed, 'cause I'm tired of being with the family, Donald. I've resented you for all these years, God, you were about 16 when you left, and no one talks about you at all. We avoid talking about you, and here you are in my head, Donald. What are you doing? I know that you were somewhere in the east the past couple of years or so. . . . I miss you. . . . I would like to talk to you 'cause something is happening to me. . . . God I think I am losing my mind. . . .

All by himself, with a little instructing, the patient has allowed at least half of his attention to go to the attentional field.

For some patients it is helpful to repeat the words which tend to externalize the therapist. Some patient statements which are addressed to the therapist only serve to budge the therapist away from the attentional field, without fully externalizing the therapist. Under this condition, the therapist can stay with the patient by repeating the right words of the patient:

Pt: (Worrying about her marriage.) I am still fighting with him. We just seem to argue over everything, no matter what. I don't know. I just get so discouraged sometimes. I can't do what he wants. Sometimes I wish he would come to see you. (The therapist has been with him, and their relationship is bad, discouraging. The last few words tended to pull the therapist just a bit away from this attentional field.)
T: Sometimes I wish he would come to see you. . . . I wish he would come to see you. . . . He is right here, and it is bad. I feel discouraged.
Pt: (Big sigh.) I wonder why I married . . . I don't know whether it's his fault or mine. I wish I had the guts to just pack it in. How can I insist that he go to therapy? I can't . . . but I wish I had the guts to tell him. I don't tell him anything. All I know how to do is fight. I fight. But I dig in my heels and never . . . I don't know . . . (I am with him, but I won't talk with him, not to him. There is distance between us, unhappy and fighting distance.)

Another way of enabling the patient to deploy more attention is by moving over to another category. Essentially, the therapist samples the various categories of attentional centers in order to come up with one or two in which most of the attention can be centered with accompanying heightened feelings. Suppose that the patient started with changes he has been noticing in himself. The patient touches upon a few changes, but only light bits of attention go to those changes.

T: I was with you somewhat. But I was not feeling much in my body. . . .
Pt: Me neither. Funny.
T: Yeah, and not all my attention was poured into it.
Pt: No.
T: OK. Let's just sample around till we find something that pulls most of our attention, that we can go into more, where our body feels something more. . . . Have there been any moments recently, like in the last day or so, when there was some sort of rising up of feelings in you? Good or bad? Let's try this and see what happens.

We can go from one category to another, each time the therapist finds himself externalized, and nothing much had happened while the therapist was sharing the patient's attentional field.

*With emphasis upon bodily sensations.* When the therapist is externalized, the aim is to enable the patient to allow most of his attention to focus upon some center so that accompanying bodily sensations are at least moderate. Often the externalized therapist will be aware of the neutral level of bodily sensations. While the patient is behaving and talking, nothing is happening in the therapist's body. Sometimes the patient's attention is focused on some center, and at other times the patient's attention is diffused or aimed at the therapist. But, in any case, the level of bodily sensations is low. That is the problem. What does the therapist do? The therapist gives further instructions which emphasize the occurrence of at least moderate bodily sensations.

It may work simply to repeat the instructions each time the therapist finds herself externalized, and with neutral bodily sensations.

Pt: . . . I try to answer my boss' questions during the committee meeting. But I know that I don't talk, uh, what should I say . . . pointedly. Jack always waits a while and then tells the boss pretty much what I was trying to say, and the boss is polite. I mean . . . but that's when I just get all frazzled. I really want to say something right here to my boss . . . I don't know what, though. There is always this little pause . . .

T: I was with you at first, and being here with the boss and Jack and in
the committee meeting. But then nothing happened in my body. Do
it all again. Let yourself be here again with them . . . good. But let
feelings happen in your body so that something happens. Do it again,
and let bodily feelings happen. Any kind, good or bad, and anywhere
in the body. OK?

The patient may need only this reminder a few times. Each time the
therapist finds herself externalized with low bodily sensations, she may
repeat the initial instructions until there is attentional centering accompanied with at least moderate bodily sensations, though the guideline
is mainly that of constant repetition of this part of the standard instructions.

Another procedure is for the externalized therapist to show the patient
exactly where bodily sensations rose, and what they were. This generally
occurs when bodily sensations rose during the course of a patient statement, only to become neutral again by the end of the statement. In the
following, the patient is attending to her son, and bodily sensations in
the therapist are quite neutral and low.

Pt: . . . There was a thing that Tommy did. He took something away
from the boy next door. Tommy is only eight, and he owns everything. He's gotta own everything. Won't share anything. Nothing.
He's always been that way. (Here is Tommy, and I sense a sort of
criticalness toward him.) I got mad at him. I always get mad at him.
There's no reason to behave like that. (I am almost saying this to
Tommy who is there in front of me.) I don't like what he
does . . . (sigh) . . . I'm gonna have to go to the dentist. I don't mind
that. He's darling. (Short nervous burst of laughter.) (With the burst
of laughter, it was as if the tension suddenly heightened in the therapist's body, as if the pressure shot up suddenly, for a moment.
During that moment the therapist was attending to the darling dentist,
and there is a quickened, almost swooningly sexual relationship with
this darling man.) Oh, I got a cavity. But my teeth are good. I can
thank my mother for that. She's got teeth like a horse, and she always
made me brush them regularly. (Bodily sensations are dead once
again, and I am externalized. I am aware of being external, and also
of the neutral level of bodily sensations in me. One way to proceed
is to highlight the earlier attentional center which was accompanied
with heightened bodily sensations.)

T: Something happened in my body especially when I was with the dentist. He was darling, and when I was with him, just for a second or two, it's like my blood pressure went up. I got all excited in my body. Things started moving inside.

Pt: Yeah . . .

T: Well, after that it all stopped and I was dead inside . . . so maybe that is the place to start again. And this time let the bodily feelings stay for a while. I can be with the dentist . . . and there . . . it's starting again. Let the bodily sensations be strong.

Pt: He's beautiful. (Little laugh.) When he leans over me and puts his face close to mine . . . I get excited. But no. No. He is gorgeous. If I was ever to have an affair, he would be the one. I never had a gorgeous man, and (starting to get more excited) he's gorgeous. But I should before I die. (Hard full laughing.)

Identify when and where the bodily sensations rose up, and what the attentional center was at the time. Tell the patient to have strong bodily sensations by going back to that moment and continuing from there. It is as if you are showing the patient how and when he was successful in allowing stronger bodily sensations to occur.

The patient may be saying words which ought to be accompanied with strong feelings. They sound like serious words. However, the therapist remains firmly externalized and bodily sensations are dead, or the therapist seems to find herself no longer attending to any center and instead is aware that nothing much was or is occurring in her body.

Pt: (In the beginning of the thirty-second session.) I am depressed. Nothing seems to mean anything anymore. Whole life is numb. . . . I was wondering what would happen if I just died. No one would care. I am so useless and empty in this life. . . .

The therapist had tried to position herself with the patient, saying the words along with the patient, and attending to the attentional center. But she is external, and nothing has happened in her body. She repeats the instructions, but indicates that the patient may say essentially the same words so as to allow bodily sensations to occur:

T: I could not be with you, not really. But mostly, nothing happened in my body. Maybe all this is important. If you want, say it all again, but this time try to let anything happen in your body. Anything. Let bodily sensations happen.

Pt: Dying is not so bad . . . what would happen if I die? . . . I may as

well . . . everyone takes up so little space . . . we talk and mean nothing. There is nothing between us . . . it's all so empty. . . . (There are
shadowy other figures around, and all without substance. I am aware
of the tension which is forming in my stomach. It is hot there, and
with tension now.) I am so alone. . . .

The therapist must be careful that some of the patient's words may
qualify as a statement of the "problem" to the external therapist, but
the accompanying bodily sensations are low or neutral, and the externalized therapist has no attentional center at all.

Pt: I'll tell you, do I have a problem. Everyone I work with. I have been
    fucked over for years. And now Sarah and I have thought about it.
    Why should I go on running the business? And believe me, I'm the
    one who runs the business. I should get out. But I can't. That's my
    problem.

Pt: Everything is fine in a way. There's nothing wrong with me. I can
    live all right. But I just don't seem really happy. Nothing makes me
    feel real good anymore. I'm not depressed, but I don't have any real
    happiness.

Pt: I used to enjoy sex. But you know . . . lately, well there is no sex.
    My wife and I . . . we don't have sex. I have lost my . . . sex means
    nothing to me. I don't have any real feelings for Penny anymore. I'm
    not that old. . . .

In each of these three excerpts, the therapist is externalized, and bodily
sensations are neutral. Accordingly, the therapist repeats the instructions with emphasis upon saying the right words in the right way so
that bodily sensations can occur with some real strength. Even when
the patient seems to label something as a problem, if bodily sensations
are low, further instructions are in order.

## REACHING THE WORKING LEVEL
## OF EXPERIENCING

So far, the therapist has shown the patient how to locate and describe
the bodily sensations and how to let attention go to some meaningful
center. If everything goes very well, here is what is occurring:

(a)  Most of the patient's attention is focused on some meaningful cen-
     ter, most of the therapist's attention is directed onto that same
     center, and very little of their attention is on one another.
(b)  At least moderate bodily sensations are occurring in the patient,
     and at least moderate bodily sensations of a similar kind are
     occurring in the therapist.
(c)  The therapist has entered into the phenomenal world of the patient.
     This is the consequence of sharing the patient's bodily sensations
     and attentional center.
(d)  Some kind of experiencing is occurring in the patient and in the
     therapist and it is occurring to at least a moderate degree. In
     short, we are at the working level of experiencing.

But it is rare for all of this to be accomplished with instructions alone.
In perhaps only 10-20 percent of the sessions does the patient follow
the instructions so well that a good measure of experiencing is now
occurring. In most sessions, the therapist must carry out other operations
in order to bring the patient to what may be called the working level of
experiencing. What else does the therapist do to attain what may be
called the working level of experiencing?

*The Criteria and Meaning of the Working Level of Experiencing*

If most of the patient's attention is on a meaningful center, and if
there is at least a moderate level of bodily sensations, then it almost
automatically follows that experiencing is occurring. Technically, the
problem is how to place the predominance of attention on the right
center, and how to allow at least moderate bodily sensations to occur.
When these two are accomplished, experiencing takes care of itself.
Reaching the working level of experiencing means enabling the patient
to attend properly and to have bodily sensations.

What are the criteria of having reached this level? How does the
therapist know when the preponderance of attention is centered, when
at least moderate bodily sensations are occurring? The key is that the
therapist has entered into the phenomenological world of the patient,
at least to some degree, i.e., the therapist is next to the patient, attending
to whatever the patient is attending to, and the therapist's body has
sensations similar to those occurring in the patient's body. Accordingly,
the perhaps surprising criterion is that (a) the preponderance of the
*therapist's* attention is on something which is constructed by the patient's

words, that is, an attentional center, and (b) at least moderate sensations are occurring in the *therapist's* body. When the patient talks in the beginning of a session, after the instructions to attend and to have bodily sensations, the therapist simply locates himself in the vicinity of the patient's phenomenological world. If the therapist's attention is not centered, if only a little of the therapist's attention is deployed onto something, then the working level of experiencing is not yet attained. If bodily sensations in the therapist are neutral or low, then the working level is not yet attained. Once the therapist has positioned himself, has taken a locus where he is ready to attend to the patient's attentional center and to undergo the associated bodily sensations, then it is the *therapist* who becomes the criterion. It is important to emphasize that the only criterion of what the patient is doing and saying, and the only criterion of what the patient's behavior and words are constructing, is that most of the *therapist's* attention is focused on some center which is accompanied with at least a moderate level of bodily sensations.

Sometimes the words and the attentional centers are commonplace and mundane. Sometimes they are dramatic. What matters is only what is occurring in the therapist. If her attention is on some center, if her bodily experiencing is at least moderate, and if a good measure is occurring in her, the working level of experiencing is reached.

The attentional center may be coterminal with whatever may be regarded as the patient's "problem" from the perspective of other approaches. For example, the working level of experiencing may occur when the patient's attention is on his being an awful drunk, and therapists from other approaches may consider the patient to be an "alcoholic," or to have a serious "drinking problem." On the other hand, it is most common that there is little or no relationship between what the therapist in other approaches regards as the "problem" or "psychopathology" and, on the other hand, what the patient is doing and saying when the working level of experiencing is reached.

Our aim is to reach the working level of experiencing. To accomplish this, the important data consist of the patient's and therapist's bodily sensations, attentional centers, and experiencings. These are the only data which are used. No other data are important. Indeed, all other data are regarded as offering very little.

If the patient says, "I grew up in Hong Kong. . . . I am going to shoot my neighbor. . . . I got my grandmother pregnant," the important data consist of the bodily sensations, attentional center, and experiencing which occur when the patient says all this. If the patient is moving about, coughing a little, holding his legs, or moving his arms around, the important data consist of the bodily sensations, attentional centers, and experiencing which occur when the patient is doing this. If the level of bodily sensations is flat, if the patient's behavior and words fail to construct anything in the attentional field, if very little of the patient's attention is on that attentional field, if, in other words, experiencing is low, then these data are worth very little. It has little importance where he grew up. Data about his intent to shoot his neighbor are unimportant data. How and when he got his grandmother pregnant is of little therapeutic import. We move in the direction of a working level of experiencing, and the behavior and words of the patient provide important data only in terms of the heightened bodily sensations, the nature of the constructed attentional field, and the level of the attendant experiencing.

*Therapist readiness and the criteria of effective therapist statements.* If an effective therapist gives the right sets of instructions to an effective patient, this working level of experiencing may be attained in five or 10 minutes. Sometimes it requires about 20 minutes or more. The patients for whom this therapy is appropriate either start right out in the first few sessions, or they quickly learn how to reach the working level after a few sessions. Reaching the working level of experiencing is not a matter of gradual learning, of slow progress over five or 10 or 20 sessions. As Gendlin indicates (1969), it is not a matter of gradual progress. Experiential patients allow the predominance of attention to focus upon a meaningful center accompanied with at least moderate bodily sensations. Other patients, those for whom experiential therapy is not appropriate, will persist in attending predominantly to the therapist and will engage in the construction of role relationships. Patients tend to fall into one of these two groups right away, rather than slowly and gradually becoming more proficient over many sessions.

In general, I find that most patients are quite ready to move to the working level; I also find that many therapists are not ready. Many therapists must construct role relationships with their patients. Many therapists are unwilling or unable to have the kind of experiencings which are occurring in patients. It is all right for the patient to experience lunacy or wildness or sexual cravings or violence or depression, but it is threatening or unpleasant for the therapist to risk having such experiencings. Regardless of the reason, many therapists end up in a role relationship. They would find it quite difficult to share the patient's bodily sensations, and even harder to share the patient's attentional center. They will be unable to enter into the patient's phenomenal world and reach a working level of experiencing. Instead, these therapists will remain rooted to the external location, with virtually all their attention on the patient, and their hesitancies will take forms such as the following constructed roles encompassing the patient:

1) The patient is weak, fragile, vulnerable. "He is not ready for strong experiencing. He cannot cope with the stress. His ego is too weak at this point. Such strong experiencing will be harmful to the patient."

2) The patient is potentially dangerous and capable of impulsive acts which are bad. "His controls are not strong enough; he might act out. If he is subjected to too much stress, he might be at the mercy of dangerous impulses. Strong affect will have dangerous consequences for him."

3) The patient needs my help and my strength to grow upon gradually. "Strong experiencing is premature; the relationship is not strong enough. He must first gain strength and trust in our relationship."

The therapist who enters into the patient's phenomenal world leaves behind such ways of constructing the patient. This therapist is ready to reach the working level of experiencing. Therapists who are not yet ready to attain the working level of experiencing will remain in an external relationship with the patient, and they will construct role relationships which are incongruent with a working level of experiencing.

The balance of this section deals with what the therapist does to reach this working level of experiencing. With some patients some of the time, the instructions are sufficient to reach the working level of experiencing. With other patients at other times, the therapist and patient may not yet have attained the working level of experiencing. Under these conditions, the therapist—already entered into the patient's phenomenal world—speaks from the locus of the patient, and engages in phenomenological description. We now turn to these two methods of reaching the working level of experiencing.

*Speaking from the Locus of the Patient*

From within the patient's phenomenological world, the therapist is mainly attending to the patient's attentional center. The rest of the therapist's attention includes what is happening in the therapist's body. This means that the therapist speaks from the locus of the patient. This also means that the therapist does not talk to the patient. So one side of this guideline is to maintain attention mainly on the attentional center and secondarily on what is occurring in the therapist's body. The other side of this guideline is that the therapist does not withdraw attention, pull out of the phenomenological world of the patient, and talk to the patient.

Consider the first statement of the patient following instructions to center attention:

Pt: I'm trying to do a good job. But, I don't know. Maybe I ain't in the right job. I don't know. I want to do the job. But . . . I try my best. I just ain't making anybody happy. Least of all me. I don't even want to go to work. My boss is OK. He's OK, I mean, he does his job all right. He says I'm doing OK . . . I don't know. I ain't got any real enthusiasm for it. Not much. I try to do a good job. But I just don't feel like going . . . (At this point bodily sensations become moderate.) Ah shit! If I quit my wife'll leave. She's said she's had it with my quitting all the time. She really means it!

Here are some therapist statements which come from the locus of the patient:

T: Oh yes, I know she really means it this time!
T: I can just about hear her screaming.
T: I wonder if she's got the guts to go through with it.

The grammar of the therapist's statements is such that the words might be spoken by the patient as well as the therapist. If the preponderance of the therapist's attention is on the wife, then the therapist's words will come from the locus of the patient. "I" will refer to the person who is attending to the wife, and that includes both patient and therapist. Even when the therapist's words do not include "I," the words come out properly when the therapist's attention is preponderantly on the wife, and not on the patient:

T: She sounds like she means it this time.
T: She won't take it any longer.
T: It won't be long. She'll be gone.

The consequences of such statements include heightened attention on the wife, heightened bodily sensations, and the occurrence of at least moderate experiencing. Now the patient attends even more to his wife. If only some of his attention had been on his wife, now perhaps most of it is on his wife.

### Phenomenological Description

The therapist can help the patient reach a working level of experiencing by doing the following:

(a) The therapist describes what occurs in his attentional field. If the therapist is attending to mother's face, that is what the therapist describes.

(b) The therapist describes prominent sensations which occur in his body. If he suddenly has butterflies in his stomach, he describes what that is like.

(c) The therapist repeats, with more and more feeling, those immediate behaviors or words of the patient which start the bodily sensations in the therapist. These are the key words and the key behaviors.

(d) The therapist stays with whatever he is describing. "Staying with" is an important guideline.

(e) The therapist uses the sensitive risings and fallings of his own bodily sensations as a trusted tracking guide.

As a package, these comprise phenomenological description. We shall take up each in turn.

*Staying with the phenomenon.* Phenomenological description means that therapist and patient stay with the phenomenon. Look at the attentional center. Let yourself see it more and more. This is the way of understanding. "The unprejudiced return to the 'things themselves,' i.e., inspection of knowledge 'itself' as given to us *directly*, with nothing mediating or interfering, reveals the intentionality or act-character of all behavior" (Buytendijk, 1950, p. 127). Describe it. Describe it carefully. Attend to it and describe it and attend to it further; ". . . the existential understanding of man and his world demands that we look at the phenomena of our world themselves, as we are confronted by them. In other words, Daseinsanalytic statements never seek to be anything more than 'mere,' albeit severely strict, careful and subtle descriptions and expositions of the essential aspects and features of all things . . ." (Condrau & Boss, 1971, p. 498). Describe each aspect and feature in detail. "By the method of phenomenology, which will admit no previous frame of reference as favored in the task of understanding the patient, the various phenomena of the patient's world as they are reported by the patient are described in greatest detail" (Needleman, 1967b, p. 30). We stay with the phenomenon; we do not deflect attention by rushing away from the phenomenon.

For example, after the therapist's instructions, the patient says: "Something's there. In me. Always. A thing. Like an inertia. It won't let anything happen. Pulls me back. There's something that keeps me in place." In some approaches, the therapist seeks to understand by rushing away from the phenomenon:

T: How do you feel about having something like that?
T: How long has it been that way? When did it first start?
T: How does it interfere in your life? Does it stop you from working? Do you think about it a lot?

These kinds of therapist statements pull the patient's attention away from the phenomenon. It is understanding of it by rushing away from it. The choice is always whether to stay with the phenomenon or move away from it.

Pt: Well, I'm ashamed. Lately . . . for the past months, maybe even a year, I don't want him to . . . George, my husband, I don't want him to touch me. Sexually . . . I can't tell him about it. But I guess I don't want sex with him.

Staying with the phenomenon may mean staying with some aspect of George or some aspect of not wanting to have sex with him. On the other hand, if the therapist deflects the patient's attention off to something else, we are not staying with the phenomenon, not using phenomenological description, and we will not move toward the working level of experiencing:

T: How do you feel about not wanting sex with him? (The patient's attention is partly drawn toward the therapist, in answering this question, and partly on some sort of feelings she is supposed to have about this.)

T: Did anything happen maybe a year ago? (The patient's attention is set to scanning her life a year ago, looking for events which might explain all of this.)

T: Well, what's so wrong with that? Sex wears out after years, often. (The patient's attention is on the therapist and on considering the proposition put forward by the therapist.)

*Experiential description of the therapist's attentional field.* We allow our attention to penetrate down into the phenomenon so that we attend to it just a bit further, so that bodily sensations become just a bit stronger, so that experiencing is carried just a bit further. The patient says: "Something's there. In me. Always. A thing. Like an inertia. It won't let anything happen. Pulls me back. There's something that keeps me in place." The therapist allows attention to go to that. Now what is there for this therapist? For one therapist, what appears is an evilness. For another therapist, what appears is a powerful force which owns the person. The therapist describes what is there and what it is like:

T1: It is something evil.

T2: Like some powerful force that owns me.

What happens? When one therapist says, "It is something evil," nothing happens. "It" is not clarified or defined or attended to more. Bodily sensations do not increase. Nothing happens to the experiencing. But when the second therapist says, "Like some powerful force that owns me," things happen. The attentional field becomes more vivid and defined. Bodily sensations become stronger. Experiencing moves ahead. Now the patient and therapist are attending to something which is in me like an inertia, will not let anything happen, pulls me back, keeps me in place—and is like a powerful force that owns me. The last few words define it just that little bit more. And now I have a chilling sensation in my back, and I start to experience a sense of being weak, giving in, succumbing. This is experiential description; ". . . some rare words have a felt effect. I call it an *experiential effect*. As these rare words come, one senses a sharpened feeling, or a felt relief, a felt shift, usually before one can say what this shift is. Sometimes such words are not in themselves very impressive or novel, but just those words have an experiential effect, and no others do. . . ." (Gendlin, 1969, p. 4).

As the therapist attends, something will appear; something will come forth and capture the attentional center. It may be its evilness, or its stone-like quality, or its being a powerful force that owns me, or its dark grey color, or its being like a heavy person who is sitting on me. Whatever aspect pulls my attention is what I describe. If I describe it and the attentional field becomes more defined, bodily sensations heighten, and experiencing carries forward, then we are on the right track.

Here is an example of describing the therapist's attentional field:

Pt: I remember my aunt was in the hospital and I visited her. She had something wrong. Not serious. Can't remember. But she asked me things. She had that same attitude toward me. Like I don't mean anything to her.

As the patient says these words, the therapist allows them to define the attentional field. What comes forth is the aunt and, as the patient says ". . . that same attitude toward me. Like I don't mean anything to her," the emergent attentional field consists of the aunt conveying that attitude.

T: She tends to look down on me. She has little respect. She never did.
Pt: She always treated me like I was dirt. Me and my father. She never liked me.

Now what happens to the therapist's attentional field? It features the aunt and her private thoughts. The therapist's attention is drawn toward the aunt's thinking that she never liked me. And with that, bodily sensations start in the therapist. She is aware of a warmth in the chest, and of the heart beating rapidly. The therapist describes the changing attentional field:

T: She is thinking, thinking that she never liked me. . . .
Pt: She doesn't! But she never comes right out . . . never! She treats me like I'm some sort of trash. Garbage! What right does she have? Why? Just because my father never went to college? We don't have money! But damn her! Damn her! Who the fuck does she think she is?

Attention is focused now, and bodily sensations are heightened in the therapist. Experiencing is carrying forward. In short, we are now at the working level of experiencing. We arrived at this working level by speaking from the locus of the patient, by staying with the phenomenon, and by using experiential description of the therapist's attentional field.

*Feelinged repetition of the critical patient words.* As the patient behaves and talks, the therapist's attention is divided between the attentional field and the sensations in the therapist's body. A sensitive attentiveness to the bodily sensations will identify those behaviors and words which are accompanied with some heightening of the immediate bodily sensations in the therapist. Some bodily sensation happens just a bit more. There is a heightening, even if it is only slight. These are the critical patient behaviors and words. When these occur, the therapist repeats just these behaviors and words, again and again, and the therapist does this in a manner which allows heightened bodily sensations to occur. This is feelinged repetition of the critical patient behaviors and words.

Pt: I remember my aunt was in the hospital and I visited her. She had something wrong. Not serious. Can't remember. But she asked me things. She had *that same attitude toward me. Like I don't mean anything to her.*

The italicized words were accompanied with a rising up of the sensations in the therapist's body. It included an inner jump or shift in the therapist's stomach region.

T: That same attitude toward me. Like I don't mean anything to her . . . that same attitude toward me . . . I don't mean anything to her . . . again . . . again . . . more feeling . . . more feeling! That same attitude . . . I don't mean anything to her! (The therapist is saying this slower and with more feelings. The heart is jumping now. Here are the critical words, and the patient joins in.)
Pt: She has that attitude toward me . . . I don't mean anything to her . . .
T: That same attitude! I don't mean anything to her! I don't mean anything to her!
Pt: That damned attitude! I don't mean anything to her!
T: Again! Again! More feeling! (The therapist is addressing both himself and the patient.) That damned attitude! I don't mean anything to her!
Pt: (With angry frustration and hurt.) I *hate* thaat attitude! I *hate* her! I don't mean a damned thing to her! Not a damned thing!

Feelinged repetition is another way of phenomenological description, and the consequence is the working level of experiencing. In the following, the patient is talking about the cancer:

Pt: . . . There are touches of it in my wrist . . . my left wrist. And in my scalp. My head . . . I go back for tests all the time. But the cancer . . . it seems to. . . . They tell me the chances are good. But I don't know. Something is so awful about it. . . . They do chemotherapy and it spreads anyhow. It used to be . . . *it just won't go away. It just moves around.* . . .

The italicized words are accompanied with an increase in facial flushing. The therapist repeats these words with some heightening of feeling.

T: It just won't go away. It just moves around. . . . It just won't go away. It just moves around! Again! Again!
Pt: It won't go away. It won't go away. It just won't go away! It won't go away! It won't go away!
T: Again, again, again! More feeling! It won't go away! It won't go away! It won't go away!
Pt: (The words are getting louder and louder, and are spoken faster and faster. There is a rising sense of desperation.) It will never go away. Never go away. It will never go away! Never! Never!!! It won't go away!!! (Now the patient is screaming out the words, and there is a terror in the way in which the words are exploded out.)

*The therapist's fluctuating bodily sensations as a tracking guide.* Phenomenological description means using one's bodily sensations as the trusted guide. If these particular words and behaviors are coupled with an increase in bodily sensations, then we are moving in the right direction. If these words and behaviors are accompanied with no increase in bodily sensations, or with dead sensations, then we are not on the right path.

About half the therapist's attention is on whatever is occurring in the therapist's attentional field, and the rest of the therapist's attention is on what is occurring in the body. In this way, the ongoing fluctuations in bodily sensations serve as a sensitive gauge or tracking guide to which a good measure of attention is always directed. No matter what phenomenon we start with, the bodily sensations will lead us in the right direction, i.e., toward attaining the working level of experiencing. We may be led over here and over there, to this aspect and that, down here and into that part over there. No matter how mixed up or shifting is the movement, the overall direction is inexorably toward the working level of experiencing.

*Phenomenological Description and the Process of Reaching the Working Level of Experiencing*

By means of phenomenological description, the therapist and patient move along until a point is reached where most of the attention is on some center, and the bodily sensations have heightened to a level where they are at least of moderate strength. As the patient behaves and talks, the therapist can attend to whatever is constructed. The more the therapist follows the guidelines of phenomenological description, a point is reached where most of the attention is on some meaningful center accompanied by at least moderate bodily sensations, and there is a working level of experiencing. That is the goal. We have achieved the crucial first step of attention-centered bodily experiencing (Figure 2.2).

In the following examples, the therapist may or may not have started by sharing the patient's bodily sensations. However, the therapist has given instructions for sharing the patient's attentional center; then, immediately following the instructions, the therapist placed himself next to the patient, ready for the patient's words to construct something within the general attentional field. As soon as the patient begins behaving and talking, the therapist follows the above guidelines of phenomenological description in a process which culminates in the working level of experiencing. The first example is taken from the initial session with a man in his early thirties:

Pt: Well, I feel worried all the time. (Nothing forms on the attentional field.) . . . just worried. More so lately. Well, I guess I always feel worried . . . no, not just worried. More like I'm tight inside. Like I'm scared . . . (Something is forming now. It is a vague something, located as if it is inside the therapist. It is a quivering tightness, but cloudy and vague.)

T: Something sort of inside, a ball maybe. And all tight up.

Pt: Yeah, and it always seems to be inside me. It gets worse . . . (While the patient is talking, there is a continuing slightly nauseous sensation in the stomach. It is slight, but that is the most prominent bodily sensation.) . . . and lately it seems to be there all the time. Like now. I am afraid. I just can't stop myself from having thoughts. . . . (Two things occur instantly. One is that the therapist's attention goes to thoughts. They are scary thoughts. Bad thoughts. And the other is that the bodily sensations jump forward. It is as if the whole stomach region clutches up just a wee bit more than it had been. But the patient continues.) I have thoughts that are there in my head and I have wondered about them. I haven't talked to anyone about them. But sometimes I get drunk. On beer. To not have thoughts. When I get drunk I feel better. (The bodily sensations have receded, and they are neutral now. Here is the slight nauseous sensation once again. The therapist's attention is still on thoughts. But now they are less definite.)

T: I'm still thinking about the thoughts, a little anyhow.

Pt: My sister is living here now. She came about a month ago and she's staying in my place till she gets a place. She's starting school, nursing. (The therapist visualizes the sister. She is in her bedroom, putting things away in some drawers. Bodily sensations are softer, but still neutral and still in the stomach region.)

T: She has her own bedroom and keeps her stuff there.

Pt: Lise is pretty. She's my youngest sister. (There is an image of her face, a sweet look on the face, an attractive looking face and hair.) I have always trusted her. (Here is a scene of childhood, in the house. Talking with Lise and telling her special things, personal things.)

T: Being with her. Younger. She is a child.

Pt: I was always the kind of sad one in the family. Quiet. But Lise was my favorite. She is six years younger. She was always the wild one. Well, she was skinny and pretty and I liked her. (The attention is focused now on Lise. She is about eight or nine, and we are together somewhere. It is vague. The bodily sensation is getting slightly stronger. There is a slight increase in the tension in the stomach. Not much.)

T: She's about eight or nine, and we are together.

Pt: (Pause.) She always laughed. And one day she hit my Dad with a broom. (Laughs.) Boy, she really belted him. (Here is a vivid image of Lise getting really mad and hitting Dad on the head with the broom. Inside the body there is a lightening up, a sort of easing and almost warmth in the stomach.)

T: (Lightly and with good humor.) Good for her!

Pt: Yeah . . . (Pause. Now the words pour out in a flood.) All I think about is Lise. I want to touch her face and her hands. I want her to stay with me. Not go to some dorm. I know that's crazy. I want to

have sex with her. She's about all I think of lately. (All of this is said
with a rush. Bodily sensations are strong, and they include a prominent tingling across the skin. The whole skin, everywhere, is alive
and excited. Now I am quite close to Lise. She is in my apartment.
I am so very close to her.)

T: I can practically reach out and touch her. Her neck, face . . . soft,
lovely.

Pt: I want to push up against her, and I want to pull her against me. My
God, I want to fuck her! (I am touching her back and buttocks. There
is sheer sex in me. I am grabbing her close. The bodily sensations are
now moderately strong. I am aware of sexual feelings across my chest,
lower torso, and especially in the genitals.)

We have now reached the working level of experiencing. Most of the
patient's attention is on the meaningful center, bodily sensations are
moderately strong, and experiencing is starting to happen.

The next patient started with a sense of depression, of things not
going right. With phenomenological description something quite different emerges as the patient reaches the working level of experiencing:

Pt: Feel heavy. Like crying. Restless, don't know what it is like. (The
therapist's attention is drawn to something heavy, like crying, restless.)

T: Fills me, and it keeps moving. (That is what the attentional field looks
like.)

Pt: Like it wants me to get mad.

T: It's talking, harshly, croaking out words at me.

Pt: I see my mother! Clear! She's got on a red robe, and her hair . . . she
is doing something to me. Grabbing me by the arm.

T: She's really mad!

Pt: I can be strong . . . I can show her. You're just an old thing! I'll show
you!

T: (The last words were accompanied with a heightening of bodily sensations in the therapist.) I can show her . . . I can show her . . . I can
show her! Again, again, again . . .

Pt: (With tension.) I can show her. I can show you! I can show you! I
can fight back!! I'll show you! (The attentional scene is vivid, bodily
sensations are strong, and we are at the working level of experiencing.)

This next excerpt is from the beginning of the 22nd session, well after the instructions for centering attention:

Pt: . . . Those are the little games that we play. I feel lonely when I do this, like putting a shell around myself. (The last words started a throbbing in the stomach of the therapist.)

T: Putting a shell around myself. Again. Putting a shell around myself. More feeling. Putting a shell around myself!

Pt: Putting a shell around myself . . . a shell around myself! (He says this louder and louder.) A shell around myself! A shell around myself! (Now the attentional field reveals a big fat body, the shell.)

T: A big fat body!

Pt: A big fat body! Big. Fat! Heavy. It feels like all fat, heavy. I am heavy. My shell. It feels like lead. My belly is huge. I am big. No one can reach me. I have no feelings. I am like lead. I am numb. No one can reach me! No one. No one at all! (The attentional field is populated with vague figures.)

T: Lots of people out there. They can't get to me.

Pt: No! No one! My sister. She wants me to . . . my mother and my father! They all want something from me. They want me to be good, and . . . and nice! (That word does it. I am suddenly warm.)

T: Nice! Nice! Nice! Nice! They want me to be nice! Nice! More, again, again, again, more . . .

Pt: I'm supposed to be nice. They are getting to me. They want to consume me. They are eating me up. They are getting to me! (Here is the working level of experiencing, with a vivid attentional field of these persons "getting to me," and the bodily sensations at the working level.)

In the following example, the patient responded to the instructions by talking at some length about his various problems. His words constructed rather vivid images and scenes for the therapist, but the therapist's bodily sensations only rose up at the very end of the long statement:

Pt: . . . and another problem I've had for a long time, and it's coming back again recently. I, ah, I have trouble with . . . I seem to salivate a lot and I swallow. Can't seem to control it and I was doing this for, oh, ever since I can remember, maybe since I was about 12. Until a year or so ago in the fall when I saw Dr. Stenmark, the psychiatrist they referred me to. And she told me that I was swallowing my sadness and, uh, it seemed to . . . discussing it seemed to help for a while. I only saw her two or three times and it helped for a while, but it came back again right away and I seemed not to have to do it anymore except once in a while, well I was aware of it more I guess. It started bothering me again and it starts up occasionally. I guess when I'm nervous about something or maybe upset about something. (So far, bodily sensations are quite low.) Then I notice that I do it and I wish it would go away but, well, I'm starting to wonder and I worry that I always got it and it'll always be there cause it's getting worse lately and I really hate it and I guess what bothers me most is *when it is getting to others. Like if I'm with someone and I keep swallowing and they start doing it too. We never discuss it but they do it too.*

Bodily sensations rise up with the last few sentences. Moreover, the therapist's bodily sensations are good ones, and they consist of bubbly laughing in the face and throat. What is constructed is the other person who is swallowing, starting to when I swallow. I do it and then they do it.

T: (Lightly, and laughing.) Look at him swallowing!
Pt: Yeah, he started . . . I got him to swallow. (My attention is on the other person who is like a puppet, and I pull the strings by swallowing. My head is very light, and there is more laughing in me.)
T: (Lightly). He's like a puppet.
Pt: (Laughing lightly.) No, no! I don't like doing this to him! I make him swallow when I do! (The scene is getting sillier. Now the other person is really like a puppet.) . . . I can get him to swallow. . . . (He laughs more.) I feel like walking around swallowing and getting everyone to swallow. (He starts laughing rather hard.) Swallow!!

We are now at the working level of experiencing. Most of our attention is on a whole bunch of people who are swallowing when we get them to. The bodily sensations are full-bodied laughing, located mainly in the face. We both are laughing rather hard. The experiencing is a gigantic sense of whimsical power and control. We have attained the working level of experiencing by engaging in phenomenological description.

The next example is taken from the beginning of the 48th session of a woman whose predominant bodily sensation consisted of a sexual throbbing in the genitals. After sharing the bodily sensations, the therapist gave the instructions for sharing the attentional center, and the patient went to a recent incident with her mother:

Pt: My mother called me last night. About 10 o'clock. When the phone rang I was startled. I was in bed with Laura and actually we were almost asleep. (Bodily sensations are still in the genitals. Attention is mainly on the phone and on mother. Attention is generalized.)

T: The phone. Calling now. Seems kind of late.

Pt: She was like a child. She was worried. She just wanted to talk. She seemed so defenseless. All she did was want to talk. Laura slept through the whole thing. I just listened mainly. (I hear mother on the phone. It is almost as if she really is a little child. A little insecure, that is all.)

T: She just sounds a little insecure.

Pt: Afterward Laura and I had sex. The best ever. We stayed up almost the whole night. It was everything . . . something about the way Mom and I were. I was close to her and no old tricks. Just honest talking. I said everything to her that made sense. I . . . (I do not see mother. Instead, I sense what it is like to be physically right next to her, almost as if we are in bed together, talking in this special way.) . . . loved talking.

T: Like with Laura on one side and something delicious and special with mother right here on the other side. I can feel what it is like to almost feel her presence.

Pt: Your voice sounds so soft and mellow. God. I do love you. I want to bring you close to me, just closer and closer . . . (soft regular deep breathing) . . . I feel like a breeze inside you. Oh that feels so good. Mmmmmmm. (We are now at the working level. The experiencing is of almost a gentle sexual swooning. Bodily sensations are warm and juicy and fill the whole genital area. Attention is largely on the physical closeness with mother.)

A working level of experiencing is reached by following the guidelines for phenomenological description. It is a process which begins with the instructions, uses the guidelines, and moves toward a point where experiencing is at least of moderate proportions, most of the therapist's and patient's attention are on an attentional center, and bodily sensations are of at least moderate proportions.

## SHARING THE PATIENT'S
## PHENOMENAL WORLD

In Chapter 5 (see Figure 5.1), a proposition was put forward that virtually all therapies fall under four versions of a single paradigm, and that experiential therapy falls under a second paradigm. This was called the phenomenological paradigm. The distinguishing hallmark of the phenomenological paradigm is that the therapist has entered into the phenomenal world of the patient. In the present chapter, the aim was to show how the therapist enters the patient's phenomenal world by sharing the patient's bodily sensations, sharing the patient's attentional center, and reaching the working level of experiencing. The purpose of this section is to describe what it is like to share the patient's phenomenal world. Bear in mind a patient whose attention is perhaps 60 to 90 percent on some focal center, who is having at least moderate bodily sensations, and in whom there is at least moderate experiencing of one kind or another. Bear in mind also a therapist who has entered into the patient's phenomenal world to some fair measure. This means that somewhere between about 50 to 80 percent of the therapist's attention is on the same attentional center shared with the patient. It also means that at least moderate bodily sensations are occurring in the therapist, and it means that some sort of experiencing is likewise occurring in the therapist.

### Reduction of Therapist Self-Consciousness

Somewhere between 50 and 80 percent or so of the therapist's attention is on the patient's highly personal and very special attentional center. To that extent, there is a reduction in the therapist's awareness of self or self-consciousness. Because most of the therapist's attention is directed toward the patient's attentional center, the therapist will have very few thoughts about what to say next, or how to formulate what to say, or whether to say this or say that. In the external therapist, a great deal of thought goes into weighing and considering what to say and how to say it. Very little of this occurs in the therapist who shares the patient's phenomenal world.

Nor does the therapist have private thoughts about the patient, or about herself, or about anything else which comes from the therapist as a separated person, an intact self: "I'm having trouble following what he is saying. . . . Sometimes I get so bored listening to this. . . . I wish

I really knew what was wrong. . . . She makes me have a headache when she gets so pulled in and sullen. . . . He is so much lighter and happier lately. . . . I like when she is so pleased with herself." Such thoughts require that the therapist attend to herself, to me and I. These thoughts tend to occur much less when most of the therapist's attention is on the patient's center of attention.

Instead of being aware and conscious of oneself, the therapist is aware and conscious of feeling scared, or of what it is like in the hospital waiting room, or of the tension in the stomach, or of the soft words spoken by the brother, or of the way father sits on the toilet and grins, or of the way it feels here at the window looking outside.

## Sharing the Patient's Experiencings

When the therapist and patient share bodily sensations which are at least moderately strong, and when most of the therapist's and patient's attention is on the same center, the remarkable consequence is that the therapist shares the patient's experiencings. As Havens (1973) puts it, by following the phenomenological method, we share the patient's reactions and feelings: "We have seen that the result of phenomenological reduction, and of our staying not only with the ideas but the experiences of the patient, is that our *feelings* are engaged. Subject to the same world as the patient [insofar as we can develop empathy], we react much as he does. [The therapist] . . . is to feel *what the patient feels.* This is the discipline of the existential method" (p. 156).

It is a matter of simple sharing, and it occurs almost automatically. All the therapist has to do is to share the moderate level of bodily sensations and allow most of her attention to be shared with and on the patient's attentional center. Merely by being cordial to letting the experiencing occur, it will occur. There is no effort, no work, no trying to figure anything out. Experiencing just happens under these conditions.

Accordingly, the therapist will be sitting by the window, looking out at her younger brother, and she will be experiencing loving closeness, soft intimacy. Or she will be undergoing the awful sense of helplessness and loss as mother angrily withdraws. The therapist will share experiencings of being rejected and unwanted, being free and loose, of driven lustful sexuality, of gentle touching, of hatred and violence. This is what occurs in the therapist who shares the patient's phenomenal world.

The patient and the therapist are quite free to share whatever experiencing occurs as the patient is sitting at the window, looking at her younger brother. It may consist of loving closeness and soft intimacy, or it may be a drawing up into a knife-edged hatred and rage, or it might be a gnawing jealousy and competitiveness. As discussed by Binswanger (1958a, 1967) and Caruso (1964), we let happen whatever experiencing comes forth, in contrast to approaches which have only two or three dimensions for making sense of what occurs in persons who, for example, sit at the window looking at their younger brothers.

In this way, the therapist truly experiences what the patient experiences. It means that ". . . the doctor 'is just as much in analysis' as the patient. He is as much a part of the psychic process of the treatment as is the patient, and is equally exposed to its transforming influences" (Jung, 1933, p. 50). This is substantially different from what occurs in the role relationship where the therapist promises to "be with" the patient, to share it all, to hold the patient's hand as they travel the therapeutic journey together. There is quite a difference between the empathic role and the actual sharing of the immediate experiencing which is gripping the patient (and therapist) right now.

The important point is that a good measure of experiencing is occurring, and the therapist is sharing this experiencing. During these moments, all that is important for the therapeutic process is that the shared experiencing is occurring. It does not matter whether the patient knows what is being experienced, or whether the patient is aware of it and can talk about it, or whether the therapist is aware of the nature of the experiencing and can talk about it.

*Phenomenological Data Exclusively Available to the Therapist Who Shares the Patient's Phenomenological World*

As long as the therapist is sharing the patient's attentional center and bodily sensations, as long as they are at the working level of experiencing, the therapist will be privy to phenomenological data which are beyond the reach of other therapists (Mahrer, 1980b). They are not available to the therapist who is external, whose attention is largely on the patient and on their interaction.

This is not a matter of degree. It is not a matter of a little more or a little less emphasis. It is a qualitative issue. Regardless of therapist sensitivity and alertness, regardless whether the approach is rational-emotive, psychoanalytic, or behavioral, regardless of the nature of the therapist and patient, the external therapist does not have access to the phenomenological data which are available to the therapist who shares the patient's phenomenal world.

If three or four experiential therapists listen to a therapeutic session to study or learn from one another, they will all listen in a similar way. They will close their eyes, align themselves with the patient, allow the patient's behavior and words to construct the attentional field. The nature of what is constructed there, the bodily sensations, and the emergent experiencings will be similar in each of the experiential therapists. They come up with similar phenomenological data. If other therapists are in the group, if other therapists do not attune themselves to the phenomenological data, if other therapists situate themselves externally as most other therapists do, then their data will be substantially different. The differences between the two sets of data are intriguing for research purposes, and perhaps somewhat disconcerting in clinical therapeutic conferences, where the two groups of therapists are using quite different sets of data.

*The patient's experiencings.* When the therapist shares the patient's phenomenal world, the therapist will have experiencings which are also occurring in the patient. The therapist who does not share the patient's phenomenal world will not have these experiencings.

When the patient is at the working level of experiencing, he may be attending to an image of his brother flexing his muscles and posing in front of a mirror. Both patient and therapist may be experiencing a sense of fear, an uncanny vigilance against being physically brutalized. Or, both patient and therapist may be experiencing an almost swooning melting into, a kind of sexualized attraction to this strong man. Whatever the nature of the experiencing, it is available to the therapist who shares the patient's phenomenal world. On the other hand, it is not available to the external therapist who is not existing within that phenomenal world. The external therapist may have all sorts of notions, reactions, clinical hypotheses, and sensitive observations. It is possible that the external therapist may even figure out that the patient is feeling fearful and vigilant, or sexually attracted. But the external therapist will not experience this, and the powerful likelihood is that the external therapist will have all sorts of other ideas and notions and inferences. Only the therapist who shares the patient's phenomenal world will share the patient's ongoing experiencings.

It is rather clear that the experiential therapist will actually share in the patient's experiencings, whereas the external therapist will not. For Freud, as an example, ". . . there was not the active seeking out of the experienced, felt life of the patient, no great empathic twisting and turning into the patient's world. Freud wanted to understand, to penetrate the most hidden reaches of the patient's motivation, but he did not want to *experience* these motivations, himself feeling them, the two, doctor and patient, living in the patient's world" (Havens, 1973, p. 162). But our proposition goes much further. The therapist who is outside the patient's phenomenological world will not even know about these experiencings, much less experience them himself. Whereas the experiential therapist will know and undergo the fear of being physically brutalized, the external therapist will neither undergo nor know that experiencing. Indeed, the experiential therapist will have access to experiencings which are simply outside the domain of the external therapist.

There are two ways in which the therapist who shares the patient's phenomenal world has exclusive access to these data. One is that the therapist has them easily and quickly. As soon as patient and therapist are at the working level of experiencing, the therapist will start sharing the patient's experiencing. Even in the first session, the therapist will right away share the patient's experiencing. It is quick and it is almost automatic. Something happens. The therapist is experiencing a fearfulness, or a sense of awe and wonder, or hurt, or antagonism. In contrast, the external therapist is deprived of these data, and typically is in the process of collecting information, of developing clinical hypotheses about the patient. The second is that the therapist who shares the patient's phenomenal world has left behind all notions about the patient and is quite free to have whatever experiencing is right here right now. In contrast, the external therapist has some kind of developing picture or sketch of the patient, a set of diagnostic or psychodynamic inferences about the patient. These become increasingly restrictive, and they constitute an increasingly powerful set of spectacles through which the therapist views the patient. Whatever might fall outside that view is delimited and prevented from intruding.

The actual data consist of the therapist's experiencings. It is the therapist who has the sense of fear and the uncanny vigilance or the swooning sexualized attraction. Our proposition may be more carefully stated as follows: When the therapist shares the patient's phenomenal world, the therapist's experiencings have a higher likelihood of being similar to the patient's experiencings than when the therapist does not share the patient's phenomenal world.

Psychotherapists have long been preoccupied with their own experiencings, both their meaning and how to use them in profitable ways. What does it mean if the therapist becomes aware of being fearful and anxious or of starting to feel quite sexual? How may the therapist use these reactions, feelings, experiencings?

One meaning, from the perspective of the external therapist, is that the therapist's own personal problems are intruding. They are interferences, which should be dealt with in the therapist's own personal therapy. Another way of explaining these therapist experiencings is that they are understandable reactions to the patient's interpersonal relations. If the therapist is feeling sexual, perhaps the patient is being especially seductive; if the therapist is bored, possibly the patient is just being boring. Within a psychoanalytic approach, this way of understanding such reactions is represented by Franz Alexander, Therese Benedek, Frieda Fromm-Reichmann, Leon Salzman, Edith Weigart, and many others. Within a Gestalt approach, this meaning is proposed by Enright (1970). How may these reactions be used? The therapist might use these reactions, for example, by openly self-disclosing them, on the presumption that such self-disclosure would lead to reciprocal self-disclosure by the patient (Jourard, 1968, 1976). Within the client-centered framework, such personal reactions to the patient may be used to enhance the therapist-patient relationship (e.g., Shaffer, 1978).

All in all, the experiencing occurring in the therapist has a radically different nature and significance, depending upon the locus of the therapist. If the therapist is in the phenomenal world of the patient, the therapist's experiencings are coterminal with those occurring in the patient; if the therapist is external, not in the patient's phenomenal world, the therapist's experiencings will not be those occurring in the patient. In other words, for the experiential therapist, one's own experiencings serve as critically meaningful and useful phenomenological data.

*The patient's attentional field.* When the therapist shares the patient's phenomenal world, the therapist is attuned to the patient's attentional field. These data are available only to the therapist who shares the phenomenal field. They are essentially unavailable to the external therapist. Although the external therapist can use all sorts of data, they do not include the patient's attentional center.

When the patient allows the preponderance of attention to focus upon some meaningful center, it is a singular event for the therapist to share. Whatever the attentional center, the therapist attends at least as much as the patient. The therapist shares in the interaction with it. The therapist is bathed in its phenomenological reality, its presence and real existence, its aliveness and its meaning. It is seen, touched, smelled, felt. All of these data are unavailable to the external therapist.

*The patient's bodily sensations.* When the therapist is in the patient's phenomenal world, the therapist will have bodily sensations which make sense within the framework of that phenomenal world. The nature of the bodily sensation, its fluctuations in strength and bodily locus, all make sense within the patient's phenomenal world. These data are available to the therapist who is in the patient's phenomenal world, and they are essentially unavailable to the external therapist.

If the therapist shares the patient's attentional center, the right behavior and words from the patient may be accompanied by a heightening of sensations in the therapist's body. The slight tension in the head becomes a more pronounced dizziness, or the heaviness in the legs turns to a muscular clamping down. Where these bodily sensations will tend to occur in the experiential therapist, they will tend not to occur in the external therapist. Where these bodily changes accompany changes in the patient's experiencing, they are generally outside the domain of the external therapist.

## Phenomenological Data: Hard, Trustworthy, and Objective

Watson argued that psychology ought to use data which are hard, trustworthy, and objective. He suggested that we concentrate upon observable data. In the carrying out of therapeutic work, experiential psychotherapists need data which are hard, trustworthy, and objective. I submit that phenomenological data meet this criterion. Gendlin (1968) trusts bodily felt events as hard data. Condrau and Boss (1971) regard the inner experiencing as objective: ". . . Kierkegaard invokes the inner experience as the real and authentic reality of the human being" (p. 491). Levitsky and Perls emphasize the trustworthy objectivity of bodily sensations and feelings: "Awareness of bodily sensations and feelings constitute our most certain—perhaps our only certain—knowledge" (1970, p. 143).

The therapist knows when she has a particular bodily sensation. "My ear started ringing. There it was, suddenly, a ringing. . . . The muscles in my right hand started to quiver. I watched my hand. It was fascinating. Nothing like that had ever happened to me . . . and then I had a headache. It was strange. Five minutes before, I had no headache. Everything was fine. Then there it was." Therapists count on these bodily sensations as very trustworthy events. They know when such bodily events occur or do not occur. These data are hard and objective, and very real.

The therapist knows when she pours most of her attention onto the patient's center of attention. "I actually saw the brother. Real as can be. It was like I was really there. . . . For a few minutes, I was seeing the cancer. It was real. It was eerie and rather startling, actually, to see the stuff as real. Sort of like waking up from a bad dream." Putting most of one's attention on the attentional center makes it come alive, and that is a phenomenon which one really knows. It is trustworthy. It is hard. It is quite objective.

The therapist knows when she is gripped with a particular kind of experiencing. It is a most singular event, one which is likewise hard, objective, and trustworthy: "For about a minute or so, I really felt completely trapped. It was all too real. I was trapped, not thinking about it, but really trapped, and I never felt anything quite like that before . . . that was weird. For a few moments, I really was controlled. I mean, those people were controlling me and out to get me. No question. It went almost too far. It was very real."

All of these are phenomenological data, and they have the characteristics of being quite hard, quite objective. For the therapist who has them, they are quite trustworthy as real and identifiable events.

# 9

# Experiential Listening:
# Being in the Patient's
# Phenomenological World

There are several ways of describing the purpose of this chapter. To begin with, Chapter 8 was concerned with how the therapist enters into the phenomenological world of the patient. Now we are ready to consider more than entry. We are ready to consider what the therapist does once he has entered into the phenomenological world.

In Chapter 8, both therapist and patient are attending to some meaningful focal center and a working level of experiencing is occurring. The therapist is located somewhere in the vicinity of the patient's operating domain, sharing the patient's attentional center and experiencing. The purpose of Chapter 9 is to describe how the therapist can be in touch with the breadth and depth of the entire phenomenological world in which the patient exists, and how the therapist can be in touch with the deeper experiencings. Entering into the world of the patient (Chapter 8), the therapist can now be and exist in the entire structure—the deepest and farthest reaches of this world. Instead of only sharing the patient's attentional center, the therapist now can attend to virtually the whole phenomenological world of which the attentional center is but a small component. Instead of only sharing the operating experiencing, the therapist now can experience the deeper potentials.

Experiential listening is being in touch with the actual form and shape of the patient's phenomenological world, and being in touch with the

282

deeper experiencings in that world. Experiential listening is the jewel of the basic practices of the experiential therapist. By means of experiential listening to the behavings and words of the patient, the therapist can now be in the deepest and farthest reaches of the phenomenological world and can undergo the deepest and farthest experiencings in that world.

The first section of this chapter describes the topographical map of the phenomenological world. The second section describes what the therapist attends to in listening experientially. The final section provides some verbatim examples of experiential listening.

## THE THERAPEUTIC NECESSITY OF BEING IN THE PATIENT'S DEEPER PHENOMENOLOGICAL WORLD

Experiential listening is the culmination of the first step (Figure 2.2). Once the patient is at the working level of experiencing, and the therapist is sharing the patient's phenomenological world, the therapist is in a position to undertake the next steps in the process. In other words, experiential listening is necessary before the therapist can carry forward the potentials for experiencing (step 2) or promote the experiencing of the relationship between the patient and the deeper potentials (step 3).

In other words, the main reason for being in the patient's phenomenological world is that the actual work of experiential therapy (steps 2-4, Figure 2.2) requires that the therapist be in touch with that world and the deeper experiencings occurring in that world. My contention is that essentially no other approach enables the therapist to attain these goals. No other approach directly enables the therapist to be in touch with (know, grasp, sense, undergo) the form and shape of the phenomenological world in which the patient exists, and no other approach directly enables the therapist to be in touch with the deeper experiencings occurring within the patient.

The method of free association does not provide these advantages. Nor does the method of developing and interpreting a transference relationship. Although these methods may provide the psychoanalytic therapist with information about the patient's deeper psychoanalytic processes, they provide little or no information on the patient's deeper existential-humanistic processes. That is, neither free association nor the transference neurosis directly provides substantial data on the patient's deeper experiencings or on the phenomenological world in which the patient is being and existing. Accordingly, the patient can become a virtuoso at free associating and developing transferences, but the work of experiential therapy cannot proceed.

The same applies to the gigantic enterprise of psychological assessment, evaluation, psychodiagnosis, and testing. Many psychotherapists use all sorts of tests and measures, interview guides, intake procedures, observational procedures, evaluation and assessment methods. By means of all these devices, the therapist can spin interesting clinical inferences about the patient's symptomatology, predisposing background, psychological resources, defense mechanisms, unconscious impulses, wishes and fears, and on and on. But when it is all over, the experiential therapist has little or no grasp of the phenomenological world in which the patient is now being or existing, and little or no grasp of the deeper experiencing which is now occurring. In other words, the experiential therapist lacks the necessary data to carry on with the work of experiential therapy.

Nor is it useful for the experiential therapist to use psychoanalytic or psychodynamic inferences about the "deeper meaning" of so-called symptoms or problems or behavioral patternings. That literature is filled with clinical axioms and lore about the deeper meaning behind handwashing, ideas of reference, fears of high places, frontal headaches, skin eruptions, aggressive outbursts, ulcers, fears of dying, trembling hands, midlife crises, loose thinking, slow learning, low back pains, and hundreds of other ways of being. As useful as such inferences are for therapists of other approaches, they are inert in providing the experiential therapist with a grasp of the immediate phenomenological world in which the patient exists, and of the patient's deeper experiencings; in short, such inferences are of little use in the work of experiential therapy.

All in all, the experiential therapist must be within the patient's full phenomenological world. But being in this world means that the therapist must have an ingrained familiarity with the topography of phenomenological worlds.

## THE TOPOGRAPHICAL MAP OF THE
## PATIENT'S PHENOMENOLOGICAL WORLD

Existential phenomenologists have wanted to plot the topography of patients' phenomenological worlds. For example, May, Angel, and Ellenberger (1958) suggested a threefold division into a world of natural events and phenomena (Umwelt), an interpersonal social world (Mitwelt), and a world of self-relationships (Eigenwelt). As a next step, existential phenomenologists wanted to uncover dimensions which apply to patients' phenomenological worlds, dimensions which would be useful in clinical therapeutics. For example, a dimension of phenomenological time was proposed, and there were investigations of how phenomenological time occurred in patients falling in the several nosological groups.

I fully accept the concept of phenomenological worlds, but my own version of existential-humanistic thinking (Mahrer, 1978a) declines a division into Umwelt, Mitwelt, and Eigenwelt, together with the therapeutic value of universal phenomenological dimensions. The topography I prefer has been derived from both my own conceptualization of the phenomenological structure of human personality, and therapeutic work with patients. By entering as deeply as possible into the phenomenological worlds of patients, by going back and forth between the fruits of this therapeutic work and related refinements in theoretical conceptualization, I have arrived at a provisional working topography of the phenomenological worlds of patients as given in Figure 9.1 and described below.

In order for the therapist to carry on the work of experiential therapy, in order to have and grasp the deeper experiencings and the immediate illuminated parts of the phenomenological world, the therapist must have an ingrained topographical map of phenomenological worlds. What are the components of the phenomenological world? When the patient behaves and talks, and the experiential therapist "listens" from within that world, what are the structural parts of the world? Experiential listening is restricted to whatever structure is presumed for the phenomenological world which is illuminated by that listening.

The map given in Figure 9.1, and the description of its parts given below, must be the one which is present in the experiential therapist who exists within the patient's phenomenological world and who receives what the patient is doing and saying. The map is to be used. It is a working map which is open to change on the basis of conceptual development of the humanistic-existential theory of human beings, and also from rigorous study of therapeutic work with patients (see Figure 1.1 and Chapter 1). But for now, provisionally, it is the working topography for the therapist who is engaged in experiential listening from within the patient's phenomenological world. What, then, are its parts?

*Operating Potential and the Center of I-Ness*

We begin with some kind of experiencing which is occurring in the operating domain. The patient is experiencing warmth and closeness, or bewilderment and confusion, or any other kind of experiencing. This experiencing is indicated as "operating potential" in Figure 9.1. What is more, there is an I-ness (or Dasein or center of one's personal identity).

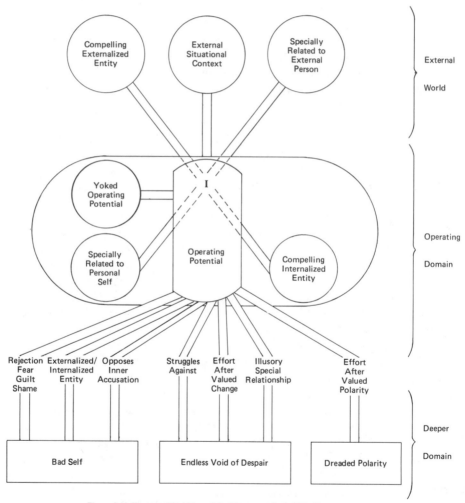

Figure 9.1. Topographical Map of the Phenomenological World

Generally, this is located within the operating domain. It is indicated as "I" in Figure 9.1. Here are two parts of the topographical map.

When the therapist enters into the patient's phenomenological world (Chapter 8), when the therapist shares the patient's bodily sensations and center of attention, here is where the therapist is located. The therapist is in the vicinity of the operating potential and shares the nature or content of the operating potential. The therapist is also in the vicinity of the sense of I-ness and shares that sense of I. Accordingly, the topographical map of the patient's phenomenological world includes the "I" or "I-ness" and the operating potential for experiencing.

*External Situational Context*

The phenomenological world includes some kind of external situational context in which the experiencing occurs. It is comprised of persons or groups, interactions and relationships, objects and things, all sorts of situational props. It is the context or scene in which the patient is right now existing, being, and experiencing. When the patient is experiencing warmth and closeness, there may be an external situational context of a few best friends, sitting in the patient's living room, happy and comfortable, looking at the patient in loving closeness.

The external situational context may be sparse and limited or richly appointed. It may be a real life scene or incident, or it may occur within a realm of fantasy, altered states of consciousness, or dream life. The patient may be a direct participant or a somewhat removed observer. The scene might be mundane or bizarre. The patient may be existing in the scene fully or slightly. Yet the phenomenological world includes some kind of external situational context.

*Specially Related to External Person*

The patient's phenomenological world may include a very special external figure with whom the patient has a very special relationship. While the patient is talking and behaving, it is as if some special other person is present, hearing all of this, receiving all of this.

Sometimes the patient is apparently talking to the therapist. Sometimes the patient seems to be talking as if to no one at all. Sometimes the patient gives a recitation of events or tells a story or issues a series of complaints. Yet the commonality lies in the presence of some special other person who is illuminated, who is present and receiving all of this.

The special other person may take the form of a parental figure whom the patient never had, or who died recently or long ago. It may be a kindly person, loving and caring, attentive and understanding. It may be a grandparent-type figure, an older sibling, an uncle or aunt. It may be a shadowy magical figure who is all-wise and all-powerful, someone who can make it all better. It may be the preciously cherished companion, the confidante, the partner. It may be a figure who nurtures and enfolds, criticizes and cajoles, is stern and tough, or powerful and strong, or sharing and embracing. But the commonality is the presence of this special other person with whom the patient has this special relationship, a person who is receiving what is coming from the patient.

### Yoked Operating Potential

While the patient is experiencing one operating potential, the phenomenological world may include a second operating potential. Both are operating potentials because the patient is capable of being both, capable of moving from one to the other, capable of experiencing both. While the patient is experiencing and being one operating potential, the other may be constructed and illuminated. They are said to be yoked to one another in the following two ways.

*The polar experiencings.* The two operating potentials are yoked to one another in some kind of polarity. The experiencing of outgoingness may be yoked with a polar experiencing of separating withdrawnness. Heterosexuality may be yoked with homosexuality or asexuality, or whatever constitutes the polarity for this person right now. The experiencing of gentleness may be yoked with a polar coldness or a polar domination or a polar assaultiveness. Whatever the nature of the dimension for this patient right now, the experiencing of one operating potential is yoked to another operating potential which is polar, and the topographical map includes the presence of the two yoked operating potentials.

The idea of yoked operating potentials is old in personality theories and psychotherapies. For example, Gestalt therapy includes such polarities as topdog and underdog. Transpersonal therapy has such polarities as child and parent. Psychoanalytic therapy has concepts such as ambivalence, and uses polarities such as manic and depressed. It is an old idea that the patient's way of being includes opposites or polarities which are yoked to one another so that being one implies and illuminates the polar other.

*The disintegrative relationship.* Typically, the relationship between the yoked operating potentials is disintegrative. That is, it is characterized by conflict, pain, disharmony. If the center of I-ness is within the operating potential, then the relationship with and from the yoked operating potential is almost always disintegrative. While experiencing heterosexuality, there are feelings of anxiety or fear, disjunctiveness or disharmony, in relationship with and from the yoked polar homosexuality. Whenever the patient is being one operating potential, there will be disintegrative feelings from the relationship with the yoked operating potential.

The patient, however, need not be in either of the two yoked potentials. Instead, the patient (I-ness) may be between the two, in the relationship between the two. This is when the patient is caught between homosexuality and heterosexuality. The patient is stuck, at an impasse, caught on the horns of the dilemma. This is the disintegrative pain of being trapped between the two polar potentials.

The topographical map includes the operating potential and a yoked potential, relating to one another in a disintegrative way.

### Specially Related to Personal Self

A patient's phenomenological worlds include special entities with which there are very special relationships. These entities may be located externally (specially related to external person, Figure 9.1) or internally (specially related to personal self). The internal "personal self" may be referred to as a whole self, a full-scale internalized individual which the patient refers to as I or me. The patient tells what *I* am like, what *my* history is, the kind of person *I* am, how *I* react and respond, the various qualities and characteristics of what this personal self is like. Or the personal self may be a single quality or characteristic. Accordingly, the patient talks about my aggression, my drinking problem, my temper, my sexuality, my sensitivity, my ego.

Whether a whole inner person or a personal quality or characteristic, there is some sort of relationship between the patient (the I or operating potential in Figure 9.1) and the specially related to personal self. The patient is protective toward the personal self, regards it as a treasured child, is disgusted with it, loves it, is stuck with it, sees it as precious, hates it. There is always some meaningfully personal relationship between the patient and the specially related to personal self.

In existential phenomenology, this is referred to as the Eigenwelt, the world of relationships with one's personal self. But the idea of a personal self, in the phenomenological world of the patient, is very old and familiar in clinical psychotherapeutics. It occurs in all the self psychologies, including client-centered therapy, transpersonal therapies, and others.

### Compelling Internalized Entity

The operating domain includes an operating potential, another operating potential to which it is yoked, a specially related to personal self, and a compelling internalized entity (Figure 9.1).

By "compelling" I mean that the internalized entity pulls the patient's attention like a powerful magnet. Virtually all of the patient's attention is compelled by this internalized entity so that the patient may become overwhelmed by it or engulfed by it. So compelling is the internalized entity that the patient's very identity may become swallowed up by it. The relationship is one of powerful compellingness.

When this compelling entity is internal, it may take the form of some body part, such as the compelling headache, ulcer, brain tumor, cancer, localized pain. Or it may take the form of some internal agency, such as the compelling fear of dying or going crazy, the temper or sexual impulse or persistent thought.

In compelling the patient's predominant attention, the internalized entity often emerges as having personality characteristics of its own. For example, it emerges as obstinate and persistent, nasty and malevolent, distant and hard to reach, aggressive and assaultive, growing and spreading, powerful and omnipotent.

### Compelling Externalized Entity

The external domain of the patient's phenomenological world includes three parts: an external situational context, a specially related to external person, and a compelling externalized entity (Figure 9.1).

Something external compels most of the patient's attention. The patient can talk or think or attend to little else. It fills the center of the patient. It may be a significant other person: spouse, parent, enemy, neighbor, sibling, child, boss, villain. It may be a group: the family, party, organization, department, neighbors, society. It may be the vision of the deceased person, God, devil, acid rain, corruption, destiny, birds.

The compelling entity is located in the external world, and it is as if the very center of gravity of the patient is now diffused and moving in the direction of that external entity. The patient raptly attends to the external entity which is defined, seen in detail. It has intactness and vividness and reality, while the patient is more diffused and vaguely ill-defined, losing integrity and demarcation as a personhood. There is little interchange between the patient and the external entity because the person is less of a substantive entity while the external entity is more of an intact thing.

The external entity is so compelling that the patient is close to being invaded or swallowed by the external entity. It is one short step from fearing the evil neighbor or the powerful God to being it, one short step for the center of the patient's identity to move into the compelling external entity.

Typically, the compelling external entity is seen as bad, mean, evil, threatening, ominous, malevolent. It is the externalized face of that which occurs, in its internalized face, as the bad and threatening cancer, persistent thought, ulcer, or awful impulse.

We now turn to the deeper domain (Figure 9.1) and to the three parts which comprise the inner phenomenological world.

*The Bad Self*

The bad self is the reservoir of everything awful, evil, monstrous, grotesque, and terrible. It includes that which the operating domain rejects and fears, denies and pushes away, feels guilt and shame about. It includes the bad qualities and characteristics which comprise the compelling entity which is externalized or internalized. It includes the badness contained in the terrible charges from some inner accusor. In psychoanalytic therapy, the bad self occurs as that which is referred to as the unconscious, especially in the form of forbidden wishes and cravings, wicked and unconscionable impulses, devilish tendencies, primitive and archaic awfulness, uncivilized and animal instincts.

*That which the patient rejects, fears, denies, feels guilt and shame about.* The negative relationship toward the bad self also serves to define it, point

toward it, illuminate its nature. Rejecting and fearing it serve to give it
shape and form. Denying it makes it real. Feeling guilt and shame about
it illuminates what it is. The patient both defines it and fends it off in
statements such as: "I would never. . . . I just couldn't. . . . The last
thing I would do is. . . . I feel bad about. . . . I am not like this or
that. . . . It would be cruel to. . . . I don't like doing this or that. . . .
I don't like being this way or that way." Sometimes the bad self is
signaled by a sudden silence or a sharp nervous laugh. Or the bad self
is illuminated by identifying persons who regard the patient as disgusting, wicked, uncivilized, hateful, loathsome, deserving rejection
and dislike, ridicule and punishment. In any case, the bad self is both
defined and avoided by the negative relationship.

*That which the patient externalizes or internalizes as the compelling entity.*
The bad self is comprised of the awful qualities and characteristics in
the entities which are so very compelling to the patient and which are
"projected" internally or externally. Indeed, what is so compelling is the
powerful possibility of the patient becoming that which is found both
in the bad self and in the compelling entity.

What is so compelling about the cancer is the unstoppable ravaging
which lurks in the deeper bad self. The relentless evilness of the compelling enemy is the relentless evilness of the bad self. God is compellingly powerful, and so is the bad self. Mother is cold, and her
compellingness lies in the coldness in the patient's own bad self. Men
are compellingly mean and cruel, and so is the deeper bad self. What
the patient externalizes or internalizes as an entity which compels most
of the patient's attention is one form of the deeper bad self (Figure 9.1).

*That which is charged by the inner antagonist.* There is a bad self contained
in a charge leveled by an inner accusor and antagonist. This prosecutor
is the conscience of common psychology, the superego of psychoanalytic
therapy. It charges the patient with being bad; it accuses the patient of
badness. It attacks the patient, criticizes and disapproves of the patient.
In turn, the patient opposes the charge by assembling evidence or by
sheer argument or by placing blame and responsibility on anything at
all.

But the charge is indeed correct and accurate, and the bad self is really
wicked, crazy, mindless, cold, wrong, evil, gross, lying, malevolent,
irresponsible, dumb, petty. What is more, the bad self excitingly loves
being evil or mischievous, devilish or outrageous, primitive or vindictive.

## The Dreaded Polarity

In the operating domain there is an operating potential and a polar potential to which it is yoked. In the same way, the phenomenological world includes a deeper potential which likewise is polar to the way the patient is, but the deeper polarity is more profound, more ominous, more dreaded. It is signaled by the patient's efforts after some highly valued way of being. There is a wanting to be some way, an insistence or urgency to be some way, a needing and trying to be some way. It may be embedded in hopes and dreams, needing and wanting, fantasies and wishes. Yet the reaching out for one pole points toward the dreaded inner polarity.

The effort after success illuminates a dreaded polarity, perhaps the awfulness of failure. The effort after being loved and accepted points toward some dreaded polarity, such as being hated and rejected, or being withdrawn and alone. When the patient reaches out toward one pole, the phenomenological world contains the dreaded internal other pole. The concept of polarities has both similarities to and differences from the doctrine of universal polarities in Jungian psychology. In existential phenomenology, there is likewise the topography of a reaching out toward one pole and the inner presence of the dreaded polarity. However, there are no grand or universal polarities such as good and evil, intellectual and emotional, maleness and femaleness, adultness and childness, outer-directedness and inner-directedness (Binswanger, 1958b, Mahrer, 1978a).

While the patient reaches out for one pole, it is as if the inner polarity knows the real truth. The inner polarity may occur as some hooded figure, a shadowy observer who sees what the patient is reaching out for and knows the truth of the inner polarity. While the patient reaches out after success, the sinister observer smiles knowingly, for the truth is that the patient is a failure. The patient's effort after being loved and accepted is laughed at by the sinister hooded figure who knows that the deeper truth consists of being hated and rejected. The patient makes efforts after being a good parent or a devoted companion or a vital and energetic youth, but the hooded figure is always present. It knows the ugly inner truth and is disgusted with the patient, or laughs at the patient, or knows better than the patient, or sees right through the patient. It knows the polar truth: The inner potential doesn't give a damn about being a good parent, has no intention of being a devoted companion, is fundamentally a tired old man.

Even the way of behaving and speaking conveys the underlying presence of the polar inner truth. The effort after some valued polarity is laced with brittleness. The excitement is thin and superficial. The joy is not genuine. There is an air of sadness and unreality in the reaching after the manifest polarity.

## The Endless Void of Despair

There is a third part of the deeper domain. It comes largely from existential concepts of the inner dark side of human beings (e.g., Binswanger, 1958a, 1967; Ellenberger, 1958; Kohut, 1971; Laing, 1962; Mahrer, 1978a; May, 1958). It consists of the inner abyss of utter nothingness and emptiness, of death, of absolute changelessness, of complete uselessness, hopelessness, and futility. It is the endless void of despair.

Once again, this inner region is often expressed in the form of a hooded figure, sinister and ominous, dark and shadowy. It knows the real truth. It is the bystander who knows, who watches and waits. Sooner or later the patient will be enveloped in the endless void of despair. It represents the inexorable truth, the inevitable final destiny of despair.

*That against which the patient struggles.* The patient struggles against something internal. That something may be in the form of some inner pressure or tendency, some problem, some inner force, some lurking inner possibility, some inner way of being, some inner state or condition, some fate or destiny. In the face of this struggle against, the underlying despairing truth is that it is all in vain, fruitless, and hopeless. The "it" against which the patient struggles will inevitably overcome the patient. Or there will be no change whatsoever. The catastrophic destiny is inexorable. There is no hope.

The patient struggles to control or overcome the sexual frigidity, the lower back pain, the violent temper outbursts, the drinking, the suicidal tendencies, the masturbation, the homosexuality, the bad thoughts, the evil ideas. The patient refuses to be the goat, the good daughter, the one who is never acknowledged, the object of their ridicule, the stable one, the unfeelinged son. The patient struggles to get out of the dilemma, to escape from the impasse, to no longer be caught and trapped. The patient struggles against the catastrophic imminence of becoming crazy, losing everything, failing miserably, falling apart, ending up this way or that way, becoming feeble and old, being over the hill, giving it all up.

In the face of each of these struggles, the underlying experiencing is that it is all in vain. Give up the struggle. The struggle is hopeless and fruitless. It will take you over. Nothing is going to change. There is no hope. Surrender to the inevitable.

*The effort after the valued change.* The patient reaches out for and makes an effort toward some valued state or condition, attainment or achieve-ment, way of being or behaving. There is the effort after becoming a better person, feeling more, being more free and spontaneous, becoming a wonderful human being, becoming transformed into a different per-son. The patient may be engaged in an effort after becoming a loving parent, a more friendly person, a better son, someone who is cared for by others, a more respected person, more accepted by the wife or boss, less self-concerned, more responsible, less anxious in crowds, less fretful in general, more sexually appealing, more assertive, one who can get along better.

Underneath all the efforts is the ominous void of despair. There is no magic cure. There will be no transformation. One will always be this way. Nothing will really change substantially. The effort is in vain, utterly fruitless. There is no hope. It will not work. The effort is naive, illusory, groundless.

*The illusory special relationship.* There is a special relationship with that special other person. Sometimes the relationship is with an external person such as the wonderful parental figure who really understands; sometimes the relationship is with the personal self (Figure 9.1). Whether internal or external, the patient is engaged with this special person in this special relationship.

But the sad truth is that it is all illusion. There is no such relationship in one's life. There probably never was. No one is this way with the patient. It is missing now, and it has always been missing. No one feels about the patient the way he does about his self. No matter how special is the patient's relationship with his precious self, it is an illusion; no one showers such a special relationship on him, and no one ever did. How wonderful it seems to have someone truly listen, and understand, and accept. But the sad truth is that such a person is missing in one's life, and the relationship is illusory. The truth is one of emptiness, nothingness, the endless void of despair.

These are the parts of the patient's phenomenological world. They comprise the topographical map of what is present when the therapist engages in experiential listening. As the patient talks, as the patient behaves, something becomes illuminated. In the external world, that something might be an external situational context, a compelling externalized entity, or a specially related to external person. Within the operating domain, what is illuminated might be a yoked operating potential, a compelling internalized entity, or a specially related to personal self. Within the deeper domain, what is illuminated may be a bad self, a dreaded polarity, or an endless void of despair. The therapist who is inside the patient's phenomenological world is ready for one of these parts to occur or come to life as the patient behaves. The phenomenological world has this structure or topography (Figure 9.1).

If the therapist does not have this topographical map, the therapist cannot engage in experiential listening. If the therapist's conceptual map of the phenomenological world does not include these parts, then the therapist will be unable to listen to or receive or grasp those parts. The therapist may be unable to hear or receive patients who are reaching out after one polarity and thereby illuminate the dreaded inner polarity—if the therapist has no map which includes a deeper polarity. If the therapist's topographical map does not include a personal self, then the therapist will not be able to listen to the patient engaging in a special relationship with that self, nor will the therapist be able to listen to the despairing emptiness of such relationships.

What I have presented here is a provisional map of patients' phenomenological worlds. It is the best I have to offer for the experiential therapist, and it is presented in a spirit of change and improvement and development. From existential-humanistic theory and from careful study of the fruits of working phenomenologically with patients, I look forward to future developments of the topographical map.

## EXPERIENTIAL LISTENING:
## WHAT THE THERAPIST ATTENDS TO

Once the therapist has entered into the patient's phenomenological world, what does the therapist attend to? Entering into the patient's phenomenological world (Chapter 8) means that the therapist shares and attends to the patient's attentional center, the therapist's ongoing bodily sensations, and the therapist's ongoing operating experiencing. In order to go deeper, in order to exist within the whole phenomenological world of the patient, equipped with the topographical map, in order to listen experientially, what does the therapist attend to?

## The Illuminated Part of One's Own Phenomenological World

The fundamental guideline is that experiential listening means attending to what occurs in one's own phenomenological world. As the patient behaves and talks, the therapist's attention goes to images occurring in the therapist's world, to deeper experiencings occurring in the therapist, to bodily sensations and feelings occurring in the therapist. The therapist may have images of a precious little self which the patient is cuddling (specially related to personal self, Figure 9.1), or images of a bunch of people in an elevator, all dressed quite formally (external situational context, Figure 9.1). The therapist may have a deeper experiencing of being delightfully and wickedly lewd and provocative (bad self, Figure 9.1). The important point is that the data are those of the therapist's own phenomenological world. Whatever is momentarily illuminated in this world becomes the important data to which the therapist attends.

Once the therapist has entered into the patient's world, the therapist's attention is ready to go to images, to deeper experiencings, and to bodily sensations and feelings which occur in her own phenomenological world. In this attentional posture, the therapist does not attend to the patient. Very little of the therapist's attention is on the patient. Instead, the therapist is affected by the patient's behavior and words. Virtually everything the patient says and does has some effect upon the therapist's images, deeper experiencings, bodily sensations and feelings. It is as if the therapist were a device or instrument which is hooked up to the patient, which is delicately sensitive to whatever the patient says and does, and which registers in the form of images, deeper experiencings, bodily sensations and feelings. Indeed, the therapist is a delicately sensitive listening device, one which picks up subtle changes in experiencing.

No matter how conscious and aware the patient is, no matter how in touch the patient may be with his world, the therapist is far more sensitive when she is inside the patient's world and attending to what is occurring in her own phenomenological world. The experientially listening therapist will be in touch with deeper experiencings, which are outside the patient's awareness. The therapist will exist in scenes and see images which are outside the patient's zone. The therapist becomes an exceedingly sensitive instrument in intimate touch with the fuller and deeper reaches of the patient, and all of this is accomplished by attending to the immediately ongoing illuminations of one's own phenomenological world.

## Imagery

The therapist's eyes are closed. The patient has been attending to her father, and the therapist's attention is likewise on father. Both patient and therapist have a tense sensation over the whole chest area. The therapist allows his attention to be ready to go to any part of the topographical map of the phenomenological world. Although some attention is generally directed at father, most of the therapist's attention is ready to go anywhere.

Then the patient talks about her father, and each word is accompanied with some kind of feeling, some intonation, a nuance here and subtlety there. All of this is received by the therapist, who sees images. There are mental pictures, fantasies. While the patient is talking and behaving, the therapist sees an old man lying on a couch, his face under a newspaper, lightly snoring. Some seconds later the therapist sees the doorway to a moderate sized apartment building, and senses himself walking up the stairs. Or the therapist is watching a mother holding a baby in her arms, smiling at the baby, and happy as can be. There is an image of a bunch of guys sitting in a cabin, laughing together and drinking beer.

The therapist attends to the images which are evoked or generated as the patient behaves and talks, and as the therapist's attention is drawn toward any part of the phenomenological world. These images are crucial data to which the therapist attends.

For example, in the following, the patient is a nurse who is attending to a recent argument with her husband: "Well, he has that look on his face . . . (he is standing nearby, a look of irritation and displeasure on his face) . . . and he picks up the broom and starts sweeping the damned kitchen! (The image is of this tall blonde fellow, angry, doing a haphazard job of sweeping up the kitchen floor, especially around and near the patient) I have a lot to do. I work hard . . . (Suddenly, there is a new image. It consists of a figure who says, 'You should sweep the kitchen floor. You are bad. You are a lazy slob.' This figure seems to be big and menacing.)

The flow of imagery is simply present when the therapist assumes the posture of experiential listening. These images sometimes are rather directly linked to the behavior and words of the patient. Generally, however, the connection is looser and more tenuous.

*Implied, alluded to images.* Some images are directly denoted by the patient's behavior and words. Other images are only implied or alluded to by the patient's behavior and words. What matters is that the therapist attend to the images, regardless of whether these images are directly denoted or only implied or alluded to by the patient's behavior and words. It does not matter whether the connection is tight or loose, close or distant, directly denoted or implied and alluded to. All the therapist does is attend to the images which are there when the patient behaves and talks.

Suppose that the patient is talking about her 10-year-old daughter. In a somewhat suggestive and critical tone of voice she says: "I know what she does when she's alone. She can't fool me. I know what she does under the covers at night, when she thinks no one knows. She can't fool me." The listening therapist may have a distinct image of the daughter in bed at night, touching her genitals, making sexual sounds, surreptitiously so that no one would know. Although the therapist sees this image concretely, the behavior and words of the patient only implied and alluded to such an image.

Sometimes the behavior and words of the patient are ephemeral, diluted, softly hinting. Yet the effect on the experientially listening therapist is to evoke a distinct image. The therapist sees a lovely little baby, a concrete image. Yet the actual behavior and words of the patient do not directly refer to a baby. Instead, the patient says: "It is so nicely formed . . . smells good, so gentle, precious . . . soft . . . like a little jewel . . ." The patient may have nothing specific in mind. Or the patient may have an image of a lovely flower. But the evoked image of a baby occurs to the experientially listening therapist, and that is the image to which the therapist attends. Even when the images may appear to be almost spontaneously unrelated to what the patient is doing and saying, they are the data to which the therapist attends (cf. Bachrach, 1968; Greenson, 1960; Reik, 1948; Schaffer, 1958).

There are no symbolic meanings, no translation of what the patient says into something else. The therapist merely assumes the posture of experiential listening, and attends to the images which are there, concrete images which are there for the therapist who is listening experientially, images which are only implied and alluded to by the behavior and words of the patient.

*Letting more ominous, deeper images occur.* There are images which are accompanied with ominous feelings in the therapist. The feelings are more threatening, more menacing, for example, a sudden clunking in the stomach, as if the bottom fell out. Or there may be a pronounced clutching up or tightening of the muscles, or the torso starts shaking and trembling. Images accompanied with more ominous bodily sensations are generally images from deeper potentials.

These images are available to the therapist who allows herself to go a little further into the deeper potential. The therapist becomes a little looser, dips further down into the deeper potential. Accordingly, the accompanying feelings are more ominous, more laced with menace, wickedness, craziness, primitiveness, more archaic.

As the patient is asserting how vibrantly youthful he is, the therapist may see an image of a shadowy figure who knows the real truth: The patient is frightened of becoming old and frail like his father. Then, dipping further, the therapist may start to have ominous feelings and bodily sensations, and the therapist sees the patient as a prematurely senile old man, sitting mindlessly in a wheelchair, mumbling inanities, and shaking all over.

The patient may be talking about himself, going on and on about every nuance of what the precious self is like. The initial image is of a parent lovingly regarding the wonderful child. But, as the therapist allows a more ominous image to occur, there is now a scene of aloneness and emptiness; no one is here with the patient who is twisted and bent in agonizing aloneness.

The patient may be struggling against the looming awful state or fate. It is the imminence of suicide or depression or death. As the therapist sinks further, she will begin to have ominous bodily sensations and ominous images. Now the images consist of a smashed body on the street below the tall building, or the dead body lying on the morgue slab, or the crazy mental patient rocking back and forth on the locked ward, or the blood pouring out of the eyes and ears and mouth of the dead person.

The content of what the patient says may consist of the negative attitudes of others. The aunt doesn't trust him. The coworker thinks of him as irresponsible. As the therapist listens by allowing the more ominous images to occur, the therapist sees the aunt yelling at him, and he is indeed a completely untrustworthy profligate. Or the image is of the coworker directly bawling him out, with full justification, as a thoroughly irresponsible child. The therapist sees the threatening, ominous, deeper image which is brought about by the patient's behavior and words.

These images occur as the therapist goes deeper and deeper, moving closer and closer to the deeper domain. As the therapist is in the vicinity of the patient's efforts after some valued polarity, the therapist will see images coming from the deeper dreaded polarity (Figure 9.1). As the therapist is inside the patient's struggles against some deeper potential, the therapist sees the images coming from that deeper potential, some kind of void of despair (Figure 9.1). As the therapist undergoes the patient's fear or guilt or shame, the therapist sees images of the deeper bad self about which the patient has the fear or guilt or shame (Figure 9.1). These images are clear and distinct; they are accompanied with ominous bodily sensations and feelings; they are the images to which the therapist attends.

*Images from key phrases.* There are key phrases which seem to be linked with certain kinds of images. The key phrases must be spoken in the right ways, and with a certain meaning and significance. I have been impressed with the regular association of these key phrases and defined kinds of images (cf. Perls, 1971, 1976).

The patient voices a stricture, a rule for living, a commandment, a universal truth or nostrum. It is given in such a way that it seems to come from out of the patient's childhood, authoritatively pronounced by some parental figure. The key component typically consists of phrases such as the following: "I should be a good boy. . . . If you don't stand up for yourself, no one will. . . . A person has to get ahead or he isn't worth much. . . . I should stick by the family. . . . My job is to make a good living for the family. . . . I should have children and be a good wife. . . . A mother's first loyalty is to her children. . . . It's my place to take care of the home. . . . You don't have a baby and then wish you never had one. . . . You must just put away bad thoughts. . . ."

Some phrases are spoken in a way which portrays an effortful seeking after precious goals and valued states or, on the other hand, menacing forces and conditions which must be avoided or gotten rid of: "I must be. . . . I'm really going to be. . . . I will finally be able to. . . . I have to. . . . I got to. . . . I desperately need to. . . . I just want so much to. . . ." These kinds of key phrases, spoken in this way, are frequently associated with images in which the whole effort is in vain, fruitless. The efforts are doomed to failure. It will not work. It won't happen. It is hopeless.

Patients may evoke images of what the bad inner self wickedly enjoys doing. At the same time, the patients' behavior and words dissociate from that, or proclaim rejection of being that way. Accordingly, the patient says: "It would be cruel to. . . . I hope that I don't. . . . I feel bad about. . . . I certainly am not. . . . I'm scared that I might. . . . I would never. . . . I couldn't. . . . If it gets any worse I might. . . . I don't like. . . ." These and similar key phrases disengage the patient from what follows, and what follows defines the contents of the evoked images: "It would be cruel to just walk out and leave him." "I feel bad about stepping on your glasses and breaking them." "I would never talk behind her back about her stealing things from stores." "I'm scared that I might rape the girl next door some night when she walks around naked like that." "If it gets any worse I might just knock someone down and beat them up."

Experiential listening means that the therapist attends to the images which are present as the patient behaves and talks. The therapist attends to these images, not to the patient or to the patient's behavior or words. Some of these images are directly connected to the patient's behavior and words. Some are implied and alluded to. Some seem spontaneously unrelated to what the patient is doing and saying. Some are accompanied with ominous bodily sensations and feelings. Some come from key phrases from the patient. All of these images occur in the phenomenological world of the therapist who is postured for experiential listening. All of these images are the data to which the therapist attends. They constitute one valuable domain of data for the experiential therapist.

### Deeper Experiencings

The second valuable domain includes the experiencing which occurs in the therapist. As the patient is behaving and talking, the therapist is experiencing something. As the therapist's attention is on whatever is illuminated within the therapist's own phenomenological world, something goes on inside the therapist. As the therapist exists within the patient's phenomenological world and sees images, some sort of experiencing will occur in the therapist. The more that the therapist lets all of this happen, the more the therapist is having deeper experiencings. These deeper experiencings are the second domain of data to which the therapist attends.

The therapist comes into closer contact with these deeper experiencings by just letting them occur. It is a matter of letting happen. There are at least three ways of letting the deeper experiencings occur:

*Fully being in the external situational context.* Almost always, the patient's behavior and words will paint some kind of scene or situational context. The experientially listening therapist will see that situational context. Generally, this scene is bothersome and threatening so that, even though the patient's behavior and words construct the scene, the patient dare not exist fully in that scene. Indeed, the patient is generally geared to avoid seeing or being in the very situational context which is evoked by the patient's own behavior and words.

The therapist does what the patient cannot do. The therapist allows himself to be in that external situational context, to live fully and completely in that scene. The therapist sees the components of the scene clearly and vividly, allows this scene to be concrete and detailed, to be fully real. The therapist steps right into the guts of the situation, lets the situation occur and play itself out in feelinged reality. By doing this, the therapist undergoes the deeper experiencing. Being and living in the scene mean having the deeper experiencing which occurs.

As the patient behaves and speaks, a situational context is constructed. It is morning. The patient is a little boy who has been forced to let his cousin sleep with him. As the patient wakes up, he is aware of peeing on the sleeping cousin. The middle of the bed is wet with warm urine, a large puddle. Here is the scene, and the therapist allows himself fully to be in this scene until some kind of deeper experiencing starts to happen. It may consist of a wickedly exciting sense of gleeful aggression. It may consist of being a baby, much too young to be continent. The more the therapist allows himself fully to be in that scene, the closer the therapist is to undergoing the deeper experiencing.

It is as if the therapist can see the situational context quite openly and clearly, and is quite willing to exist completely in that scene and to allow whatever experiencing is there to happen. And when it does, the therapist pays attention to the nature of this deeper experiencing, for it is the valuable data of experiential listening.

*Being the compelling internalized or externalized entity.* The overall principle is that the therapist just lets happen whatever starts to happen, and the deeper experiencing will occur. The same guideline applies to compelling internalized or externalized entities. When the patient's attention is forcibly drawn by some entity, the therapist does what the patient rarely dares to do, i.e., let oneself be drawn the last step into being that compelling entity. The entity pulls and compels the patient toward being it, being incorporated into it, and the therapist just lets it happen. Then the therapist has the deeper experiencing.

The compelling entity may be the cancer, the looming madness, the evil man in the next apartment, or the devil. With most of the patient's (and therapist's) attention on it, the therapist lets go and gives in to being whatever it is. Then the therapist experiences the savageness of the cancer, the wildness of the looming madness, the malevolent control of the evil neighbor, or the depravity of the devil. Whatever the nature of the deeper experiencing, that becomes the valuable data to which the therapist attends.

*Succumbing to the deeper experiencing.* The therapist will almost always be attending to whatever images are evoked by the patient's behavior and words. At the same time, the therapist will sense the outer edges of some kind of deeper experiencing. It is as if the deeper experiencing is subtly present, available, able to be sensed by the therapist. As given in Figure 9.1, the therapist can sense the leading edge of some kind of deeper bad self, some kind of deeper void of despair, some kind of deeper dreaded polarity. The next step is for the therapist to let it happen, i.e., to succumb to the deeper experiencing. Give in just a bit further to the experiencing which is there.

While the imagery consists of some specially related to external person or specially related to personal self, the therapist may sense the experiencing of all that as illusory (see Figure 9.1). Letting that happen further, the therapist now experiences the despair of emptiness and aloneness; there is no such external person; there are no such special relationships. At first the therapist undergoes the experiencing of being caught between two yoked operating potentials. One cannot be the good son, loyal and devoted, nor can one be the bad son, cold and uncaring. Then, allowing oneself to sink further into this underlying experiencing, the therapist is filled with a good measure of the endless void of despair: It is the deeper experiencing of being forever caught, hopelessly mired in the agonizing impasse for the rest of one's life. Or the therapist undergoes what it is like to struggle against the looming unreality, the catastrophic world of madness. Allowing oneself to succumb to the sensed deeper potential, the therapist experiences the awful consequences of the eternal struggle: Nothing will ever change, the struggle may as well go on forever. These are various forms of the endless void of despair, and they are arrived at by succumbing to the deeper experiencing which begins to be present.

The same is done when the underlying experiencing is some form of bad self or dreaded polarity (Figure 9.1). The therapist will start to experience the deeper potential a little. There may be a sensing of an inner uncomfortableness or unease, or perhaps even an intense terror or wrenching avoidance. Below the bad feeling is the hinting or sensing of the deeper experiencings. All the therapist does is succumb. Let it happen more. Give in. Then the therapist is undergoing the deeper experiencings.

As the therapist succumbs more and more, the therapist will experience the deeper potential more and more. These are the important data to which the therapist attends. But the more the therapist succumbs, and the more the therapist enters into the bowels of the deeper experiencing, the more a curious phenomenon occurs. When the therapist is just below the operating domain, in the zone between the operating domain and the deeper potentials (Figure 9.1), the form of the deeper potential is bad. It is sensed as threatening, awful, grotesque. When the therapist succumbs a little further, down into the domain of the deeper potentials, a curious change occurs. It is as if the very form of the deeper potential changes from its bad form to a good form. What starts out as the terrifying imminence of madness becomes a peaceful freedom from suffocating pressures, or an exciting spontaneity, or a wonderful impulsiveness. Instead of being experienced in a terrifying form, it now emerges in a form which is felt as tranquil and harmonious or delicious and wickedly delightful or even exciting fun. This is the curious change in form, from bad to good form (Mahrer, 1978a), which occurs as the therapist allows herself to succumb more and more to the looming, imminent deeper potential.

*Bodily sensations.* Experiential listening means being attuned to one's own deeper experiencings. At times these are signaled or manifested in the form of bodily sensations. In any case, attending to deeper experiencings includes attending to bodily sensations. As the patient is behaving and talking, the therapist's attention may be drawn toward bodily sensations which rise up and invite attention. These may include a headache, the skin across the forehead becoming tight, cold feet, a pounding in the stomach, the face feeling flushed and warm, butterflies in the stomach, a slight cramping in the buttocks, a soreness in the lower back, a sense of rising and floating, a general drowsiness and heaviness, the hands becoming numb, a hot hollowness in the chest, nausea, internal pulling and twisting, an inability to move arms and legs, the tongue feeling swollen and thick, the whole body feeling much smaller or larger, a sensation of wetness on the skin or blood pouring from the back or ears. When the therapist's attention is drawn toward these bodily sensations, they constitute valuable data.

*Thoughts*. Deeper experiencings also occur in the form of thoughts. The therapist is attentive to cognitions, ideas, words and sentences, inner voices. When the therapist is in the posture of experiential listening, these thoughts make sense within the phenomenological world shared by patient and therapist. No matter what the thoughts refer to, they are expressions of the deeper experiencing.

The imagery may include the old uncle who is droning on and on about his idyllic boyhood. As this is occurring, the therapist may be aware of a thought: "I don't want to hear any more of this" or "I could set fire to his chair if I had the guts" or the therapist hears a voice saying: "What bullshit." All such thoughts are data to which the therapist attends.

Experiential listening, then, means that the therapist attends to the images which occur in one's own phenomenological world, as well as to one's own deeper experiencings. Experiential listening means that the therapist enters into the patient's phenomenological world. Once the therapist has entered into this world, the therapist has access to two realms of precious data: one's own flow of images and one's own flow of deeper experiencings.

The basic practices of experiential psychotherapy culminate in experiential listening. It may take a few minutes or 15-25 minutes or even more, but each session reaches a point where the patient's attention is predominantly on some center accompanied with at least moderate bodily sensations, and the patient is experiencing. At the same time, the therapist has entered into the patient's phenomenological world, exists in the deeper phenomenological world of the patient, and is attending to meaningful images while undergoing deeper experiencings. This is the foundation for all the work of experiential therapy.

### EXAMPLES OF EXPERIENTIAL LISTENING

The purpose of this section is to serve as both demonstration and training. It serves as a demonstration of experiential listening, and it provides a set of opportunities for the therapist to develop and refine the skills of experiential listening.

I have selected excerpts from tapes of the work of my own graduate students, from tapes of patients with whom I have worked, and from tapes of other experiential psychotherapists. In each excerpt, the patient is at the working level of experiencing. That is, the patient's attention is largely on some meaningful center, not the therapist, and the bodily sensations are at least at a moderate level. If a sentence or a phrase or so is at this working level of experiencing, it is italicized. Otherwise, the entire excerpt is at the working level of experiencing.

If the therapist assumes the posture of experiential listening, then the therapist will have access to a phenomenological scene (images) and to some kind of deeper experiencing. The therapist will see (exist in) imagery and that imagery will be the phenomenological scene. It will be present, and will have reality. In addition, the therapist will experience something from the deeper potential. Accordingly, each excerpt is followed by the phenomenological scene and the deeper experiencing which is there for the experiential therapist or reader who assumes the experiential posture and who listens experientially. It would be better if these excerpts were on tapes. To reduce the disadvantage somewhat, I have tried to describe something of the way in which the patient's words were spoken.

The first aim of the reader should be to have one's own phenomenological scene and deeper experiencing. This is more important than the degree of similarity to the phenomenological scene and deeper experiencing in the text. I have been impressed with the commonality among experiential therapists who listen to the same excerpts. Yet this commonality includes a range of emphases. From the same excerpt, some phenomenological scenes and deeper experiencings are more concrete, while others are more vague. Some are of a lighter vein; others are somber. Some are mundane, while others are bizarre. Some are more hesitant, while others are more certain. The reader may regard the phenomenological scenes and deeper experiencings as reasonably illustrative of those which would be obtained from a group of experiential therapists.

I encourage the reader to go over each excerpt several times until it seems to be real, until the reader can listen to the words spoken in some way which has presence. Listen to the words again and again until you are existing in some phenomenological scene (seeing some kind of imagery), and until you have some kind of deeper experiencing. If the phenomenological scene and deeper experiencing are similar to those given following each excerpt, all well and good. If there are differences, at least you have engaged in experiential listening so as to have some kind of phenomenological scene and deeper experiencing. And that is probably more important, especially if they have a presence and a reality to them. By following the basic practices, you should be able to engage in experiential listening.


## A. External Situational Context

The behavior and the words of the patient invoke a concrete scene, an external situational context. This scene, rather than some kind of deeper potential, is illuminated. Once the therapist sees this external situational context, the deeper potential occurs when the therapist moves further into the scene, exists and lives in it.

1) *Direct encounters.* An external situational context is constructed, and there are key words or key actions which come from the patient. The therapist sees this scene as if the patient says these key words or carries out these key actions directly toward the other person. The therapist witnesses direct encounters even though these words and actions are not directly targeted toward the other person. Typically they are aimed at no one in particular.

1.1 Pt: (Slowly, as if near tears.) I'm in the crib near my parents' bedroom. Crying. Crying so hard . . . (There are soft tears.) I feel so bad. It doesn't work. I'm sick of it all, crying and . . . I want to be picked up by them. Please just lift me up and pick me up . . . (Still softly crying.) I don't like being stuck in a box. (Now there is some beginning annoyance.) I'm alive but they never give me life. They are nice people *but they'd rather play with each other than me.*

In the phenomenological scene, the patient is in a crib and the parents are in bed in the room. They are looking at one another, talking together and touching. There is a flavor of sex in the bed. But the patient is crying loudly, making a lot of noise. He is quite present and very intrusive: "Play with me! Stop playing with each other. I'm going to bother you! Pay attention to me, dammit!" The patient is jumping up and down, making loads of noise. The deeper experiencing is that of being an intruder, a real bother, unwanted and ignored, but nasty and petulant, protesting.

1.2 Pt: (With increasing agitation.) It's getting worse. Much worse . . . I think I'll have to go back to the hospital. I'm beginning to think I got to . . . (Now the voice is sharper and harder.) *My husband isn't treating me right. He isn't nice to me. . . .*

In the phenomenological scene, the patient is yelling at the husband: "I'm going to punish the hell out of you. You bastard. It'll all your fault. I'm going to make you squirm. I'm going to make you feel rotten!" The husband is present. He is downcast, guilty, and responsible. The deeper experiencing consists of vindictiveness, punitiveness, retribution.

1.3 Pt: (She is describing her close friend with whom she is currently living.) . . . Ellen is beautiful. She is strong and doesn't really need anyone. She is the kind of person who knows what she is and what she wants. Occasionally she gets uncertain. But she is like a cat. No matter what happens, she always lands on her feet. She is competent. Not like me. (Pause, now there is a bit of hurt defensiveness in the voice.) She thinks of me as, oh, stupid sort of, not like her. But nice. She thinks of me as nice. . . . Ellen always has a look. Chilling. Ellen is haughty. She knows that I am slow in picking things up, and she helps me, but *I know she really doesn't respect me, or like me. . . .*

In the phenomenological scene, the patient is talking directly to Ellen: "I know that you don't respect me, or like me." Ellen is a powerful force, an authority. The patient is looking directly at Ellen, and is saying these words with strong feeling. Ellen is almost a wee bit shocked to hear these words. The deeper experiencing consists of a sense of justified defiance, being on an equal footing with Ellen. There is a risked excitement and, around the edges, the tip of a fear of Ellen's retaliation.

1.4 Pt: (He is attending to the image of his mother who died three years ago.) Sometimes she is there, close to me. She comes when I am falling asleep and she whispers to me. She said, "You'd better straighten it out. Try to straighten it out." *So I am going to. I don't know how, but I am going to do something.*

In the phenomenological scene, the words are being spoken directly to the mother: "Yes, mother. I am going to straighten it out. I don't know how, but I am going to do something." Patient and mother are looking directly at one another. It is evening. He is lying in bed, and mother is right by the bed, within reaching distance. The deeper experiencing is warm closeness with mother, comfort and security in her presence. It is a good experiencing of loving closeness and bonding with mother.

1.5 Pt: It never happened before. I thought . . . I thought I was normal and something bad was happening . . . but . . . I am not! They really are going to hurt me! And . . . I can't do anything about it! . . . I am an insect. . . . There's nothing left anymore! I don't know . . . I know people aren't talking about me . . . but I did fear everybody! *I never did what they wanted me to do. That's so easy! It's easy to do what others tell you! . . . Just do what they say!*

The prominent feature of the phenomenological scene is "they." The patient is saying words directly to "them": "I never did what you wanted me to do. That's so easy! It's easy to do what you tell me! Just do what you say!" The patient is screaming these words directly at them. There are two or three "they" persons here with the patient. They consist of family: father, mother, an aunt or uncle, maybe an older brother or sister. The scene is charged. They are shocked, angry. They do not like hearing words like these. The deeper experiencing is that of defiance, confrontation, standing up to them.

1.6 Pt: (Attending to his father.) God he drank . . . he was a slob, a slob! I never trusted him. He'd get drunk and had that crazy look in his eye. I could never know what he'd do. . . . *I never liked the drinking. . . . I always thought he was an animal!*

In the phenomenological scene, father is present. Indeed, the scene is charged, and there is a kind of confrontation between the patient and the father. The patient says the following directly to father: "I never liked your drinking . . . I always thought you were an animal!" The deeper experiencing is that of fighting father, standing up to him, yelling at him, risking some sort of outbreak.

1.7 Pt: (He is attending to his grandmother.) She sits in that chair like a monarch. Old and crippled. She squawks and I'm supposed to come running. That voice. It's not even human. "Jeffrey!" Croaking. Yelling. She never thinks. Just what she wants. She wants a bath. Read to me. *She never thinks about me and what I want. I hope she dies. But she will never die.* Hmmph. *She'll live another ten years, the witch! And she'll never think about me and what's going on in my life!*

The patient is here with the grandmother. She is being yelled at by the patient: "You never think about me and what I want. I hope you die. But you'll never die. You'll live another ten years! You witch! And you'll never think about me and what's going on in my life." Grandmother is angry, shocked, extremely upset. The deeper experiencing is that of anger, defiance, standing up to the oppressor.

2) *Stopping short of the concrete scene.* Sometimes the patient stops with just an abrupt silence or a phrase or two which just trails off. Sometimes a concrete scene is signified by a few vague words. An entire scene is thereby alluded to without its ever being directly mentioned. The words just point toward some scene without denoting or signifying anything directly. But the therapist is witness to a complete scene. Its content is wicked, mischievous, tabooed, scary, nasty, exciting—i.e., threatening. Or it is horrendous, terrifying, catastrophic.

2.1 Pt: (Talking of the other fellow at work.) . . . He stays working through the lunch hour. He always does. He is a hard worker. I go for lunch. Always. We all do. But not him. I must say that I . . . I don't like . . . I think sometimes *he doesn't really get all that much done with the extra hours. He wants to be the assistant director. Maybe he'll get it . . . maybe he won't . . . I wish . . . (abrupt ending.)*

In the phenomenological scene, the wish comes true. He does not get to be assistant director. In fact, something awful happens to him. He got into some sort of trouble, and now he is packing his things and leaving the plant. He was fired. Here he is, walking away. Nothing worked out for him. The deeper potential is the experiencing of gloating, revenge, sweet vindication. It feels beautiful.

2.2 Pt: (She says this in a tone of dejection.) The kids . . . I'm all by myself. . . . (She and her husband were divorced about seven months ago.) I don't think I can handle them all by myself . . . it's too much. . . . *Sometimes I wonder if I can get through it. . . .*

The phenomenological scene is one in which she does not get through it. She cannot handle them by herself. In fact, she is sitting in the corner on the ward of the mental hospital. She is utterly depressed, overcome by it all, alone and withdrawn. Someone else has to be concerned about the kids because she is mindless, unaware of the kids, blank about most everything. The deeper experiencing is being free—free of the children, of the responsibilities, of all the stresses and problems.

2.3 Pt: (He is rather tense and upset.) How would I feel with a woman? I think I don't know how to deal with one. I act as if I don't have the least idea. I treat them like they are alien things. I've never gotten close to one. I don't even have the fantasies of real men! Seems like those fantasies are a secret! I've only known what men are like, not women. . . . Most of my sexual experiences have been with men, not women. *I know what that's like.* (Abrupt stop. Pause and silence.)

The phenomenological scene shows what sexual experiences with men can be like. It is filled with anger, hurt, and fighting. The patient is with a man, and they are angrily arguing with one another. The other man no longer wants to be with him. The other man has had sex with someone else, and the patient knows it. The two are yelling at each other, and there are bitter, hurtful, nasty words. The deeper experiencing is that of sexualized fighting, sexualized anger and resentment, hurt and rejection.

2.4 Pt: (She is agitated, and attending to her husband.) But I have to be protective. Otherwise, I won't have any kind of security. I'll wait. Wait and see. (Even more agitation.) *I have too much to lose now. If I lose him . . . no way can I lose him!*

In the phenomenological scene, she has indeed lost him. He is gone, and so is her security. The specific scene is one in which she is living in a cheap apartment, not the fine home. She is sitting in a tiny kitchen, eating inexpensive food by herself. There is very little money. The husband is living far away, and there is no further connection with him. The deeper experiencing is rage, rage about her circumstances, rage at her husband, depressed rage about the way she is living and the way she has ended up.

2.5 Pt: . . . I want somebody to comfort me and cheer me up, and she does that, and I, I (he is a little tearful) . . . I want that . . . I need that so much. I (tears) . . . at the same time . . . I'm afraid that (tears) I'm just *letting myself be opened up for more hurt* . . . (Hard tears.)

In the phenomenological scene, the patient is letting himself be opened up for more hurt. The awful scene occurs. The patient is leaning back, helpless, exposed, fully vulnerable. She is yelling at him, hurling all the nasty cutting remarks that hurt the patient deeply. Then, in a burst of violence, she rips open his chest and belly, tears at his guts, rips apart his viscera. The deeper experiencing is being assaulted, being ripped apart, damaged.

2.6 Pt: . . . and then Dad grabbed me and he started kissing me. What do I do to get away? The next morning I woke up and I wondered if it really happened. He was fine. As if nothing happened. He dropped me off, and never said anything, nothing at all. Whenever I go back to Springfield I gotta make sure that somebody's with me. Sometimes when he gets to drinking . . . I don't know what would have happened. I don't know what I could have done. It bothers me an awful lot. I take lots of time off . . . thinking it might happen again. I don't know how to keep in contact with him, and keep it at a distance. . . . If I phone him and I know he isn't that interested, I know I'd feel bad. . . . *Fathers should be helpful. Lots of my girlfriends have fathers and such and nothing like this kind of thing.* . . .

The patient stops short of a phenomenological scene in which she is alone at her father's place. Both are filled with sex, and he is grabbing her all over, touching her breasts and legs, touching her all over. On her part, the patient is barely resisting him. Indeed, she is saying, "Take me. I'm yours. Grab me. Be strong. Assault me. Take me." In this scene, the deeper experiencing is incestuous lust, the deliciousness of being sexually taken.

2.7 Pt: (Attending to his mother-in-law.) . . . Sadie has been living with us for almost two years. *I guess she is somehow more of a friend than my wife is. We have tea alone together at night. It is peaceful . . . in many ways I miss having a real wife.*

In the phenomenological scene, the mother-in-law is his real wife. The two are alone in a room. They are only a few feet from one another.

They are laughing with one another and touching one another. She is dressed for bed, and he too is ready to go to bed. Sex is stirring in both of them. The deeper experiencing is the warmth of sexuality, the sense of sexual closeness and intimacy, the stirrings of sexual arousal.

3) *The implied scene.* While the words and behavior of the patient refer and denote one scene, there is another which is more implied, one step away. This implied scene makes sense of the scene which is more directly referred to and denoted by the patient's words and behavior. Sometimes the implied scene is the extension or natural outcome of the denoted one. In 3.1 to 3.4, the implied scene is threatening, frightening; in 3.5 to 3.8, it is pleasant, sexual, wicked.

3.1 Pt: (Tearful, angry, pleading with her father to accept her.) Father, you misinterpreted what I wanted to do. *You look, but you never really see me. You look, and all you see is the bad, the bad side. You never see the good.* Look at me. *You never encourage anything, any kind of involvement* . . . just in the family, and then, *you weren't there.* Really. Just physically.

The phenomenological scene is the straightforward extension of what she is constructing. Father is not really there, does not really see her, never encourages, has no involvement, sees her badness. The father is about 20 feet away from her, not attending to her. She is simply not a significant part of his thoughts. When he does think of her, however, he thinks of her as a bad person, someone with whom he wants little or no relationship. On her part, the patient is indeed the essence of badness. She is hunched up, angry, snarling noises in his direction. The deeper experiencing is that of hatefulness, badness, being rejected and overlooked.

3.2 Pt: (In a scene when she was nine, and her mother comes on a visit to her and hands her a Christmas gift.) . . . I don't *want* your lousy gift. I don't want anything from you. Take your gift. It's not a gift. It's not! Dammit, just leave me alone. . . . *You're never around anyhow. You just come here 'cause you're guilty.* Well, stay away! Leave me alone!!

The phenomenological scene is extended out of the notion that the mother does not really want to be there with the patient; it is true. The mother coldly and angrily tells the patient that she is right. "I'd prefer never to see or hear from you. I'd rather stay away. I only visit every so often because I do feel just a little guilt. If I didn't have any, I'd never see you or even think about you." And from now on that's the way it will be. In this scene, the deeper experiencing is that of being absolutely unwanted, quite rejected and meaning nothing in the life of the mother.

3.3 Pt: (Attending to her husband.) . . . He doesn't really care what happens to us. . . . He is gone . . . off . . . living with . . . who knows what. . . . He has a responsibility! And the way he talks to the kids. I listen. He doesn't know. He stalls them with promises, but he will never give them anything. He doesn't even care about them. I always knew it. Wait. Some day the kids will find out too. *But they adore him. No matter what, they call him Daddy. And they think about him almost all the time. But it's his decision. He is the one who wanted to leave.* . . .

There, for a brief moment, her behavior and words imply a phenomenological scene in which what happens is precisely what she is so fearful will happen. The husband the kids are together, and they are happy. They touch and laugh. Finally they are all together and secure, a real family, warm and pleased with each other. They are all looking at one another lovingly. And she is not at all present. The deeper experiencing is the bitter anguish of being left out, of being discarded, of keeping them from happiness with one another, of being unwanted.

3.4 Pt: (In a kind of dream-like state, describing a flow of images.) . . . I see something like dancing moonbeams. Up and down and curving, going in motion. Regular. They seem to be variations on green, some are dark and . . . most of them are light. Now their movements are almost indiscriminate . . . and . . . I see campsites and brush and fires . . . back to the moonbeams. I like this. The colors seem to change from greens to yellows and blues . . . now back to greens. They seem to be flickering. How lovely they are. It's almost like they were on a velveteen background. (And now more slowly.) Beautiful . . . like they are shimmering . . . so soft . . . gentle . . . little things . . . lying on a velveteen . . . so soft and gentle. . . . (She stops. There are tears.)

In the phenomenological scene, there is a baby. This is the concrete referent implied by words such as soft, gentle, little, lying on a velveteen . . . there is a dream-like, unreal quality to the baby. It is as if the baby died or never really was. In this scene, the deeper experiencing is painful. It is that of loss or despair of a baby.

3.5 Pt: (A 17-year-old girl talking about her boyfriend.) . . . So I waited for him to call, and he didn't call. I called up Stell and we went cruising around, near where he lives. And just like you'd think, there he was, just walking toward Cremo's like it was all planned . . . Sounds nice, doesn't it? But *we just can't get together. He just runs whenever I talk to him about . . . us.* He tells me that he wants to be sure that he can be with other girls. . . . That just gets to me. *I wrote him a letter about the whole thing and I never did send it . . . no nerve.* (Laughs.)

The more directly denoted scene is one in which she is alone with him, and she is telling him that she likes him. Maybe she is even reading the letter to him. But the more implied scene is one in which they are in a bedroom, away from everyone. They are naked and in bed, touching and holding one another, whispering and wiggling. The deeper experiencing is a mixture of romanticized sexuality and excited eroticism.

3.6 Pt: (He is tense and agitated throughout these statements.) Now when I go along and I see a couple, I look at the man. . . . I look at his face and at his balls. . . . I am a little attracted, and that's sick. They walk toward me and I try to look away from him. At her. Like a little experiment and I get funny sometimes. Why do I do that? I dunno!

Here is a rather vivid scene. However, the implied phenomenological scene is one in which the patient sees nothing but the attractive other man. The patient plasters himself up against the other man and kisses him passionately, pressing his body flat against the other man. The deeper experiencing is wild and passionate homosexuality.

3.7 Pt: (The conservative, staid, older businessman is attending to his new secretary.) She does do the work well. Besides, she is not only efficient and intelligent, *she is an attractive woman, girl, woman . . . long black hair. Very pretty. And she walks so . . . evenly. I like to watch her. Sometimes I catch myself just looking at her. . . .*

There is another scene implied by this rather vivid scene in which he is looking at the lovely woman. In the implied scene, they are alone in her apartment. She is full of sexuality, and she wants sex with him. She is slowly, seductively taking off her clothes, lying on her bed, invitingly. She is full of sexuality. The deeper experiencing is sexualized lusty passion.

3.8 Pt: (Shaking, agitated.) It scares me . . . I feel like I'm falling into a hole. Death . . . I'll fall into this hole. I'll be without reason. . . . People will say I'm psychotic. I don't want to give up. . . . They'll take me to a hospital, and I'll be psychotic.

The phenomenological scene which she defines is one in which she is a raving psychotic, completely without reason. She is surrounded by people who have taken her to the hospital and who chant that she is crazy. In the midst of these people, she runs in circles like a banshee, screaming lunacies at them, doing obscene things in front of them. The deeper experiencing is that of being wildly free, shocking them all, offending them and loving it.

4) *Parental figures invoking rules.* These external situational contexts consist of parental figures who make pronouncements in a controlling authoritative manner about what life is like, rules for living, homilies on life, rules for how the patient should and should not be.

4.1 Pt: (She is attending to the way things were when she grew up.) It was hard to feel comfortable. Never really. I mean like always work. . . . There's always something I gotta do. I mean, *you gotta do your homework 'cause you always leave it to the last minute* . . .

The phenomenological scene includes a mother. Mother is standing there, a little annoyed, and somewhat critical. She is saying words to the patient: "You have to do your homework because you always leave it to the last minute." In this scene, the deeper experiencing is that of being bad, a bother, criticized and yelled at.

4.2 Pt: (Attending to how he is supposed to be. He speaks with feeling, haltingly.) . . . I don't know. I can't cope with, how would I say . . . I can't cope with the . . . uh . . . (sighs) the verbal, uh . . . portion that I have to say out loud. Uh. Here's how I feel and here's why I feel like this . . . but *I'm supposed to make it clear out loud, and I have*

*to . . . I'm supposed to say just exactly how I feel. . . . I* seem to sense
and know and I . . . I probably have a good idea of why I'm feeling
the way I am, but *I can't say it to . . . to the person who . . . to hear it . . .*

In the phenomenological scene, there is a parental figure who is demanding and authoritative. This person is critical of the patient. "You
mumble. You don't say it straight. Now try to say it clearly this time.
And get it right. Say exactly how you feel." Here are the rules. However,
the patient is not complying. He is not going to say it directly; he is not
going to tell; he is not about to do what the parental figure wants. In
this scene, the deeper experiencing is that of defying, standing up to,
resisting, confronting the big authority.

4.3 Pt: Shit! I can't say, "Yes, darling" and then know damn well it is
just a bunch of shit. "Yes, dear. I'll be good and never crazy, and
never feel threatened." If it's not in accordance with what he wants,
then he won't love me. Then Mr. Big'll be annoyed with his lady
(dripping with angry hostility). Well, *it's time to be more secure than
insecure! I have this fucking mask I live in. For years I've been glued inside
this mask. You have to be nice! You have to be screwed once a month by the
master! Spread your legs and never wave your ass in the air or get horny!
Just open your legs! I feel like a whore when I get screwed!*

In the phenomenological scene, there is a big man present. He is her
father and her husband and "man." He is stern and disapproving of
the patient. "You are bad! You must serve your master. He fucks you
when he wants. Be a good sexual wife. You are not supposed to have
sexual feelings except when he wants you. You are not supposed to be
seductive except with him and when he wants. Otherwise you are a
wicked whore!" In this scene, she has been caught by her father. He
found her in a state of lust, being full of passion, moaning and groaning
as her body is writhing in passion. The deeper experiencing is that of
being wickedly sexual, a devilishly wanton woman, a seductively passionate being.

### B.  Bad Self

The behavior and words of the patient construct and illuminate a
deeper potential. The deeper potential is an inner self which is bad. It
has characteristics and tendencies which are awful, frightening, mon-

strous, wicked. In addition, there is the patient who is struggling to cope with the bad self in some way.

By shifting into the bad self, what first occurs is the nature of the experiencing. Then, from within this deeper experiencing, the phenomenological scene takes shape. Its general contours are already present. But its specific nature occurs only after the nature of the deeper experiencing is illuminated.

1) *Defining and rejecting the bad self.* The patient's behavior and words first define rather concretely what the bad self is like, what it wants to do, how it wants to be. Then the patient's behavior and words reject the bad self, pronounce that the patient would never be that way, hates being that way, could never be that way; in short, the patient rejects the bad self which is defined. The deeper experiencing is that which is occurring within the so-called bad self as it is doing whatever it is doing. The phenomenological scene is that in which the so-called bad self is doing whatever it is doing.

1.1 Pt: (She is attending to her friend.) She doesn't have any idea about her husband. What he's doing with Ann. She's . . . just doesn't know. *I could never tell her. Oh, I'd never say such a thing to her. She'd be cut to pieces to hear something like that. I couldn't be that nasty to her . . . or to anyone.*

In the phenomenological scene, the bad self is indeed telling the friend. It is saying things to her, and she is cut to pieces hearing these things. The bad self is deliciously nasty in saying, "Your husband is cheating on you! He is screwing Ann behind your back!" In this scene, the deeper experiencing is the joy of being nasty, wicked, hurting her friend, making her friend squirm, tearing her friend apart.

1.2 Pt: My project is progressing but I don't care. I guess I'm holding the fort. Tidying over situations. Swaine is doing all right. *I can't complain about him. I mean I wouldn't put the blame on him. Not really. I couldn't do that.*

In the phenomenological scene, the bad self is complaining about Swaine, putting the blame on him. The patient is upset and angry. There are about five people in his office, and he is screaming at Swaine, documenting how Swaine has screwed up the project. "How could you be so stupid? I ought to fire you! The project is falling apart, and it'sbecause of you, you damned idiot!" The deeper experiencing is that of attacking, assaulting, destroying.

1.3 Pt: Well, his breath was just awful. But *of course I would never ever say that to him. That would be rude. You just don't act that way. I couldn't.*

In the phenomenological scene, the bad self is being rude. It says things directly to the man: "Your breath is just awful! You stink!" The deeper experiencing is that of firm openness, toughness, transparent bluntness.

1.4 Pt: Must I dodge the responsibility? He won't return the call, and I know that when they call. So I say to them, fine, he'll call you back. But I know he won't. He's such a coward, and he faces up to absolutely nothing. . . . *I have no desire to take over his life.* So how can I pass the telephone message on to him? . . . *He didn't even get home till 12:30. . . . I don't want to go through life making his decisions for him.*

In the phenomenological scene, the bad self carries out the desire to take over his life, making his decisions for him. The patient is sitting in the chair in the evening. She is relaxed and happy, the boss. Her husband is answering phone calls, being dutiful and responsible, a little scared of her, but being a good little boy. The deeper experiencing is that of invincible power, absolute control.

1.5 Pt: (She is talking about her husband.) We went driving with Keith's friend. It was fun. We were laughing and silly. We did a little drinking. Not much. Then we stopped and had supper together. I felt happy. So did Roger. We talked a lot at supper, and I didn't feel tense or scared much. Actually I felt quite good. I felt like making love that night. I think he loves me. . . . (Pause.) *I can't leave him. He feels guilty enough. I just can't put the blame on him. It would be cruel to leave him.*

In the phenomenological scene, the bad self leaves the husband, is delightfully cruel in putting the blame on him, and makes him thoroughly guilty. He is crying, tears streaming down his face, while he feels like he is fully to blame. He is almost writhing in guilt. "Please . . . please . . . I'll be different . . . please!" But her mind is made up and she is leaving him. The deeper experiencing is that of being brutal, cruel, tough, vicious, righteous.

1.6 Pt: (She is attending to her father.) My father . . . does he want me to be crazy? . . . He doesn't want me to be crazy. I have it in me. But I don't want to be. I have something, a little girl in me. I want to be a person. *I don't want to be his little girl! He should have other little girls. I don't ever want to be his little girl.*

In the phenomenological scene, the bad self is being his little girl. She is nestled in his lap, curled up, loved and comforted. Daddy's arm is around her, patting her gently. The deeper experiencing is the warm closeness of being Daddy's little girl, loved and protected.

1.7 Pt: I'd say, "Mother, I don't want you to come to my house!" That makes me so uncomfortable. It hurts me. God! I'm 30 years old. (And now, addressing mother.) I don't want your criticisms. I wish you'd treat me the way you treat your friends. . . . I've stopped playing all those games with you. 'Cause of that my sister and I never got along. We hated each other. (Now mother fades away.) She's it. I'll never be close to my mother. I know that. *But I have something. My own family now. I'm a grown woman. I'm not her daughter. . . . I don't need her!*

In the phenomenological scene, the bad self needs mother, needs mother desperately. She is a little child to her mommy. Indeed, she is a little child, curled up on mommy's lap, and mommy is bathing the little girl in beatific love. The deeper potential is the experiencing of little girlness, of being loved and nurtured as a little girl.

2) *Labeling it as a problem; the bad self loves it.* Not only is the patient coping with a bad self, but the emphasis is on the valence of the feeling as the bad self does whatever it does. The patient labels the bad self as a problem about which the patient is worried and bothered; certainly the feeling is not one of pleasure, not at all. However, the bad self revels and delights in being that way; it is sheer pleasure to be that way. The bad self loves being that way.

2.1 Pt: (A woman who is referring to her stepfather.) . . . Men can have my body but never my mind. Two men did, and I know that more would. But he (her stepfather) would just talk about dirty things. I was only 18 or 19, and I had repulsions against him. He'd talk about what happens in your mouth when you eat a guy . . . shit! . . . Oh, what the hell. I know that I'm just like him. *Steve (her stepfather) was sexual, and I realize now that I am sexual too and . . . and I tried to fight that all my life. . . . We all are. But all he talks about is sex and I get insulted.*

The deeper experiencing is the open, free, delightful, wonderful experiencing of sexuality. Within the general scene which she sketches, the specific phenomenological scene is one in which she and Steve are fully aroused. He is on his back on the bed and his legs are spread. She is on her knees, with her tongue and mouth all over his penis and testicles. She and Steve are moaning and happily sexual. It is wonderful.

2.2 Pt: (Distraught.) I got to. I'll do anything. How do I get rid of it? I'll lose everyone. (Crying.) My father, Dennie (her first husband), and now Bill (the man she is presently married to). It's like a plague. Hiding and thinking it'll get better. I don't know what to do. . . . *I'm just never there when they need me.* I don't know what happens. Like I . . . (crying) . . . *What happens to me? I gotta get rid of it. I just got to. I can't live with that anymore.*

The deeper experiencing is that of never being there when significant men need me, and furthermore, being this way is delightful, sheer pleasure. It is the wonderful experiencing of being tough and firm, doing whatever the hell I want to do, being superior to these men. In the phenomenological scene, she is powerful, muscular, big. There is a man who is on his hands and feet in front of her, groveling in passive weakness, his face turned upwards in pleading submission and helplessness.

2.3 Pt: (In his late thirties.) One thing as well . . . that's been bothering me over the last few years, and uh, but . . . in my relationships with women . . . I'm so . . . well, it's a double thing . . . they are fairly good in a sense, on one level . . . at least . . . I relate fairly well. I'm fairly open. I'd like to be more . . . I'd like to *give of myself more . . . more. Give myself of my emotions more.*

The deeper experiencing is that of not giving of oneself to women, not being emotional with women. It is the sheer enjoyment of teasing them, defying them, being removed and cold to them. In the phenomenological scene there are four or five women who are beseeching him for his love, his concern, his feelings for them. But he is stoic, cold, removedly staring at them in stony disdain.

2.4 Pt: (There is agitation in his voice.) Well, when Christine (his wife) isn't home for a day or even for the afternoon . . . it's awful. I get these thoughts about cruising . . . going to a gay bar . . . I . . . Sometimes I . . . it gets so bad sometimes I hide the car key. I want her to take both keys so I can't have the car. I hide the key sometimes so I can't get the car. It's like a fight and I get all tight inside and I feel nervous all over. It's terrible. I'm so scared that I'll give in. I get so scared. I just don't know any longer. . . .

The deeper experiencing is that of having given in, of cruising, going to gay bars. It is the experiencing of being filled with open homosexual excitement. In the phenomenological scene, he is at a gay bar, looking over the body of the other man, lingering on his neck, his arms, and shoulders. He is almost on the verge of swooning into the other man, so filled is he with sexual excitement. They are very close to one another, both breathless and tingling.

3) *It is not my fault; the bad self loves being that way.* The patient gives excuses and explanations as if to some agency which is charging or accusing the patient. Not only is the charge true, but the bad self loves being whatever way it is accused of being.

3.1 Pt: (After describing a big fight with his sister, and how she collapses into crying and begging forgiveness.) . . . and I dunno. Well, she acts crazy and she . . . it's awful. I can't say anything to her. . . . *I got so mad at her 'cause I'm under a lot of tension. A new location and inventory and things go wrong!*

It is as if some shadowy agency is saying, "You are mean. You are bad. You actually like tearing apart that poor little girl." The deeper experiencing is that of being mean, cruel, hurtful, powerful, controlling. In the phenomenological scene, he is standing erect, godlike, and his sister is draped on the floor, her arms wrapped around his legs. She is beaten, submissive, tears pouring down her face, looking up in adoring worship of her lord.

3.2 Pt: (He is telling about meeting his friend at the airport.) I think the reason I forgot is that I get engrossed in things so much that I screen everything else out, and when I was done, I was shocked that it was after seven and the plane was due in at seven. I've always been that way.

It is as if some shadowy figure is leveling an accusation: "You didn't want to meet him! You had no reason whatsoever for not being there! You are bad!" The deeper experiencing is the delightfully wicked pleasure of saying no, of having the other person squirm, of being defiantly aggressive. In the phenomenological scene, the patient sees the other person arriving at the airport. No one is there to meet him, and he is hurt, let down, frustrated and a little angry. The whole section of the airport is filled with a kind of cackling laughter. Ha ha! No one is there to meet you!

3.3 Pt: (She is upset, complaining.) . . . I was ready to hold down my bitching, *but he wouldn't find time for me. Rich just wouldn't talk with me.* He just sat there, watching the tube. *I didn't want to fight.* I don't know . . . that's not the main thing. I didn't want to watch. . . . *He expected me to be there and to do what he wanted to do. That's unfair!*

It is as if some shadowy figure is accusing the patient: "You are bad! You always fight! You bitch all the time. You should be nice and do what he wants. You shouldn't complain!" The deeper experiencing is the sheer joy of fighting, of loving to bitch at him, of incessant complaining, of never doing what he wants, of not having to be nice. In the phenomenological scene, Rich is cowering in front of the television, hurtfully stung by every word she hurls at him as she screams at him, bitches at him unmercifully.

4) *I am not bad; yes you are.* The patient is already sensing the badness, already succumbing to the truth of his badness. The deeper experiencing is that of being utterly bad, of deserving and earning the accusation. In the phenomenological scene, some agency is charging the patient with being thoroughly bad, and in the background is the incident which proves his badness.

4.1 Pt: (He is attending to the secretary whom he finally took to supper. They held hands and touched and hinted at their mutual willingness to have an affair together.) . . . *I don't feel bad at all.* After all these many years . . . I feel sort of like a new person. It all went along so easily. She was wonderful. I don't know why I never did that before. *No one knew. It was discreet. . . . I think I am like a lot of people. We saw others . . . they too, well . . . maybe they were doing the same thing there.*

In the phenomenological scene, his wife, her parents, his parents, and his two children are in the room with him. They are agreeing with the wife, and they are looking angrily at him with narrowed eyes and hard faces. The wife is yelling at him, "You are bad. Everyone knew. No one would ever do anything like that! We all hate you. I'm leaving you and the children are going with me. We are never going to speak to you again!" The deeper experiencing is that of being rotten, deserving of massive punishment, being a bad husband, a bad father, a bad son, a thoroughly disgusting person.

4.2 Pt: (Attending to one of the medical residents whom the patient supervises.) Benny was there in the corridor. Afterwards. The meeting. He missed. It's the second in a row. Just drifts around I guess. He . . . I told him about missing the meeting and he looked . . . annoyed at me. . . . *I know I expect a lot. He seemed miffed. I want some responsibility from him. There's nothing wrong with that. He should be that way. What's wrong with that?*

In the phenomenological scene, a figure is criticizing the patient: "You are bad. You expect much too much. He has a right to be miffed with you. You expect much too much responsibility from him. It is wrong. You dominate them and get on their backs. You are awful." The deeper experiencing is that of being cold and inhuman, excessively dominating, and of being punished and scolded for being bad.

4.3 Pt: (He is attending to his younger brother who is still at home.) Had palsy all his life. His left eye is bad. Something's wrong with it. It's an eye that doesn't look, doesn't work. Glaucoma? He used to take pills. *I couldn't take care of him anymore. I had to go away. That's part of it. I got so I just couldn't stand it. . . . I stayed for a while.*

In the phenomenological scene, a figure is yelling at the patient: "You are bad! You should have stayed and taken care of him. He needs you! You should be with him. What kind of an uncaring sonuvabitch are you anyway? You are bad!" In the background, the younger brother is at home, lost and hurt. He is crying, "Where is Patrick? Why did he leave me?" The deeper experiencing is a cruel coldness, a self-centered in-humanness which deserves being hated and punished.

4.4 Pt: (She has been attending to a recent affair she had. Then she switches.) That's happened and that's that. *It's good that it finally happened, 'cause then we had that talk.* Paul's been under strain lately and we've never talked. We just don't talk. *That thing with Brian was just a way of showing Paul that our marriage was over.* It was bad for me. We talked that one as far as we can go. We have decided to end it. We both agreed the thing with Brian just showed how flawed our marriage was anyhow. *There was no other way. It had to end that way.*

In the phenomenological scene, a figure is screaming at her, "You are bad! You are dirty and sneaky! You broke up the marriage. Paul deserves someone better than you, you bitch! You're a worthless piece of shit! Adulteress!" In the background, she is carrying on the sneaky, sordid affair, a terrible person doing an awful thing. The deeper experiencing is that of being tainted, dirty, an animal deserving of hateful punishment.

5) *They mistreat me; you deserve it.* The patient complains and whines and nags about others. They are bad; they mistreat and are unfair to the patient. The deeper experiencing is that of being the bad one; it is the patient who is awful, and not the other one; the patient is mistreated because he deserves it.

5.1 Pt: (Bitterly complaining.) I see this guy from Montreal. He is a cartographer, and he's doing just fine. Real fine. He just got here about six months ago and he's moving right along . . . Jesus! . . . There's this girl. About two years older than me. . . . She's going to be the associate director! She's barely my age! . . . What the fuck! That's a senior position . . . but I'm not getting anywhere. I can barely hold onto my crappy job. . . . She has less education than me . . . was in the position less. She hasn't been with the government long. . . . They always get the job. They get . . . breaks! And I don't get any-where . . . I feel like a stepping stone. Christ! I go nowhere. I don't know. They get ahead and I stand still!

A shadowy figure whispers the truth: "It's because they are good and you are bad. They have talent. They are competent. They deserve to get ahead. You are a loser. You are incompetent and inadequate." The deeper experiencing is being a loser, being incompetent, being inadequate, being a fuck-up. In the phenomenological scene, he is at work. He looks and acts like a drunken imbecile. He is dressed in peculiar clothes, and everyone else looks well-dressed. He makes gutteral noises like a dumb animal, and others speak elegantly. He is carrying papers from one to the other as an office boy.

5.2 Pt: (Attending to the faces.) I know that they are after me. They are there. Faces. The eyes mainly. With awful expressions . . . (Moans.) I see their eyes. They leer at me! They look at me! And they just look. I can't stand it anymore. They leer! They hate me! It's like I can't get away from them.

The shadowy figure whispers the truth: "It's because they know how rotten you are." The deeper potential is the experiencing of sexual rottenness, degradation, a sickening sexual low life. In the phenomenological scene, she is doing all sorts of awful sexual acts of perversion and degradation: masturbating in church, sniffing her father's underwear, sucking off a neighborhood dog, sticking dirty objects in her rectum and vagina. And all the while, she is being denounced by the good people in her family, the community, and the world.

5.3 Pt: (He is quite upset, with attention upon his mother.) . . . but sometimes I'm just not sure of myself. Not really sure about things. I get scared. I get scared. It's hard for you to understand. You have an image of me. Like Burt Reynolds. Macho and strong. I'm supposed to make a decision and that's it. I say to her, what do you think? Just help me. Sometimes I really get mixed up . . . I don't know. . . . She gets such a look on her face if I . . . *I know I'm grown.* . . .

She is right; he is wrong. The deeper experiencing is that of a little baby, a squalling infant. In the phenomenological scene, mother is screaming at him. Her face is contorted with rage, and she is absolutely disgusted with him. He is lying on his back on the floor in front of her, making baby gurgles, his arms and legs jerking like a little baby, drool coming out of his mouth.

5.4 Pt: (In the hospital room, visiting his uncle.) . . . and he asks me questions. What am I doing? What kind of a job do I have? Why don't

I have a better job? Why don't I have a steady job? He's an accountant, a businessman. Like steel. Cold. No emotion. He regards me like a balance sheet. *I don't mean nothing to him. I'm a kid who doesn't mean a damned thing to that computer. Ticks everything off like a balance sheet. I'm not his son. I'm a piece of shit. I'm here by accident. I am the son of his sister—an outcast, a loser, a guy who didn't make it. . . .*

The deeper experiencing is that of being a complete and thoroughly unwanted piece of shit, a loser, a deserved outcast. In the phenomenological scene, the uncle is yelling at him all the things the uncle really feels about him. He is worthless; no one wanted him; he shouldn't even be alive; just go away; he is a failure. And the patient is the living truth of all those accusations.

5.5 Pt: (She is attending to her husband.) . . . Daniel was a hard baby. It was my third child. I don't know where Sid was. He wasn't at the hospital. Who knows where he was? He showed up . . . some time. . . . He is so damned irresponsible. He never remembers me, like on my birthdays, and anniversaries. When we are at parties . . . he acts like a dolt. He . . . I'll be holding a cigarette, and he won't even notice enough to light it. And if I forget something . . . I was just holding it, and he just went on with his dumb talk. Interrupts! Anyone can be talking, and he just . . . he breaks in. With dumb things. Like he doesn't even notice what is going on. . . .

The shadowy figure listens, unimpressed: "No, Christine. Sid is the good one. You are the one who is bad. You are whining and complaining. Sid is a fine man; you are a shrew." The deeper experiencing is that of being the cackling shrew, ugly and complaining, nagging and bitching. In the phenomenological scene, she is bitching and yelling at Sid. All the people at the party are standing around good old Sid, looking at her in disgust for the awful person that she is.

6) *The compelling internal/external entity.* The bad self occurs as the internal or external entity which is so compelling that the patient is drawn into being it. In the phenomenological scene, the patient is doing what the compelling entity was doing. In 6.1-6.3, the compelling entity is internal. In 6.4-6.7, the compelling entity is an external person, who, in 6.8-6.12, is deranged. In 6.13-6.14, the entity is a generalized external agency such as God, the communists, or society.

6.1 Pt: The headache is all over. Bad. Hurts. Feels heavy. If I turn . . . move my head . . . it hurts, gets heavy . . . stops me. All over the head. Inside and out. Feels like . . . heavy . . . all inside and . . . seems to fill the head. Just too much. *Like a live thing . . . if it could . . . it would burst the skull. Coming out. Pushing out. Feels like it could burst my skull open. . . .*

The phenomenological scene is one in which the patient is doing just this, i.e., is bursting, crashing out, exploding. Here is incredible inner energy exploding outwards in a wild and powerful blast. However, the scene is cloudy and without exact particulars. The deeper experiencing is that of explosive blasting, crashing, bursting.

6.2 Pt: (Attending fixedly at the cancer.) I have always thought of it as . . . uh . . . pinkish red. That's all. I never thought about it. (Pause.) Grainy . . . no . . . maybe reddish . . . I never thought about it. (Pause.) Maybe about like a lump . . . I think like a lump. But inside me. I never thought about it . . . hard to find. It is nasty . . . I mean it is slippery . . . it moves . . . I don't know. (Getting upset.) I keep seeing funny things there . . . it comes and goes. It moves around. *It is nasty! Still pink . . . (Very upset.) . . . It's . . . well, it gets flesh and eats it! . . . I feel awful . . . it eats flesh . . . I don't want to see it anymore.*

In the phenomenological scene, the patient is the active one who is eating flesh, tearing at the soft exposed flesh with teeth snapping and ripping. The victim is a living creature who is being torn apart, bite by bite, as the patient devours more and more. The deeper experiencing is that of sheer animal attacking, cannibalistic devouring, ripping, tearing, devouring.

6.3 Pt: (Attending to the headache.) It is like a force, a kind of energy. Feels like a gas. Heavy gas. Inside and pressing. It gets heavier and hurts. That's when it hurts. Like now . . . sometimes it stops. Breaks up. It gets lighter somehow. Sometimes it gets like that. . . . It's at the front, over the forehead. *Pounding.* No, it's throbbing. . . . *It hurts! Like it . . . wants to hurt! Like it's just, well, and it, well, wants to hurt! . . . Now it is more in the back of the head. Oh . . .*

In the phenomenological scene, the patient is mercilessly pounding another person, hitting the other person again and again. The patient is never going to let that other person go, and will torture the helpless other person again and again and again. The deeper experiencing is that of being merciless, of hurting, pounding, smashing.

6.4 Pt: (The mother is intent upon her six-year-old daughter, angrily describing the way the daughter is.) . . . I was talking to Fred on the phone. I saw her, out of the corner of my eye. I know when she's up to something. Saw her do it again. The same thing always happens when I'm on the phone or when she thinks I'm not going to know what she's up to. She thinks I'm busy and she thinks I'm not going to watch her. *She has thoughts, that one.* I could see her sneaking into her room. *I know she's going to mess around in there. I know what she does. She shouldn't do that. She hides, but I know. . . . She's tricky, that one. . . . She thinks she's so smart. She shouldn't do those things!*

In the phenomenological scene, mother is in her room, sneaky, hiding, not letting anyone know. She touches her breasts and her nipples, the clitoris and the vagina—stroking, caressing. Soon she is groaning and moaning, writhing and twisting, but always vigilant so that no one comes in the room. The deeper experiencing is that of masturbatory eroticism, hidden sexual ecstasy.

6.5 Pt: (The husband is attending to his wife.) How the hell can she be so . . . it's her baby too . . . but she gets all pissed off when he cries at night. She just ignores him. Lets him alone most of the time. Never plays with him. *She . . . she just leaves him alone! . . . She has no right to leave him alone all the time. He is a good baby! But she acts like she'd rather spend all her time with her girlfriends.*

The phenomenological scene is one in which he is free, not married. He is single, with three or four buddies at a bar. They are laughing and chatting together. No responsibilities. He has a great apartment. The deeper potential is being free, without responsibilities.

6.6 Pt: (After complaining about his wife. She bothers him. He doesn't like sex with her. At this point his attention is almost fully drawn into her.) . . . She gets taken over. Her hips move. Whole body moves. She isn't herself. She is sex, all sex . . . she's not herself. A sex thing. Churning. *Her hips are hot and moving . . . like the sex in her. All over her. Whole genitals seem big . . . and got her . . . just a wanting. Craving.*

*All over wanting. Needing. All over the body. Whole body . . . sexed . . . whole body.*

In the phenomenological scene, the patient is a wild, sex-crazed animal, hot and moving, churning. His whole body is twisting and lust-filled. He is grabbing and hunching, lurching and writhing. The deeper potential is crazed sexuality, pure eroticism.

6.7 Pt: (A male who is describing a scene from when he was a young adolescent.) My father'd lie on my raft when the sun was out. Liked . . . always was looking at girls. Healthy slender ones, with high breasts, and the bellybutton showing. He'd use my raft. He'd just take it—and he'd float on the water. I'd see his penis. *His balls would show in the trunks. Bulging and even showing sometimes . . . hairy . . . big and heavy. . . . His penis was revolting. It was a flaccid penis. He is fat, heavy. Blubbery. More like a fat drunk. He's revolting. That's awful.*

The phenomenological scene is one in which the patient is lying naked on the raft. He is huge, big-chested, with an enormous erection and big hairy balls. There are lovely slender young women around, tittering and very much attracted. "Look at this! Great, huh! Want to fuck! Look at me, ladies! Take a look at this!" The deeper experiencing is gross sexual exhibitionism, sexual display.

6.8 Pt: (Complaining about her mother who incessantly yells at her, relentlessly attacks her.) She has that terrible look on her face. That voice. It never stops. It goes on and on and screeches. Never stops. She follows me wherever I go in the house. Can't get away from her. Yelling at me: "Look at your room. You never clean it. What kind of a person are you? Do you think I'm going to run around after you? What is this? I can't stand it any longer." She is raving! She is out of her mind. Yelling and screaming!!

In the phenomenological scene, the patient is raving wildly at some other person. Her voice is screeching and out of control. She is running back and forth, saying somewhat bizarre things to and about the other person who is both the victim and the subject of all the lunatic screaming. The deeper experiencing is that of being deranged and irrational, out of control.

6.9 Pt: . . . *My father would drag her around the floor, screaming at her, and my mother would just lie there, dragged around, limp, like a rag!* Not doing anything. She would talk to the birds we had, canaries . . . but I could never make out what she said, and she'd never let me hear. . . . I was scared of her 'cause of that. And I think I was scared of the birds. She'd scream crazy if I'd put my finger in the cage to try to pet them . . . worried about my hurting them. . . . *She thought my dad was always attracted to her sister. Yelled that she knew about them. God! I remember when she died . . . she hung herself in the garage . . .*

In the phenomenological scene, the patient is now deranged and suicidal. She is wild and lunatic, out of contact with everyone, and completely taken over by craziness. She has crazy ideas and even hangs herself in the garage. In the final vignette, the patient is a crazy woman who is hanging from the rope in the garage, dead. The deeper experiencing is wild, uncontrolled lunacy.

6.10 Pt: She would put a sheet around her and sit in the closet. I remember feeling terrified when kids would come over. Like I had to make sure I didn't think about my mother in the closet. Sometimes she would rock and make noises there. . . . She said that people were recording her voice. She would accuse me of recording her voice and fooling her. Lying. I'd cry sometimes. *She was a paranoid schizophrenic they said . . . in the closet. Sweating. Rocking. With the sheet . . .*

In the phenomenological scene, she is in the closet, a crazy woman, sitting and rocking, with the sheet wrapped all around her. She is in another world, without thoughts. She is deranged and crazy. The deeper experiencing is being crazy, completely withdrawn.

6.11 Pt: (After incessantly complaining about his parents. He is in a scene in which he is about 10 years old.) *They are pounding each other, and she is kicking him. (Screaming.) There was a broken glass somewhere. I think she knocked it off the counter. There is hatred! Hatred! I said if you don't stop (patient is yelling at them) I'll kill you! . . . I want them to stop! I've had enough! I have to stop this fight. They always fight!*

In the phenomenological scene, the patient is beserk—rushing at the parents, assaulting them, hurling them against the wall. He is filled with wild and uncontrollable power as he is out of his mind. The deeper experiencing is wild and uncontrolled crazy physical assaultiveness, smashing and bashing.

6.12 Pt: (Attending to the face of the person she had known some years ago, and recently met again. The person had been in a car accident.) She was not attractive anymore. Ruth had been attractive. I see her face. Carefully. *The eye . . . the red blotches, and the rumpled skin . . . they're almost moving. Seeing them up close. Red blotches. Like festering sores. Blind in the eye. Ugly. I feel weak. I . . . there. Her face. Different. Oh. Ugly. Red. Ugly. See them up close . . . like something is wrong with me. Really wrong. I've always had headaches. Scared that something's wrong. Blind. Like an accident. My face will change. Be ugly. Scarred, it hurts . . . my eyes. . . .*

In the phenomenological scene, the patient is walking along the street. Some oncoming people are horrified, others just look away, a few gasp. She is aware of her grotesque face, scarred and disfigured. The deeper experiencing is that of being a demented monster, an ugly gargoyle who is deranged.

6.13 Pt: (Attending to the communists.) It really does nothing, no good. You can't fight them. They are too well organized. They train. Yeah, they train for years. *They know the ropes all right. And they take their time. Years maybe. Thirty, forty years. Then they got control. And in . . . thirty, forty years, they'll control the world.*

The phenomenological scene is one in which we are in control of the world. We are sitting in a huge building, and it is the center of the whole world. We are in charge of the world. We are the ones who run the entire world. The deeper experiencing is that of complete control, complete domination, sheer power.

6.14 Pt: I get kind of light-headed when I think of how hostile people are. It's everywhere. You can't do anything. You can't be yourself. No way. *Society won't let you. It won't let you. It won't let you do anything. It won't let you be yourself. Society decides what you're supposed to be. It forces everyone to conform. And if you don't (smashes one fist into the other open hand) . . . it'll punish you. It determines everything. No way. You gotta conform. It forces everyone. It takes away your individuality.*

The phenomenological scene includes a massive superperson: society. It is huge and gray, and powerful. It yowls. It owns every petty little human being. Power. Strength. People are walking around in chains. The deeper experiencing is power, sheer, forceful, magnificent, omnipotent power.


## C. The Dreaded Polarity

The behavior and words of the patient build a deeper potential which is the polarity of the way the patient is being. What is illuminated is both the content of the deeper polarity and the antimony between that and the patient's way of being.

1) *I am like this; no, you are the polarity*. The patient struggles to paint a picture of being a particular kind of person. For example, the patient is adult or successful or free or strong or sound. However, the dreaded truth is that the inner process is not that way at all; indeed, it is the polarity. The patient is a child or a failure or a slave or weak or full of disabling problems. Once the inner polarity is revealed, the therapist undergoes the deeper experiencing. From within the perspective of the deeper experiencing, a phenomenological scene occurs. The phenomenological scene is built by the nature of the deeper experiencing from the materials supplied by the patient, i.e., from what is directly denoted by the speaking and behaving patient.

1.1 Pt: (Looking at mother.) I'm better, Mom. I really am. You'd be proud of me. *I can take care of my own finances now. And I'm not sloppy anymore. I'm starting to keep my place neater. Even my drawers are sort of clean. Not the way I was. And I'm going to university. My grades are fair, Mom. And I even do yoga in the mornings like you. But I'm still heavy. . . .*

The deeper experiencing is that of being a fat, disgusting little boy. He is sitting on the floor in his room. His shirt is dirty, his pants are rumpled, his belly is sticking out of the shirt, and one torn sock is on his foot. The room is a complete mess, and so is he. His mother has just entered the room, and the look on her face is full of the horrified disgust she feels for him.

1.2 Pt: This will be my second book. The first did well. It was selected by about 30 colleges. *I am sort of an authority on stress materials. It's a new field, and I'm one of the leaders. Right now I'm working on a special manual for engineers. They sought me out. So that one should do well. Yes, I've done rather adequately.*

The deeper experiencing is that of being a failure whose work is worthless. In the phenomenological scene, some of the engineers are mentioning good work and good books in the field. One mentions his name and they look at one another. Most of them are quizzical. They never heard of him. One does. He raises his eyebrows and gestures in a way which instantly dismisses him as a nothing.

1.3 Pt: *I have earned everything I have. Nothing was given to me.* I owe my father for qualities I guess. But *nothing else.* I have been fortunate. But life has been good to me. I own one of the largest newspapers in the state, and *it has taken effort, real effort. Over years.*

The deeper experiencing is that of being a worthless incompetent who rides on the coattails of his father. In the phenomenological scene, he is sitting on the beach at the resort, drinking; meanwhile, back in the newspaper, the top executives are screaming about the worthless owner who doesn't know what the hell is going on; if his father only knew that the son is screwing up the business.

1.4 Pt: I am free to do what I want. Anything. I am free. No one holds me down.

The deeper experiencing is that of being held down, restrained, unable to be free, controlled. In the phenomenological scene, the patient is on his back. A massive agency is sitting on his chest, and the patient cannot even move his arms or legs. He is not even struggling.

1.5 Pt: (The husband is describing how wonderful his life could be if . . .) I think of seeing people. Friends. I don't like being in the way. I don't know. I'd play basketball on Saturdays, and I'd see women when I wanted to. Great. I'd do that. Well, I'd meet people. Interesting people. I'd do that if I wanted. And if I didn't want to, well, then . . . I could study what I wanted to. It'd be great. Free. No expectations.

The deeper experiencing is being stuck, caught, not free, controlled, a prisoner. In the phenomenological scene, he is sitting on the back porch, daydreaming. Suddenly a voice booms out of the back door:

"Jerome, get in here and wash your hands for dinner!" In an instant, the daydreams are shattered, he jumps to his feet and rushes inside the house, the dutiful good little boy.

1.6 Pt: (In his late thirties.) . . . My gut is hard. I keep myself in perfect shape. (Laughs.) No fat. I work out every day. Rest on Saturdays. Six days a week. Do 200 sit ups and 200 leg raises, every day. Very few work out like that . . . maybe I'm a fanatic.

The deeper experiencing is that of being soft, weak, frail, fat, over the hill. In the phenomenological scene, he is sitting with a bunch of guys in their early twenties. They are slim and trim, lean and muscular. He is fat, bloated, out of shape and lying to them about what a jock he used to be.

1.7 Pt: I've never had any real problem. Oh I've had worries, but nothing serious. I've known some who had serious stuff. Had to go to the hospital. But I'm sound. I've always had the capacity to think right.

The deeper experiencing is that of being a looney, a crazy nut. In the phenomenological scene, she is standing in the middle of the ward, talking utter twaddle about moonbeams and gravel. Even the other patients are looking at her as one who is completely flipped.

1.8 Pt: *I've had three years of analysis!* God, I hope it did something. I was awful. *But I got straightened out. It worked. I'm OK now. I am all right!*

The deeper experiencing is that of being insane, out of his mind, a bizarre nut. In the phenomenological scene, the men in the white coats are putting him in the ambulance. "There now, uncle Ezra, it's time to go back to the moon. You have your appointment with your analyst, and you don't want to be late."

1.9 Pt: (She is attending to her mother.) I know I have to stand up to her. *I just have to give it to her.* Just let go. I ought to kick her fat, disgusting belly. That's what I ought to do. *I'm not afraid.* I want to kick your fat disgusting belly. I want to shove it in! Really hard. *I want to smash the toe of my boot into your belly.* Once I do that I'll be free. *I'm not afraid to kick her.* I'll kick her in the belly. *She's nothing to be afraid of*. She's not even strong. *She's old and weak. I should have kicked you, you bitch. . . . I have to do it. . . .* I'd rather be a whole person and proud of myself.

The deeper experiencing is that of being a frightened, cowardly, passive little wimp, cowering and whining. In the phenomenological scene, mother is powerful. She fixes the patient with a piercing look, and stands with her hands on her hips. The patient is pressed into the wall, cowering and trembling, slowly sliding to the floor, cringing.

2) *I have impact, substance, worth; no, you are nothing.* There is some urgency or effort after having some significance and meaning in regard to others. One must have impact or substance or worth, whether good or bad, pleasant or unpleasant. However, the dreaded truth is the polarity; it is the experiencing of being invisible, nothing, of having no impact or substance, of being nonexistent. Out of the deeper experiencing emerges the phenomenological scene which is congruent with the deeper polarity and which is built from the materials of what the patient is saying and doing.

2.1 Pt: I'm screaming at him. Get the hell out of here! You're no kind of father. What does he care about the kids? Nothing! Lorrie is upset. So is Joan. I get everyone upset. He is awful. With him, Bob, I go bananas. He is infuriating. Shit! Why can't you pay the money you should? You don't have to come around. I get so damned mad at him. *I want to hurt him. I really want to hurt him. I want to make him squirm, that bastard. . . .*

However, the deeper experiencing is that of being without impact or substance, having no effect whatsoever, being a nonexistent nothing. In the phenomenological scene, she is with her husband and the kids. It is as if her words lose their substance a foot or so from her mouth, and they dissipate before reaching them. Not only do the husband and kids pay no heed to her words, but they do not even acknowledge her presence. Then she stops, and is aware that they are together, and she is not even present; she is an invisible nothing.

2.2 Pt: (He is talking in a somewhat hushed voice, laced with some excitement.) She thinks of me as pretty much of a normal person.

*(Little laugh, mild.) There is a lot about me that she doesn't know. . . . She doesn't even suspect . . . I don't think anyone does. (Intimately, engagingly provocative.) I've lived with it for years.* Even before we were married.

The deeper experiencing is emptiness, nothingness, having no impact or effect, being without substance. In the phenomenological scene, the patient runs frenetically from person to person, trying to get them interested, ensnared. But people just walk by, not noticing. There is no secret, no enticing treasure. What is more, there is no person; the patient has no impact upon anyone. They do not even look at him. He is invisible.

3) *We are like this with one another; no, it is the polarity.* The patient struggles to paint a picture of a given interpersonal relationship. I am like this with him; he is like this with me; we are like this with one another. The dreaded deeper truth, however, is the polarity. First, the deeper experiencing occurs, the inner polarity. Then the phenomenological scene is built from the denoted referents, and congruent with the nature of the deeper experiencing.

3.1 Pt: (He is talking about his son.) I'm going to let him in the business as soon as he graduates. *He'll do well. He'll be a good addition to the firm. He'll be a real asset. Why, he has a natural affinity for people and for organization. Ever since he was little he had this common sense and the ability to think ahead. Yes, he'll do all right.*

The deeper experiencing is that of hating the son, regarding him as a worthless loser, an embarrassing mistake. In the phenomenological scene, the patient is screaming at the son: "Give you a job? Never! You're a worthless sonuvabitch! Get the hell out of here, you worthless bastard!" The son is standing there with a sullen look on his face, picking his nose, looking like an imbecile.

3.2 Pt: (A woman in her late thirties, attending to the younger woman to whom she is quite attracted.) Diane showed up about an hour late. Never mentioned anything about my having everything all set. She waltzes in and starts the stereo. She never mentions anything at all. *But that is the way she is. She is cute. Nothing ever bothers her. I guess that is the way she grew up. Her mother was like that too. They are kind of silly, both of them. I guess I am more sober, and I worry about things more. I count on her a lot. She is happy. More than I am. I try to be more like her. I have started being happier. Like Diane, and not letting things bother me.*

The deeper experiencing is the rageful hurt of being overlooked, of being little or nothing in the world of the other person. In the phenomenological scene, the patient tries to scream and yell, to get Diane to acknowledge her by at least feeling bad. But Diane barely hears. Instead, she just plunks herself down in the chair, drinks a beer, then gets up, and leaves the apartment, with not a bit of acknowledgment of the patient.

3.3 Pt: (Sniffling and crying.) I don't know if she would react that way . . . she's not a very . . . warm, affectionate person . . . Mother. Yet *I know you worry about me. . . . I know she does.*

The deeper experiencing is being fully unwanted, rejected, worthless. It is a bitter hurt and disappointment. In the phenomenological scene, mother speaks: "No, I don't give a damn about you. I don't want you. I never wanted you!" Mother's upper body leans forward threateningly toward the patient, and her face is aimed right at the patient, eyes piercing down into the patient who is plunged into shocked flooding tears.

3.4 Pt: (Attending to his father.) . . . Father, I'm not going to be your little boy. All that is over. The past is gone. Let's both give up the past. Speak to me as a man. Talk *to me. Why don't I start to respect the man you are, the person you are—and you the man I am. Person to person. I am a man, with my own concerns, my own responsibilities.*

The deeper experiencing is that of being an unwanted little baby, an object of disgust and scorn. In the phenomenological scene, the patient is a six-foot, 28-year-old infant, much too large for the crib in which he is lying. His thumb is in his mouth, and he is making slurping sounds. His father is standing next to the crib, looking down on his son: "My God, what a disgusting piece of crap!"

3.5 Pt: (He is attending to his mother.) You are evil! You are wrong! You don't care what any other person feels. You're like a huge worm! I wish I could squash you! You're fat, bloated. And you do nothing about it. I don't understand you. You're wicked, selfish, the most egotistical person I know. *I don't want to be your son anymore. I'm going to get away from you!*

The deeper experiencing is that of being one with mother, the archaic union, blood of her blood, flesh of her flesh. In the phenomenological scene, he is pressed into her body like a baby. Arms and legs are in mother's flesh so deeply that he is virtually ingrained into her body. His head is encompassed within her breasts. All is peaceful and one.


## D. The Endless Void of Despair

The behavior and words of the patient both construct and illuminate a deeper potential which consists of the experiencing of the endless void of despair. It is the black bottomless pit of giving up, of fruitless dreams, of inhumed hopes and wishes, shattered illusions, changelessness. Precariously perched at the very edge of the endless void of despair, the patient is, instead, trying and making efforts, dreaming and reaching out.

1) *Give up, the awful state is going to occur.* The patient knows or senses some awful state which is much too present. The inner pull is to give in to it, stop struggling; there just is no escape whatsoever. It is going to take one over. The awful state is going to occur. The patient's words and behavior first construct and illuminate the deeper experiencing, the nature of the state of complete giving up. Next emerges the phenomenological scene in which the giving up occurs.

1.1 Pt: (In a tone of agitation and terrible worry.) Every week or so it's just there! I get the need! I can think of nothing but booze! (And then, dejectedly.) All those years. Counseling and AA and . . . everything . . . I fought. Years . . . I keep some hidden and then I get some nerve or something and I get rid of it. I play crazy games. I hide the key . . . I go crazy trying to remember where I put the key. . . . (All of this is said in almost desperation, agitatedly.)

The deeper experiencing is that of being a complete alcoholic, a drunken mindless boozer. There is no more agitation or struggle. In the phenomenological scene, the patient is sitting alone on the bed in the room. It is a cheap hotel in a rundown part of town. He is jobless and friendless, sitting drunken and dejected on the bed. He is mindless.

1.2 Pt: My God, that is like a pus inside, here. It is my sickness. That hate! I know my stomach and my intestines are rotting with it. It is going to kill me. *It is so fucking deep.* I need help. *I gotta get rid of it. I got to. I just got to!*

The deeper experiencing is the despair of abandoning the struggle, giving up to the inexorable rotting. It is the experiencing of the wholesale rottenness. In the phenomenological scene, the entire person is taken over by the pussy rottenness. It has invaded the whole body, not just the stomach and intestines. The whole body is greenish black with pussy rottenness, and there is no person anymore.

1.3 Pt: (Depressed.) I don't want to end it all . . . I don't know . . . (Pause.) There are times when I get out of it. *I'll get out of it. I know I have a lot to live for . . . a lot to do. I have things to do. I have to! I gotta keep thinking of these things. I'm young yet. . . .*

The deeper experiencing is the despair of giving up and succumbing to the awful state; it is the final peacefulness of death; it is all over. In the phenomenological scene, the patient's body is still. The face is at peace; the muscles are no longer tense. The patient is dead and still.

1.4 Pt: (After a long hurtful silence.) *I don't want to be just a big dummy.*

The deeper experiencing is that of being the big dummy. It is painful and hurtful, but there is no other way. It is the experiencing of being the complete dummy, and nothing but the complete dummy. In the phenomenological scene, the patient is sitting in class. The object of ridicule and scorn, all the other children are attending to him, laughing at him, looking at one another in shared derision. It is a fact that he is indeed the class dummy.

1.5 Pt: *I am afraid of . . . becoming psychotic. When I talk to them, people . . . I fear them. Strange thoughts. Getting worse . . . I get so full of anxiety, and hide it. . . . Everyone seems OK, but . . . I don't know what it means to live anymore.*

The deeper experiencing is that of numbness, withdrawal, the utter finality of endless and inexorable deranged separation. It is the state of craziness, with no connections with people. In the phenomenological scene, real people just go about their business. They move about, do things, talk with one another, shake hands and make love. But all of this normal living goes on around the patient who sits in another world, nearby. She is not in their world, nor are they in hers.

1.6 Pt: (Quiet tears are there.) I woke up early, and I was so low. So depressed. It got worse as the day went on. I had those thoughts of just doing away with myself again. . . . I didn't want to see anyone . . . thought I'd never make it through. (Crying quietly.) . . . I don't know . . . each day is so hard. Getting harder . . . I don't know.

The deeper experiencing is the despair and the peace, the agony and the still quietness of nothingness, emptiness, death. In the phenomenological scene, he is sitting in a state of total withdrawnness. There are no thoughts confounding his head, nor are there persons in his world. He is still and existing by himself. There are no people anywhere. His head is clear and free of any thoughts whatsoever.

1.7 Pt: (Breathing hard and rapidly, flipping his head from side to side.) . . . I think I am going crazy. There are crazy thoughts . . . I have always . . . I'm so scared that I'll hurt someone. I'm getting worse. I can't get my mind off of it . . . faces . . . I'm scared they are after me, and I know that's crazy . . . but I am so close. I feel it. . . .

The deeper experiencing is that of being utterly deranged, out of his mind, and wildly assaultive. It is the experiencing of hurting people, and doing so as a lunatic. In the phenomenological scene, the patient is with a bunch of people and they are all that way. He attacks them and they attack him. Faces swerve at him menacingly, with an aggressive swoosh, and he knocks off the heads of some others. In all, it is crazy bedlam, utter aggressive madness.

1.8 Pt: (Woman in her middle thirties, attending to mother.) . . . I don't think she's ever trusted me. She has always hounded me, treated me like I had no responsibility. I can't relax with her. I can't ever feel responsible. Comfortable. I get these tense feelings in my chest whenever I'm with her, and, shit, it's always been that way. *I have to be tightened up against her. I have to be guarded against her. Just get in her presence and the defenses go up. Sometimes I want to say, "Go away and leave me alone." God, I wish I could tell her, just once. . . .*

The deeper experiencing is that of no longer fighting; instead, the patient is helplessly exposed and vulnerable; there is no intactness, instead, the patient no longer exists; it is the unresisting passivity which leads to complete dissolution of one's being. The phenomenological scene is one in which the patient loses all body integrity, becomes utterly helpless and exposed and vulnerable. Mother comes closer and closer, and then actually assimilates and incorporates the patient who is becoming increasingly transparent and invisible as she is disappearing.

1.9 Pt: (The feelings quickly reach high intensity, and the words are splattered out in a rush.) . . . And she says something about retarded children. And I start thinking that my head is full of fog. I am full of fog in my head and I have thoughts. . . . *Who are we? Why are we here? People say words like robots. The words come out of them. I see them and they are mechanical and little, run like machines. My voice is not like my voice. These don't seem like my hands. They have been here all my life, but they're not mine. What am I here for? Who am I? Thoughts are there, but they are enemies that are in my head!*

When the patient gives up, when the struggle is over, the deeper experiencing is that of being dead, mechanical, a robot—and having no awareness. It is being one of them, without thoughts, without questionings. I am a robot; I do and move and behave. In the phenomenological scene, mechanical words issue from the patient who is being with mechanical persons who issue mechanical words. The whole world is comprised of robots, and the patient is one of them.

1.10 Pt: I would get mad at her. I would get annoyed and they would all look at me as if I was weird or something. I used to be more impulsive, more like that. Used to challenge. (Laughs.) I don't know. Used to be more like that. I liked myself better like that. I used to talk a lot to people and get drunk and be silly. No one would push me around then. But guys wouldn't like me like that. They'd say he wasn't ideal. *It happened gradually.* I used to have so much confidence it was scary. They'd think he had contempt for people. People aren't good enough for him. I want to be the first, smartest, the best. I want people to respect me, think of me as special. *But something happened.* I married Ann and worked at Bingham's, and *gradually changed.* When I was in Vancouver, I met a gal and it was great making love. I knew

I shouldn't sleep with her. But I couldn't have any other desire. Then we moved to Toronto and *it happened again*. I knew I'd find another woman, and I did. *Now I'm constipated, dull. Haven't slept with a woman in years. I'm a good husband now. I follow the tradition. I don't sleep around.*

When the struggle is over, the deeper experiencing is that of being dead, a slug, without life, without feelings, without excitement. In the phenomenological scene, he is with his wife. They have finished eating, and they both lean back in their chairs, looking dully at one another. There is nothing to say. They are both slugs, mindlessly staring at one another.

2) *Your hopes and dreams are fruitless; they will never be realized.* There are hopings, wishings, dreamings, efforts after and strugglings after. But they are fruitless and in vain. Underneath is the endless void of despair; give up, it is all for nothing. The deeper experiencing is the despair of having given up the hopes and dreams. Then the phenomenological scene is present, consistent with the deeper potential and constructed out of the roots of the hopes and dreams.

2.1 Pt: When I sell these two paintings, I'll have enough money to move to Oregon and set up the kind of studio Quent and I have talked about for years. I'll have the money. *There'll be enough to pay the bills, and then I'll finally be able to do it like I always planned.*

The deeper experiencing is that of being a loser, a failure; it is the experiencing of the despair of fruitless dreams. In the phenomenological scene, the patient is sitting, depressed, in the same old apartment. They have not moved to Oregon, and the truth is that they never will. There is not enough money to pay the bills, and there never will be. There are no more plans. In the corner is a hooded figure chanting, "I told you so. I told you it would never work."

2.2 Pt: (A woman who has been describing the kind of store she would like to start.) . . . This town could use a shop like that. I've always wanted to have my own place, a little place. I think I'm ready now. Oh it sounds so great. I love the planning. Jan and I have been scouting around for just the right location. . . . I am happy. I feel just so good. And there's the spot. Right on Mayfair Street. It's just right. There are some little shops there. I love this. . . . *I don't see why I can't do it.* . . .

The deeper experiencing is that of knowing it will never occur, of being silly and frivolous, being a groundless dreamer, full of silly plans, of being full of hare-brained schemes, of being a dumb ninny. In the phenomenological scene, her head is down and she is half angry and half despairing. Some other hooded person is annoyed with her, is bawling her out as a frivolous ding-dong full of silly dreams. That other figure is grounded in reality and has a solidly accurate understanding of the patient.

2.3 Pt: I'd like bodies all around me. Men and women. Maybe three or four. Lovely slender women who ooze sex. With me in bed. This would be the best. We all would be naked and touching, one climax after the other. Sex would be perfect. We are all open and touching and sex, sex. Hair, wet and moist. Bodies all around.

The deeper experiencing is deadness, coldness, tightness. It is the experiencing of sexlessness, being wooden. In the phenomenological scene, the patient is walking by himself through a park in the spring. Couples are walking together affectionately; they are lying on the grass, touching. But the patient is pulled inside his outer clothes, withdrawn and wooden.

2.4 Pt: (Groaning, feeling rotten, hurting.) I want everything from her. But she's just not that way. I want to love her, to be with her always. I know she has a life of her own. But it gets me so much when she just leaves me. I get into the bed and . . . God . . . the way it all is . . . I don't know what to do. She doesn't understand. She just won't understand. *Why can't she see? Why can't she see? God, what can I do? How can I live? Doris, oh Doris. Don't you know how it feels? Just know. Just know what it's like. Please! Please!*

The hope is that Doris will be here, and she will be affectionately understanding. Underneath is the deeper experiencing, the utter despair of hopelessness, emptiness, aloneness. In the phenomenological scene, Doris is completely out of his life, leading a life of her own. She never sees him, never thinks of him. He cries, and nobody hears the agonizing wailing.

2.5 Pt: (He is attending to the woman.) I have been so supportive of her. While he (the other man) was gone, I did everything for her. Got this feeling. I want to see her sound and happy, but she told me that she wanted to take some time to make up her mind. She made that decision because of what someone told her about me. I gave her a chance to make a rational decision . . . but she's going downhill, and she needs me, if she'll only come to her senses. *She's been running around with him for nearly six months now. If he keeps up with her, he'll get her pregnant, 'cause I know him. He's done that sort of thing before.*

The dream is that she will come to her senses and appear before him, having seen the truth of what he has been saying, throwing herself into his arms. However, the deeper experiencing is the despair of fruitless and unrealizable dreams. It is the experiencing of abject hopelessness, of losing out, of having no one. In the phenomenological scene, he is alone. In a different part of town, the woman and the other man are lying in bed, lost in one another, whispering intimately, and very happy.

3) *It will never change.* The patient's behavior and words denote some state which is awful and an implication that it will change. There is a wisp of hope or an insistence on change; there is a grounding in pain and an implication that it might or must change for the better. The despairing deeper experiencing is that nothing is going to change; the awful state is going to remain. The phenomenological scene is built by the deeper experiencing from the contents of what is denoted in the patient's behavior and words.

3.1 Pt: (She is almost whispering, and her words are filled with depression.) I don't know what is happening anymore. I'm just not getting anywhere. Selling is no good, not really for me. Maybe nothing is. I don't know. I tried it and thought maybe. . . . I was at home, and in bed with Sue. Things aren't going well with her either. I don't know. I'm confused. We don't get along anymore. Maybe we never really did, not really. I don't know. I'm so confused about things, about myself. Maybe I can get free of things, the pressures, I don't really seem to ever get out from them. Nothing works. I've done what I can, maybe. I feel so unsatisfied, and not knowing what can be done. A couple of days ago I was at the center, and I saw Jack. He's a guy that I used to sleep with. Once. I thought I got pregnant, but I wasn't. I *couldn't look at him. Got scared like I used to. Feel bad. Can't be trusted. I know if he. . . . I feel sometimes like a pervert. . . . I'll always make the same mistakes.* (Crying.)

Here is a little wish and hope that things somehow can be different, and, separate from that, the deeper experiencing of utter hopelessness. Nothing will ever be any different. There is abject despair. It is the experiencing of always and forever being not quite heterosexual and not quite homosexual; there is no sexual place for her; she is a sexual misfit. The phenomenological scene includes an endless column of men on the left and women on the right, and her life consists of going from one to the other, always between the two columns, and always scared and confused and desperately unhappy.

3.2 Pt: (Attending to his sick old mother.) When she asks me about when I am coming home, I don't know. I try being all right. She is so old and just hanging on. And orders me about so. . . . Sometimes I wish she would die already. . . . Aw, I shouldn't say that. I worry so much about her, about what to do. . . . I wish I could get away. . . . I don't know. I just don't know. . . .

The deeper experiencing is being forever caught and stuck in these feelings, torn by these feelings, never free. In the phenomenological scene, he is an old man, bent over and decrepit, with a long white beard. Standing and feebly shaking by the side of her weed-covered grave—she died 30 years ago—he is still worried about her and angry at her, tied to her and struggling to be free of her. It is cold and wet, but there he is.

3.3 Pt: (The words are spoken in a kind of hopeless depression, and they are addressed partly to oneself and partly to anything or anyone, but not to the therapist.) I don't know . . . am I getting anywhere . . . accomplishing? . . .

The deeper experiencing is that of complete hopelessness and despair—painful emptiness of dashed hopes. The phenomenological scene is that of being still, of no movement. The world is receding. Things are becoming colorless and deadened. Everything is still. From all around comes a whispered voice: "No!"

3.4 Pt: (In a high state of agitation. He is yelling.) I'll be damned if I'm going to suffer anymore! No more! I've had enough! I'm going to jump on people! I'm not going to take any more shit from everyone!

The deeper experiencing is the agony of forever being the little wimp upon whom everyone shits, the beaten one who is the brunt of others. In the phenomenological scene, he is a beaten, broken man, and a crowd of people wait their turn to shit on him. He is already under a pile of feces about six feet high. The crowd is composed of young children, feeble old people, women and men, big people and little people, everyone.

3.5 Pt: (Woman in her late twenties.) . . . *I want to be myself. I want to find myself.* So many people just run through their lives without ever really knowing what they are like. I can be like them. Dead. Dead persons. *I must know what I am like. Can I be myself?* Can I find out and be myself? Sometimes I wonder if I should be myself. *I must. I must be whatever I am. I must be whatever I really am.*

The deeper experiencing is the despairing anguish of being empty, unfinished, without possibilities. It is the dawning of the utter iron truth that this is all there is; there is no more. In the phenomenological scene, the patient is looking inside herself for the exciting golden possibilities, the precious wonderful inner person, but there is nothing inside—it is an empty space.

4) *The illusory special relationship with one's self.* What is characteristic is the almost forced specialness of the patient's relationship with the precious self. The deeper despair shines through the forced relationship, the needing and brittle shallowness of the special relationship. While the denoted scene portrays the patient and the special self in special relationship, the more ominous deeper experiencing lurks as the despair of the awful truth, i.e., the hurtful absence of just such a relationship.

4.1 Pt: (Continuing on and on with a description of the continuous flow of feelings.) . . . and I feel it now in the jaw. It's tense. Dropping down to the shoulders and the neck. Over the shoulders. It feels like things are thawing out there. In the neck and shoulders. My shoulders are moving. Into a defensive posture. Pattern. They both seem like they're getting ready for a defensive posture. Now . . . now they are moving. The shoulders are hunching forward now. Almost maybe starting to be in a fetal position. Interesting. The muscles in the neck and shoulders are tightening just a bit, again as if something is going to maybe attack, or threaten. Maybe sort of getting ready to ward off an assailant, or some sort of an assault. The upper body is getting ready to crouch over. Maybe like when a cat gets ready. Stretches. It is alive, just a little tension, and it's just about equal in both shoulders.

The patient's behavior and words denote a scene in which he is captivated and charmed by the self, wholly interested in every wonderful detail of its body and the flow of feelings and possibilities in the self. But there is a more ominous deeper experiencing: It is the despair and hurt of no one really caring, the painful emptiness of this kind of relationship with a genuine human being. In the phenomenological scene, the patient is a little child, sitting cross-legged on the floor. The family is in the room, but no one fondles him, no one bathes him in loving care. Instead, they are like cold figures who do things near and around him, but not to and with him.

4.2 Pt: (Telling about a secret act.) No one is there. I live alone. I wrap myself up tight in a blanket. A big, warm, favorite blanket of mine. I have had it for years. Blue and green. I shut the door and make sure that no one is there. And no one will come in. I put on diapers. I have three of them. Like a baby. Keep them in a drawer, hidden. No one knows. I have plastic pants that I put over the diaper. I have two baby bottles, and I fill one with either orange juice or milk. It is so nice. I have a big black horse. Soft. I hold the horse. Close. Against my chest. Here. First I take a shower, a long nice shower. Then I put baby powder all over, careful. I am clean and smell good. Then I can lie here for a long time. I love this. It feels so good.

The patient's behavior and words touch a deeper experiencing: the utter despairing emptiness of simple loving care. In the phenomenological scene, there is a baby and a parental figure. The baby and the parent are in the same room, even within reaching distance of one another. But there is no loving mutuality, no touching fondly, no caressing, no comforting or being comforted. Instead, there is the painful absence of all of this.

4.3 Pt: (Gliding from one aspect to another of what she is like.) I just have never really gotten started. It's like waiting. Maybe like being stuck. Well, for many years I . . . I am kind of waiting. Sort of like in the wings. There are all kinds of potentials. I wanted to act for some time. It's like my potentials are there and just waiting for the right time and the right place. I think I'm not mean or bad in any way. I mean, I haven't got any bad problems. I know that sometimes Fred thinks that I'm . . . I don't, well, try hard enough. I've always had not enough willpower. It's something that I've lacked. My father was like that too. But I guess lots of people are like that. I need the right break. Thank God I don't have problems. Well, some. But not bad ones. I mean, my friend Sheila has real problems. I think that I give up easily. Maybe that's something I can work on. Like having, oh, like not pushing hard enough. I got B's in school. I know I have the ability and . . . but I don't get down and work. I think I sometimes have a sluggishness in me. Yeah.

The deeper experiencing is the hurtful despair of no one there to help, to guide, to see all the possibilities. In the phenomenological scene, she is a little girl who is the center of the concerned attention of the older people. They are talking about helping her, showing her how, lovingly regarding her as full of all sorts of capacities and potentials. But then it becomes clear: they are not real people; they are dream-like images which fade away. Now the child is alone. No one is there; no one was there.

4.4 Pt: I know that I tend to worry too much. . . . Sometimes I just worry and worry and it's always unnecessary. Everything turns out OK in the end. But I fret. I know that I obsess all the time about every little thing. It is silly. What a worry wart. And there's no real reason for it. I worry about every little detail about things. I've always been that way since I was, oh, maybe a teenager. Worry, worry. And in the end . . . well . . . I think I'm getting better. I don't worry so much about family things anymore. I am getting better and maybe in a few years I just won't worry so much at all. . . .

The deeper experiencing is the hurt and despair of no one attending to him, being lovingly concerned with him; it is the sore absence of such a relationship. In the phenomenological scene, the patient is sitting by himself, quietly, staring at the empty space. No one is around. The patient is imagining a parent who is understanding and lovingly concerned, someone who is with her son, close to her son. It is a dream, an illusion.

4.5 Pt: . . . and I don't *do* anything. I go right back into thinking all the horrible, obsessional thoughts from way back when. They don't go away, and it's as if I want it to be that way you see, somewhere inside. I mean, consciously I don't, but somewhere there I want it to be that way, see? And uh, and then after that I started to think and I said if she really knew me (laughs) she'd hate me (laughs). You know, maybe that's why I do it. Maybe that's why I'm so nice. But it's not true, I said . . . you know, it's like this argument was going on. I said it's not true. I'm being me, and whether I'm nice or not, I don't know. I'm sure if I say something insulting to her she'll tell me about it. Uh, I expect that she would, and I said, and I'm not being anybody else except who I am, and I say why can't I trust? You know, and somehow I can't trust. OK, there's a lack of trust, and I'm scared.

The deeper experiencing is that of emptiness, aloneness, the hurt and anguish of no one who is lovingly concerned. In the phenomenological scene, the patient is a little girl, sitting at the big round table. Everyone is talking to each other—Mommy and Daddy and her sister and two brothers. But no one is looking at her. No one ever bathes her in loving pure attention.

4.6 Pt: (Seeing an image of himself as a little boy.) I used to sit in a favorite spot in the woods behind the house. Sunshine. Really soft and pretty. I loved to sit with my back against a tree. I loved doing that. There was a kind of other-worldliness about it all. It was my spot. Like my world. As if no one else knew about it. I would go there and sit and let thoughts come to me. Sometimes hours would go by. I can see myself not sleeping, but just . . . drowsy. I had little hands and I was skinny. Never strong. I used to sit with one leg tucked under the other. . . .

The deeper experiencing is the painful anguish of no one there, no one attending to him exclusively, no one caressing and loving him. In the phenomenological scene, he is sitting in the middle of his room. On the floor around him are some toys, his baby shoes, a spool he used to play with, an old cap from when he was four years old, and about a hundred pictures of him. He is sobbing and writhing in hurt.

4.7 Pt: (Tight, a little cold and metallic.) I see my desk. It is all cluttered. Don't really want to do anything. Looking at the papers, memos. A rage. A feeling of rage. Anger. It keeps me from doing anything at work. It makes me late all the time. Don't even get there till sometimes. . . . Impulses . . . have to watch impulses. Otherwise I'll smash everything and get wild. (Still tight, still a little cold and metallic.) They are always there, like ready. They have to be watched, all the time. It's like they are waiting, and they'll slip out. . . .

Instead of a whole self, the patient's special relationship is with a part of the self. Nevertheless, the deeper experiencing is the despairing loneliness of no one who is there to bathe him in loving attention. In the phenomenological scene, he is a very little boy who is reciting the specialness of a tiny toy computer. On it is written: "The Impulse of Anger." But there is no one there, no one who is wholly entranced and concerned with the impulse of anger.

4.8 Pt: I have come to terms with my anger. (In his voice there is a quality of interest, and no anger.) . . . Much better in the last ten years or so. Over the years I've gotten real insight into my anger. . . . Workshops have helped tremendously. It flares up every so often; sometimes I just can't think what gets it started. But in general I think that I've become rather comfortable with it. An occasional flare-up, nothing more. . . . I understand what it is made of. The thing that trips it off when it finally gets started. . . . Yes, I think it's more under control now. All in all it's just not so much of a problem anymore now that I got enough insight into what it's all about.

Instead of a whole self, the patient's special relationship is with a part of the self. The deeper experiencing is the agonizing sadness of being alone, of nobody here to play with him, to love and be concerned with him. The patient is a little boy, sitting alone in the backyard, with a toy truck. He is crying. No one is with him.

4.9 Pt: I have always had this problem. Get dissatisfied. I become dissatisfied and just pack it all in. All my life I guess. Well certainly since I started university. It's sort of a game, when I can laugh about it. I try something and then complain. It's the grumbling that I don't like. Just start becoming dissatisfied. It doesn't take long to start. And I just can't seem to do anything about it. I want to find more ways to fight it. But it isn't easy. It's really something. . . . Lately it's been almost getting to be too much. What I've been doing for years and years is filling up my life with all sorts of activity to sort of make it disappear, and go away . . . but that doesn't seem to work. Being busy from morning to night doesn't seem to work . . . so I just don't seem to know just what to do . . . maybe fight it in some way. Like dissolve it. Maybe make it disappear . . . but, I don't know . . . It's something I can hardly fathom . . .

Instead of a whole self, the patient's special relationship is with a part of the self, identified as a grumbling dissatisfaction. However, the deeper experiencing is the painful despair of the utter absence of a companion, a play partner, an adoring best chum. In the phenomenological scene, the patient is playing all by himself. There is no companion, and there just won't be one. The play materials may include a few toys, a game or two, a little pot or beer or a bedroom. But the scene is dominated by the emptiness.

5) *The illusory relationship with the special other person.* As the patient behaves and talks, the denoted content becomes predominated by the presence of a very special listener, the magical other person who receives the story in a most special way. But the whole scene is illusory, and the despairing truth is that there is no one like that, as wonderful and precious as such a special relationship might be.

5.1 Pt: We have been having marital difficulties since we have been married. I am thinking of leaving my husband. . . . I should be able to because we haven't been happy for 12 years. We had to get married. We had some ups, but mostly downs until we came to terms with it. I had dated other fellows at college and at work. Then our relationship developed. It was a lot more than just loving, and crying. Then we got married. Then he started attacking me verbally. At first it was because of my lack of education. But I proved that. Then he attacked my physically. I was fat. So I kept myself in shape. Still, he perceived me as fat. I think he came to terms with the fat, but he still attacked me, for 12 years he attacked all that I do. . . . I have to prove to him, but I turned all my hate on him. Then I'd get it in the arm. He'd hit me, but somehow I didn't realize he was doing all those things. . . . I feared for my life . . . even when he said he did it in jest. I'm not sure of my feelings for him. He depresses me . . . he depresses me, but I don't know why. . . . I can't just let go. I'm afraid of hurting him. I have guilt feelings. . . . Without even knowing me, he just whops me with his hand, which is an unrealistic situation. . . .

The denoted scene is one in which the husband is hitting her, beating her, attacking her. But the story is being told to a kindly, caring, understanding figure who is present as the patient is telling about how pitiable her life is. This other figure is induced to say, "Oh, too bad. I am sorry. Maybe we can do something about that. I understand and have concern for you." But the more ominous phenomenological scene is the absence of all that. There is no such person in her life. She wants so much to have someone like that, but there is no one at all. Instead, there is emptiness. The deeper experiencing is the hurt and pain of no one being there, the loneliness of no one like that.

5.2 Pt: (She is distraught, scattered, glum) I know that I am too old to be in school. But it is important. School is . . . too much for me. I think a lot about quitting. I sit down with the homework and know I should be doing it, but I can't get . . . maybe the energy. I have to do all the housework, and we have a big family. It's not easy . . . I can't get down or behind. Yet I know there are times when I get that way. I know I complain a lot. My husband tells me . . . and I try to keep everything in order. My family. I stay up late at night. I work hard and everything. I should finish school in maybe a year at this rate. . . . I dunno . . . being so old . . . I wish I were . . . some of the others are practically daughters. I mean, I could be their mother. . . . I don't see how I can take care of all the things at home. . . .

In the phenomenological scene the patient is almost whining, complaining, asking for understanding, sympathy. And there is another figure, the one to whom all of this is being said. Either this other parental figure is gentle, understanding, empathic: "I understand; it is a great deal to ask. Maybe we can do something about it." Or the other figure is disgusted and frustrated: "What a baby you are, whining and complaining. Grow up!" Underneath this scene is the more ominous one. Would it not be wonderful to have someone like that, really? But there is no one. Nor has there ever been someone like that. It is illusory. The deeper experiencing is the hurt of having no one, the pain of aloneness, the anguish of the emptiness in one's life.

5.3 Pt: (Freely giving of her valuable thoughts.) I visualize Jan not as Jan. . . . Jan becomes my mother. That's the way my thoughts go. From visualizing to accepting it as a fact. Then I start thinking that once that happens she'll start making demands. Telling me what to do. These thoughts only come after the visualizing, and when the image is accepted as true. Then she'll tell me that I can't go out with men. I can't do this. Men are like that. If she says things when I'm in a clear mood, I can be honest with her. But when I have trouble knowing what is getting her to talk that way, I have to figure out what she really means and why she might be saying that. Usually I know why, uh, what is getting her to do that. My thinking just goes quickly most of the time. I know that she has no one to yell at, and I am the best one now. But I can't indicate that I know this about her, not in a way so'd she'd feel funny. If she persists, it's a different matter. Sometimes I want to take some time just to figure it out. But in the mornings I do my yoga and my normal school thinking. I read and I think, and in the afternoons I go to school and socialize. So it depends what state I am in when she tells me. I used to have more direct reactions, but my thoughts changed in the last year and I figured out how to listen to what she says. . . .

While the initial scene includes a kindly and interested figure, listening attentively, the more ominous deeper scene is one in which the patient is telling all of this to no one. No one is there to hear this, no one is listening. The deeper experiencing is the anguished hurt of the absence of such a figure, the despair of no such relationship.

5.1 Pt: (Complaining, plaintive, whining. She is in her late twenties.) . . . and there just aren't any jobs. And nobody cares . . . I tried to get one by answering the ads. But I can't find any. When I call, I get vague answers, and usually the job . . . there isn't any. When I call. Cathy doesn't care. She just goes to school and she's busy all the time. And when I tell her, she is always too busy. She even expects me to make all the suppers. Sometimes. I can't. 'Cause I gotta keep looking for a job. And if I come home late, she gives me that look like she hasn't . . . uh . . . she doesn't like my coming home late. But she can come home whenever. And then she gets mad at me 'cause she says I wasn't home when she called . . . about the library or something. I can't be home all the time, and listen to the phone. . . .

In the denoted scene, she is sitting with her mother in the kitchen, and she is bitching and complaining about something. Mother is friendly, listening. The two of them have plenty of time and they are trading talk about some other person, complaining. They tell stories to each other about that other person. The more ominous scene is one in which mother is not there, nor is anyone else there. The patient is alone, empty, without that special other one. The deeper experiencing is that of needing and wanting, yet desperately missing that other person; it is being alone, despairingly.

5.5 Pt: . . . She tells me to leave. Divorce . . . I think I'm so mixed up that I'll be like this always. How can I get out? How? What should I do? I did this myself. Not her. She . . . she was just there. And this is not the first time. My whole life was like this. I am in it now. I am caught. It is my trap. My own making, I can't blame Rita. I used her. Now I think of dying. It almost seems peaceful. No, I won't kill myself. But the thoughts are there. It is the peacefulness of it. I haven't solved anything, and I don't think I will. I get tired. Or I get filled up like the problem has no way out. I sometimes cry. But when it is all over, I am where I started. I can't get out. . . . (Here the attention becomes even more focused, and the level of bodily feelings rises.) *Please, what am I going to do? All I know is I'm in no shape to find my way out. I need help. I need someone to lead me by the hand and lead me out. . . . I don't care if it hurts.* (Crying hard.)

In the phenomenological scene, the wonderful person who takes him by the hand and leads him out of the turmoil fades. There is no one there. The whole image was an illusion. No matter how needy and helpless is the patient, there is no one there to help him. The deeper experiencing is that of the grinding hurt of being without anyone, being alone, having no one there.

# 10

# *After Experiential Listening:*
# *The Next Steps*

The basic practices culminate in experiential listening. In each session, the patient and therapist begin by getting their bodies settled in the chairs. Sometimes the patient describes what is occurring right now in the body, and the therapist allows a similar occurrence in his body. Then the patient is to let the experiential process begin. Attention is to be let go. It floats and drifts over here and over there until the patient moves into an experiential state where attention is preponderantly on some meaningful center (and not the therapist), and bodily sensations are at least moderate. Experiencing is moving ahead.

The therapist has shown the patient how to do all this. When the patient is attending, having some bodily sensations, and is beginning to experience, the therapist allows himself to share all of this. A good measure of the therapist's attention is poured onto the patient's attentional center, the therapist has bodily sensations somewhat similar to the patient's, and experiencing is likewise occurring in the therapist. In short, the therapist shares a fair measure of the patient's phenomenological world. Here is where the therapist "listens" experientially. The therapist is now living in some kind of phenomenological scene and is undergoing some kind of experiencing.

Basic practices include everything the therapist does to reach this point. In the series of steps which comprise experiential psychotherapy (Figure 2.2), we are now ready for steps 2 or 3. That is, the therapist is now ready to carry forward the experiencing which is made alive and present by experiential listening. Or, the therapist is now ready to "work" the relationship between the patient and the deeper potential which is made alive and present by experiential listening. The next steps of the therapeutic process absolutely require that the therapist remain within the patient's phenomenal world. Experiential listening is the culmination of the basic practices, and is essential for carrying through the next steps of therapy.

The first section of this book provided the reader with an overview of all of the five steps which comprise each session. In this chapter, my aim is to walk with the reader through steps 2-5. Beginning with experiential listening, I want to illustrate how the therapist carries forward the potentials for experiencing (step 2), how the therapist furthers the experiencing between the patient and the deeper potential (step 3), how the therapist and patient undergo the experiential being of the deeper potential (step 4), and how the therapist and patient culminate the work of each session with the opening up of changes in the patient's ways of being and behaving in the extra-therapy world (step 5). The purpose of this chapter is to provide an introduction to the steps which occur after experiential listening and to the methods for undertaking each of the steps.

For those therapists who are already familiar with these methods, this chapter illustrates how to use these methods, in combination with experiential listening, to go through the next steps. For those less familiar with experiential methods, this chapter will serve as an introduction to the advanced practices of experiential psychotherapy.

In the balance of this chapter, we shall take up where experiential listening ended. That is, we shall begin with some of the examples of experiential listening given in Chapter 9, and illustrate the methods used by the therapist to proceed through the next steps. Once the therapist shares the patient's phenomenal world, is privy to some phenomenological scene and experiencing, what methods are used to proceed through the next steps?

## CARRYING FORWARD THE POTENTIALS FOR EXPERIENCING

When the therapist is within the phenomenological world of the patient, sharing the phenomenological scene and the experiencing, there are two options. One is for the therapist to carry forward whatever experiencing is occurring. The other is for the therapist to work the relationship between the patient and the deeper potential. We shall discuss the first option first.

There are two practical aims of carrying forward the potential for experiencing. One is to enable whatever experiencing is present and occurring to be more present and more occurring. Whatever it is, whatever the nature and content of this experiencing, it is to occur more, in heightened amplitude. The second practical aim is to open the way for the patient to be the deeper potential, to disengage from the substantive structure of the person one is (the operating domain) and to undergo the profound change of being the deeper potential. These are the two practical, functional aims of this step. Together, these two aims mean that the process of experiential psychotherapy is moving ahead.

What does the therapist do to carry forward the potential for experiencing? What are the methods?

*The Therapist Clarifies the Phenomenological Scene*

The therapist sees the phenomenological scene a little more clearly; the therapist lets the scene be more present. There may be color or sound or movement or action. Whatever it is, the therapist attends further to any or all aspects of the phenomenological scene. The therapist lives more in the scene, interacts with its components, is real and present in the scene, makes it alive and vibrant, relates and interrelates with it, becomes a part of it. In short, the therapist clarifies the phenomenological scene.

In the following, the conservative, staid, older businessman is attending to his new secretary:

Pt: She does do the work well. Besides, she is not only efficient and intelligent, she is an attractive woman, girl, woman. . . . Long black hair, very pretty. And she walks so . . . evenly. I like to watch her. Sometimes I catch myself just looking at her.

In the therapist, these words evoke a scene in which the two are alone in her apartment. She is full of sexuality, and she wants sex with him. She is slowly, seductively taking off her clothes, lying on her bed, invitingly. She is full of sexuality. There is also the experiencing of sexuality. But the therapist's attentional pull is more onto the aroused woman than the inner experiencing. The therapist clarifies what is present and real:

T: Gorgeous, just gorgeous, and look at the way her body moves. I see her there on the bed.
Pt: Her waist is so slender.

That defines her waist, and the therapist now sees her lovely slender waist and her hands slowly moving over her waist:

T: Oh yeah! And her fingers touching, moving over the waist.
Pt: (Slowly.) I think she's beautiful. Just beautiful. I know I shouldn't think about her so much, but I can't help it. Sometimes I just catch myself wanting, wanting to be with her, be with a woman like her. Maybe in her apartment.

The therapist is with her now, in the apartment:

T: Her lovely hair . . . her body, so beautiful. In the apartment . . . her bedroom.
Pt: She's the kind of woman I've always . . . always wanted. I want someone like her. God, I need someone like her. I could just let myself go! I want to be with a woman like that!!

The experiencing carries forward as the therapist clarifies whatever components of the phenomenological scene are made present and real by the words of the patient. Here is the carrying forward of an impetuous sexuality, a sense of urgent sexual wanting. This experiencing carries forward as the therapist clarifies the phenomenological scene evoked in the immediate words of the patient.

Another example is taken from experiential listening in Chapter 9. This man is crying lightly as he says the following:

Pt: I woke up early, and I was so low. So depressed. It got worse as the day went on. I had those thoughts of just doing away with myself again . . . I didn't want to see anyone . . . thought I'd never make it through. (Crying quietly.) . . . I don't know . . . Each day is so hard. Getting harder . . . I don't know.

In the therapist there is an experiencing of both despair and peace, a kind of agony and the still quietness of nothingness, emptiness, death. However, the therapist's attention is more drawn to a phenomenological scene of sitting in a state of total withdrawnness. There are no more doubts confounding the head, nor are there persons in his world. The therapist is still, and existing all by himself. There are no people any-where. His head is clear and free of any thoughts whatsoever. It is this scene which the therapist describes:

T: There's no one around. No one. No people. It's empty or something.
Pt: They don't know what it's like.

"They." Vague and shadowy images appear, gray and ephemeral. The therapist clarifies "they":

T: Ah! "They." Gray and fleeting. People, more like shadows.
Pt: Debbie (his ex-wife whom he sees occasionally). I called her. She didn't want to talk to me. It's useless.

In the therapist, the phenomenological scene includes Debbie far away, maybe a mile or so, and happy.

T: She's smiling, happy. I don't affect her much. She's far away, very far away. Yeah, and saying something. Words! I don't like the words!

Now the experiencing carries further forward:

Pt: It's over! She really doesn't give a damn! God, I hate that! Why? My God, why? (His voice is loud and shaky.) She really doesn't give a good fucking damn! She's cold as ice! I hate that! That bitch got rid of me! She doesn't want to be with me! I can't stand that!!!

Here is the carrying forward of the experiencing of being a rejected, obnoxious, pouty little child who must have his own way.

Experiential listening provides the therapist with a phenomenological scene and an experiencing. When the therapist clarifies this scene, even as it changes, the consequence is the carrying forward of the experiencing.

## The Therapist Expresses the Experiencing

When the therapist is more drawn into the experiencing, rather than the phenomenological scene, the therapist may express the experiencing. This may be the operating or the deeper experiencing. Whichever is more present, the therapist allows the experiencing to occur rather fully and with open intensity. This means the heightened experiencing affects the quality and tone of voice, and even a measure of physical-bodily postures and movements. If key words and phrases are filled with feeling, these may be repeated. In any case, the therapist expresses the experiencing within the context of the phenomenological scene, and in straightforward, direct interactive relationship with significant figures.

She is describing what it is like with her brother-in-law. He has come for a four-day visit, and now, the third day, he is in the kitchen, leaning close to her, talking:

Pt: Well, his breath was just awful. But of course I would never ever say that to him. That would be rude. You just don't act that way. I couldn't.

Within the therapist, the "bad self" is being precisely rude. It says things directly to him: "Your breath is just awful! You stink!" The deeper experiencing is that of firm openness, toughness, transparent bluntness. The therapist expresses the deeper experiencing in just these words:

T: Your breath is just awful! You stink!
Pt: (She shrieks in sudden laughter and then continues.) Well he does!
T: (Openly addressing the brother-in-law.) You do! Oh you really do!
Pt: (Laughing.) Go take a shower! I'd like to tell him! Yeah, go take a shower . . .
T: (Completing the statement.) . . . and use soap! You'll like it! Hell, I'll like it! We'll all like it!
Pt: And brush your teeth. Yeah, try brushing your teeth. Check with me. Check with me first. No brushee no eatee! You got bad breath! Oh do you have rotten breath! Yech!

Here is an enjoyable sense of firm openness, toughness, transparent bluntness. It is carried forward through the therapist's direct and open expression. In one swift shift, the patient moves from sitting on the deeper potential to open and free expression. Carrying forward ordinarily refers to greater experiencing of operating potentials. Occasionally it is the deeper potential which is gracefully allowed to occur simply and directly. In our schema of steps (Figure 2.2), the patient has moved directly to step 4, the experiential being of the deeper potential.

The next excerpt from Chapter 9 illustrates the therapist expressing the operating potential. The patient is attending to his father, and is agitated as he sputters:

Pt: God he drank. . . . He was a slob, a slob! I never trusted him. He'd get drunk and had that crazy look in his eye. I could never know what he'd do. . . . I never liked the drinking. . . . I always thought he was an animal!

Experiential listening reveals a phenomenological scene in which the therapist is confronting father, and the scene is charged. The therapist is saying the following directly at father: "I never liked your drinking. . . . I always thought you were an animal!" Within the therapist is the experiencing of standing up to him, fighting him, yelling at him, risking some sort of outbreak. With scary anger, the therapist's arms raise, fists clenched:

T: I never liked your drinking! I always thought you were an animal! I never liked your drinking!!! I always thought you were an animal!!!
Pt: (Somewhat hesitantly.) I did. (Pause.) I could never tell him. He was awful. (And then, with rising feeling.) You just wouldn't listen. You never listen to anybody.
T: You got it? You're not supposed to listen. Specially to an anybody like me.
Pt: Well, shit! It's true!!! Yeah, it's true I'm scared of you! I'm terrified of you! I've always been terrified of you! We all are! You're not a father! You're an animal!!!

Experiential listening paints a different picture now. In the phenomenological scene the therapist is holding father by his shoulders, touching him, real contact. The experiencing is that of closeness, warmth, the desperate wanting of a father:

T: (Arms outstretched, touching father.) Look, look at me! Dammit, I love you. Do you hear? I love you.
Pt: (A whole mixture of feelings. He is scared, voice trembling. There is also excitement in his voice, and tears are tumbling down his cheeks.) Don't you see? I've always wanted you to love me. Should I beat you up? Do I have to shake the hell out of you? You asshole! Can't you see I love you? I love you! Listen to me! Dad, Dad. You're such an asshole. You get drunk and act like a fucking asshole. Everyone's scared of you. I've always been scared of you. But . . . But

I . . . am I some sort of nut 'cause I love my Daddy? I do! I love you!
Listen! I love you, I love you, I love you . . . (Big sigh. Then, quieter,
more calmly.) I love you.

Experiential listening provides the phenomenological scene and the
experiencing. When the therapist expresses the experiencing, the consequence is that the patient's experiencing carries forward.

## The Therapist Welcomes the Experiencing

One method of carrying forward the experiencing is for the therapist
to serve as the vehicle or avenue of its expression. A second method is
for the therapist to welcome the experiencing. This consists of letting
it occur within the therapist. It is an acknowledgment of what it feels
like, a description of how it is, what it does to the therapist's insides
and feelings and imagery. Welcoming the experiencing means letting
it affect the therapist in any way it does, a kind of easy and graceful
letting it occur within the therapist, whether the form and effect are
pleasant and enjoyable or scary and bothersome. It is a letting-be, an
integrative welcoming of whatever the experiencing is like.

In the following excerpt from Chapter 9, he is attending to the woman
who is moving further and further away from him. He is groaning and
hurting:

Pt: I want everything from her. But she's just not that way. I want to
love her, to be with her always. I know she has a life of her own. But
it gets me so much when she just leaves me. I get into the bed
and . . . God . . . the way it all is . . . I don't know what to do. She
doesn't understand. She just won't understand. Why can't she see?
Why can't she see? God, what can I do? How can I live? Doris, oh
Doris. Don't you know how it feels? Just know. Just know what it's
like. Please! Please!

For the experientially listening therapist, the phenomenological scene
is one in which Doris is completely out of his life, leading a life of her
own. She never sees him, never thinks of him. The deeper experiencing
is the utter despair of hopelessness, emptiness, aloneness. This is what
the therapist lets happen, and welcomes:

T: Well, it's all empty inside. Hollow, really empty. And I can feel the tears all starting, they're filling up my whole face. But it's the emptiness, in my whole chest, really empty.

Pt: She's really gone. I mean sooner or later. It'll happen. (Almost mechanically.) It'll be over. She'll leave.

Although the words are spoken mechanically, the experiencing within the therapist heightens with an added element:

T: It's hollow now and . . . and hot. Yeah, it's hot inside. Funny! My whole insides are empty and hot.

Pt: But she doesn't give a damn. She doesn't care. (With more feeling.) I think I'm gonna cry. Yeah, there are tears. I think I'm gonna bawl and I don't want to. But, oh, I feel sort of like collapsing. I think I'm gonna cry. 'Cause she's gone. She really is gone! I think she really is gone!

T: Now it's different! Oh yeah! Now there's a yelling. I can almost hear the yelling. It's filling me up in my face. I can sense the yelling.

Pt: Doris is gone. I mean she will someday be out of my life forever. (Now he raises his voice as if telling the world.) She's gone! She's out of my life. And I'm alone. I'm really alone. She left me!!! I am alone!

The therapist describes what this is like inside:

T: My lip is going out. There it goes. And I look around. Very quiet. No one's here. Very peculiar.

Pt: I've never been alone. I don't know what the hell's . . . I don't wanna be alone! I hate being alone! I hate the whole idea. I've never been alone, ever! What the hell am I gonna do? I'll rot! How the hell could she leave me? Nobody leaves me! I'll rot. I can't stand being alone. Why am I alone? I don't know what to do. I don't know how to be alone!

The patient is backing slowly into the experiencing of being alone. It could occur as a pit of utter agonizing despair; it could occur as a first flush of a kind of autonomy. But it carries forward as the therapist welcomes the experiencing, takes it in and describes what it is like inside.

In the next excerpt, the patient is telling about having failed to meet his friend at the airport, and he is just a little guarded and defensive:

Pt: I think the reason I forgot is that I get engrossed in things so much that I screen everything else out, and when I was done, I was shocked that it was after seven and the plane was due in at seven. I've always been that way.

The experientially listening therapist is in a scene at the airport. No one is there to meet the friend, and the friend looks hurt, let down, frustrated and a little angry. The whole section of the airport fills with a kind of cackling laughter. Within the therapist, there is an experiencing of delightful wickedness, a pleasureable aggressive defiance. The therapist welcomes this and describes what it is like:

T: Ooo. This feels wicked. Hmmm. Yes . . . I feel nasty, sort of secretly, like if no one's looking, then I'd laugh my head off. I can picture him, there at the airport, everyone laughing at him. I like this. Oh, I shouldn't feel like this.

A sort of welcoming description of the experiencing allows the patient to sample that also:

Pt: (A last ditch attempt to feel bad.) He's my friend!
T: Right! (Snickers.)
Pt: I'm always on time!
T: Right!
Pt: (Out it comes.) Serves him right! I'm always the nice one, the push-over. He never even asked me to meet him. I just think I'm supposed to. I never wanted to meet him in the first place! But no, I don't have guts enough to ever stand up for myself. I'm the nice little pushover. I didn't want to! I don't have to do it! Once, just once! Why the hell can't I say no? Just no!! That's OK. Other people do. They can say no, especially to me. Oh yeah, they say no to me. But not good old Melvin, no! Not me! I just do whatever I think they want me to do 'cause I'm Melvin the pushover! No. No. No. I can't ever say no to anyone. No, I don't want to. No, I don't. But I can't. Ever! Ever! Shit!!!

Here are three methods which enable the carrying forward of experiencing. Once the therapist is within the patient's world, experiential listening provides the therapist with a phenomenological scene and some inner experiencing. From within that phenomenological world, the therapist attends to the phenomenological scene, describing whatever presents itself. Or the therapist expresses the inner experiencing, or welcomes and tells what it is like. Used singly or together, these methods result in the carrying forward of experiencing. Whatever it is, whatever its nature and content, it now happens more. In addition, the way is opened up for the fourth step, in which the patient has the opportunity to disengage from the entire operating domain and to undergo the shift into being the deeper potential.

## EXPERIENCING THE RELATIONSHIP WITH DEEPER POTENTIALS

Experiential listening means that the therapist exists, at least to some extent, in the patient's own world. The therapist is in touch with some ongoing phenomenological scene and some ongoing experiencing. One option is for the therapist to carry forward whatever experiencing is present. A second option is for the therapist to further the relationship between the patient and a deeper experiencing.

The therapist is already at least somewhat within the phenomenological world of the patient. As the patient is attending to something, is behaving and experiencing, experiential listening may well allow the therapist to be in quite close touch with the deeper experiencing. Instead of expressing it out into the phenomenological scene, instead of welcoming and describing what it is like, the therapist may allow himself to "be" this deeper experiencing, to let it fill the therapist.

Now the main avenue is between the therapist, as the agent or voice of the deeper experiencing, and the patient. Experiential listening may highlight the relationship between the patient and the deeper experiencing and, as the incorporated deeper experiencing, the therapist furthers this relationship. This is the internal encounter, a two-way, back-and-forth relationship between patient and therapist as the voice of the deeper experiencing.

There are two interrelated practical consequences to the working of this internal relationship. One is that the relationship inevitably proceeds in the direction of an easing, a softening. There is integrative closeness where before there was distance and separation. There are feelings of oneness and inner harmony, where before there was fear, anxiety, fractionation. Second, as with the carrying forward of the potentials for experiencing, the patient is brought to a point of friendly closeness to the deeper potential, and is ready to undertake the momentous shift out of the operating domain and into the very being of the deeper potential.

The method consists of integrative encountering. The therapist, as the voice of the deeper experiencing, encounters the patient, pointedly relates to and with the patient. But it is a precious kind of encountering, an integrative encountering. That is, the therapist need not fear and avoid the deeper experiencing. Instead, the therapist can enjoy it, can play with being it, can express and be the good form of it. The therapist can welcome the very being of it, and allow it to fill and suffuse him. It can bubble and percolate in the therapist, play itself happily and joyfully. The therapist can have fun being that which the patient recoils from and must avoid and oppose. The therapist, in short, can relate to the patient as the good form of the deeper experiencing, the pleasant, joyous, gay form. This is the method of integrative encountering, for the encountering moves in the direction of integration between the patient and the deeper potential.

We return to some of the examples of experiential listening in Chapter 9. When experiential listening illuminates the patient and the deeper potential, the therapist encounters the patient as the voice and being of the illuminated deeper potential. That is one way of describing the method. Another way goes like this: When experiential listening illuminates the deeper potential, the deeper potential comes to life and interacts with the patient. If the deeper potential were to come alive, and talk to the patient, what would it say? How would it be? This is not the bad form of the deeper potential, the form seen by the patient who avoids the deeper potential, who erects barriers against it and is terrified by it. It is its own deeper potential, its own good form of the experiencing. It feels good, and it is quite free to be playful and spontaneous, and to relate with the patient lovingly and intimately. Experiential listening invests the therapist with the deeper potential, enables the deeper potential to come alive through the voice of the therapist who interacts with the patient:

Pt (Woman in her late twenties.): I want to be myself. I want to find myself. So many people just run through their lives without ever really knowing what they are like. I can be like them. Dead. Dead persons. I must know what I am like. Can I be myself? Can I find out and be myself? Sometimes I wonder if I should be myself. I must. I must be whatever I am. I must be whatever I really am.

Experiential listening sensitizes the therapist to a despairing anguish of being empty, unfinished, without possibilities. It is the utter reality that this is all there is, there is no more. In the phenomenological scene, the patient is looking inside herself for the exciting golden possibilities, the precious wonderful inner person, but there is nothing inside; it is an empty space.

Blending into this deeper experiencing, letting it fill him, the therapist relates to the patient:

T: Like some golden little flower inside your soul? A lovely treasure? It's all empty! That's it! See, it's hollow.

Pt: What do you mean? (There is a tension and gathering of strength.)

T: What do you think—you're going to evolve into some wonderful human being?

Pt: (More tense and wary.) I want to be myself.

T: What is all this drivel? "Can I be myself? Can I find out and be myself?" What kind of crap is that?

Pt: There's more to me than this. I want to grow. I want to be the person I am.

T: You're grown. That's it. Story's over. You ain't nothing but a very common woman. Nothing to grow. That's it!

Pt: (Shocked, angry, scared, hurt.) *No!*

T: *Yeah!* See! Inside? Nothing. It's all empty! Unless you want to pretend. You want to pretend? Go ahead, pretend. But the game is over.

Pt: (In laugh-shock.) No . . . no . . . no . . . that's not true at all. I've always been ready to just let myself be . . .

T: Well that's over. . . .

Pt: (Continuing) . . . what I am. There's so much more to me. I . . . there is! I am so much more! I am!

T: Sorry.

Pt: (In a high state of tension.) I am! I am! I can be so much more! What! How can you. . . ? That's crazy! I've spent·my whole life . . . but that's crazy! There is more to me. I've been searching my whole life! What are you saying? No! There is much more to me. There is more. There is a whole person I can be! There is more!

T: Yeah, well lemme look around for something. I don't see much anywhere. You see something I don't see?

Pt: (Hard breathing.) I don't know what to say. I can't. . . . I don't know what to say. This is crazy . . . it's funny! I can't believe this. (Pause. Then much more quietly and softly.) I should be falling apart. (Pause.) What's going on! I feel OK . . . strange . . . I feel . . . calm . . .

T: Watch out. That's the emptiness.

Pt: Maybe. Why do I feel all right? I feel all right.

There is a beginning harmony between the patient and the deeper potential, the absence of a nascent inner jewel of a human being. The encountering is moving toward a more integrative relationship with what had existed as a deeper emptiness, a vacuum of nothingness.

In the next excerpt, the patient is attending to his younger brother. Instead of staying in the family and taking care of the brother, he left; now he is explaining how that was all right:

Pt: Had palsy all his life. His left eye is bad. Something's wrong with it. It's an eye that doesn't look, doesn't work. Glaucoma? He used to take pills. I couldn't take care of him anymore. I had to go away. That's part of it. I got so I just couldn't stand it . . . I stayed for a while.

Experiential listening reveals a deeper cruel coldness, a self-centered inhumanness which deserves being hated and punished. The therapist speaks as the voice of this deeper potential:

T: Sure you did. You put in your time. What the hell? Fuck him.
Pt: No, I should have stayed.
T: Well, go ahead and beat yourself—as long as you can have your freedom. It's great!
Pt: I'm bad.
T: Yeah, you are. May I have a piece of this? How's this: "You are bad, you are really bad. You are an uncaring, cold, sonuvabitch bastard. Cold and uncaring." Pretty good. Your turn. Now you can beat yourself. Go ahead. Then my turn again.
Pt: I should have stayed.
T: Great. You stay. I want to have freedom. I love being on my own. It's great!
Pt: Shut up!!
T: Whatever you say, sir!
Pt: *Shut up!!!*
T: *As long as I can have my apartment. I loved getting out! It was time!*
Pt: *Shit!* I never wanted to take care of the little bastard anyhow! I didn't do it 'cause I wanted to. I did it 'cause I expected some reward! Like putting in good time. I hated it. I never wanted to be in that shitty family anyhow. It was like putting on an act for years. For fucking

years! Good old Bobby! Fuck! No! I lied for 20 fucking years! Like an exchange! Well now I'm collecting. If I was honest I would have said no a thousand years ago!

T: Welcome to the family of the cold bastards. Cruel.

Pt: Well it feels like me for once. Jesus! What a liar I've been!

T: Hello, you cold cruel bastard.

Pt: There are lots of us. Oh what a waste. What a shitty waste. (Pause.) My head is dizzy. My headache's gone. It's been there all the time. I feel dizzy.

T: Go home and take care of him.

Pt: (Laughing.) I think I've hated him from the day he was born.

T: (Laughing.) Before.

Pt: (Laughing.) Yeah, before. I'm dizzy. My head is very light. Clear. Wow! (Pause.) Feels a little strange.

One of the practical aims of this internal encountering is that there is an easing of the relationship between the patient and the deeper potential. The relationship becomes more integrated and open. This means that the patient and deeper potential are closer to one another. In other words, this method brings the patient to the same point as the methods of carrying forward the potentials, i.e., now the patient is ready to consider the fourth step in the experiential process.

## EXPERIENTIAL BEING OF THE DEEPER POTENTIAL

Each session opens with the therapist outside the patient, the teacher who shows the patient how to focus attention (Chapter 7). Next, the therapist enters into the patient's phenomenological world (Chapter 8) and is able to listen experientially (Chapter 9). Sharing the patient's phenomenological scene and experiencing, the therapist carries forward that experiencing (step 2) and/or engages in the integrating of the relationship between the deeper potential and the patient (step 3). The next step is for the patient to undergo the massive and profound disengagement from the continuing, substantive personhood or operating domain, and to negotiate the momentous shift into the very being of the deeper potential. It is a matter of allowing oneself to be a qualitatively new and different person. Sometimes this radical shift occurs by itself. More often, the therapist must return to the external location and serve as the teacher of the methods of undertaking this shift.

*Therapist and Patient Succumb to the Wholesale Deeper Potential*

One method is for the therapist to give instructions for just giving in to being the wholesale deeper potential, completely succumbing to whatever it is. Almost always, steps 3 and 4 culminate in some given phenomenological scene and some specific deeper experiencing which is present and imminent. Now the patient has the choice of remaining the person whom he is or letting himself be the wholesale deeper potential in fully complete and saturating experiencing. The choice resides with the patient whether to do this or not, whether to do this now or not.

In an earlier excerpt, the patient was hurting in relation to Doris, who is moving further and further away from him. The therapist helps raise up the deeper experiencing of hopelessness, emptiness, aloneness. Now the experiencing is carried forward, is intruding into the patient, and is occurring with greater amplitude and intensity. The patient is close enough to succumb to the inner sense of hopelessness, emptiness, aloneness.

It is here that the therapist gives instructions on what to do and how to do it. The therapist describes the nature of the deeper experiencing, and invites the patient to just let go, to succumb; instead of pulling back away from it, just surrender completely into the abject pit of being completely alone. Doris is forever gone. He is left, abandoned wholly. He "can't stand being alone. Why am I alone? I don't know what to do. I don't know how to be alone!" Now he is to let the worst occur. We know the awful situation; we know the catastrophically imminent deeper experiencing. The next step is to let it all occur.

Following the instructions, and the patient's choice to succumb, the therapist again returns into the phenomenological world of the patient, and engages in experiential listening. The patient takes the next step:

Pt: (Whispering.) I am all by myself. I am really alone. Alone. Really alone. I don't know what to do. How to live. I can't believe . . . I can see the floor. I feel like I'm on the floor. The floor seems hard. Hard. I'm finally alone. Really alone. No one . . . no one's here. I've always been terrified of being like this. I somehow always knew that I'd end up like this. All my life I've been scared to death of being old and all alone. An old man with nothing and no one. She's gone. She's really gone. And there's no one to come, nobody's gonna come for me. (These words are accompanied with heightened feeling. It is as if an inner panic grabs hold. He stops abruptly.)

T: No one's going to come. No one. No one's gonna come for me. Again, again! No one's gonna come for me!

Pt: (He is crying in a state of near panic.) Nobody's going to come for me! Ever!!! (Long hard crying.) I'll be all by myself. Why? Tell me please! I want somebody to come for me. You promised. (Now the tears are very hard and the crying has an almost desperation to it.)

The therapist is aligned with the patient, sharing the phenomenological world in which, right now, the therapist is sitting on the floor with arms outstretched, as if talking to the ephemeral other figure. The experiencing is the terrifying anguish of being left alone.

T: You . . . you . . . well, someone's here . . .

Pt: (Still crying.) No . . . no (long pause). I waited. I wanted my Daddy to come back, but he never did. You never came back for me. You never made it all better. I've been alone my whole life. I was all by myself. Waiting . . . (There is a lightening here.)

T: And that's pretty dumb.

Pt: I think I've been in mourning my whole life.

These words sent a chill down the therapist's back. In an almost eerie way, these words seem to be coming from someone other than the patient. In a flash, the therapist is in a scene where he has just awakened suddenly as if from a long sleep. The experiencing is that of being kind of independent and autonomous, a whole person:

T: Well! I feel like I just woke up!

Pt: (Similarly, as if continuing to be the other or new or different person.) These are my arms and legs . . . I can feel my heart here. My face is heavy, like the skin is heavy . . . I feel like I'm in a meadow looking around at the grass. It's pretty. It smells fresh . . . sort of lazy too. (Pause.) . . . This is silly . . . I feel real tall. Real big, and like I'm jumping, you know, like being real light? I like this. It's peculiar. I feel real light! This is funny! I can feel my arms and my legs and my whole body, like it belongs to me. Like I just got them . . . yeah . . . I like this . . . I feel light and bouncy. Sunshine and nice . . .

The rule almost always holds. When the patient wholly succumbs to the deeper experiencing, opens up and penetrates through its pain and hurt, then the curious change takes place. It emerges in its good form.

Here the disintegratively bad form of the abject and hurtful aloneness is disclosed as a kind of intactness, a freedom, a bodily oneness, a joyful independence and autonomy. Momentarily, at least, the patient has undergone a significant shift into being the good form of the heart of the deeper potential. It is the consequence of succumbing wholesale to the deeper potential.

*Therapist and Patient Undergo the Primitive Reversal: Doing to Them What They Did to You*

A second method of experientially being the deeper potential typically occurs within the context of those precious, early, primitive scenes in which other figures are the agents or expressors of deep potentials for experiencing. Carrying forward the potentials for experiencing (step 2) and experiencing the relationships with deeper potentials (step 3) tend to open up increasingly significant early moments of heightened experiencing. In these scenes, there are critical moments when the preponderance of attention is on the other person who is the active agent of the experiencing. That is, the other person is carrying out the experiencing; the center of gravity lies within that other person and not the patient. Accordingly, the invitation is for the therapist and patient to reverse the action; the therapist and patient are to do to the other person what the other person does to the patient. This is the method.

Let us return to the patient who confronted his father, stood up to the animal, saying, ". . . I never liked the drinking . . . I always thought he was an animal!" Carrying this forward culminated in an experiencing of some closeness and love: ". . . am I some sort of nut 'cause I love my Daddy? I do! I love you! Listen! I love you, I love you, I love you. . . ." The opening up of this experiencing brought therapist and patient into earlier incidents more highly charged with the experiencing. In the present session, as in several previous sessions, the experiential track led to an incident in which the patient was four years old, playing in the garage by himself. Suddenly his father burst into the garage and was rushing back and forth yelling at the little boy. The father than slumped to the floor and bawled like a baby, his whole body lurching with the heaving of the wrenching tears. The patient was dumbfounded, awestruck. He was frozen with shock even as the father looked directly at him beseechingly, tears pouring down his face.

No one spoke of this incident. Only years later did the patient connect this incident with the sudden death of the grandfather in a car accident.

Instead, this incident was framed by itself in a special room in the patient's memory, unconnected with the rest of his life except through the opening up of the deeper experiencing of a buried love-yearning for his father. Throughout his current life, the patient respected some people, was friendly with his wife, enjoyed friends; but he rarely experienced love. He knew what it was like to be afraid of his father, to keep a safe distance between himself and other "animals," and that insured against the experiencing of a highly charged love.

In this garage incident, the patient's whole center of gravity resided in father. The patient was raptly transfixed onto father. The choice is whether the patient is ready to do to the father what the father did to him. The patient must reverse the direction and do what the father did to him. The patient must yell, slump to the floor, bawl like a baby, allow his body to lurch and heave with wrenching tears, and look beseechingly at his father, tears pouring down his face. Such ways of being were distinctly alien.

He sat for a while, then started:

Pt: You're sitting there, Daddy. I know that my . . . grampa was just killed . . . (Long pause. Tears are starting. He cries. Then he cries and cries, louder and louder.) I loved my Grampa! I loved him! (He screams out:) *Noooo! Please noooo!* (More hard crying.) Daddy, he's dead!!! My grampa is dead! Daddy. (Hard racking crying.) Oh Daddy. I love you!!! Daddy! Daddy! (Long hard crying.) Do you understand? He's dead! They killed him with a car. I loved him! I love you! Daddy I'm scared. I'm so scared that I'll die! I don't wanna die anymore. I can't stand this! Please don't let me die! Please Daddy! (He cries and cries, whimpering and groaning. Then there is a pause.) Oh Daddy, I love you so much! So much . . . I love you. (Accompanying the tears is a pleasant buoyancy throughout the chest and head.)

There are primitive incidents and scenes in which key persons do "it" to the patient; these key persons express and carry out the experiencing. The mother or father controls and dominates the little patient; the other person is mean and cruel to the little patient; the other figure rejects and hates the little patient. In reversing this direction, the surprisingly unthinkable task is for the patient, in the reality of that early scene, to do to them what they did to the patient. The patient pours out control and domination over mother or father; the patient explodes with meanness and cruelty to the other person; the patient is energized with rejection and hatred toward the other figure. By means of this method, carried out fully within the context of the early scenes, the patient achieves the momentous shift out of the personhood or operating domain in which he had continuously existed, and undergoes the profound and cataclysmic being of the deeper potential.

*Therapist and Patient Undergo New Experiencing in Redivived Critical Moments*

The carrying forward of experiencing (step 2), and the experiencing of relationships between the patient and the deeper potential (step 3) bring the patient much closer to a deeper potential. In addition, these two steps tend to disclose earlier scenes and situations in which the deeper potential might have occurred or started to occur. These are the critical moments when the patient failed to let the deeper potential come forth. Accordingly, the method is to return to these critical moments, and this time, to undergo new experiencing as the deeper potential. The patient moves out of the person whom he is, and enters into the full experiential being of the deeper potential in a fresh and new experiencing within the context of the early critical moment.

Let us return to the conservative, staid businessman who moves into heightened sexual experiencing within the context of a phenomenological scene involving his secretary. That vignette ended with his more open sexual experiencing: "She's the kind of woman I've always . . . always wanted. I want someone like her. God, I need someone like her. I could just let myself go! I want to be with a woman like that!!"

Further carrying forward of that experiencing and further experiencing of the relationship between the patient and the deeper potential disclosed a critical moment which seemed to have occurred when he was about six years old. His older sister is remembered as being in bed with him and her girl friend. The girl friend was inspecting his sister's genitals, and he especially recollected their giggling together. He too was silly and laughing, and it seemed as if they were all being naughty and wicked. The critical moment occurred when the girl friend just reached out and touched his penis. He was shocked, and he screamed. It seemed that his mother immediately burst into the room and that was the abrupt end of the recollected memory. But he vividly remembers the details of the critical moment when the girl friend grabbed his penis and he screamed.

The method calls for the patient to return to that instant and, this time, to allow himself to be the wholesale experiencing of sexuality. The therapist tells the patient what to do and how to do it. When the patient chooses to do so, he returns to that scene, enters into the critical moment, and instead of screaming in shock, allows himself to undergo the deeper sexual experiencing:

Pt: Touch me, Lise! Go ahead. Touch me. I like your pretty black hair. Yeah! Touch me. Oooh! (Laughs.) Shhh! Touch me again!

T: I like the way your fingers . . .

Pt: . . . That feels good. (Laughing.) Closer! Both of you! Ooh! Rub up against me. . . . My penie feels good. C'mon, touch my penie more! (Laughs.)

T: It's getting bigger! Hey look! It's getting bigger!

Pt: Wanta get a wash rag and rub it! (He is very excited.) Touch it more! C'mon, both of you touch it more. Yeah! Yeah! (He is wiggling all over.) Touch me touch me touch me touch me more touch me more . . . I love this! More more more more more more!!! (Hard and raucous laughing.) More more more more more more!!! Yeah yeah yeah. . . . Wheeeee! I like this! *I love this!!!* (He laughs and laughs.) . . . *that's fun!!*

Through this method, the patient has allowed himself to undergo the shift into being the deeper potential, and to "be" this deeper potential within the context of the early critical moment.

The patient has now had a taste of being a whole new person. For anywhere from a few seconds to perhaps 20 minutes, he left the old personality behind, the worn-out old personality with all the problems and conflicts. He was able to be the deeper personality—not the one he continually avoids and fears, the one he dares not be, not the one he sees from his jaundiced side of the disintegrative relationship. Instead, he was able to taste and feel what it is like to be the lived deeper potential. The more he carried forward the potentials for experiencing, the more he experienced the integrative relationship between himself and the deeper potential, then the more he was able to be a deeper potential which is fresh and alive, sound and harmonious. And this is the culmination of the first four steps of therapy. Now the patient is ready for the final step.

## BEING-BEHAVIORAL CHANGE IN THE EXTRA-THERAPY WORLD

From the opening of the session to this point, the patient has gone through four significant experiencings. The mildest (step 1) is the experiencing of getting ready. That is, the patient allowed a preponderance of attention to focus on some meaningful center so that bodily sensations came alive and some kind of experiencing began to occur a little. It is here that the therapist joins into the patient's phenomenological world and begins experiential listening. Up to this point the therapist was engaging in those practices which are basic to experiential psychotherapy, i.e., those which lay the groundwork for the next steps.

The second experiencing (step 2) is the carrying forward of the potential for experiencing. It is experienced more, probably beyond the point where the person ordinarily experiences. Experiential listening is necessary for the therapist to facilitate this step. Third, the patient experiences an integrative relationship with the deeper potential. In this, the patient undergoes something new: a touch of a new, welcoming, peaceful, harmonious relationship with a transformed, mutated, good form of the monstrously awful deeper potential. Experiential listening is likewise a necessary precondition for this third step. Finally, the patient experiences the momentous shift out of the person in which he has been encased and from which he has functioned virtually his entire life—and the profound sampling of an altered state of being, namely, the vitalized and integrated deeper potential, a genuinely new personhood. From these experiencings comes the opportunity to be and behave in the extra-therapy world as a new and changing person. The patient has tasted significant change in the therapy context; now the time has come to consider the world without. This is the final step in the session.

### Therapist and Patient Risk New Ways of Being/Behaving

This method typically begins with the actual changes which occurred in the session itself. Each of the previous steps included some kind of experiencing. Quite often these are new experiencings; the patient is being different, is behaving differently, and is experiencing something different. The choice is innocent enough: If the patient allows such changes to occur in the therapy, maybe the patient has a choice of being, behaving, and experiencing in a similar way in one's actual life. Another choice is also innocent enough: If the way of being and behaving and experiencing seems good, pleasureable, even rather exciting, maybe the patient can reconstruct his life in ways which allow for these pleasant experiencings or ways of being and behaving. The therapist and patient consider all of these changes to a point where there is a little risk, i.e., to a point where the imminent reality of these new ways of being and behaving actually starts to grip the patient somewhat.

One patient was able to experience what it is like to stand up to his father, to fight him directly, even to yell at him. In carrying forward the experiencing, described earlier, the patient was able to say and be and experience the following—all of which is new:

Pt: . . . You just wouldn't listen. You never listen to anybody . . . well, shit! It's true!!! Yeah, it's true. I'm scared of you! I'm terrified of you! I've always been terrified of you! We all are! You're not a father! You're an animal!!!

Even more, this opened the way for further experiencing of closeness, warmth, a love-yearning for father. Again, these are new ways of being, behaving, and experiencing:

Pt: . . . Can't you see I love you? I love you! Listen to me! . . . am I some sort of nut 'cause I love my Daddy? I do! I love you! Listen! I love you, I love you, I love you . . .

Subsequently, in being the deeper potential (step 4), the patient was able to experience something quite new and deep, i.e., a fully open intimacy with father, a bodily letting-go of childlike helplessness and vulnerability. He was able to cry like a baby, and all the following is new:

Pt: . . . Daddy I'm scared. I'm so scared that I'll die! I don't wanna die anymore. I can't stand this! Please don't let me die! Please Daddy! (He cries and cries, whimpering and groaning. Then there is a pause.) Oh Daddy, I love you so much! So much . . . I love you. (There is a pleasant buoyancy throughout the chest and head.)

Consider the possibility of being and behaving and experiencing in these new ways in one's actual life. Consider how one must be and behave in order to build the kind of immediate world in which one might actually be and behave and experience all of these in a new and changing world. The patient starts with the unexpected:

Pt: My father's a doctor.

T: What?

Pt: Yeah, he's been in practice for about 40 years in Brookfield. And I don't go to doctors. I think I'm going to go to him. And I could. Well, I could ask him to check me over. Ha! Yeah! I could do that. (Laughs.) He'd love that! I could ask him to give me a checkup. I never ever thought of anything like that. My grampa was a general practitioner. Dad too. I really would like that!

T: Well, that'd be new. Hello Dad!

Pt: And I think I'll take Martin (his son) along. I think I'd like Martin to be a doctor too. I could take him. I've never been on a trip with Martin, just him and me. Sure, we could drive there and spend a few days with Dad. I haven't even seen him since he remarried and that's maybe something like five years. Five years!

T: A reunion, a real reunion, the three generations.

Pt: Sure! First time. I'll tell Stella (his wife) . . . that . . .

T: Something's happening . . . I'm getting dizzy . . . and I feel like something's lifting . . .

Pt: I feel different . . . a little nervous maybe . . . I could talk with Stell. I don't ever really talk with Stell anymore. I think I want . . . jeez, I feel like a little baby. I feel like crying. . . . (He leans over and down.) I want to be in her lap. I want her to put her arms around me. I feel like I want to be held. (Long pause.)

T: I'm warm. (Long pause.)

Pt: I think I fell asleep. I feel a little shaky, like a baby. I want to be with her. I think I want to talk with her and tell her something. (Laughs.) I don't know what, something. I want to talk with her. I miss her. I miss my wife. I love her.

Here are risked new ways of being, new ways of behaving, new experiencings.


*Therapist and Patient Risk Letting Go of Old Ways of Being/Behaving*

Therapist and patient actually confront the utterly real possibility of letting go of old ways of being and behaving which insured that the patient will indeed feel rotten, and insured that the patient would not experience the deeper potential. It is as if the new and changing patient can now see how (the other) he constructed a world fittingly designed to make him miserable. And then the risk is to consider, seriously, the letting go of one or two of those old ways.

We turn now to the patient who was so hurting in relation to Doris as she moves further and further away from him. There was the anguish of hopelessness, emptiness and aloneness without her. As he succumbed to the utter aloneness, to the terrible waiting for the Daddy who never would come, the change occurs. He dipped into a new sense of bodily intactness, a freedom, a joyful independence and autonomy.

Later, therapist and patient turn to the world which can be, the extra-therapy life. They consider ways in which the patient insures a painful sense of hopelessness, emptiness, and aloneness, how the patient's ways of being and behaving construct such a painful world expressly designed to maintain such unhappiness:

Pt: Well at work, yeah at work. All the time at work. I'm so good at getting promoted. I am good. So I get promoted to jobs that are always over my head. I do it so well! And then I want Daddy to come bail me out. My big boss is supposed to help me. Yeah, come be with me and make it all better. And he never does. Then it gets worse and worse and I get transferred or get another job. I feel so damned alone and abandoned and like there's never a Daddy who comes. I'm perpetually waiting for my Godot, my boss Daddy. It's sick! I'm the best son to a father who never shows up. I'm a professional. And all I do is suffer! What a rotten life!

T: But good at it! Oh I'm skilled!

Pt: Forty years of practice! What the hell do I expect?

T: To get better and better, that's all.

Pt: It really is crazy.

T: So? So let it go, you asshole!

Pt: (Snorts.) That would mean giving up my job I suppose. (Pause.) Why not? Why not! I could stay in the ministry and do what I really want to do. I could. I really could. I always manage to get over my head. I could resign . . . that doesn't feel so bad. Hell, it feels good! I'll resign. I could do what I am best at. I always start out at that and then I weasel my way to the top. What a waste. Resigning feels good. No, thank you. No more of this shit . . .

T: And! And? There's more?

Pt: My ulcer.

T: Yes, my ulcer.

Pt: I'm thinking of my ulcer. It hasn't hurt the whole time here. (Pause.)

Uh . . . I . . . my body . . . it feels good. I somehow don't think I'll keep my ulcer anymore . . . funny . . . I don't think I want that damned thing. (Pause.)

T: I am seeing Doris . . .

Pt: Me too. I don't blame her a bit. I don't . . . what a waste with her. (Little laugh.) I drive her away.

T: What? I couldn't hear.

Pt: I drive her away! Whatever she does is not enough. Yeah. I spend most of my time arranging so I can't count on her. I . . . I'm ashamed of it. I get in fights with her and then wait for days till she is supposed to come to me and somehow figure out what's wrong and make it better. Oh that poor kid! I really am ashamed.

T: Wait for days till she is supposed to come to me . . .

Pt: I take care of my ulcer. I get worse. I stay away from her. I wait for her and she never comes and then I feel so sorry for myself. (Big sigh.)

T: Maybe, just maybe, it can be let go.

Pt: That would be very hard. I am too good at that. I would have to grow up a little, a lot. That would mean no more games with her. Maybe even no more fights like that. Oh, that would be big. It's like saying goodbye to a friend. I mean me. I'd have to stop pouting with my ulcer. Stop sitting in mourning for her. Like I am now. That's a big order.

T: Wow, yeah.

Pt: This is serious. This is really pretty damned serious. It means I'd have to give up my pouting. That's kind of scary. And no more setting her up. That's a very tall order.

T: You bet!

Pt: Why doesn't it feel bad? It doesn't. It almost feels exciting. Like maybe there's a possibility. Something I can do. It feels like, ah, like something's opening up maybe. It's a little exciting.

Here is a risking of a letting go of some old ways of being and behaving. It is a consideration of changes in one's extra-therapy world.

### Therapist and Patient Risk Opening Up the Awful Ways of Being/Behaving

Now that the patient has had a taste of being the deeper potential, the very idea of being that way in one's actual life is almost unthinkable.

Here is where therapist and patient consider the (unthinkable) possibility of changing one's world to accommodate the (unthinkable) experiencing. Here is where therapist and patient consider what the life really could be like, how the patient could be and behave, if the inner experiencing were to take over his life for the (unthinkable) foreseeable future.

This is half serious play. Therapist and patient really consider what the life would be like. It is a genuine glimpse into what might indeed occur and how the patient might well be and behave. They face the risk of opening up the awful ways of behaving. It always has the sense of: "Oh my God, it really could be like that; it is quite possible." On the other hand, it is playful and light, jesting and fanciful. In this integrative confronting of the risk, therapist and patient honestly and openly face the risk of what realistically could transpire.

The staid and conservative businessman began with a naughty glance at his lovely secretary, and ended up in bed with his sister and her girl friend. He loved the open sex, the laughing giddiness of wicked and hidden sex play among the three of them, the unfettered wholesale experiencing of kiddy sexuality. Let us pick up the dialogue when therapist and patient are risking the consideration of actually letting this way of being and behaving open up into his life:

T: Prostitutes! That's it. You could hire a high class whore—sorry, "companion"—for the weekend. You could hire her when you go to Montreal for the weekends.
Pt: No! Never!
T: It'd be easy.
Pt: I could never do that!
T: Well try, dammit.
Pt: I wish I could. I can't.
T: Well, wish a little harder.
Pt: I'd have to be out of my mind, or drunk.
T: See! You're already starting to figure out a way. Good. Go on.
Pt: I could never do that.
T: (In a prissy manner.) Pity.
Pt: (Laughing.) It would be the end of my marriage.
T: (Laughing.) Now we got some changes going. Great. So now you're fucking high-class whores and you're going to end the marriage. Great . . . wait, I got an idea. How about you and your sister and her girl friend reenacting the bed scene the way it should have occurred? Yeah! What a great idea! Can you arrange that?

Pt: They're over 50 years old for Christ sakes!!!

T: Well then it's about time. Another 20 years and you'll all be too rickety.

Pt: (Laughing.) I could just see it.

T: How the hell could you arrange that?

Pt: (Laughing.) You know! I think it would be fun! (He laughs hard.) If I could do that I could do anything!

T: Anything . . . like what?

Pt: Everyone fools around with their secretaries!

T: How would you get her to play around with your penie?

Pt: I wish I could get anyone to play around with my penie!

T: (Mockingly shouting out to the world.) Hey anyone! I want to get someone to play around with my penie! Anyone listening? Call 784-8341.

Pt: That's the wrong number!

T: (Laughing.) Well, you do it!

Pt: No! This is crazy! I'm not going to do any of this! (Laughs.) Not that I haven't thought about it. It would destroy my life.

T: A little more feeling please. That didn't sound very convincing.

Pt: I love my wife.

T: Could you try that line again? Please? I mean, if your wife were here, that would not give her maximum security.

Pt: I'm beginning to think my whole life is a joke.

T: Listen to this, folks. Here's where the staid conservative businessman sees his whole life flash before him. It's the beginning of . . . what do they call it?

Pt: Insight.

T: Yeah, insight.

Pt: I don't do anything.

T: Yes you do. You make sure that you never get in bed with your sister and her girl friend and have great wonderful fun with . . . uh . . . with . . . (whispers) sex.

Pt: (Pause.) I've always thought about all that. But it's like I never acknowledge that I'm the one who thinks about it. All my life it's like I have sex on my mind and live my whole life so that it never happens, like I never thought about it. Look at me! I don't even look like a dirty old man.

T: Aha! Out of the closet comes the dirty old man.

Pt: That'll be my next life.

T: You could write books about it.

Pt: That's what I read! I stash them away in my workshop! I read dirty
books. I always have! And I always thought I could write them!

T: You do? You really do? Well, that's the ticket! Write the greatest sexy
books ever written!

Pt: I could! . . . (Laughs.) This is crazy! What am I doing? Somehow this
seems crazy. I mean crazy. But I think it could happen. I almost wish
I could have it happen.

T: What?

Pt: I don't know. (Laughs.) Any of it. (Laughs.) I am so mixed
up . . . and I don't even feel bad. Except that I think I'm wasting my
whole life. Yeah.

This is the final step in the process of a session of experiential psychotherapy. In this final step, the therapist and the patient experience
the risked possibility of actual changes in ways of being and behaving
in the world which the patient constructs and in which the patient exists.

The aim of this book has been to describe the basic practices which
(a) culminate in the therapist's sharing the patient's phenomenological
world and engaging in experiential listening, and (b) are necessary for
the subsequent steps of experiential psychotherapy. The aim of this last
chapter has been to introduce the methods of undertaking the next steps:
the carrying forward of experiencing, experiencing the relationship between the patient and the deeper potentials, experiencing the being of
the deeper potentials, and the experiencing of being-behavioral change
in the extra-therapy world. The methods of undertaking these steps
comprise the advanced practices of experiential psychotherapy.

# References

ALEXANDER, F. The dynamics of psychotherapy in the light of learning theory. *American Journal of Psychiatry*, 1963, *120*, 440-448.

ALEXANDER, F. and FRENCH, T. M. *Psychoanalytic therapy*. New York: Ronald Press, 1946.

ANGYAL, A. *Neurosis and treatment: A holistic theory*. New York: Wiley, 1965.

BACHRACH, H. Adaptive regression, empathy, and psychotherapy: theory and research study. *Psychotherapy: Theory, Research and Practice*, 1968, *5*, 203-209.

BAR-LEVAV, R. Behavior change—insignificant and significant, apparent and real. In A. Burton (Ed.) *What makes behavior change possible?* New York: Brunner/Mazel, 1976. Pp. 278-303.

BENEDEK, T. M. Control of the transference relationship. In F. Alexander and T. M. French (Eds.) *Psychoanalytic therapy*. New York: Ronald Press, 1946. Pp. 173-206.

BERGIN, A. E. Some implications of psychotherapy research for therapeutic practice. *Journal of Abnormal Psychology*, 1966, *71*, 235-246.

BINSWANGER, L. The existential analysis school of thought. In R. May, E. Angel, and H. F. Ellenberger (Eds.) *Existence: A new dimension in psychiatry and psychology*. New York: Basic Books, 1958a. Pp. 191-213.

Binswanger, L. Insanity as life-historical phenomenon and as mental disease: The case of Ilse. In R. May, E. Angel, and H. F. Ellenberger (Eds.) *Existence: A new dimension in psychiatry and psychology*. New York: Basic Books, 1958b. Pp. 214-236.

BINSWANGER, L. *Being-in-the-world: Selected papers of Ludwig Binswanger*. J. Needleman (Ed.) New York and London: Harper Torchbooks, 1967.

BORDIN, E. S. Inside the therapeutic hour. In E. A. Rubenstein and M. B. Parloff (Eds.) *Research in psychotherapy*. Washington, D.C.: American Psychological Association, 1959. Pp. 235-246.

Boss, M. *Psychoanalysis and Daseinsanalysis*. New York: Basic Books, 1963.

BREUER, J. and FREUD, S. *Studies in hysteria*. New York: Nervous and Mental Diseases Publications, 1936.

BUBER, M. Guilt and guilt feelings. *Psychiatry*, 1957, *20*, 114-129.

BUCKLEW, J. *Paradigms for psychopathology: A contribution to case history analysis*. Chicago: Lippincott, 1960.

387

BUCKLEW, J. The use of symptoms to assess case history information. *Multivariate Behavioral Research*, 1968, Special Issue, 157-168.

BUGENTAL, J. F. T. The person who is the psychotherapist. *Journal of Consulting Psychology*, 1964, 28, 272-277.

BUGENTAL, J. F. T. *The search for authenticity: An existential-analytic approach to psychotherapy.* New York: Holt, Rinehart and Winston, 1965.

BUGENTAL, J. F. T. *Psychotherapy and process: The fundamentals of an existential-humanistic approach.* Reading, Mass.: Addison-Wesley, 1978.

BUGENTAL, J. F. T. *The search for existential identity.* San Francisco, Jossey-Bass, 1979.

BUYTENDIJK, F. J. J. The phenomenological approach to the problem of feelings and emotion. In M. L. Remert (Ed.) *Feelings and emotions.* New York: McGraw-Hill, 1950. Pp. 127-141.

BYLES, M. B. *Journey into Burmese Silence.* London: George Allen and Unwin, 1962.

CARKHUFF, R. R. and BERENSON, B. G. *Beyond counseling and therapy.* New York: Holt, Rinehart and Winston, 1967.

CARUSO, I. A. *Existential psychology.* New York: Herder and Herder, 1964.

CAUTELA, J. R. The application of learning theory "as a last resort" in the treatment of a case of anxiety neurosis. *Journal of Clinical Psychology*, 1965, 21, 448-452.

CHANG, CHEN-CHI. *The practice of Zen.* New York: Harper and Row, 1959.

COLBY, K. M. Discussion of papers on therapist's contribution. In H. H. Strupp and L. Luborsky (Eds.) *Research in psychotherapy.* Vol. 2. Washington, D.C.: American Psychological Association, 1962. Pp. 95-101.

CONDRAU, G. and BOSS, M. Existential analysis. In J. G. Howells (Ed.) *Modern perspectives in world psychiatry.* New York: Brunner/Mazel, 1971. Pp. 488-518.

DEIKMAN, A. J. Implications of experimentally induced contemplative meditation. *Journal of Nervous and Mental Diseases*, 1966, 142, 101-116.

DENES-RADOMISLI, M. Existential-Gestalt therapy. In P. Olsen (Ed.) *Emotional Flooding.* New York: Penguin Books, 1977. Pp. 25-39.

DREIKURS, R. Adlerian psychotherapy. In F. Fromm-Reichmann and J. L. Moreno (Eds.) *Progress in psychotherapy.* New York: Grune and Stratton, 1956. Pp. 111-118.

EIGEN, M. The recoil in having another person. *Review of Existential Psychology and Psychiatry*, 1973, 12, 52-55.

ELDRED, S. H., HAMBURG, D. A., INWOOD, E. R., SALZMAN, L., MAYERSBURG, H. A., and GOODRICH, G. A procedure for the systematic analysis of psychotherapeutic interviews. *Psychiatry*, 1954, 17, 337-345.

ELLENBERGER, H. F. A clinical introduction to psychiatric phenomenology and existential analysis. In R. May, E. Angel, and H. F. Ellenberger (Eds.) *Existence: A new dimension in psychiatry and psychology.* New York: Basic Books, 1958. Pp. 92-124.

ELLIS, A. Requisite conditions for basic personality change. *Journal of Consulting Psychology*, 1959, 23, 538-540.

ENRIGHT, J. An introduction to Gestalt Techniques. In J. Fagan, and I. L. Shepherd (Eds.) *Gestalt therapy now.* New York: Harper and Row, 1970. Pp. 107-124.

FENICHEL, O. In H. Fenichel and D. Rapaport (Eds.) *The collected papers of Otto Fenichel: First series.* New York: Norton, 1953.

FISCHER, W. F. *Theories of anxiety.* New York: Harper and Row, 1970.

FISKE, D. W. *Measuring the concepts of personality.* Chicago: Aldine, 1970.

FRANK, J. D. *Persuasion and healing: A comparative study of psychotherapy.* Baltimore: Johns Hopkins Press, 1961.

FRANKL, V. E. *From death camp to existentialism.* Boston: Beacon Press, 1959.

FRANKL, V. E. *Psychotherapy and existentialism: Selected papers on logotherapy.* New York: Penguin, 1967.

FREUD, S. The dynamics of the transference. In: *Collected papers of Sigmund Freud.* Volume II. London: Institute of Psychoanalysis and Hogarth Press, 1924.

FREUD, S. Analysis terminable and interminable. In J. Strachey (Ed.) *Standard edition of the complete psychological works of Sigmund Freud*. Vol. V. London: Hogarth Press and the Institute of Psychoanalysis, 1953.

FROMM-REICHMANN, F. *Principles of intensive psychotherapy*. Chicago: University of Chicago Press, 1958.

GENDLIN, E. T. Experiencing: A variable in the process of therapeutic change. *American Journal of Psychotherapy*, 1961, *15*, 233-245.

GENDLIN, E. T. *Experiencing and the creation of meaning*. Toronto: The Free Press of Glencoe, 1962.

GENDLIN, E. T. A theory of personality change. In P. Worchel and D. Byrne (Eds.) *Personality change*. New York: Wiley, 1964. Pp. 100-148.

GENDLIN, E. T. Existentialism and experiential psychotherapy. In C. Moustakas (Ed.) *Existential child therapy*. New York: Basic Books, 1966. Pp. 206-246.

GENDLIN, E. T. Client-centered: the experiential response. In E. F. Hammer (Ed.) *Use of interpretation in treatment*. New York: Grune and Stratton, 1968. Pp. 208-227.

GENDLIN, E. G. Focusing. *Psychotherapy: Theory, Research and Practice*, 1969, *6*, 4-15.

GENDLIN, E. T. Therapeutic procedures with schizophrenic patients. In M. Hammer (Ed.) *The theory and practice of psychotherapy with specific disorders*. Springfield, Ill.: Charles C Thomas, 1972. Pp. 333-375.

GENDLIN, E. T. *Focusing*. New York: Everest House, 1978a.

GENDLIN, E. T. The body's releasing steps in experiential process. In J. L. Fosshage and P. Olsen (Eds.) *Healing: Implications for psychotherapy*. New York: Human Sciences Press, 1978b. Pp. 350-368.

GOLDSTEIN, A. P., HELLER, K., and SECHREST, L. B. *Psychotherapy and the psychology of behavior change*. New York: Wiley, 1966.

GOTTSCHALK, L. A. (Ed.) *Comparative psycholinguistic analysis of two psychotherapeutic interviews*. New York: International Universities Press, 1961.

GREENSON, R. Empathy and its vicissitudes. *International Journal of Psychoanalysis*, 1960, *41*, 418-424.

HALEY, J. The art of psychoanalysis. In S. I. Hayakawa (Ed.) *Our language and our world*. New York: Harper, 1959. Pp. 113-125.

HALEY, J. Control in psychotherapy with schizophrenics. *Archives of General Psychiatry*, 1961, *7*, 340-353.

HALEY, J. *Strategies of psychotherapy*. New York: Grune and Stratton, 1963.

HALPERN, H. An essential ingredient in successful psychotherapy. *Psychotherapy: Theory, Research and Practice*, 1965, *2*, 177-180.

HARTMANN, H. Psychoanalysis as a scientific theory. In S. Hook (Ed.) *Psychoanalysis, scientific method and philosophy*. New York: New York University Press, 1959. Pp. 3-35.

HATHAWAY, S. R. Clinical intuition and inferential accuracy. *Journal of Personality*, 1956, *24*, 223-250.

HAVENS, L. L. *Approaches to the mind: Movement of the psychiatric schools from sects toward science*. Boston: Little, Brown, 1973.

HAVENS, L. L. The existential use of the self. *American Journal of Psychiatry*, 1974, *131*, 1-10.

HAVENS, L. L. *Participant observation*. New York: Jason Aronson, 1976a.

HAVENS, L. L. Existential therapy. In J. Masserman (Ed.) *Current psychiatric therapies*. New York: Grune and Stratton, 1976b. Pp. 67-77.

HEIDEGGER, M. *Being and time*. New York: Harper and Row, 1963.

HOBBS, N. Sources of gain in psychotherapy. *American Psychologist*, 1962, *17*, 741-747.

HOGAN, R. A. and KIRCHNER, H. Preliminary report on the extinction of learned fears via short-term implosive therapy. *Journal of Abnormal Psychology*, 1967, *72*, 106-109.

HOLT, H. The problem of interpretation from the point of view of existential psychoanalysis. In E. F. Hammer (Ed.) *Use of interpretation in treatment*. New York: Grune and Stratton, 1968. Pp. 240-252.

HORA, T. Tao, Zen and existential psychotherapy. *Psychologia*, 1959, *2*, 236-242.

HORA, T. The process of existential psychotherapy. *Psychiatric Quarterly*, 1960, *34*, 495-504.
HORA, R. Psychotherapy, existence, and religion. In H. M. Ruitenbeek (Ed.) *Psychoanalysis and existential philosophy*. New York: Dutton, 1962. Pp. 70-81.
JANOV, A. *The primal scream*. New York: Putnam, 1970.
JOURARD, S. M. *Disclosing man to himself*. New York: Van Nostrand Reinhold, 1968.
JOURARD, S. M. Changing personal worlds: A humanistic perspective. In A. Wandersman, P. Poppen, and D. Ricks (Eds.) *Humanism and behaviorism: Dialogue and growth*. Oxford: Pergamon, 1976. Pp. 35-53.
JUNG, C. G. *Modern man in search of a soul*. New York: Harcourt, Brace, 1933.
KEEN, E. *Three faces of being: Toward an existential psychology*. New York: Appleton-Century-Crofts, 1970.
KELMAN, H. Kairos: The auspicious moment. *American Journal of Psychoanalysis*. 1969, *29*, 59-83.
KIESLER, D. J. Some myths of psychotherapy research and the search for a paradigm. *Psychological Bulletin*, 1966, *65*, 110-136.
KOHUT, H. *The analysis of the self*. New York: International Universities Press, 1971.
KOVACS, A. L. The intimate relationship: A therapeutic paradox. *Psychotherapy: Theory, Research and Practice*, 1965, *2*, 97-104.
KUBIE, L. S. The nature of psychotherapy. *Bulletin of the New York Academy of Medicine*, 1943, *19*, 183-194.
LAING, R. D. *The divided self: A study of sanity and madness*. Baltimore: Penguin, 1960.
LAING, R. D. Ontological insecurity. In H. M. Ruitenbeek (Ed.) *Psychoanalysis and existential philosophy*. New York: E. P. Dutton, 1962.
LAING, R. D. *Self and others*. New York: Pantheon Books, 1969.
LAMBERT, M. J. and BERGIN, A. E. Psychotherapeutic outcome and issues related to behavioral and humanistic approaches. In A. Wandersman, P. Poppen, and D. Ricks (Eds.) *Humanism and behaviorism: Dialogue and growth*. Oxford: Pergamon Press, 1976. Pp. 173-188.
LAWTON, G. Neurotic interaction between counselor and counselee. *Journal of Counseling Psychology*, 1958, *5*, 28-33.
LEVITSKY, A. and PERLS, F. S. The rules and games of Gestalt therapy. In J. Fagan and I. L. Shepherd (Eds.) *Gestalt therapy now*. New York: Harper and Row, 1970. Pp. 140-149.
LOEVINGER, J. Three principles for psychoanalytic psychology. *Journal of Abnormal Psychology*, 1966, *5*, 432-443.
MAHRER, A. R. A preface to the mind-body problem. *Psychological Record*, 1962, *12*, 53-60.
MAHRER, A. R. Analysis of a fragment of a dream. *Voices: Journal of the American Academy of Psychotherapists*, 1966, *2*, 40-41.
MAHRER, A. R. The goals of intensive psychotherapy. In A. R. Mahrer (Ed.) *The goals of psychotherapy*. New York: Appleton-Century-Crofts, 1967a. Pp. 162-179.
MAHRER, A. R. The goals and families of psychotherapy: Summary. In A. R. Mahrer (Ed.) *The goals of psychotherapy*. New York: Appleton-Century-Crofts, 1967b. Pp. 259-269.
MAHRER, A. R. The goals and families of psychotherapy: Discussion. In A. R. Mahrer (Ed.) *The goals of psychotherapy*. New York: Appleton-Century-Crofts, 1967c. Pp. 276-287.
MAHRER, A. R. The goals and families of psychotherapy: Implications. In A. R. Mahrer (Ed.) *The goals of psychotherapy*. New York: Appleton-Century-Crofts, 1967d. Pp. 288-301.
MAHRER, A. R. Self-change and social change. *Interpersonal Development*, 1970a, *1*, 159-166.
MAHRER, A. R. Interpretation of patient behavior through goals, feelings, and context. *Journal of Individual Psychology*, 1970b, *26*, 186-195.
MAHRER, A. R. Some known effects of psychotherapy and a reinterpretation. *Psychotherapy: Theory, Research and Practice*, 1970c, *7*, 186-191.
MAHRER, A. R. Personal life change through systematic use of dreams. *Psychotherapy: Theory, Research and Practice*, 1971, *8*, 328-332.

MAHRER, A. R. Theory and treatment of anxiety: The perspective of motivational psychology. *Journal of Pastoral Counseling*, 1977, 7, 4-16.

MAHRER, A. R. Metamorphosis through suicide: The changing of one's self by oneself. *Journal of Pastoral Counseling*, 1975a, 10, 10-26.

MAHRER, A. R. Therapeutic outcome as a function of goodness of fit on an internal-external dimension of interaction. *Psychotherapy: Theory, Research and Practice*, 1975b, 12, 22-27.

MAHRER, A. R. *Experiencing: A humanistic theory of psychology and psychiatry.* New York: Brunner/Mazel, 1978a.

MAHRER, A. R. Sequence and consequence in the experiential psychotherapies. In C. Cooper and C. Alderfer (Eds.) *Advances in experiential social processes.* New York: Wiley, 1978b.

MAHRER, A. R. Turning the tables on termination. *Voices: Journal of the American Academy of Psychotherapists*, 1978c, 13, 24-31.

MAHRER, A. R. The therapist-patient relationship: Conceptual analysis and a proposal for a paradigm-shift. *Psychotherapy: Theory, Research and Practice*, 1978d, 15, 201-215.

MAHRER, A. R. Experiential psychotherapists: A "prognostic test" and some speculations about their personalities. *Psychotherapy: Theory, Research and Practice*, 1978e, 15, 382-389.

MAHRER, A. R. An invitation to theoreticians and researchers from an applied experiential practitioner. *Psychotherapy: Theory, Research and Practice*, 1979, 16, 409-418.

MAHRER, A. R. The treatment of cancer through experiential psychotherapy. *Psychotherapy: Theory, Research and Practice*, 1980a, 17, 335-342.

MAHRER, A. R. Research on theoretical concepts of psychotherapy. In W. De Moor and H. R. Wijngaarden (Eds.) *Psychotherapy: Research and Training.* Amsterdam: Elsevier/North Holland Biomedical Press, 1980b. Pp. 33-46.

MAHRER, A. R. Value decisions in therapeutically-induced acute psychotic episodes. *Psychotherapy: Theory, Research and Practice.* 1980c, 17, 454-458.

MAHRER, A. R. Humanistic approaches to intimacy. In M. Fisher and G. Stricker (Eds.) *Intimacy.* New York: Plenum, 1982. Pp. 141-158.

MAHRER, A. R., LEVINSON, J. R. & FINE, S. Infant psychotherapy: Theory, research and practice. *Psychotherapy: Theory, Research and Practice*, 1976, 13, 131-140.

MAHRER, A. R., and PEARSON, L. The working processes of psychotherapy: Creative developments. In A. R. Mahrer & L. Pearson (Eds.) *Creative developments in psychotherapy. Volume I.* Cleveland: Case Western Reserve University Press, 1971. Pp. 309-329.

MALONE, T. P., WHITAKER, C. A., WARKENTIN, J., and FELDER, R. E. Rational and nonrational psychotherapy. *American Journal of Psychotherapy.* 1961, 15, 212-220.

MATARAZZO, J. D. The practice of psychotherapy is art and not science. In A. R. Mahrer & L. Pearson (Eds.) *Creative developments in psychotherapy.* Cleveland: Case Western Reserve University Press, 1971. Pp. 364-392.

MAUPIN, E. W. Zen Buddhism: A psychological review. *Psychedelic Review*, 1965, No. 5.

MAY, R. Contributions of existential psychotherapy. In R. May, E. Angel & H. F. Ellenberger (Eds.) *Existence: A new dimension in psychiatry and psychology.* New York: Basic Books, 1958. Pp. 37-91.

MAY, R. On the phenomenological bases of psychotherapy. *Review of Existential Psychiatry and Psychology*, 1964, 4, 22-36.

MAY, R. *Psychology and the human dilemma.* Princeton: D. Van Nostrand, 1967.

MAY, R., ANGEL, E., and ELLENBERGER, H. F. (Eds.) *Existence: A new dimension in psychiatry and psychology.* New York: Basic Books, 1958.

MEEHL, P. E. *Clinical versus statistical prediction.* Minneapolis, Minnesota: University of Minnesota Press, 1954.

MULLAN, H. and SANGIULIANO, I. *The therapist's contribution to the treatment process.* Springfield, Ill.: Charles C Thomas, 1964.

NARANJO, C. *The unfolding of man.* Menlo Park, Cal.: Stanford Research Institute, 1969.

NEEDLEMAN, J. Preface. In J. Needleman (Ed.) *Being-in-the-world: Selected papers of Ludwig*

*Binswanger*. New York: Harper Torchbooks, 1967a. Pp. viii-xvii.

NEEDLEMAN, J. The concept of the existential a priori. In J. Needleman (Ed.) *Being-in-the-world: Selected papers of L. Binswanger*. New York: Harper Torchbooks, 1967b. Pp. 9-31.

NICHOLS, M. and ZAX, M. *Catharsis in psychotherapy*. New York: Gardner Press, 1977.

OUSPENSKY, P. D. *In search of the miraculous*. New York: Harcourt, Brace & Company, 1949.

OUSPENSKY, P. D. *The fourth way*. London: Routledge and Kegan Paul, 1957.

PATTERSON, C. H. Relationship therapy and/or behavior therapy? *Psychotherapy: Theory, Research and Practice*, 1968, *5*, 226-233.

PERLS, F. S. *Gestalt therapy verbatim*. Toronto: Bantam, 1971.

PERLS, F. S. *The Gestalt approach and eyewitness to therapy*. New York: Bantam, 1976.

POLSTER, E. and POLSTER, M. *Gestalt therapy integrated*. New York: Brunner/Mazel, 1974.

POPPEN, P. J., WANDERSMAN, A. and WANDERSMAN, L. P. What are humanism and behaviorism and what can they say to each other? In A. Wandersman, P. J. Poppen and D. Ricks (Eds.) *Humanism and behaviorism: Dialogue and growth*. Oxford: Pergamon Press, 1976. Pp. 3-32.

RACHMAN, S. *The effects of psychotherapy*. Oxford: Pergamon Press, 1969.

RADO, S. *Psychoanalysis of behavior: Collected papers*. Volume I. New York: Grune and Stratton, 1956.

RADO, S. *Psychoanalysis of behavior: Collected papers*. Volume II. New York: Grune and Stratton, 1962.

REIK, T. *Listening with the third ear*. New York: Farrar, Strauss & Co., 1948.

ROGERS, C. R. *Client-centered therapy*. Boston: Houghton-Mifflin, 1951.

ROGERS, C. R. The necessary and sufficient conditions for therapeutic personality change. *Journal of Consulting Psychology*, 1957, *21*, 95-101.

ROGERS, C. R. The characteristics of a helping relationship. *Personnel and Guidance Journal*, 1958, *37*, 6-16.

ROGERS, C. R. The interpersonal relationship: the core of guidance. *Harvard Review*, 1962, *32*, 416-429.

ROGERS, C. R. The concept of the fully functioning person. *Psychotherapy: Theory, Research and Practice*, 1963, *1*, 17-26.

ROGERS, C. R. Implications of recent advances in prediction and control of behavior. In R. S. Daniel (Ed.) *Contemporary readings in general psychology*. Boston: Houghton-Mifflin, 1965. Pp. 375-380.

ROGERS, C. R. The interpersonal relationship in the facilitation of learning. In R. R. Leeper (Ed.) *Humanizing education: The person in the process*. Washington, D.C.: Association for Supervision and Curriculum Development, 1967. Pp. 1-18.

ROGERS, C. R. *On becoming a person*. Boston: Houghton-Mifflin, 1970.

ROSE, S. Intense feeling therapy. In P. Olsen (Ed.) *Emotional flooding*. New York: Human Sciences Press, 1976. Pp. 80-95.

SCHACHTEL, E. G. *Metamorphosis*. New York: Basic Books, 1959.

SCHAFFER, R. Regression in the service of the ego. In G. Lindzey (Ed.) *Assessment of human motives*. New York: Rinehart, 1958.

SCHEFLEN, A. E. *Psychotherapy of schizophrenia: A study of direct analysis*. Springfield, Ill.: Charles C Thomas, 1960.

SCHEFLEN, A. E. Natural history method in psychotherapy: Communicational research. In L. A. Gottschalk and A. H. Auerbach (Eds.) *Methods of research in psychotherapy*. New York: Appleton-Century-Crofts, 1966.

SCHOFIELD, W. *Psychotherapy: The purchase of friendship*. Englewood Cliffs, New Jersey: Prentice-Hall, 1964.

SCHUTZ, W. C. *Joy*. New York: Grove Press, 1967.

SCHUTZ, W. C. *Here comes everybody*. New York: Harper and Row, 1971.

SCHUTZ, W. C. Encounter. In R. Corsini (Ed.) *Current psychotherapies*. Itasca, Illinois: Peacock, 1973. Pp. 401-443.

SHAFFER, J. B. P. *Humanistic psychology*. Englewood Cliffs, New Jersey: Prentice-Hall, 1978.

SHOBEN, E. J., Jr. Psychotherapy as a problem in learning theory. *Psychological Bulletin*, 1949, *46*, 366-392.

SHORR, J. E. *Psycho-imagination therapy*. New York: Intercontinental Medical Book Corporation, 1972.

SHORR, J. E. *Psychotherapy through imagery*. New York: Intercontinental Medical Book Corporation, 1974.

STAMPFL, T. G. Implosive therapy. In P. Olsen (Ed.) *Emotional flooding*. New York: Penguin, 1977. Pp. 62-79.

STAMPFL, T. G. & LEVIS, D. J. Essentials of implosive therapy: A learning theory based psychodynamic behavioral therapy. *Journal of Abnormal Psychology*, 1967, *72*, 496-503.

SULLIVAN, H. S. *Conceptions of modern psychiatry*. New York: Norton, 1953a.

SULLIVAN, H. S. *The interpersonal theory of psychiatry*. New York: Norton, 1953b.

SUZUKI, D. T. *Zen Buddhism*. Garden City: Doubleday, 1956.

TRUAX, C. B. Effective ingredients in psychotherapy: An approach to unraveling the patient-therapist interaction. *Journal of Counseling Psychology*, 1963, *10*, 256-263.

TRUAX, C. B. & CARKUFF, R. R. New directions in clinical research. In B. G. Berenson and R. R. Carkuff (Eds.) *Sources of gain in counseling and psychotherapy*. New York: Holt, Rinehart and Winston, 1967. Pp. 358-391.

VAN DUSEN, W. The theory and practice of existential analysis. *American Journal of Psychotherapy*, 1957, *11*, 310-322.

VESPE, R. Ontological analysis and synthesis in existential psychotherapy. *Existential Psychiatry*, 1969, *7*, 83-92.

WARKENTIN, J. and WHITAKER, C. A. Time-limited therapy for an agency case. In A. Burton (Ed.) *Modern psychotherapeutic practice*. Palo Alto, Cal.: Science and Behavior Books, 1965. Pp. 249-304.

WATTS, A. *Psychotherapy east and west*. New York: Ballantine Books, 1961.

WHEELIS, A. W. How people change. *Commentary*, 1969, May, 56-66.

WHITAKER, C. A. and MALONE, T. P. *The roots of psychotherapy*. New York: Blakiston, 1953.

WHITAKER, C. A., WARKENTIN, J., and MALONE, T. P. The involvment of the professional therapist. In A. Burton (Ed.) *Case studies in counseling and psychotherapy*. Englewood Cliffs, New Jersey: Prentice-Hall, 1969. Pp. 218-256.

WILHELM, R. *The secret of the golden flower: A Chinese book of life*. London: Routledge and Kegan Paul, 1962.

WYSS, D. *Psychoanalytic schools from the beginning to the present*. New York: Jason Aronson, 1973.

# Name Index

Alexander, F. 10, 142, 155, 158, 159, 174
Angel, E. 41, 285, 294
Angyal, A. 212

Bachrach, H. 142, 299
Bar-Levav, R. 54
Benedek, T.M. 142
Bergin, A.E., 24, 164
Binswanger, L. 41, 53, 54, 55, 208, 276, 293, 294
Bordin, E.S. 142
Boss, M. 15, 42, 43, 54, 60, 91, 155, 263, 280
Breuer, J., 54
Buber, M. 57
Bucklew, J. 57, 176
Bugental, J.F.T. 56, 148, 248
Buytendijk, F.J.J., 262
Byles, M.B. 59

Carkhuff, R.R. 22, 143
Caruso, I.A. 161, 276
Cautela, J.R. 11
Chang, Chen-Chi, 59
Colby, K.M. 6
Condrau, G. 15, 42, 43, 91, 155, 263, 280

Deikman, A.J. 59
Denes-Radomisli, M. 47
Dreikurs, R. 184

Eigen, M. 184
Eldred, S.H. 23
Ellenberger, H.F. 41, 54, 55, 233, 285, 294

Ellis, A. 142
Enright, J. 47, 167, 279

Feldey, R.E. 56
Fenichel, 172
Fine, S. 87
Fischer, W.F. 140, 210
Fiske, D.W. 141
Frank, J.D. 22, 161
Frankl, V.E. 74
French, T.M. 142, 155, 158
Freud, S. 54, 176
Fromm-Reichmann, F. 141, 142

Gendlin, E.T. 8, 10, 26, 27, 45, 47, 50, 54, 78, 90, 178, 200, 202, 226, 250, 259, 264
Goldstein, A.P. 142
Goodrich, G. 23
Gottschalk, L.A. 142
Greenson, R. 142, 299

Haley, J. 69, 147, 150, 157, 160
Halpern, H. 147, 167
Hamburg, D.A. 23
Hartmann, H. 141
Hathaway, S.R. 141
Havens, L.L. 41, 43, 54, 56, 57, 141, 167, 233, 248, 275, 278
Heidegger, M. 150
Heller, K. 142
Hobbs, N. 142, 155
Hogan, R.A. 60
Holt, H. 41, 42

# Subject Index